A Franz Boas Reader

The Shaping of American Anthropology, 1883–1911

D120148

Franz Boas
1906

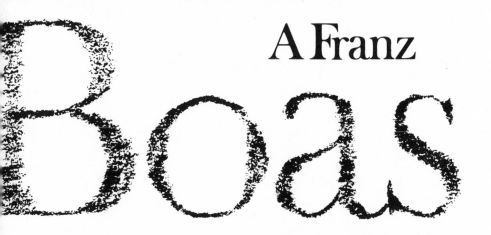

A Franz

Boas

Reader

The Shaping
of American
Anthropology,
1883–1911

Edited by
George W.
Stocking, Jr.

The University of Chicago Press
Chicago and London

The University of Chicago Press, Chicago 60637
The University of Chicago Press, Ltd., London

© 1974 by George W. Stocking, Jr.
All rights reserved. Originally published 1974
University of Chicago Press edition 1982
Midway Reprint edition 1989
Printed in the United States of America

Library of Congress Cataloging in Publication Data

Boas, Franz, 1858–1942.
  A Franz Boas Reader

  Originally published: The shaping of American
anthropology, 1883–1911. New York : Basic Books, 1974.
  Bibliography: p.
  Includes index.
  1. Anthropology—Addresses, essays, lectures.
  2. Boas, Franz, 1858–1942—Addresses, essays,
lectures.   I. Stocking, George W., 1928–.
  II. Title.
  [GN6.B57. 1982   306   81-21851
  ISBN 0-226-06243-0   AACR2

❧ PREFACE

In view of the number of volumes of Franz Boas materials that have been published in the last few years,[1] a venture to reprint more Boas requires at least a word of explanation. In a nutshell, that explanation boils down to this: there is still no single volume that treats the total range of Boas' anthropological endeavor during the decades in which he reshaped American anthropology, defining the major lines of its subsequent development down to the mid-twentieth century. The closest in conception to the present volume is perhaps the selection Boas himself made, at the very end of his career, of what he considered his more important shorter anthropological writings (Boas 1940). Obviously, that selection remains the definitive illustration of his anthropological viewpoint as he wished it to be preserved. Not surprisingly, it is rather heavily weighted toward the latter half of his very long career. Over two-thirds of the sixty-two selections were originally published after Boas was fifty, that is to say, after his basic viewpoint was defined, after his most influential works were completed, and after his dominance in the profession was already established. From the point of view of a person still active to the year of his death at eighty-four, such a weighting—and the small but subtly significant changes introduced in some of the earlier pieces—doubtless seemed justified. But thirty years later, when it has become possible to see Boas as an historical figure (Stocking 1968a) as well as a focus of theoretical controversy (Harris 1968; White 1963), a strong case can be made that his own selection stands in need of supplement.

The problem with someone whose vigor continued so long is that we lose sight of his prime. There is a tendency to think of Boas as a figure of the 1920s—when the oldest living generation of his students had their earliest contact with him. But by present standards, he was then due for retirement. In fact, his prime lay in the two decades around the turn of the century. By 1906 he had already been honored by a *Festschrift* (Laufer 1906); 1911 was the year in which he published his most impor-

---

[1] Throughout this volume, I have used the parenthetical citation style of anthropological journals, indicating simply author, year, and page number (where necessary). Full citations will be found in the bibliography at the end, which includes references to the following recent Boas publications: Boas 1888 (rep. 1964); Boas 1911a (rep. 1966); Boas 1938 (rep. 1965); Boas 1940 (rep. 1966); Boas 1945 (rep. 1969); Boas 1966; Rohner 1969.

tant work in each of the three areas of his anthropological interest (Boas 1911a, b, c).

The present volume, then, attempts to present Boas in his context and in his prime. It also attempts to present him in his totality. Although *Race, Language, and Culture* (Boas 1940) covered the major aspects of his substantive anthropological work, the focus defined by its title excluded aspects of his career that were perhaps as important and frequently as time-consuming as his actual scientific work. I have therefore included a number of selections intended to illustrate Boas' role in the propagation of anthropology and in its application to various issues of general public concern.

Having defined the goals of this volume in such ambitious terms, it is necessary to enter two caveats. On the one hand, I have not attempted to portray Boas in the full round of personal biography—although I did choose as frontispiece a portrait in which his dueling scars are visible. The focus has been on Boas' professional life, although needless to say, a good bit of his personality is revealed in the process. On the other hand, my attempt to contextualize is limited by the fact that this is a Boas reader, and the selections are all from his pen.

Even within the limits of the goals above defined, the problem of selection has been quite difficult. Prior to the end of 1911, there are close to four hundred entries in Boas' bibliography (Andrews et al. 1943). However, since Boas' own selection is still in print, and the present volume can in any case only be regarded as supplementary, the problem is somewhat simplified by excluding anything that appears in *Race, Language, and Culture*—as well as other materials recently reprinted elsewhere. Obviously, a principle of exclusion is not itself a solution to the problem of selection—especially if it means omitting such crucial statements as "The Limitations of the Comparative Method of Anthropology" (Boas 1896a). But on the whole I think that I have been able to find previously unreprinted pieces that illuminate the major aspects of his overall viewpoint, and in general the principle has stimulated the recapture of a considerable number of Boas' writings that have until now not been readily accessible.

Every rule, of course, must have its exceptions. As far as the principle of nonduplication is concerned, there are five: the essay on "Alternating Sounds" (cf. DeLaguna 1960), which contains in germ most of Boasian anthropology; the letter to Zelia Nuttall (cf. Parmenter 1966), which is the definitive statement of his plans for the propagation of anthropology; a small selection from "The Aims of Ethnology" (cf. Boas 1940), which I have included in order to recapture an aspect of his early viewpoint that he later preferred to suppress; the 1906 commencement address at Atlanta University; and the short piece on "Freedom to Teach" (cf. Boas 1945). As far as the limitation of date is concerned, I have found it impossible not to include several statements on public issues from the period of

World War I, as well as Boas' own brief retrospective statement of the early influences on his anthropological outlook. Beyond this, limits of space have forced several compromises with the goal of comprehensiveness: There is little specifically relating to Boas' work on primitive art and nothing on his brief, but methodologically groundbreaking, excursion into archaeology (Adams 1960; Gamio 1959; Mason 1943).

The only other point to make about selection is that I have included a number of letters from Boas papers in several different repositories. I did this in part because there were several aspects of his career that seemed most economically handled in this fashion, and also because such letters provide a kind of insight that the published record can never yield. Since the papers in the American Philosophical Society alone number more than 60,000 items (Stocking 1968b; cf. Boas 1972), the problem of selection might seem even greater here. However, there were a number of letters that stood out as particularly significant, and others that were generally representative of a particular aspect of his endeavor. Although the sample is very small, on the whole it seems to me to add an important dimension to this volume.

In general, I have tried not to compromise the integrity of each selection as originally conceived. With several evident or indicated exceptions, each is a self-contained unit and is here reproduced in full. Rather than encumber the volume with "[sic]'s," let me say that I have tried my best to reproduce the text as it was in the original. Here and there in the letters I have introduced a word in brackets to clarify meaning, and I have exercised a silent editorial discretion in a few instances where it seemed clear that the original contained a typographical error, or where spelling or punctuation might create a real problem of understanding. For the most part, however, I have left Boas' rather archaic and idiosyncratic usage of commas, semicolons, and colons as in the original; and I have not presumed to pretty up his often rather difficult and sometimes even obscure Germanic constructions.

Although with several exceptions I have not attempted to annotate Boas' texts, I have included as an introduction a paper originally presented to the Wenner-Gren Foundation Conference on "The Nature and Function of Anthropological Traditions," 17–21 April 1968, under the title "The Boas Tradition in American Anthropology." Never previously published, it was written with its present function in mind, and I have found it necessary to make only a very few revisions. Hopefully, it offers a statement of some of the major intellectual assumptions and most general characteristics of Boasian anthropology. To supplement it and to provide a more specifically focused context, I have written brief introductory sections for each of the major groups of selections. Readers interested in more extended explication of particular phases of Boas' work should consult my *Race, Culture and Evolution* (Stocking 1968a) or the other sources referred to in the introductory sections.

Finally, there is the acknowledgment of debts. Over the last decade the American Philosophical Society has in various ways supported my researches on Boas. I would like to express my gratitude not only to the Society, but specifically to Mrs. Gertrude Hess, who was for a long time extremely helpful to me, and to Mrs. Carolyn Milligan, who has been equally helpful since Mrs. Hess's retirement as Associate Librarian. Beyond this, I would like to acknowledge the Society's permission to publish a number of letters from the Boas Papers, as well as that of the Smithsonian Institution's National Anthropological Archives to publish two from the old Bureau of Ethnology Archives, and that of the Pitt Rivers Museum to publish two from the papers of E. B. Tylor. I would also like to express my appreciation to Franziska Boas and other members of the Boas family for their gracious encouragement. As far as the substance of the book is concerned, I would like especially to thank three friends and colleagues: Dell Hymes, who offered comments on an early outline; David Schneider, who criticized a draft of the introductory essay; and Ray Fogelson, whose comments on a later version of both outline and introduction were, as usual, extremely helpful. Finally, I should express my appreciation to Lita Osmundsen, Director of Research of the Wenner-Gren Foundation, and to Stanley Diamond, editor of a proposed volume of the papers of the 1968 Conference, for graciously consenting to the publication of my introductory essay in this volume.

CONTENTS

A Franz Boas

Reader

The Shaping
of American
Anthropology,
1883–1911

INTRODUCTION

THE BASIC
ASSUMPTIONS
OF BOASIAN
ANTHROPOLOGY

Although German-born and deeply rooted in the intellectual traditions of his homeland, Franz Boas more than any other man defined the "national character" of anthropology in the United States. There has been debate over whether it is appropriate to speak of a Boas "school" (White 1966, pp. 3–4), but there is no real question that he was the most important single force in shaping American anthropology in the first half of the twentieth century. And while his influence has been greatly attenuated in the last two decades, it continues to be felt down to the present day, in some cases even in the work of anthropologists who are conscious of no specific debt to him. To take a closer look at the fundamental assumptions of Boas' anthropology may therefore serve other purposes than those of individual intellectual biography. It may also provide the basis for a more systematic investigation of Boas' broader intellectual influence. It may tell us something about what differentiates American anthropology from other national anthropological traditions. And it may cast light on certain enduring epistemological antinomies that characterize anthropological inquiry generally.

Let us begin with certain issues in the debate Boas carried on in 1887 with Otis Mason and John Wesley Powell over "the occurrence of similar inventions in areas widely apart" (cf. below: Part II, Selection 7).

Although this debate has been discussed previously (Buettner-Janusch 1957), its implications have not been exhausted. Nor will I attempt to exhaust them here, but only to emphasize those which seem to me fundamental to Boas' anthropology. Furthermore, I will be less interested in the light this analysis casts on the discontinuities between Boasian anthropology and the nineteenth-century evolutionary tradition that preceded it, than in what it tells us about Boasian anthropology itself, in the context of another major anthropological current of the twentieth century. Finally, what I say about post-Boasian anthropology will be brief and in a sense hypothetical: That is to say, I will not pretend to offer a complete historical account, but simply part of a framework in which such an account might be constructed.

In the broadest sense, the issue between Boas and Mason had to do with the concepts of causality and classification. One of the explanations that Mason put forward for the "occurrence of similar inventions"—and the one that was at issue between him and Boas—was the traditional evolutionist notion of "independent invention": "In human culture, as in nature elsewhere, like causes produce like effects. Under the same stress and resources the same inventions will arise." Against this, Boas argued that in Mason's "enumeration of causes of similar inventions, one is omitted, which overthrows the whole system: unlike causes produce like effects" (Boas 1887c, p. 485). In responding to Boas' attack, Mason granted that this was an "ingenious" suggestion, which might explain certain "superficial" similarities of culture. He felt, however, that it would not win widespread acceptance, "in the face of the axiom that 'like effects spring from like causes'" (Mason 1887, p. 534). Boas replied that the axiom at issue was one that could not be "converted": "though like causes have like effects, like effects have not like causes"—which, in the context of what immediately preceded, and of Boas' at this point still rather awkward English, should clearly be read as "like effects do not necessarily have like causes" (Boas 1887d, p. 589). Although neither man appealed to philosophical authority, the issue ("the plurality of causes") was one that can be found in more recent textbooks on logic (Cohen and Nagel 1934, pp. 269–272), and Boas was apparently following John Stuart Mill on the question. However, it is not to my present purpose to pursue either the history or the merits of the dispute. I would rather like to suggest that much of Boas' basic anthropological orientation can be extrapolated from the position he took on this issue. In arguing this, I do not mean to suggest that historically Boas in fact deduced his anthropology from this premise, but rather to assert that there is an inner consistency to Boas' anthropology, and that it may contribute to our historical understanding to view it in terms of its inner logic.

Implicit in the issue of the likeness of effects was the general problem of classification, which is a focus of concern in much of Boas' early work. At various points Boas attacked what he was wont to call "premature" or "arbitrary" classification. The attack on Mason in fact centered on Mason's attempt to define "families, genera, and species" of ethnological phenomena that could then be treated comparatively. Involved in this was the determination of "like effects" by prior definition. Mason argued that "whoever attempts to classify material must first have in mind certain notions, ideas, or characteristics by means of which he will separate one object from another," which Mason referred to as "classific concepts" (Mason 1887, p. 534). Boas, on the other hand, characteristically abjured definition almost entirely as, in effect, a prejudgment of the likeness of effects. Characteristically, he started not from conceptual definition, but from the actual distribution of empirical phenomena. When W. J. McGee suggested that a proposal Boas offered in 1896 for a study of physical characteristics of American Indians was a racial "classification," Boas responded that it was merely "a geographical tabulation of observed facts" (BAE, Boas to McGee, 12 September 1896). In practice, Boas may have taken for granted that one could deal with distinguishable and separable units in the external world, but he eschewed any abstractions from these: "The object of our study is the individual, not abstractions from the individual under observation" (Boas 1887c, p. 485). The issue is particularly evident in his physical anthropology, which was largely directed against any attempt to subsume the range of distribution of measured physical differences within an idealized type. The "type" of any distribution was to be defined not in terms of its average value, but in terms of the total distribution of variants. An apparently "normal" distribution (that is, an apparently like effect) might often result from the intermixture of two different groups, as he argued was the case with the measurement of head-forms among Great Lakes Indians (Boas 1893, pp. 573–574; cf. below, Part II, Selection 10).

Classification was also complicated by another factor: the viewpoint of the observer. A classic statement of the issues involved here is contained in the article "On Alternating Sounds" (Boas 1889b; cf. below, Part II, Selection 9). Here the problem was inverted, in that Boas dealt with the apparent unlikeness of phenomena that were in reality the same: with the tendency of the hearer to classify as two different sounds a third sound that did not exist in his own language. But the basic approach is much the same, and depended on the fact that apparently similar sounds were really variants around an average, which were subsumed within a single category by processes of association and habit. The establishment of categories was thus heavily conditioned by the prior experience and point of view of the observer, and the central point of the article was in fact the arbitrariness of traditional classification and the inadequacy of analogies based on apparent similarity as the basis for classification.

Association and habit in the observer had their analogues in the historical processes conditioning the phenomena observed, which might also create apparent likenesses in the effects whose causes were under investigation. Since the "physiological and psychological state of an organism at a certain moment is a function of its whole history," appearances were frequently deceptive: "The outward appearance of two phenomena may be identical, yet their immanent qualities may be altogether different" (Boas 1887d, p. 589). Indeed, "the historical intricacy of the acting causes" was so complex in the realm of ethnology that "the development of similar ethnological phenomena from unlike causes" was "far more probable" than its alternative (Boas 1887c, p. 485).

Historical processes, furthermore, did not move in lockstep: different aspects of human life were affected in different ways by different historical or developmental processes. Thus, in interpreting physical characteristics, we must "consider each measurement as a function of a number of variable factors which represent the laws of heredity and environment." The correlation of two measurements would be "close when they depend largely upon the same factor, slight when they depend largely upon distinct factors" (Boas 1893, p. 574). Classification would be the more arbitrary the larger the number of factors it attempted to include, and classification in terms of one factor would produce quite different results from classification in terms of another—a proposition that at its broadest level was expressed in Boas' argument that race, language, and culture were not now and probably never had been closely correlated (Boas 1911a, pp. 1–10).

Summarizing, we might say that for Boas, the likeness and the classification of effects were not the starting point of investigation, but a goal arduously to be obtained. It was not a matter of definition or analogy: It was both in origin and in discovery a historical more than a logical problem. It could only be accomplished by getting behind appearances, transcending the point of view of the observer, and untangling the historical complexity of the processes affecting human life to arrive at categories that were not founded "in the mind of the student" (Boas 1887d, p. 614), but were somehow derived from, consistent with, and in a sense internal to, the phenomena themselves.

At this point, we are led easily to a second issue in the Boas-Mason debate that is equally illuminating of Boasian anthropology: the relationship of "elements" and "wholes." Mason, like evolutionist ethnologists generally, was not particularly interested in cultural wholes, and indeed Powell, in his later contribution to the argument, even denied their meaningful existence for the ethnologist (Powell 1887, pp. 612–613). But from Boas' point of view, the issue was central. As posed in this debate, it had to do with the practical problem of museum arrangement. Mason defended an arrangement of specimens that grouped together artifacts from various levels of culture designed to satisfy generic human needs: cooking utensils, weapons, and musical instruments, each in their own evolutionary sequence. It was these technological species that Boas attacked as "rigid abstractions": "In ethnology, all is individuality"

(Boas 1887d, p. 589). But the individuality Boas was defending was not simply the individuality of the element—though he, too, in fact based much of his ethnological theorizing on an analysis of the relationship of elements. The individuality that most concerned Boas was rather that of the element in its "surroundings," which Boas defined not simply in the present, but as the product of "the history of the people, the influence of the regions through which it passed in its migrations, and the people with whom it came into contact" (Boas 1887d, p. 588). If one would "understand the single specimen," one must see it in relation to "the productions [of a given tribe] as a whole" (Boas 1887c, p. 485).

Here again, the "likeness of effects" was at issue: a rattle could not be viewed simply as a means of making noise. It might also be, "besides this, the outcome of religious conceptions, as any noise may be applied to invoke or drive away spirits" (Boas 1887d, p. 588). It might, in short, have a number of meanings. It was the fact that they had different inner meanings that made outwardly similar effects fundamentally unlike. Furthermore, meaning was the concept that mediated the relations of elements and wholes. Insofar as it implied a causal direction, the movement was from whole to element:

From a collection of string instruments, flutes, or drums of "savage" tribes and the modern orchestra, we cannot derive any conclusion but that similar means have been applied by all peoples to make music. The character of their music, the only object worth studying, *which determines the form of the instruments,* cannot be understood from the single instrument, but requires a complete collection from the single tribe. [Boas 1887c, p. 486; my emphasis]

Although Boas' concern with the meanings of cultural wholes had important consequences for American anthropology, much of his activity as ethnologist was, paradoxically, based on the analysis of elements. The reasons for this will be referred to later. At this point I would simply recall that the medium of his critique of evolutionary ethnology in the period between 1887 and 1896, when he drew together the argument on "The Limitations of the Comparative Method of Anthropology," was in fact a study of the distribution of folk-tale elements (Boas 1891b, 1896a, 1896b). This should not, however, obscure his underlying concern with the integration of elements in a single culture. Both tendencies—and the tension between them—are evident in remarks he made on tribal mythologies in 1898. "The mythologies of the various tribes as we find them now are not organic growths, but have gradually developed and obtained their present form by the accretion of foreign material." But although often adopted ready-made, this foreign material was "adapted and changed in form according to the genius of the people who borrowed it." On the one hand, culture was simply an accidental accretion of individual elements. On the other, culture—despite Boas' renunciation of organic growth—

was at the same time an integrated spiritual totality that somehow conditioned the form of its elements (Boas 1898, p. 673; cf. below, Part III, Selection 12).

Especially after 1900, when his critique of evolutionism was by and large accomplished, Boas became more concerned with the ways in which the "genius of a people" integrated the elements that the almost accidental accumulation of historical processes brought together in a single culture. However, his thought on this issue was by no means systematic and has to be extracted from writings that were nominally on somewhat different topics. Thus, prior to 1900 he suggested that because membership in Kwakiutl secret societies gave certain "advantages and prerogatives," there was a tendency among the Kwakiutl to create new societies, each of which required its own set of validating traditions. Although the Indians did not set out consciously to invent these, their imaginations, impelled by status-striving and heightened by fasting, received in hallucination the required traditions—"the material for which was necessarily taken [by imitation] from the existing ideas [of the tribe], or from the ideas of neighboring tribes" (Boas 1897, pp. 633–634). Two decades later, Boas argued that folklore and mythology were founded on "events that reflect the [everyday] occurrences of human life, particularly those that stir the emotions of the people." At the same time, because the "power of imagination of man" was "rather limited," people much preferred to "operate with the old stock of imaginative happenings than invent new ones." Their imagination thus "played with a few plots, which were extended by means of a number of motives that have a very wide distribution," and which each group selectively borrowed and adapted "under the stress of a dominant idea" or institution characteristic of their own culture (Boas 1916a, pp. 515–520, 880–881; 1916b, pp. 319–326). Although in each of these examples Boas was concerned with specific issues relating to folklore, by implication he suggested something about the general dynamics of cultural processes—the processes by which "the genius of a people" acted to mold borrowed elements to a traditional pattern.

The problem of "the genius of peoples" was more directly at issue in Boas' work on racial differences in mental function. Boas explained many aspects of both primitive and civilized behavior in terms of "secondary explanations" or rationalizations of customary behavior whose actual origins were lost in tradition, but which were highly charged with emotional value. Certain circumstances—the violation of norms, the process of socializing children—tended to bring this customary behavior sharply into group consciousness, and it was rationalized in terms that might have little to do with its actual origin. But if secondary explanations were arbitrary as far as the individual custom they explained was concerned, they were not arbitrary in relation to the culture as a whole. They depended on the general cultural context, and on the range and character of the clusters of ideas brought into association with one another within that context (Stocking 1968a, pp. 221–222). Furthermore, in tribes where there were small groups of chiefs or priests who had charge of certain ceremonials, there arose an esoteric doctrine which systematized "the heterogeneous mass of beliefs and practices current in the tribe" (Boas 1902, pp. 872–874).

One level of integration of elements into cultural wholes was thus the conscious one of secondary explanation. But there was also a deeper level at which integration took place. It was particularly in relation to language that this level was a matter of concern to Boas. On the one hand, there seemed to be a universalistic underpinning to language, in the sense that there was in all men a tendency to classify phenomena. At the deepest level, Boas seemed to feel that this tendency expressed itself in certain broadly defined categories that were universal. Thus all languages classified actions in terms of time and place. And even in relation to culture, one finds occasionally in Boas residual hints of Bastian's *Elementargedanken*—elementary cultural categories that would be found underlying all cultural diversity. But except at this very general psychological level, Boas saw the tendency to categorization expressed in diversity rather than uniformity: "the groups of ideas expressed by specific phonetic groups show very material differences in different languages, and do not conform by any means to the same principles of classification" (Boas 1911a, p. 21). These different classifications would develop unconsciously as an historical reflection of "the chief [cultural] interests of a people" (Boas 1911a, p. 22). Furthermore, different languages varied in the categories that were obligatory—that *had* to be expressed in order for communication to take place. Although Boas did not himself elaborate the analogy in detail, he did argue that the very unconsciousness of these linguistic processes told us much about the processes of culture in general: "the common feature of both is the grouping-together of a considerable number of activities under the form of a single idea, without the necessity of the idea itself entering into consciousness." The "analogy of ethnology and language" made the latter "one of the most instructive fields of inquiry in an investigation of the formation of the fundamental ethnic ideas," since its operations were never obscured by the mechanism of secondary explanation (Boas 1911a, p. 66). Implicit in all this was the notion that the integration of elements into wholes was something more than a conscious process of secondary explanation. This conscious integration was founded on a substratum in which the underlying categories and dominant ideas of the culture, although ultimately themselves historical products, were *a priori* in the sense that they "develop at present in each individual and in the whole people entirely sub-consciously, and nevertheless are most potent in the formation of our opinions and actions" (Boas 1911a, p. 64). Ultimately, if only by analogy, it was at this unconscious level that cultural elements had their profoundest integration in "the genius of a people."

In arguing Boas' underlying concern with the integration of elements and wholes, it is important, however, to emphasize the character of this integration. It was on the one hand a psychological integration. It was founded on ideas, not on external conditions. And although the meanings in which it was expressed were inherent in the whole rather than constructed out of the relationships of elements, it was nevertheless internal to the individual actor. Its obligatory character was not externally imposed, but based on unconsciously internalized categories, on the processes of imitation and socialization, and on deceptively self-conscious secondary explanations. It was also an historical integration. The accidental accretions of culture contact, the constant manipulation of elements, and the retrospective systematization of secondary explanation, pulled in various directions to create a kind of dynamic, moving, or processual integration which, although founded on a substratum of unconscious categories and dominant ideas, was never fully stable, but subject to change and drift. In this context, it was a rather loose kind of integration. True, one can find in Boas' study of the Chilkat blanket interesting suggestions of an implicit approach to the dynamics of cultural integration in rather formalistic terms (Boas 1907a, p. 373). And his approach to language, although much less structuralist than some writers have suggested (Stocking 1968c), nevertheless led directly to subsequent structuralist points of view. But his linguistic paradigm, as Hockett has suggested, was one of "item and process," not "item and arrangement," and this is true of his overall approach to cultural integration. For Boas, the integration of wholes was not a matter of necessary or logical relations of elements. Its character was best described, not in terms of "structure" or "system," but in terms of "meaning," of "theme," of "focus," and of "pattern" (cf. Aberle 1960; Hockett 1954; Hymes 1961b). In all this, it reflected its origin in the rather loose romantic conception of the "genius" or *Geist* of a people.

Implicit in Boas' view of causality and classification and in his conception of the relation of elements and wholes was a much broader issue: the nature of science in general and of anthropology as a science. To place Boas' views on all these matters in context, it is necessary to go behind the Boas-Mason debate itself and consider certain aspects of the personal and intellectual background in which Boas' scientific viewpoint was elaborated.

Boas' scientific orientation has to be understood in terms of his peculiar position within and between two traditions in German thought that were themselves undergoing reformulation in this period. On the one hand, he was from his youth clearly influenced by "the historicist spirit of romantic idealism"; on the other, he came of age in the period when "the hairy philosophy of monistic materialism" was at its high point in Germany (Gillispie 1960, p. 321). Both interests were reflected in his university studies: the one, in Ritterian geography; the other, in physics. His doctoral research on the color of sea water raised certain issues about the effect of the viewpoint of the observer on the quantitative measurement of perceptual phenomena. The scientific researches of his postdoctoral years were a series of attempts—first in psychophysics, then in geography, and then in ethnology—to test how far the quantitative, deterministic, and mechanistic assumptions of contemporary physical science (which in the beginning he clearly accepted) would apply to the study of psychic phenomena of various sorts. At one point in the development, he was inclined to an extreme "geographic determinism," but his studies eventually led him to the conclusion that the influence of geography was an "extremely complex matter" that was affected by any number of psychological factors, which in turn could only be elucidated historically (cf. below, Part I, Selections 3 and 4; Part II, Selection 6; Stocking 1968a pp. 135–160). This personal intellectual odyssey—which was unified by a concern with epistemological problems—involved on the one hand a questioning of certain assumptions of nineteenth-century physical science, at least insofar as they were carried over into the study of human phenomena. On the other, it involved a reassertion of the legitimacy of a quite different approach to the study of such phenomena. But its outcome was, to say the least, ambiguous, and that ambiguity is not without significance for twentieth-century American anthropology.

Boas' "Study of Geography" (1887e) may be regarded both as a statement of the inner tension in his scientific viewpoint and as a measure of the extent to which the balance in this tension had shifted in the six years after he received his doctorate in 1881. Here Boas distinguished two different conceptions of the nature of scientific inquiry. Both had the same starting point: "the establishment of facts." Both had the same ultimate end: "to find the eternal truth." But their relationship to facts and their approach to truth were quite different. The difference was that between the "physical" and the "historical" methods. "The physicist compares a series of similar facts, from which he isolates the general phenomenon which is common to all of them. Henceforth the single facts become less important to him, as he lays stress on the general law alone." The historian, on the other hand, denied that the "deduction of laws from phenomena" was the only approach to "eternal truth." There was also the method of "understanding," and for those who chose this route, the attitude toward the individual fact or event was quite different from the physicist's: "Its mere existence entitles it to a full share of our attention; and the knowledge of its existence and evolution in space and time fully satisfies the student, without regard to the laws which it corroborates or which may be deduced from it." Insofar as the historian was interested in law, it was in order to explain the actual history of "the phenomena from which it had been deduced."

A second issue on which historians and physicists differed was the legitimacy of the study of phenomena having "a merely subjective" as opposed to an "objective unity." Physicists would grant the legitimacy of certain types of historical studies. But even here, the physicist did not study "the whole phenomenon as it represents itself to the human mind, but resolves it into its elements, which he investigates separately"; and insofar as he was interested in the history of these elements, it was in order to create "a systematical arrangement" whose order was "objective." On the other hand, the historian insisted on the equal scientific validity of the study of more complex phenomena whose elements "seem to be connected only in the mind of the observer"; and in studying them, he was interested not in the elements, but in "the whole phenomenon."

Both approaches were legitimate and necessary forms of scientific inquiry. Each of them was founded on a different characteristic of the human mind, so that a choice between them could "only be subjective." However, the historical—or more broadly, after Alexander von Humboldt, the cosmographical—approach operated as a necessary corrective to certain tendencies inherent in the physical, which had its origin in the "aesthetic disposition" to "bring the confusion of forms and species into a system." When otherwise unrestrained, this disposition could lead to the Epicurean argument that "It does not matter . . . if an hypothesis is true, but all probable explanations are of the same value, and the choice between them is quite insignificant." In fact, however, the relative value of theories was measured by their "truth." Naturalists had therefore always to examine "the truth of their theories by applying them to new phenomena, and in these researches those phenomena are the most important which seem to be opposed to the theories." Cosmography, on the other hand, arose out of the "affective" impulse, the "personal feeling of man towards the world" around him. The cosmographer was interested in the phenomenon itself, "without regard to its place in a system"; like Goethe, he tried "lovingly . . . to penetrate into its secrets until every feature is plain and clear," until its "truth" could be affectively apprehended. Here, then, was the effective counter to the Epicurean tendency of the physical method: "As the truth of every phenomenon causes us to study it, a true history of its evolution alone can satisfy the investigator's mind, and it is for this reason that Epicurus's probable or possible explanation is not at all satisfactory to science" (Boas 1887e, passim).

Although much of Boas' argument can be interpreted either as growing directly out of his own scientific experience or out of issues specific to the tradition of German geography, it is also clearly related to the traditional distinction in German thought between the *Naturwissenschaften* and the *Geisteswissenschaften*, between the sciences dealing with physical nature and those dealing with human spiritual activity. As applied to the study of man, the tendency of Kantian thought, in the words of Talcott Parsons, was toward a "radical dualism" that "favored the reduction of all phenomenal aspects of man, especially the biological, to a 'materialistic' basis, and produced a radical hiatus between this and his spiritual life." Post-Kantian idealist interest in the latter, Parsons argues, led in two directions: "detailed, concrete history" of the Rankean sort, on the one hand; and on the other, Hegelian philosophy of history, which, after being subjected to a relativizing critique by Wilhelm Dilthey, eventuated in the concept of discrete individual *Geisten* associated with specific historical periods or cultural traditions. Both of these currents shared an opposition to positivistic natural science, to the reduction of human behavior to physical or biological causality, and to any sort of "general analytic theory." They were also, each in its own way, empiricist and concrete in outlook—the second current, in the sense that it resisted "any attempt to break down the concrete whole [of a *Geist*] analytically." *Geisten* were "organic," although not in a biological sense, and were to be almost intuitively "understood" as totalities of meaning rather than broken down by "atomistic" analysis (Parsons 1949, pp. 473–485). Dilthey's *Einleitung in die Geisteswissenschaften* was published in 1883, and in the preceding year he assumed a chair at the University of Berlin. Later references to Dilthey's work indicate that Boas had been influenced by him, and it is clear that his conception of the "historical" method— which partook of both the Rankean and the Hegelian currents—should be viewed in this framework.

It would be a mistake, however, to think of Boas only in this context. He was by inclination and training a *Naturwissenschaftler*, thoroughly grounded in the tradition of atomistic analysis of elements and of mechanistic causal determinism. But he had received his training in a period when the epistemological assumptions of classical physics and the nature of causality and scientific law were themselves beginning to be questioned by certain physicists and philosophers, and the questions that were stimulated by his doctoral dissertation are perhaps best viewed in this context (Gillispie 1960, pp. 493–521; Passmore 1957, pp. 322–345). However, Boas' own dissatisfaction with traditional physics did not lead him like Ernst Mach to question the reality of traditional physical substances, to regard scientific laws as conventional hypotheses whose "truth" was simply a matter of their continuing utility, or to formulate a radically sensationalist epistemology. Nor did Boas' reaffirmation of the historical method lead him, like Wilhelm Dilthey and his neo-Kantian successors, toward a redefinition of the metaphysical presuppositions of historical inquiry or to an unqualified assertion of the separateness of natural and historical science. If historical method was different than physical method, it was not therefore outside of or distinct from science: It was rather another way science had of looking at the phenomena of nature, whether sentient or dead. Perhaps because he left Europe at a time when these newer currents had not reached the flood, perhaps because his own epistemological interests led him into a quite different area of study, Boas' scientific and historical outlooks remained in important respects within nineteenth-century traditions.

It is in this context that one must interpret his differences with Mason over the nature of anthropology as a science. Mason's view of science seems to have been unaffected by any of these currents. He had no questions about the "axioms" of causality nor about the distinction between historical and natural scientific method. Like many cultural evolutionists of a slightly earlier period, he was still trying quite straightforwardly to apply to the study of human historical phenomena "the methods and the instrumentalities of the biologist" (Mason 1887, p. 534). On the other hand, if Boas' viewpoint was in some respects reflective of more modern influences, it was nevertheless a rather complex mélange of the *Geistes-* and *Naturwissenschaftliche* viewpoints that does not yield itself easily to historical interpretation. Clearly, he was opposed to deductive and analogical methods, which he felt ran counter to the impulse of recent biology and physics. These might help to define problems, but they could not establish scientific laws, which Boas clearly conceived in quite different terms than modern philosophers of science. Scientific laws existed in nature, external to the mind of the observer. They were not probabilistic or conventional statements, but reflections of "eternal truth." In attempting to discover them, the "method of starting with a hypothesis" was "infinitely inferior" to a "truly"—one might almost say "rigidly"—"inductive" approach (Boas 1896a, p. 905). It was as part of this induction that history entered anthropological science as the necessary basis for the derivation of "the laws and history of the development of the physiological and psychological character of mankind" (Boas 1887d, p. 588). "Tracing the full history of the single phenomenon" served a twofold purpose: on the one hand, it stripped away the "influence of surroundings" so that one could get at the physiological and psychological substructure of man; on the other, once "phenomena arising from a common psychical cause among all tribes" could thus be isolated, a comparison of "histories of growth" could lead to the discovery of "general laws" of human development (Boas 1887d, p. 588; 1896a, p. 907).

In this framework, the historical and the physical methods were no longer, as they had been in "The Study of Geography," alternative approaches. In anthropological research, history, although subordinated to the goal of scientific law, was nonetheless prior to it. Only through history could cultural laws be established.

But if the historical and physical approaches were thus integrated in theory, the ambiguities within and the tensions between them had by no means been resolved. The "single phenomena" whose history Boas would have traced had, to say the least, a somewhat indefinite character. At one level, they were the *Geisten* of whole cultures, and if Boas objected to the "rigid abstractions" of technological genera and species as "classifications" existing "only in the mind of the student," he had no question that tribal cultures, although phenomena "having a merely subjective connection," were nevertheless directly and concretely observable and distinguishable, "without making artificial classifications." But if they were to be studied analytically only in terms of internally derived categories, the problem of analyzing a culture or a language as it appeared to the native himself was, to say the least, complicated by the fact that its categories were unconsciously based and obscured by secondary explanation. Furthermore, at another level the "single phenomena" were clearly conceived in elementary rather than holistic terms. In practice, Boas' historical method was perhaps archetypically exemplified by his quasi-statistical study of the distribution of folk-tale elements. In practice, Boas conceived of history in rather traditional and indeed somewhat positivistic terms. Carried on in an area where the traditional documentary materials of historical inquiry were largely lacking, subjected both to the standards of evidence of traditional historiography and to the same rigorous criteria that Boas applied to inductions in the physical sciences, history was itself so difficult and complex as to be almost impossible to realize. Boas seems later quietly to have acknowledged this by a change in one word of the reprinted version of his "Limitations of the Comparative Method." In 1896, induction involved a study of the "actual history of definite phenomena"; in 1940, it involved the study of the "actual relations of definite phenomena" (Boas 1896a, p. 277; 1940, p. 905). In the process, the goal of historical reconstruction had, to say the least, been drastically modified. Finally, at the very broadest level, one cannot help but sense a conflict between history's role in checking the Epicurean tendencies of physical science and making possible a closer approach to "eternal truth," and the revelation of historical ethnology that "civilization is not something absolute, but that it is relative, and that our ideas and conceptions are true only so far as our civilization goes" (Boas 1887d, p. 589). And indeed in the long run, the search for "eternal truth" succumbed more and more to skepticism; there is a consistent tendency in Boas' thought toward increasing doubt of the possibility of establishing valid categories for the comparison of cultural phenomena, and a consequently growing skepticism as to the possibility of establishing significant "laws" in the cultural realm (Kluckhohn and Prufer 1959, p. 24). All of which suggests that the relation of history and physical science was for Boas less one of complementarity than one of mutual inhibition. And indeed in later life and after his death he was criticized for a double failure: "he does not write histories, and he does not prepare scientific systems" (Redfield, in Eggan 1955, p. xii; cf. Boas 1936).

But if Boas did neither of these, he nevertheless did much to define twentieth-century American anthropology. In the first place, it is worth noting in passing his contribution to the embracive conception of anthropology that has been most peculiarly characteristic of the United States. Since it came into fairly wide usage around 1860, the implicit etymological inclusiveness of the term "anthropology" has by no means always been realized in practice. On the European continent, the tendency from the beginning was to distinguish (physical) "anthropology" from "ethnology." In England, the greater inclusiveness of the tradition that culminated in A. C. Haddon was transformed into a rather narrowly defined "social anthropology" quite separate from the physical study of man. In the United States, men like John Wesley Powell and Daniel Garrison Brinton espoused an embracive anthropology and spent some effort detailing the content of its subdivisions, but they did little empirical research in what they called "somatology" (Brinton 1892). In contrast, Boas—who through Bastian and Virchow had ties to both the "cultural" and the "physical" halves of the German anthropological tradition—made physical anthropological research an integral part of his professional activity. Along with the evidence of culture and of language, it provided an important approach to "the problem of the early history of mankind" (1899, p. 106). True, Boas trained few students in physical anthropology, and he made only a brief excursion into archaeology. But he nevertheless provided a model of multifaceted research competence that influenced a number of his students and did much to maintain the embracive conception of anthropology that even to this day continues to give a special character to the discipline in this country.

Within the embracive anthropological orientation embodied in his own researches on race, language, and culture, the scientific viewpoint defined by Boas' thought on causality and classification, on the character of wholes and elements, and on the relationship of the historical and physical methods was applied with a consistency that has not perhaps been fully appreciated heretofore. At the broadest level, I have suggested already that his attitude toward classification was manifest in his insistence on the distinction between race, language, and culture as the reflection of three distinct classificatory points of view and three quite different sets of historical processes. But the argument can be carried somewhat further. In each of these three areas, the main impact of his work was critical, and his criticism can be viewed as an attack on prevailing classificatory and typological assumptions, whether these were the "rigid abstractions" of the three European races, of isolative, incorporative, and inflective languages, or of the evolutionary states of savagery, barbarism, and civilization. In each area what was involved was an attempt to show that the allegedly differentiating criteria did not march in lockstep, but were affected in complex ways by interacting historical processes.

In each area, the impact of his criticism was relativistic both in a methodological and an evaluative sense—races, languages, and cultures could be neither studied nor ranked from a Europocentric point of view. In each area, his emphasis was on the empirical study of the actual distribution of phenomena, and the collection and publication of large masses of data—whether head measurements or the texts of folk-tales and myths—to provide the basis for future inductive study. There were, of course, asymmetries. The problem of the relation of wholes and elements presented itself in a different way in relation to race than in relation to language and culture. In its basis, if not in its manifestations, race was a physical rather than a spiritual phenomenon. Its unity was not a matter of "inner form" or *Geist*. But even here there is an analogy between Boas' focus on the local population as an historically conditioned unit and his focus on historically conditioned linguistic and cultural wholes. Furthermore, in each area classification was a goal to be achieved, rather than the starting point of investigation. In each area it depended on the prior study of the historical processes that conditioned the apparent likeness of effects in the present. And since these interacting processes had operated in the past as well as the present, one could never assume that the earlier stages of any phenomenon were necessarily simpler ones. The bias was always toward complexity. The most illuminating cases for study were those—like the Northwest Coast—in which interacting historical processes had eventuated in extremely complex outcomes. The most important cases were always those which provided exceptions to some rule or law. And in all three areas, Boas became more and more skeptical as to the possibilities of historical reconstruction, genetic classification, or the derivation of scientific law. His retreat from laws in the study of culture is paralleled in his physical anthropology and in his increasing reservations about the possibility of establishing a classification of languages on the basis of morphological characteristics. In each area, what remained in the end was the study of process in the present.

Taken as a whole, Boas' anthropology, both in its critical and its constructive aspects, was rather self-consciously conservative. In science, if not in politics, the term was one he and his students used with approbation. And although embracive, his anthropology was also somewhat insular. Boas was from the beginning a bit patronizing towards much of American science, but his emigration attenuated the German influence; as a result, his anthropology remained for some time much within the framework that was elaborated in the 1880s and 1890s. At the same time, it was a self-consciously innovating break with what had gone before, and it embodied a crusading attitude that sought to propagate "the anthropological point of view" in other disciplines and among the public at large. Despite the inner tension between the historical and physical methods, it saw itself, and presented itself to the public at large, as scientific anthropology, especially in relation to the speculative evolutionary theory which it displaced. Dubious of analogies, opposed to deduction, suspicious of hypothesis and of theory, it was a spare discipline that accepted rather little in the way of support from other scientific points of view, especially from the biological sciences that had provided a model for evolutionary anthropology.

In order to place Boasian anthropology in better perspective, it may be helpful briefly to compare it with another viewpoint that has been very influential in the twentieth century: the tradition that flows from Durkheim through Radcliffe-Brown into modern British social anthropology. There are in fact more similarities between Boas and these two figures than one might offhand suspect, but on the issues of the Boas-Mason debate the differences are quite explicit. For Durkheim, to deny that like effects have like causes was to deny "the principle of causality." For Durkheim, the subject matter of sociology was social "facts," which were to be "defined in advance by certain common external characteristics." These must be considered "independent of their individual manifestations," and "from without, [rather than] from the point of view of the consciousness experiencing them." They were to be treated in relation to "social types" or "species," and the species was to be defined by its "average type." Species were to be classified in terms of the "nature and number of the component elements and their mode of combination," taking as a basis most simple, undifferentiated, single-segment society, and proceeding through a limited number of possible combinations—all in terms of explicit biological analogies. "The first origins of all social processes" were to be sought, not in the past, but "in the internal constitution of the social group." Because the relation of cause and effect was "logical" and not merely chronological, there was "a very important role of deduction in experimental reasoning," in which "one well-constructed experiment often suffices for the establishment of a law." If social facts were a separate order of phenomena from psychological, and sociology was "not an auxiliary of any other science," there was no essential discontinuity in method between sociology and other sciences, and Durkheim quite explicitly defended the use of analogies derived from biology (Durkheim 1895, passim).

Although Radcliffe-Brown departed from Durkheim in some respects, the basic assumptions were still the same. At a number of points he made it clear that like effects were the result of like causes. If his central problem was "meaning," meaning was to be construed in terms of function. The relation of elements and wholes was that of a "closely connected system" in which every custom was functionally integrated in terms of an explicit biological analogy, and causal relations were not to be sought in history but in the requirements of the ongoing system. Furthermore, social anthropology—which Radcliffe-Brown was at some pains to distinguish from ethnology, precisely on the grounds of its rejection of history—was to be in every sense one of the natural sciences (Radcliffe-Brown 1922, passim; 1923).

In short, although both the Boas tradition and the tradition of British social anthropology emerged in reaction to evolutionary anthropology, their reactions took quite different directions. Stated oversimply, one might say that the latter gave up the dimension of time, while retaining many of the methodological assumptions; the former retained the dimension of time, but abandoned the methodological assumptions. As Radcliffe-Brown noted in 1923, evolutionism contained both an historical and a scientific component. In reaction against it, Boasian anthropology moved in the direction of history; British social anthropology in the direction of science.

In the context of their differences of basic assumption, it is hardly surprising that Boasians found little of value in Durkheim. Goldenweiser's review of the *Elementary Forms of the Religious Life* seems best understood in this context. Many of his criticisms in fact flowed from precisely those fundamental differences in assumption that we have been considering. Goldenweiser objected to Durkheim's "apparently innocent" definition of religion as involving in fact "a whole series of hypotheses"; he criticized the attempt to derive a law from a single instance; he criticized Durkheim's data on empirical grounds; he argued that totemism was not a single phenomenon, but a series of "aggregates of various cultural features of heterogeneous psychological and historical derivation" (Goldenweiser 1915). Similarly, it is not surprising that Boasians had little communication with British social anthropology. Certain of these same issues of assumption (notably the question of the point of view of the observer and the complexity of historical causation) were clearly involved in Kroeber's early debate with Rivers on kinship terms (Kroeber 1909). Somewhat later, Radcliffe-Brown quite properly noted the basic differences in outlook implicit in Kroeber's "Eighteen Professions," which in many respects may be regarded as a kind of manifesto of Boasian anthropology (Radcliffe-Brown 1923; Stocking 1968a, pp. 267–268).

At this point, of course, we come back to an issue raised in the opening of this paper: the extent to which it is appropriate to identify Boas with subsequent American anthropology, or Boas' students as a "school." Without attempting to settle this issue here, I would suggest (as a hypothesis deserving further study) that Boas' students did tend to share the underlying assumptions I have been discussing, and that to a very great extent their anthropology developed along lines implicit in these assumptions. One can distinguish temporal phases of development; and one can distinguish what might be called "strict" Boasians (Spier, Lowie, and Herskovits), "evolved" Boasians (Benedict and Mead), and "rebelling" Boasians (Kroeber, Radin, and Sapir). But the character of development or rebellion was usually to take one aspect of Boasian assumption and to carry it farther than Boas himself would accept. And in general, much of twentieth-century American anthropology may be viewed as the working out in time of various implications in Boas' own position. After the critique of evolution itself, which culminated in Lowie's *Primitive Society* (1920), the next phase was a development out of Boas' approach to history in terms of the geographical distribution of culture elements, a trend which culminated in the culture area studies of the 1920s and the mapping of trait distributions in the 1930s. The second major phase developed out of Boas' interest in "the genius of a people," and eventuated in the 1930s in studies of acculturation, of culture pattern, and of culture and personality. The general movement was thus from criticism to historical reconstruction to the psychological study of cultural process and total cultural integration in the present (cf. Erasmus 1953). But the overall movement also had an internal consistency in the sense that Boas' anthropology made certain types of anthropological questions more relevant than others.

Starting in the mid-1930s, however, "science" began to assert itself more strongly against "history" in American anthropology (cf. Harris 1968, pp. 605ff). As Robert Redfield pointed out in 1937 (Eggan 1955, p. xi), the shift took place in the context of Kroeber's attempt finally to sort out the mixture of history and science in Boasian assumption (Kroeber 1935; cf. Boas 1936)—and, one might add, of the prior shift in Boasian anthropology from historical reconstruction to present process. The reassertion of more "scientific" points of view began first under the stimulus of Radcliffe-Brown at Chicago, and continued in the 1940s in the work of such diverse figures as George Murdock, Julian Steward, and Leslie White. There were attempts to combine the more scientific viewpoints with a Boasian historical orientation (Eggan 1954). However, by the middle 1950s there were signs of more general dissatisfaction with the Boasian viewpoint (Ray 1955; Wax 1956), and since that time Boas has been subjected to sharply critical evaluation by several neoevolutionist writers (White 1963, 1966; Harris 1968). While the variety of the newer viewpoints strains a bit within the rubric "scientific," and more particularistic historical orientations have not completely disappeared, the anthropology of the last two decades has been much more concerned with comparison and generalization, with the universal characteristics of human nature and sociocultural development (Wolf 1964, pp. 13–24). Indeed, some might argue that Boas is rapidly receding into the historical past of American anthropology.

To suggest this, however, is to minimize neither the historical impact nor the lasting contribution of Boasian anthropology, and it is quite possible that the contemporary relevance of the Boasian viewpoint is far from exhausted. At a level which I have chosen not to treat here, but which I have discussed at length elsewhere (Stocking 1968a; cf. Spier 1959), I would suggest that it is out of Boas' critique of evolutionary assumptions that certain of the most fundamental orientations of modern American cultural anthropology derive: on the one hand, the rejection of the traditional nineteenth-century linkage of race and culture in a single hierarchical evolutionary sequence; on the other, the elaboration of the concept of culture as a relativistic, pluralistic, holistic, integrated, and historically conditioned framework for the study of the determination of human behavior.

The concept of culture has since 1950 undergone an increasingly self-conscious reanalysis (Kroeber and Kluckhohn 1952; Wolf 1964). Culture is now seen less in terms of inventories of material artifacts and concrete behavioral manifestations and more in terms of codes and rules, symbolic structures, and systems of meaning. Even so, the recent development of the concept can be viewed as a convergence of the Boasian "pattern" and the Durkheimian "structural-functional" theories of culture (Singer 1968). The complexities of this convergence are beyond the scope of this paper (the Durkheimian tradition itself was by no means homogeneous or unilinear, and led not only to Radcliffe-Brown but also to Lévi-Strauss). Nevertheless, it is worth noting that some recent approaches to the study of culture bear at least analogous similarities, if not direct historical connections, to certain aspects of Boas' thought. These are most evident in the systematic elaboration of linguistic models and in the attempt to establish "emic" categories through linguistic analysis. Lévi-Strauss's references to Boas (Lévi-Strauss 1963, pp. 18–21) and componential analysts' references to Kroeber's 1909 paper, which was heavily influenced by Boas (Stocking 1968c; Hymes 1964, p. 695), both suggest historical relationships that might be more systematically explored. In this context, specific aspects of Boas' thought may be more directly relevant to current anthropological inquiry than his recent eclipse might lead one to think.

Be that as it may, at a more general level it may be argued that the Boasian orientation, broadly construed, will always be relevant to anthropological inquiry. The past record of attempts to develop a natural scientific social or cultural anthropology gives some ground for skepticism that such inquiry will ever be wholly subsumed by "science." Certainly the bright hopes of the 1930s have faded somewhat among British social anthropologists. It has been almost a decade since Rodney Needham suggested:

Sociological laws of functional interdependence have not yet been established in social anthropology, no general theory has so far emerged, and a succession of testable hypotheses have led (where they have led anywhere) not to abstract formulae of social life but to empirical generalizations. Rather than now possessing a solid theoretical basis . . . social anthropology is in a state of conceptual confusion expressed in proliferating technical taxonomies and definitional exercises, each new field study offering enough "anomalous" features to lead to yet more typological and methodological pronouncements. We have reached a point of empirical plenitude and propositional futility at which Leach's precept that in anthropological analysis "we must take each case as it comes" inspires both relief and hope. As he persuasively writes, "ethnographic facts will be much easier to understand if we approach them free of all . . . *a priori* assumptions. Our concern is with what the significant social categories are: not with what they ought to be." With these words we are back to Durkheim and Mauss, back to 1903. [Needham 1963, p. xli]

From a somewhat different perspective, one might say that we are not so far from Boas. The skepticism of general theory and sociological laws, the rejection of *a priori* assumption, the focus on the individual ethnographic case—Boas' shade must smile with satisfaction!

The Radcliffe-Brownian tradition is of course only one current of scientism in anthropology. The "scientific" impulse has been a part of anthropology for a long time, and will undoubtedly continue to be a fruitful stimulus to inquiry. But one need not accept F. W. Maitland's turn-of-the-century prediction that "by and by anthropology will have the choice between being history and being nothing" to join Boas in doubting that science will ever carry the day completely (cf. esp. Boas 1932, pp. 257–258). From this point of view, the issues of the Boas-Mason debate and the antinomies in Boas' own intellectual position may have general epistemological resonance—if not specific methodological relevance—for a long time to come.

PART I

THE BACKGROUND OF BOAS' ANTHROPOLOGY

The five background pieces I have selected move from the general to the particular—from the sweep of the late-nineteenth-century anthropological context through Boas' own family background to what was perhaps his most important single anthropological experience.

The occasion of the first deserves some comment. As an adjunct to the Louisiana Purchase Exposition held in St. Louis during 1904, there was a Congress of Arts and Science, which was attended by many of the world's leading intellectual figures, and which has since been described as the "coming of age" of American scholarship (Coats 1961). The program within each discipline was headed by two papers, one historical, the other on the current state of theory. American anthropology was at this point in a state of incomplete transition (cf. Darnell 1969, 1971c). The leading figures of the nineteenth-century social-evolutionary tradition (Lewis Henry Morgan, Daniel Garrison Brinton, and John Wesley Powell) were all dead (Resek 1960; Darnell 1967; Darrah 1951). The intellectual leader of the discipline was clearly Boas; but the man who organized the anthropological section of the congress was W. J. McGee, who had been Powell's right-hand man at the Bureau of American Ethnology until forced out of the bureau after Powell's death (McGee 1915). Unlike many of the Washington anthropologists, McGee was rather friendly to Boas, but he was nonetheless a social evolutionist of the older school; and when it came to allocating responsibilities at the congress, he took the theoretical paper for himself, over Boas' objection. An

unwilling historian, Boas had more motive than most scientists for viewing the history of his discipline in terms of his own theoretical viewpoint.
We get here, then, Boas' own myth-history of anthropology, with what
was to become the typically Boasian overemphasis on the impact of
Darwinism, a diminution (by virtual omission) of the American evolutionary tradition, and an outcome in a characteristically Boasian set of
problems and methodological orientations. Even so, the piece remains
today one of the better short treatments of the subject, perhaps in part
because Boas' historical viewpoint led him to see anthropology itself as
an historical product—its almost accidental present unity facing possible
fragmentation under the stress of increasingly rigorous demands for specialized training in each component subdiscipline.

Not surprisingly, Boas emphasized the German contribution to his discipline, and the second selection focuses in greater detail on this aspect of
his background. Its special interest lies in the fact that Rudolf Virchow,
whom Boas first met in meetings of the Berlin Anthropological Society
during the winter of 1882, was as close as any man could be to Boas'
model of the natural scientist. Like Boas, Virchow was methodologically
conservative, institutionally activist, and politically liberal; and he, too,
was fired by what Boas much later called "the ice-cold flame of the passion for seeking the truth for truth's sake" (Boas 1945, p. 1). Aside from
obvious parallels in physical anthropology, there are many analogies
between Virchow's critical view of Darwinism and Boas' own later attitude to cultural evolution. Beyond this, one notes even the significance of
details of phrasing: Virchow took a leading organizational role in German science, and "*therefore* it is no wonder that his views have wielded
a far-reaching influence"—a lesson Boas himself took very much to heart.

With the third and fourth selections, we turn from anthropological to
biographical context, the best brief statement of which is contained in
reminiscences Boas offered in 1938 (cf. Stocking 1968a, pp. 135–160;
Kluckhohn and Prufer 1959). To supplement these, I have included
(with minor deletions) one of a series of letters discussing his career and
research plans that Boas wrote in the early 1880s to his Uncle Abraham
Jacobi, a "forty-eighter" who had established himself as a leading physi-
cian in New York City. Feeling his academic prospects in Germany
threatened by a rising wave of anti-Semitism, Boas was already in 1882
considering emigration to the United States, and his letter was intended
to support an application for a fellowship at Johns Hopkins. His parents,
however, preferred to keep him in Germany, and with their support he
continued his studies in Berlin. There, during the following year, his
interest in Eskimo migration patterns developed into plans for an
extended research expedition, and in June 1883 he embarked for Baffinland aboard the sailing ship *Germania*.

Over the next fifteen months in "the sublime loneliness of the Arctic,"
Boas found among the Eskimo confirmation of his conviction that "the

idea of a 'cultured' individual is merely relative." His letter-diary for this period is preserved in his papers, but rather than forestall its future publication by including portions here, I have incorporated instead a popular account that Boas wrote after his return. By this time, his geographical interests had receded into the background, and he was definitely committed to a lifetime study of man.

 SELECTION 1

The History of Anthropology ~ 1904

I have been asked to speak on the history of anthropology. The task that has been allotted to me is so vast, and the time at my disposal is so short, that it will be impossible to do justice to the work of the minds that have made anthropology what it is. It would even be futile to characterize the work of the greatest among the contributors to our science. All that I can undertake to do is to discuss the general conditions of scientific thought that have given rise to anthropology.

Viewing my task from this standpoint, you will pardon me if I do not first attempt to define what anthropology ought to be, and with what subjects it ought to deal, but take my cue rather from what it is and how it has developed.

Before I enter into my subject, I will say that the speculative anthropology of the eighteenth and of the early part of the nineteenth century is distinct in its scope and method from the science which is called "anthropology" at the present time, and is not included in our discussion.

At the present time, anthropologists occupy themselves with problems relating to the physical and mental life of mankind as found in varying forms of society, from the earliest times up to the present period, and in all parts of the world. Their researches bear upon the form and functions of the body as well as upon all kinds of manifestations of mental life. Accordingly, the subject-matter of anthropology is partly a branch of biology, partly a branch of the mental sciences. Among the mental phenomena, language, invention, art, religion, social organization, and law have received particular attention. Among anthropologists of our time we

Address at the International Congress of Arts and Science, St. Louis, September 1904, as published in *Congress of Arts and Science*, ed. H. J. Rogers, 8 vols. (Boston: Houghton Mifflin, 1906), 5: 468–482. Also published in *Science* 20 (1904): 513–524.

find a considerable amount of specialization of the subject-matter of their researches according to the divisions here given.

As in other sciences whose subject-matter is the actual distribution of phenomena and their causal relation, we find in anthropology two distinct methods of research and aims of investigation: the one, the historical method, which endeavors to reconstruct the actual history of mankind; the other, the generalizing method, which attempts to establish the laws of its development. According to the personal inclination of the investigator, the one or the other method prevails in his researches. A considerable amount of geographical and historical specialization has also taken place among what may be called the "historical school of anthropologists." Some devote their energies to the elucidation of the earliest history of mankind, while others study the inhabitants of remote regions, and still others the survivals of early times that persist in our midst.

The conditions thus outlined are the result of a long development, the beginnings of which during the second half of the eighteenth century may be clearly observed. The interest in the customs and appearance of the inhabitants of distant lands is, of course, much older. The descriptions of Herodotus show that even among the nations of antiquity, notwithstanding their self-centered civilization, this interest was not lacking. The travelers of the Middle Ages excited the curiosity of their contemporaries by the recital of their experiences. The literature of the Spanish conquest of America is replete with remarks on the customs of the natives of the New World. But there is hardly any indication of the thought that these observations might be made the subject of scientific treatment. They were and remained curiosities. It was only when their relation to our own civilization became the subject of inquiry that the foundations of anthropology were laid. Its germs may be discovered in the early considerations of theologists regarding the relations between Pagan religions and the revelations of Christianity. They were led to the conclusion that the lower forms of culture, more particularly of religion, were due to degeneration, to a falling-away from the revealed truth, of which traces are to be found in primitive beliefs.

During the second half of the eighteenth century we find the fundamental concept of anthropology well formulated by the rationalists who preceded the French Revolution. The deep-seated feeling that political and social inequality was the result of a faulty development of civilization, and that originally all men were born equal, led Rousseau to the naïve assumption of an ideal natural state which we ought to try to regain. These ideas were shared by many, and the relation of the culture of primitive man to our civilization remained the topic of discussion. To this period belong Herder's *Ideen zur Geschichte der Menschheit*, in which, perhaps for the first time, the fundamental thought of the development of the culture of mankind as a whole is clearly expressed.

About this time, Cook made his memorable voyages, and the culture of the tribes of the Pacific Islands became first known to Europe. His observations and the descriptions of Forster were eagerly taken up by students, and were extensively used in support of their theories. Nevertheless, even the best attempts of this period were essentially speculative and deductive, for the rigid inductive method had hardly begun to be understood in the domain of natural sciences, much less in that of the mental sciences.

While, on the whole, the study of the mental life of mankind had in its beginning a decidedly historical character, and while knowledge of the evolution of civilization was recognized as its ultimate aim, the biological side of anthropology developed in an entirely different manner. It owes its origin to the great zoölogists of the eighteenth century; and in conformity with the general systematic tendencies of the times, the main efforts were directed towards a classification of the races of man and to the discovery of valid characteristics by means of which the races could be described as varieties of one species, or as distinct species. The attempts at classification were numerous, but no new point of view was developed.

During the nineteenth century a certain approach between these two directions was made, which may be exemplified by the work of Klemm. The classificatory aspect was combined with the historical one, and the leading discussion related to the discovery of mental differences between the zoölogical varieties or races of men, and to the question of polygenism and monogenism. The passions that were aroused by the practical and ethical aspects of the slavery question did much to concentrate attention on this phase of the anthropological problem.

As stated before, most of the data of anthropology had been collected by travelers whose prime object was geographical discoveries. For this reason the collected material soon demanded the attention of geographers, who viewed it from a new standpoint. To them the relations between man and nature were of prime importance, and their attention was directed less to psychological questions than to those relating to the dependence of the form of culture upon geographical surroundings, and the control of natural conditions gained by man with the advance of civilization.

Thus we find about the middle of the nineteenth century the beginnings of anthropology laid from three distinct points of view: the historical, the classificatory, and the geographical. About this time the historical aspect of the phenomena of nature took hold of the minds of investigators in the whole domain of science. Beginning with biology, and principally through Darwin's powerful influence, it gradually revolutionized the whole method of natural and mental science, and led to a new formulation of their problems. The idea that the phenomena of the present have developed from previous forms with which they are genetically connected, and which determine them, shook the foundations of the old principles of classification, and knit together groups of facts that hitherto had seemed disconnected. Once clearly enunciated, the historical view of the natural sciences proved irresistible, and the old problems faded away before the new attempts to discover the history of evolution. From the very beginning there has been a strong tendency to combine with the historical aspect a subjective valuation of the various phases of development, the present serving as a standard of comparison. The oft-observed change from simple forms to more complex forms, from uniformity to diversity, was interpreted as a change from the less valuable to the more valuable, and thus the historical view assumed in many cases an ill-concealed teleological tinge. The grand picture of nature in which for the first time the universe appears as a unit of ever-changing form and color, each momentary aspect being determined by the past moment and determining the coming changes, is still obscured by a subjective element, emotional in its sources, which leads us to ascribe the highest value to that which is near and dear to us.

The new historical view also came into conflict with the generalizing method of science. It was imposed upon that older view of nature in which the discovery of general laws was considered the ultimate aim of investigation. According to this view, laws may be exemplified by individual events, which, however, lose their specific interest once the laws are discovered. The actual event possesses no scientific value in itself, but only so far as it leads to the discovery of a general law. This view is, of course, fundamentally opposed to the purely historical view. Here the laws of nature are recognized in each individual event, and the chief interest centres in the event as an incident of the picture of the world. In a way the historic view contains a strong æsthetic element, which finds its satisfaction in the clear conception of the individual event. It is easily intelligible that the combination of these two standpoints led to the subordination of the historical fact under the concept of the law of nature. Indeed, we find all the sciences which took up the historical standpoint for the first time soon engaged in endeavors to discover the laws according to which evolution has taken place. The regularity in the processes of evolution became the centre of attraction even before the processes of evolution had been observed and understood. All sciences were equally guilty of premature theories of evolution based on observed homologies and supposed similarities. The theories had to be revised again and again, as the slow progress of empirical knowledge of the data of evolution proved their fallacy.

Anthropology also felt the quickening impulse of the historic point of view, and its development followed the same lines that may be observed in the history of the other sciences. The unity of civilization and of primitive culture that had been divined by Herder now shone forth as a certainty. The multiplicity and diversity of curious customs and beliefs appeared as early steps in the evolution of civilization from simple forms of culture. The striking similarity between the customs of remote districts was the proof of the uniform manner in which civilization had developed the world over. The laws according to which this uniform development of culture took place became the new problem which engrossed the attention of anthropologists.

This is the source from which sprang the ambitious system of Herbert Spencer and the ingenious theories of Edward Burnett Tylor. The underlying thought of the numerous attempts to systematize the whole range of social phenomena, or one or the other of its features,—such as religious belief, social organization, forms of marriage,—has been the belief that one definite system can be found according to which all culture has developed; that there is one type of evolution from a primitive form to the highest civilization, which is applicable to the whole of mankind; that, notwithstanding many variations caused by local and historical conditions, the general type of evolution is the same everywhere.

This theory has been discussed most clearly by Tylor, who finds proof for it in the sameness of customs and beliefs the world over. The typical similarity and the occurrence of certain customs in definite combinations are explained by him as due to their belonging to a certain stage in the development of civilization. They do not disappear suddenly, but persist for a time in the form of survivals. These are, therefore, wherever they occur, a proof that a lower stage of culture, of which these customs are characteristic, has been passed through.

Anthropology owes its very existence to the stimulus given by these scholars and to the conclusions reached by them. What had been a chaos of facts appeared now marshaled in orderly array, and the great steps in the slow advance from savagery to civilization were drawn for the first time with a firm hand. We cannot overestimate the influence of the bold generalizations made by these pioneers of modern anthropology. They applied with vigor and unswerving courage the new principles of historical evolution to all the phenomena of civilized life, and in doing so sowed the seeds of the anthropological spirit in the minds of historians and philosophers. Anthropology, which was hardly beginning to be a science, ceased at the same time to lose its character of being a single science, but became a method applicable to all the mental sciences, and indispensable to all of them. We are still in the midst of this development. The sciences first to feel the influence of anthropological thought were those of law and religion. But it was not long before ethics, æsthetics, literature, and philosophy in general were led to accept the evolutionary standpoint in the particular form given to it by the early anthropologists.

The generalized view of the evolution of culture in all its different phases, which is the final result of this method, may be subjected to a further analysis regarding the psychic causes which bring about the regular sequence of the stages of culture. Owing to the abstract form of the results, this analysis must be deductive. It cannot be an induction from empirical psychological data. In this fact lies one of the weaknesses of the method which led a number of anthropologists to a somewhat different statement of the problem. I mention here particularly Adolf Bastian and Georg Gerland. Both were impressed by the sameness of the fundamental traits of culture the world over. Bastian saw in their sameness an effect of the sameness of the human mind, and terms these fundamental traits *Elementargedanken*, declining all further consideration of their origin, since an inductive treatment of this problem is impossible. For him the essential problem of anthropology is the discovery of the elementary ideas, and, in further pursuit of the inquiry, their modification under the influence of geographical environment. Gerland's views agree with those of Bastian in the emphasis laid upon the influence of geographical environment on the forms of culture. In place of the mystic elementary idea of Bastian, Gerland assumes that the elements found in many remote parts of the world are a common inheritance from an early stage of cultural development. It will be seen that in both these views the system of evolution plays a secondary part only, and that the main stress is laid on the causes which bring about modifications of the fundamental and identical traits. There is a close connection between this direction of anthropology and the old geographical school. Here the psychic and environmental relations remain amenable to inductive treatment, while, on the other hand, the fundamental hypotheses exclude the origin of the common traits from further investigation.

The subjective valuation which is characteristic of most evolutionary systems was from the very beginning part and parcel of evolutionary anthropology. It is but natural that, in the study of the history of culture, our own civilization should become the standard, that the achievements of other times and other races should be measured by our own achievements. In no case is it more difficult to lay aside the *Kulturbrille*—to use von den Steinen's apt term—than in viewing our own culture. For this reason the literature of anthropology abounds in attempts to define a number of stages of culture leading from simple forms to the present civilization, from savagery through barbarism to civilization, or from an assumed pre-savagery through the same stages to enlightenment.

The endeavor to establish a schematic line of evolution naturally led back to new attempts at classification, in which each group bears a genetic relation to the other. Such attempts have been made from both the cultural and the biological point of view.

It is necessary to speak here of one line of anthropological research that we have hitherto disregarded. I mean the linguistic method. The origin of language was one of the much-discussed problems of the nineteenth century, and, owing to its relation to the development of culture, it has a direct anthropological bearing. The intimate ties between language and ethnic psychology were expressed by no one more clearly than by Steinthal, who perceived that the form of thought is molded by the whole social environment of which language is part. Owing to the rapid change of language, the historical treatment of the linguistic problem had developed long before the historic aspect of the natural sciences was understood. The genetic relationship of languages was clearly recognized when the genetic relationship of species was hardly thought of. With the increasing knowledge of languages, they were grouped according to common descent, and, when no further relationship could be proved, a classification according to morphology was attempted. To the linguist, whose whole attention is directed to the study of the expression of thought by language, language is the individuality of a people, and therefore a classification of languages must present itself to him as a classification of peoples. No other manifestation of the mental life of man can be classified so minutely and definitely as language. In none are the genetic relations more clearly established. It is only when no further genetic and morphological relationship can be found, that the linguist is compelled to coördinate languages and can give no further clue regarding their relationship and origin. No wonder, then, that this method was used to classify mankind, although in reality the linguist classified only languages. The result of the classification seems eminently satisfactory on account of its definiteness as compared with the result of biological and cultural classifications.

Meanwhile the methodical resources of biological or somatic anthropology had also developed, and had enabled the investigator to make nicer distinctions between human types than he had been able to make. The landmark in the development of this branch of anthropology has been the introduction of the metric method, which owes its first strong development to Quetelet. A little later we shall have to refer to this subject again. For the present it may suffice to say that a clearer definition of the terms "type" and "variability" led to the application of the statistical method, by means of which comparatively slight varieties can be distinguished satisfactorily. By the application of this method, it soon became apparent that the races of man could be subdivided into types which were characteristic of definite geographical areas and of the people inhabiting them. The same misinterpretation developed here as was found among the linguists. As they identified language and people, so the anatomists identified somatic type and people, and based their classification of peoples wholly on their somatic characters.

The two principles were soon found to clash. Peoples genetically connected by language, or even the same in language, were found to be diverse in type, and people of the same type proved to be diverse in language. Furthermore, the results of classifications according to cultural groups disagreed with both the linguistic and the somatic classifications. In long and bitter controversies the representatives of these three directions of anthropological research contended for the correctness of their conclusions. This war of opinions was fought out particularly on the ground of the so-called Aryan question, and only gradually did the fact come to be understood that each of these classifications is the reflection of a certain group of facts. The linguistic classification records the historical fates of languages and indirectly of the people speaking these languages; the somatic classification records the blood relationships of groups of people, and thus traces another phase of their history; while the cultural classification records historical events of still another character, the diffusion of culture from one people to another and the absorption of one culture by another. Thus it became clear that the attempted classifications were expressions of historical data bearing upon the unwritten history of races and peoples, and recorded their descent, mixture of blood, changes of language, and development of culture. Attempts at generalized classifications based on these methods can claim validity only for that group of phenomena to which the method applies. An agreement of their results—that is, original association between somatic type, language, and culture—must not be expected. Thus the historical view of anthropology received support from the struggles between these three methods of classification.

We remarked before that the evolutionary method was based essentially on the observation of the sameness of cultural traits the world over. On the one hand, the sameness was assumed as proof of a regular, uniform evolution of culture. On the other hand, it was assumed to represent the elementary idea which arises by necessity in the mind of man and which cannot be analyzed, or as the earliest surviving form of human thought.

The significance of these elementary ideas or universal traits of culture has been brought into prominence by the long-continued controversy between the theory of their independent origin and that of their transmission from one part of the world to another. This struggle began, even before the birth of modern anthropology, with the contest between Grimm's theory of the origin and history of myths and Benfey's proof of transmissions, which was based on his learned investigations into the literary history of tales. It is still in progress. On the one hand, there are investigators who would exclude the consideration of transmission altogether, who believe it to be unlikely, and deem the alleged proof irrelevant, and who ascribe sameness of cultural traits wholly to the psychic unity of mankind and to the uniform reaction of the human mind upon the same stimulus. An extremist in this direction was the late Daniel G. Brinton. On the other hand, Friedrich Ratzel, whose recent loss we lament, inclined decidedly to the opinion that all sameness of cultural traits must be accounted for by transmission, no matter how far distant the regions in which they are found. In comparison with these two views, the third one, which was mentioned before as represented by Gerland, namely, that such cultural traits are vestiges or survivals of the earliest stages of a generalized human culture, has found few supporters.

It is evident that this fundamental question cannot be settled by the continued discussion of general facts, since the various explanations are logically equally probable. It requires actual investigation into the individual history of such customs to discover the causes of their present distribution.

Here is the place to mention the studies in folklore which have excited considerable interest in recent times, and which must be considered a branch of anthropological research. Beginning with records of curious superstitions and customs and of popular tales, folklore has become the science of all the manifestations of popular life. Folklorists occupy themselves primarily with the folklore of Europe, and thus supplement the material collected by anthropologists in foreign lands. The theorists of folklore are also divided into the two camps of the adherents of the psychological theory and those of the historical theory. In England the former holds sway, while on the Continent the historical theory seems to be gaining ground. The identity of the contents of folklore all over Europe seems to be an established fact. To the one party the occurrence of these forms of folklore seems to be due in part to psychic necessity, in part to the survival of earlier customs and beliefs. To the other party, it seems to owe its origin to the spread of ideas over the whole continent, which may, in part, at least, be followed by literary evidence.

However this controversy, both in folklore and in anthropology, may be settled, it is clear that it must lead to detailed historical investigations, by means of which definite problems may be solved, and that it will furthermore lead to psychological researches into the conditions of transmission, adaptation, and invention. Thus this controversy will carry us beyond the limits set by the theory of elementary ideas, and by that of a single system of evolution of civilization.

Another aspect of the theories here discussed deserves special mention. I mean the assumption of a "folk-psychology" (*Völker-psychologie*) as distinct from individual psychology. "Folk-psychology" deals with those psychic actions which take place in each individual as a social unit; and the psychology of the individual must be interpreted by the data of a social psychology, because each individual can think, feel, and act only as a member of the social group to which he belongs. The growth of language and all ethnic phenomena have thus been treated from the point of view of a social psychology, and special attention has been given to the subconscious influences which sway crowds and masses of people, and to the processes of imitation. I mention Steinthal, Wundt, Baldwin, Tarde, Stoll, among the men who have devoted their energies to these and related problems. Notwithstanding their efforts, and those of a number of sociologists and geographers, the relation of "folk-psychology" to individual psychology has not been elucidated satisfactorily.

We will now turn to a consideration of the recent history of somatology. The historical point of view wrought deep changes also in this branch of anthropology. In place of classification, the evolution of human types became the main object of investigation. The two questions of man's place in nature and of the evolution of human races and types came to the front. The morphological and embryological methods which had been developed by biologists were applied to the human species, and the new endeavors were directed to the discovery of the predecessor of man, to his position in the animal series, and to evidences regarding the direction in which the species develops. I need mention only Huxley and Wiedersheim to characterize the trend of these researches.

In one respect, however, the study of the human species differs from that of the animal series. I stated before that the slight differences between types which are important to the anthropologist had led to the substitution of the metric or quantitative description for the verbal or qualitative method. The study of the effects of natural selection, of environment, of heredity, as applied to man, made the elaboration of these methods a necessity. Our interest in slight differences is so much greater in man than in animals or plants, that here the needs of quantitative precision were first felt. We owe it to Francis Galton that the methods of the quantitative study of the varieties of man have been developed, and that the study has been extended from the field of anatomy over that of physiology and experimental psychology. His researches were extended and systematized by Karl Pearson, in whose hands the question, which was originally one of the precise treatment of the biological problem of anthropology, has outgrown its original limits, and has become a general biological method for the study of the characteristics and of the development of varieties.

We may now summarize the fundamental problems which give to anthropology its present character. In the biological branch we have the problem of the morphological evolution of man and that of the development of varieties. Inseparable from these questions is also that of correlation between somatic and mental characters, which has a practical as well as a theoretical interest. In psychological anthropology the important questions are the discovery of a system of the evolution of culture, the study of the modifications of simple general traits under the influence of different geographical and social conditions, the question of transmission and spontaneous origin, and that of "folk-psychology" versus individual psychology. It will, of course, be understood that this enumeration is not exhaustive, but includes only some of the most important points of view that occupy the minds of investigators.

The work of those students who are engaged in gathering the material from which this history of mankind is to be built up is deeply influenced by these problems. It would be vain to attempt to give even the briefest review of what has been achieved by the modest collector of facts, how his efforts have covered the remotest parts of the world, how he has tried to uncover and interpret the remains left by the races of the past.

I think we may say, without injustice, that his work is directed principally to the explanation of special problems that derive their chief interest from a personal love for the particular question and from an ardent desire to see its obscurity removed and to present its picture in clear outlines. Nevertheless, the well-trained and truly scientific observer will always be aware of the general relations of his special problem, and will be influenced in his treatment of the special question by the general theoretical discussions of his times. It must be said with regret that the number of anthropological observers who have a sufficient understanding of the problems of the day is small. Still their number has increased considerably during the last twenty years, and consequently a constant improvement in the reliability and thoroughness of the available observations may be noticed.

One or two aspects of the research work of the field anthropologist must be mentioned. The studies in prehistoric archeology have been given a lasting impulse by the discussions relating to the evolution of mankind and of human culture. Two great problems have occupied the attention of archeologists,—the origin and first appearance of the human race, and the historical sequence of races and of types of culture. To the archeologist the determination of the chronological order is an important one. The determination of the geological period in which man appeared, the chronological relation of the earliest types of man to their later successors, the sequence of types of culture as determined by the artifacts of each period, and approximate determinations of the absolute time to which these remains belong, are the fundamental problems with which archeology is concerned. The results obtained have the most immediate bearing upon the general question of the evolution of culture, since the ideal aim of archeology practically coincides with this general problem, the solution of which would be contained in a knowledge of the chronological development of culture. Of course, in many cases the chronological question cannot be answered, and then the archeological observations simply rank with ethnological observations of primitive people.

The field-work of ethnologists has been influenced in several directions by the theoretical discussions of anthropologists. We do not need to dwell on the fact that the scope of ethnological research has become more extensive and exhaustive by taking into consideration more thoroughly than before the whole range of cultural phenomena. More interesting than this is the stimulus that has been given to historic and psychological observation. On the one hand, the theory of transmission has induced investigators to trace the distribution and history of customs and beliefs with care, so as to ascertain empirically whether they are spontaneous creations, or whether they are borrowed and adapted. On the other hand, the psychic conditions that accompany various types of culture have received more careful attention.

These detailed archeological and ethnological studies have retroacted upon the theories of anthropology. The grand system of the evolution of culture, that is valid for all humanity, is losing much of its plausibility. In place of a simple line of evolution there appears a multiplicity of converging and diverging lines which it is difficult to bring under one system. Instead of uniformity, the striking feature seems to be diversity. On the other hand, certain general psychic facts seem to become discernible, which promise to connect "folk-psychology" with individual psychology. The trend of this development is familiar to us in the history of other sciences, such as geology and biology. The brilliant theories in which the whole range of problems of a science appears simple and easily explicable have always preceded the periods of steady empirical work which makes necessary a complete revision of the original theories, and leads through a period of uncertainty to a more strictly inductive attack of the ultimate problems. So it is with anthropology. Later than the older sciences, it has outgrown the systematizing period, and is just now entering upon the empirical revision of its theories.

Our sketch of the history of the prevailing tendencies in anthropology would be incomplete without a few remarks on the men who have made it what it is. What has been said before shows clearly that there is hardly a science that is as varied in its methods as anthropology. Its problems have been approached by biologists, linguists, geographers, psychologists, historians, and philosophers. Up to ten years ago we had no trained anthropologists, but students drifted into anthropological research from all the sciences that I have mentioned here, and perhaps from others. With many it was the interest aroused by a special problem, not theoretical considerations, that decided their course. Others were attracted by a general interest in the evolution of mankind. The best among them were gradually permeated by the fundamental spirit of anthropological research, which consists in the appreciation of the necessity of studying all forms of human culture, because the variety of its forms alone can throw light upon the history of its development, past and future, and which deigns even the poorest tribe, the degraded criminal, and the physical degenerate worthy of attentive study, because the expressions of his mental life, no less than his physical appearance, may throw light upon the history of mankind.

Even now the multifarious origin of anthropology is reflected in the multiplicity of its methods. The historian or the political economist who comes in contact with anthropological problems cannot follow the methods of the biologist and of the linguist. Neither can the anthropologist of our period fill the demands for information of all those who may need anthropological data. It might almost seem that the versatility required of him will set a limit to his usefulness as a thorough scientist. However, the solution of this difficulty is not far off. We have seen that a great portion of the domain of anthropology has developed through the application of the new historical point of view to the mental sciences. To those who occupy themselves with this group of problems, anthropological knowledge will be indispensable. Though the anthropological point of view may thus pervade the treatment of an older branch of science, and help to develop new standpoints, the assistance that anthropology renders it does not destroy the independence of the older science, which in a long history has developed its own aims and methods. Conscious of the invigorating influence of our point of view and of the grandeur of a single all-compassing science of man, enthusiastic anthropologists may proclaim the mastery of anthropology over older sciences that have achieved where we are still struggling with methods, that have built up noble structures where chaos reigns with us, the trend of development points in another direction, in the continuance of each science by itself, assisted where may be by anthropological methods. The practical demands of anthropology also demand a definition and restriction of its field of work rather than constant expansion.

The historical development of the work of anthropologists seems to single out clearly a domain of knowledge that heretofore has not been treated by any other science. It is the biological history of mankind in all its varieties; linguistics applied to people without written languages; the ethnology of people without historic records, and prehistoric archeology. It is true that these limits are constantly being overstepped, but the unbiased observer will recognize that, in all other fields, special knowledge is required which cannot be supplied by general anthropology. The *general* problem of the evolution of mankind is being taken up now by the investigator of primitive tribes, now by the student of the history of civilization. We may still recognize in it the ultimate aim of anthropology in the wider sense of the term, but we must understand that it will be reached by coöperation between all the mental sciences and the efforts of the anthropologist.

The field of research that has been left for anthropology in the narrower sense of the term is, even as it is, almost too wide, and there are indications of its breaking up. The biological, linguistic, and ethnologic-archeological methods are so distinct, that on the whole the same man will not be equally proficient in all of them. The time is rapidly drawing near when the biological branch of anthropology will be finally separated from the rest, and become a part of biology. This seems necessary, since all the problems relating to the effect of geographical and social environment and those relating to heredity are primarily of a biological character. Problems may be set by the general anthropologist. They will be solved by the biologist. Almost equally cogent are the reasons that urge on to a separation of the purely linguistic work from the ethnological work. I think the time is not far distant when anthropology pure and simple will deal with the customs and beliefs of the less civilized people only, and when linguistics and biology will continue and develop the work that we are doing now because no one else cares for it. Nevertheless, we must always demand that the anthropologist who carries on field-research must be familiar with the principles of these three methods, since all of them are needed for the investigation of his problems. No less must we demand that he have a firm grasp of the general results of the anthropological method as applied by various sciences. It alone will give his work that historic perspective which constitutes its higher scientific value.

A last word as to the value that the anthropological method is assuming in the general system of our culture and education. I do not wish to refer to its practical value to those who have to deal with foreign races or with national questions. Of greater educational importance is its power to make us understand the roots from which our civilization has sprung, to impress us with the relative value of all forms of culture, and thus serve as a check to an exaggerated valuation of the standpoint of our own period, which we are only too liable to consider the ultimate goal of human evolution, thus depriving ourselves of the benefits to be gained from the teachings of other cultures, and hindering an objective criticism of our own work.

 SELECTION 2

Rudolf Virchow's Anthropological Work

In Rudolf Virchow science has lost one of its great leaders, Germany one of her great citizens, the world one of its great men. For sixty years Virchow has devoted his strong mind and his indefatigable energies to advancing the work of mankind. The sciences of medicine, anatomy, pathology and anthropology count him as one of their great men. For long years he has been a power in German political life, always upholding the cause of personal freedom.

The beginnings of his anthropological work almost coincide with the beginnings of modern physical anthropology in Germany. Among the

Science 16 (1902): 441–445.

men who laid the foundation of this science no one has done more to shape, guide and foster it than Rudolf Virchow. His interest in anthropology, which was destined to impress the mark of his personality upon the young science, developed during the time when he investigated the causes of cretinism and the conditions determining the growth of the skull. The similarities between pathological forms of the skull and those found among different races of man probably led him to researches on the variations of form of the human body. The scope of his anthropological interests expanded rapidly and the impetus which he gave to anthropological work, particularly in physical anthropology and in prehistoric archeology, was so great that the development of these two branches of science in Germany may be said to center in Virchow's activity.

At the time when Virchow took up his work, anthropology was still in its first beginnings. During the eighteenth century Von Sœmmering and Blumenbach in Germany, and Camper in Holland, had directed their attention to a study of the anatomical characteristics of the races of man, but the new anthropology did not arise until the second half of the past century. The strong impetus which the theory of evolution gave to all sciences, combined with the immediate interest in the early history of European nations, and the increasing knowledge of foreign races were the principal factors that contributed to the formation of modern anthropology.

Virchow, through his eminent faculty for organization, has advanced the whole field of anthropology. He took a leading part in the formation of the German Anthropological Society, of the *Berliner Gesellschaft für Anthropologie, Ethnologie und Urgeschichte*, and in the establishment of the monumental *Archiv für Anthropologie* which occupies a high rank in anthropological literature. The two societies soon became the centers of anthropological activity in Germany. The German Anthropological Society devoted its energies to the study of the physical characteristics and of the earliest history of the Germans. Under Virchow's lead this society undertook to collect statistics relating to the distribution of the color of skin, eyes and hair in Germany, and observations were collected in all the public schools of the country. The results of this extended inquiry, which include a cartographic representation of the distribution of types in Germany and a discussion of their probable history, were published by Virchow.

The *Berliner Gesellschaft für Anthropologie, Ethnologie, und Urgeschichte* soon became a center to which flowed a flood of anthropological material from all parts of the world, and where important scientific questions were discussed by the most competent authorities. Through its intimate relations with German travellers the society became of valuable assistance in the development of the Berlin Ethnographical Museum, which owes its origin and greatness to Adolf Bastian. Owing to Virchow's influence the society gradually acquired a large and valuable collection of human crania and skeletons. Among the subjects discussed before the society European archeology always held a prominent place, and Virchow took a lively part in this work which has contributed much to the growth of the prehistoric collections in Berlin.

As director of the Pathological Institute and Museum of the University of Berlin, Virchow had further opportunities to advance our knowledge of the anatomy of races, and he accumulated much valuable anthropological material in this Institute. His studies of prehistoric archeology brought him also into close contact with students of folk-lore and he became one of the founders of the *Museum für Volkstrachten.*

It will thus be seen that Virchow took the leading part in the organization of anthropological work in Germany. Therefore, it is no wonder that his views have wielded a far-reaching influence, so much so, that without a knowledge of his work the peculiarity of German physical anthropology and of German prehistoric archeology can hardly be understood.

Most important is his attitude toward the theories relating to the descent of man. His views regarding this question were determined by his fundamental researches on the functions of the cell in the animal organism. He formulated his views in the words that every cell is derived from another cell. No matter how much the forms of the cells may vary, every new form is derived from a previous form. Cells, in the course of their lives, may change their forms according to age and according to the influences to which they are subjected. Such changes take place both in the healthy and in the sick organism, and often it is impossible to draw a sharp line between normal or physiological, and abnormal or pathological, changes. Virchow himself expresses these views in the words that in reality there is no distinct line of demarcation between physiological and pathological processes, that the latter are only physiological processes which take place under difficult conditions. The cell which changes its form during its lifetime may, therefore, be said to be variable; or, in Virchow's words, it possesses mutability. From his point of view the whole question of the origin of species centers in the problem of the relation between the mutability of the organism and the mutability of the cell. The comparison of the forms of organisms and organs may form the starting point of researches on variability, but the study of the variations of the whole organism or organ must be based on the study of the variations of the constituent cells, since the physiological changes of the whole body depend upon the correlated physiological changes that take place in the cells. Without a knowledge of the processes that take place in varying cells, it is impossible to determine whether a deviation from the normal form is due to secondary causes that affect during their period of development organs already formed, or if it is due to primary deviations which develop before the first formation of the varying organ.

Two questions, therefore, arise: the first, if secondary deviations may become hereditary. For this no convincing proof has been found. The second question is whether primary variations do occur, and if so, whether they are hereditary.

Led by these points of view Virchow demands that researches on the origin of species be based on researches on the mutability of cells and groups of cells, and he declines to speculate on the origin of species, until through researches on tissues a sound foundation has been laid. Sometimes it would seem as though Virchow doubted the scientific value of the theory of evolution. I do not think this is the case. He merely emphasizes again and again the methodological point of view, that the understanding of the forms of the body must be based on a knowledge of the forms, mutual relations, and functions of the cells and that, therefore, the question of "mutability" must be settled by researches on these lines.

Furthermore his position rests on the general scientific principle that it is dangerous to classify data that are imperfectly known under the point of view of general theories, and that the sound progress of science requires of us to be clear at every moment, what elements in the system of science are hypothetical and what are the limits of that knowledge which is obtained by exact observation. To this principle Virchow has adhered steadfastly and rigidly, so much so that many an impetuous student has felt his quiet and cautious criticism as an obstacle to progress. On this account he has suffered many hostile attacks—until generally the progress of research showed that the cautious master was right in rejecting the far-reaching conclusion based on imperfect evidence. There are but few students who possess that cold enthusiasm for truth that enables them to be always clearly conscious of the sharp line between attractive theory and the observation that has been secured by hard and earnest work.

There are two anthropological problems which are important in their relation to the theory of evolution; the one that of the antiquity of man, the other that of the interpretation of anatomical characteristics of the lower races. The evidence in regard to the anatomical form of early man is very scanty, and for many years the discussion centered in the interpretation of the Neanderthal skull, which possesses a number of peculiar characteristics, particularly an exceedingly low head and very large superciliary ridges. Virchow demonstrated that the skull had undergone many pathological changes, and he took the position that it was unsafe to base on this single specimen a new race which might be considered a precursor of man. He preferred to consider the skull as an individual variation until other similar finds would give corroborative evidence. Virchow was equally cautious in the interpretation of theromorphic variations in the forms of the human body. He maintained that such forms are not necessarily cases of atavism, but that they may be due to peculiar physiological processes; and that without special investigation of their origin they cannot be considered as proof of a low organization of the races among which they are found with particular frequency. There is no proof that such forms are connected with a low stage of culture of the people among whom they are found. They occur, for instance, among the Malays and among the ancient Peruvians, both of which races have attained high stages of culture.

We cannot, in the scope of these notes, enter upon Virchow's numerous investigations bearing upon the anatomy of the races of man. Many of them contain discussions of general principles. His researches on the physical anthropology of the Germans and his description of American crania may be mentioned as specially important.

His investigation of the anatomical characteristics of the Germans led him naturally to studies in prehistoric archeology to which he devoted much of his time and energies. For a long time forms of the body were considered a characteristic of nationalities. Forms of skulls were described as Teutonic and Slavic; there were Turanian and many other kinds of skulls. Nobody has done more than Virchow to show that this view is untenable. The question of the history of the Slavic settlement of eastern Germany has received much attention on the part of German archeologists and is still far from being entirely cleared up. While methods of burial, prehistoric objects, names of places, plans of villages and houses are good indications for ancient Slavic settlements, the anatomical forms of the present population and of ancient skeletons do not allow us to draw any inference regarding the nationality of the ancient inhabitants, because neither Germans nor Slavs present a uniform and characteristic anatomical type. Virchow has always maintained that the limits of human types do not coincide with the dividing lines of cultures and languages. People who belong to the same type may speak different languages and possess different forms of culture; and on the other hand —as is the case in Germany—different types of man may be combined to form one nation.

These phenomena are intimately connected with the intricate migrations of the races of Europe; with the invasions of southern Europe by Teutonic peoples and the development of north European culture under the influence of the cultures of the eastern part of the Mediterranean Sea. The gradual introduction of metals and the disappearance of the culture of the stone age is one of the phenomena that are of great assistance in clearing up the relations between the ancient inhabitants of Europe. The change of culture indicated by the introduction of bronze indicates that the new culture arose in the far East. This is the reason which induced Virchow to undertake extensive prehistoric studies in Asia Minor and in the region of the Caucasus. His studies in prehistoric archeology, which apparently are so remote from his original anatomical work, are in reality closely connected with his researches on the early history of the races of Europe. Anatomical data alone cannot solve these intricate problems, and Virchow's extensive activity in the field of prehistoric archeology is another proof of his thorough and comprehensive method which utilizes all the available avenues toward the solution of a scientific problem.

Physical anthropology and prehistoric archeology in Germany have become what they are largely through Virchow's influence and activity. His method, views and ideas have been and are the leading ones. His greatness as a scientist is due to the rare combination of a critical judgment of greatest clearness and thoroughness with encyclopedic knowledge and a genius for grasping the causal relation of phenomena. His critical judgment was so strong that, in an address delivered in the summer of 1900, he was even led to doubt the desirability of the strong preponderance of his influence upon current opinion. With profound admiration and gratitude we regard his life's work which has determined the course of a new science.

   SELECTION 3

"The Background
of My Early Thinking"

The background of my early thinking was a German home in which the ideals of the revolution of 1848 were a living force. My father, liberal, but not active in public affairs; my mother, idealistic, with a lively interest in public matters, the founder about 1854 of the kindergarten of my home town, devoted to science. My parents had broken through the shackles of dogma. My father had retained an emotional affection for the ceremonial of his parental home, without allowing it to influence his intellectual freedom. Thus I was spared the struggle against religious dogma that besets the lives of so many young people.

An early intense interest in nature and a burning desire to see everything that I heard or read about dominated my youth. Philosophical questions were therefore remote from me during my adolescent period,

Opening paragraphs from "An Anthropologist's Credo," *The Nation* 147 (1938): 201–204. Later revised and reprinted in *I Believe*, ed. Clifton Fadiman (New York: Simon and Schuster, 1939), pp. 19–29.

and I lived in the surrounding world without speculation, naively enjoying every new impression.

As I remember it now, my first shock came when one of my student friends, a theologian, declared his belief in the authority of tradition and his conviction that one had not the right to doubt what the past had transmitted to us. The shock that this ouright abandonment of freedom of thought gave me is one of the unforgettable moments of my life. A second shock was a series of conversations with an artistically gifted elder sister to whom my materialistic world seemed unendurable. I am inclined to think that these incidents had a permanent influence on my life because they stand out so clearly in my memory.

My university studies were a compromise. On account of my intense emotional interest in the phenomena of the world, I studied geography; on account of my intellectual interest, I studied mathematics and physics. In preparing my doctor's thesis I had to use photometric methods to compare intensities of light. This led me to consider the quantitative values of sensations. In the course of my investigation I learned to recognize that there are domains of our experience in which the concepts of quantity, of measures that can be added or subtracted like those with which I was accustomed to operate, are not applicable.

My reading of the writings of philosophers stimulated new lines of thought, and my previous interests became overshadowed by a desire to understand the relation between the objective and the subjective worlds. Opportunities to continue this line of study by means of psychological investigations did not present themselves, and by a peculiar compromise, presumably largely dictated by the desire to see the world, I decided to make a journey to the Arctic for the purpose of adding to our knowledge of unknown regions and of helping me to understand the reaction of the human mind to natural environment. A year of life spent as an Eskimo among Eskimos had a profound influence upon the development of my views, not immediately, but because it led me away from my former interests and toward the desire to understand what determines the behavior of human beings. The first result of my attempts to explain human behavior as a result of geographical environment was a thorough disappointment. The immediate influences are patent, and the results of this study were so shallow that they did not throw any light on the driving forces that mold behavior.

The psychological origin of the implicit belief in the authority of tradition, which was so foreign to my mind and which had shocked me at an earlier time, became a problem that engaged my thoughts for many years. In fact, my whole outlook upon social life is determined by the question: how can we recognize the shackles that tradition has laid upon us? For when we recognize them, we are also able to break them.

SELECTION 4

Psychic Life from a
Mechanistic Viewpoint

[April 10, 1882]

DEAR UNCLE,

At your request I am sending my Doctor's diploma and testimonials from my teachers.

My course of study and my plans for future work are as follows: after I completed my course at the Gymnasium in Minden, Westphalia, in 1877, I began my studies at the University of Heidelberg. I stayed only one semester at Heidelberg, studying especially mathematics and physics. The following four semesters I spent at Bonn, spending most of my time on mathematics, physics, and botany, and beginning the study of geography. The last four semesters I studied at Kiel, mainly geography and physics, [though] I gave some time to philosophy. At the end of the summer semester, 1881, I graduated and received my doctor's degree. My examination subjects were geography, physics, and philosophy; my dissertation [was] "Beiträge zur Erkentniss der Farbe des Wassers" [*Contribution to the Understanding of the Color of Water*]. I returned to Minden in October, 1881, in order to enjoy [compulsory] military duty until October, 1882.

The objectives of my studies shifted quite a bit during my university years. While in the beginning my intention was to regard mathematics and physics as the final goal, I was led through the study of the natural sciences to other questions which prompted me also to take up geography, and this subject captured my interest to such an extent that I finally chose it as my major study. However, the direction of my work and study was strongly influenced by my training in natural sciences, especially physics. In the course of time I became convinced that my previous materialistic *Weltanschauung*—for a physicist a very understandable one —was untenable, and I gained thus a new standpoint which revealed to

Draft of a letter to A. Jacobi, preserved in the Boas Papers, American Philosophical Sociey, along with a translation, presumably the work of Helene Boas Yampolsky, who worked for several years on the preparation of the papers. The present translation was modified slightly on the advice of David Nicholas, my research assistant at the University of California, Berkeley, who compared Mrs. Yampolsky's translation with the original German.

me the importance of studying the interaction between the organic and the inorganic, above all between the life of a people and their physical environment. Thus arose my plan to regard as my life's task the [following] investigation: How far may we consider the phenomena of organic life, and especially those of the psychic life, from a mechanistic point of view, and what conclusions can be drawn from such a consideration? In order to solve such questions I need at least a general knowledge of physiology, psychology, and sociology, which up to now I do not possess and must acquire.

I am sorry I cannot send you any of my papers in time. [Here follows a list of the psychophysical papers Boas published in 1882.] I have for the present given up my psychophysical work, as there was no time to make experiments during my military training. [Here follows a reference to a paper in physics shortly to be published.] At present I am studying the dependence of the migration of the present-day Eskimo on the configuration and physical conditions of the land. This is, of course, a very extensive piece of work and cannot be finished so soon. I am taking it up chiefly from a methodological standpoint, in order to discover how far one can get, by studying a very special and not simple case, in determining the relationship between the life of a people and environment.

If I should in the near future have an opportunity to study, I would try to solve these questions. In addition, I wish to finish up and summarize my psychophysical studies, for which I need more material for observation before I can finish up properly. I have further a few smaller meteorological studies which I should like to finish up as quickly as possible, so that I may give all my energy to working on the question which I have chosen as my life's work.

 SELECTION 5

A Year Among the Eskimo

If I undertake to describe some of my Arctic experiences I cannot entertain you with exciting adventures, such as shipwrecks and narrow escapes, for such were not my share. My narrative must be that of the daily life of the inhabitants of these ice-bound coasts, the Eskimo. They were my companions in all my journeys. I used to travel from

Bulletin of the American Geographical Society 19 (1887): 383–402.

village to village, and thus their fortunes were my fortune. The little adventures of their life were my adventures, and I hope what my description may seem to be wanting in exciting scenes and imminent dangers will be made good by the fact that my experiences are those of a whole people, that my difficulties and dangers were such as the Eskimo have to brave and to struggle with throughout their lives.

When our ship first approached the gloomy shores of Baffin Land—one of the large islands forming the Arctic archipelago—the Eskimo descried us, manned a boat, and boarded our schooner. Little did I think that within a short time I should look at yon little filthy fellow, with long hair and sparkling eyes, with feelings of hearty interest, not to say friendship; little did I think how warmly they would welcome me in their small huts.

After a few days the ship left us, and I was alone with my servant among the Eskimo. I think it is unnecessary to describe their low statures and flat faces; their neatly finished skin dresses, and the long-tailed jackets of the women, who carry their children about in the huge hoods of their jackets, or in their wide boots, which reach to the hips. Neither will I speak about their swift craft, the kayak, which they skilfully manage with the double-bladed paddle.

September and the first days of October were spent with brief excursions in the neighborhood of the place where I had landed, for it was too late in the season to undertake extensive journeys. The brown slopes of the mountains began to be covered again with a white coat of snow, and ice was forming in the bays. Only a few weeks more and gales were raging over the sea; ice was forming rapidly, and winter had come. The Eskimo had built snow huts and stone houses, which were covered with shrubs and turf. Large lamps were burning inside, affording light and heat. The ice-floes had consolidated under the shelter of the land, and the men went out every day to hunt seals at the edge of the floe. There they stood waiting for a seal to rise. As soon as the hunter sees it the harpoon is thrown, and the carcass drawn upon the ice. The hunters must watch the state of the weather; for if a sudden gale blowing from the land should arise, the ice is liable to break, and to be carried into the sea. I recollect a young man who was thus cut off from the land, and found himself unable to return to the coast. For eight days he drifted to and fro at the mercy of the winds. Heavy snow-falls covered the drifting ice, the swell broke up the floe, and death stared at him continually. Yet he did not despair, nor even lose his temper, but in mockery of his own misfortune he composed the following song:

> Aya: It's glorious on the ice!
> Here it's nice.
> Behold my lonesome path!
> All snow and slush and ice!
> This is nice!

> Aya: It's glorious on the ice!
>   Here it's nice.
>   Behold my native land!
>   Its snow and slush and ice!
>   This is nice.
> Aya: Awaking from my slumbers in the dawn,
>   Monotonous fields of ice
>   And gloomy lanes of water
>   I behold.
> Aya: O when I reach the land
>   It will be nice!
>   When will this roaming end?
>   When will I be at home?
>   Then it's nice!

As it grew colder the floe grew more extensive, and about the beginning of December the sea was sufficiently frozen over for travelling. This is the time of the year when the natives visit one another, and therefore it was the most favorable season for my travels and explorations. I had purchased a sledge and dogs, and in the beginning of winter made short excursions in order to learn how to drive a sledge. In December I started on my first journey, and henceforth until about the end of July I was continually moving about, surveying the coasts and the interior of Baffin Land.

I used to stay in the Eskimo villages and to survey the neighborhood. As soon as this work was finished, I proceeded to the next village, and thus worked my way all along the coast. In the villages I lived with the Eskimo in their snow-houses. Generally I proposed to a man who was well acquainted with the country to join me for a few days, and as I had better dogs and a better sledge than the Eskimo, my offer was gladly accepted. Such trips lasted generally about a fortnight, and during that time the man went sealing while I was surveying.

I shall describe one day of such travels, as this will convey a fair idea of the out-door life of the Eskimo in winter.

Early in the morning the woman cooked the breakfast, while the man prepared the sledge. The latter consists simply of low runners connected by a number of crossbars. When in use, the bottom of the runners is covered with a coating of ice, that the sledge may glide more smoothly over the snow. The load consisted of our sleeping-bags, my astronomical instruments, our hunting gear, snow-knives, a lamp, and a lump of seal meat and blubber. After this light load was secured by lashing, the dogs were harnessed up and put into the sledge. Now we were ready to start. On the first day of a journey the dogs are generally well rested, and then it is difficult to keep them back until all is ready. As soon as the driver cries "H!" off they go down the snow-banks, down over boulders of ice that are piled up on the shore. The sledge bounces over all obstacles, and it requires all the strength and attention of the traveller to hold to it and to keep clear of projecting rocks and pieces of ice.

When the sledge gets to the unbroken floe which covers the sea, the harnesses and traces of the dogs must be looked after before the party is ready to proceed. When all is in good order, the travellers sit down on the sledge, the driver in the front part; he takes up the whip, which is about twenty-five feet long, and off they go.

It is very pleasant to ride on a light sledge drawn by good dogs, when the ice is level and the snow hard. Under such circumstances one can easily accomplish about seventy miles in a day's drive. But even then driving is a hard work and requires considerable skill and attention. After a short while one or the other of the dogs will get lazy. Then the driver calls out his name and lashes him; but it is necessary to hit the dog called, for if another is struck, he feels wronged and will turn upon the dog whose name has been called; the leader, who will not allow any fighting among his dogs, enters into the quarrel, and soon the whole pack is huddled up in one howling and biting mass, and no amount of lashing and beating will separate the fighting animals. The only thing one can do is to wait until their wrath has abated, and then to clear the traces, which have become so entangled that they must be restrung.

But caution is necessary in doing so. The dogs are made to lie down by lashing their heads gently. While the traces are being strung, the leader looks back cunningly, and as soon as all is ready he jumps to his feet, all other dogs follow him, and away they go before the driver can fairly get hold of the sledge. Or, if one succeeds in that, the whip and mittens will remain behind and it is necessary to drive back in a wide circle in order to recover them.

Before I was acquainted with all the peculiarities of the dogs, I frequently spoke to my companion, asking him the names of promontories, bays, islands, etc. While we were talking the dogs turned round and all of a sudden sat down, facing us as though they wanted to know what we were talking about. They absolutely allow no conversation between the travellers, but one has always to speak to them. The driver will say: "Aq aq—now run, now run! Ah! do you see yon island, yon little island? There is a house on it, a nice little house! Now run!" and so on. If he wants to turn to the right, he throws his whip to the left and sings out: "Aua, ja aua, au aua," and as long as he continues to do so, the dogs turn more and more to the right. If it is very cold, one has to run now and then by the side of the sledge, in order to keep warm, and thus one is fairly tired out when it is time to stop and to make a camp.

The first thing to be done is to build a snow-house. Snow blocks are cut with a knife or a dove-tail saw and then arranged so as to form a vault. Of course, such a house, which is built for a single night only, is very small, but nevertheless it takes about two hours to finish it. Then the fire is lighted and some snow is melted. While one of the men is engaged in this work, the other unharnesses the dogs and takes the harnesses into the house. The sledge is unloaded and every thing carried into the hut, as else the dogs would devour it. It takes about four hours until the travellers are ready for their meal, which invariably consists of raw, frozen seal meat and water. As I was provided with better cooking accommodations than the Eskimo have, we were able to cook coffee or soup, and this was a great attraction for the Eskimo when travelling with me. The clothing is not taken off during the night, but kept on until a longer stay is made. These snow-huts do not get very warm during a single night, when the glass is 40° or 50° below zero, though the door is sealed with a snow-block and the lamp is kept burning all night. Therefore the nights are rather uncomfortable, particularly as the houses are so small that one cannot sit with extended legs. I was generally glad to get under way again in the next morning and to pursue my journey.

I described here the travelling over smooth ice and over hard snow. When the traveller has to pass fields of rough ice, and when deep and soft snow obstructs the way, travelling is even more laborious. The driver has to go on the right side of the sledge, and to push it on, and to steer it past the boulders of ice with the whole of his strength. He must stimulate the dogs continually; and nevertheless they will sit down every few minutes and look piteously at their master, as though they wanted to say: "We cannot do any more." When sudden snowfalls overtake travelling parties, their lives are even sometimes endangered. Seals do not frequent the broken floes, and besides, the snow conceals their breathing-holes. In winter we were overtaken by an occurrence of this kind. Our party consisted of three, an Eskimo, my servant, and myself. As it was my very first trip we did not know much about travelling. When about twenty-five miles distant from the settlement I intended to visit, a snowfall set in which covered the ice with from two to four feet of snow. Our dogs were absolutely unable to move on, and so we had to leave behind sledge, dogs, and every thing, and to make our way to the settlement on foot. After a laborious march of about three miles, fog set in, we struck a floe of rough ice, and erelong we had lost our way. The compass was of no use, as I did not know the position of the place. Fortunately, after a few hours, the moon made her appearance and the fog lifted. But only after a march of thirty hours at a temperature of 48° below zero, and all the time travelling over rough ice, and for many hours through deep snow, did we succeed in finding the village. My unfortunate servant had frozen his feet, and had to stay in that place for several months.

It was at this time that I learned to know Eskimo hospitality. When we entered the hut my new friend was eager to help us to throw off our clothing, and we were given a warm bed. While we were asleep a seal was cut, though, in consequence of the bad weather, provisions were scanty; and a hearty meal was cooked, which was served to us as soon as we awoke. Meanwhile the "lady of the house" had dried our clothing and was busy mending it. In short, we were made as comfortable as possible. In the evening all were assembled in our home, some sitting on the ledge, some squatting or standing on the floor, eager to hear of our misfortune. During the night a gale was blowing, which hardened the snow; and therefore several men set out the next morning to fetch our provisions and our dogs. Such are the incidents and difficulties of winter travelling; but it is agreeable and pleasant as compared to sledging in summer. Then the ice is covered with water to a depth of three or four feet. The traveller has to wade through this ice-cold lake, and he must be careful to avoid the large whirlpools which form over each seal hole, and the rapid streams which gush down the cracks that cross the flow in every direction. And all is glaring in a bright blue and white, which hurts the eyes and causes snow-blindness.

But I will return to my winter journeys. I said before that while I was surveying, the Eskimo used to go sealing. The hunting of seals is a very tiresome and disagreeable work in winter. The seals scratch holes through the ice, in which they rise to breathe. The dogs scent these holes, and when one is found, the hunter waits by its side until he hears the breathing animal. Sometimes he will stand there motionless for a whole day, the harpoon in his right hand, the harpoon line coiled up over his left arm. As soon as he hears the animal he throws the harpoon vertically downward.

In spring another method of hunting is used. At this season the seals crawl upon the ice and lie by the side of their holes, sleeping and basking. Every now and then the cautious animal raises its head and looks around to ascertain whether somebody is approaching. The Eskimo, who wear seal-skin clothing at this time of the year, lie down on the ice and creep up to the seal. When the animal looks up they will lie down and imitate its movements. When it lies down again they approach it cautiously. At last they get near enough to strike it with the harpoon.

In the beginning of winter I had occasion to see one of the great festivals of these Eskimo, which is of more than common interest, as it is closely connected with their religious ideas. When late in the fall storms rage over the land, and again release the sea from its icy fetters; when the floes are pressed one against another and piled up in wild disorder, the Eskimo believes he hears the voices of the spirits which inhabit the mischief-laden air. They beleaguer the villages and bring sickness and death, bad weather and failure in hunting. The worst of these spirits are Sedna, mistress of the under-world, and her father, to whom the dead Eskimo fall.

The old legends which mothers relate during the long winter nights to their timidly listening children, tell of Sedna: Once upon a time there lived a man with his daughter Sedna on a lonely place. His wife had been dead for a long time, and the two led a quiet life. Sedna grew up to be a beautiful girl, and the young men came in from all around to sue for her hand, but none of them could win her proud heart. One spring-time, when the ice had broken up, a fulmar flew from over the sea and wooed Sedna with enticing song. "Come to me," he said, "come into the land of the birds, where there is never any hunger. My tent is made of beautiful bird-skins; my brethren, the fulmars, shall bring you all your heart may desire; their feathers will clothe you; your lamp shall always be filled with oil, your pot with meat." Sedna could not resist such wooing, and they went together into the land of the birds. When at last they reached the country of the bird, after a long journey, Sedna discovered that her spouse had shamefully deceived her. Her tent was covered with wretched fish-skins, full of holes, that gave free entrance to the wind and snow. Instead of white reindeer-skins, her bed was made of hard walrus-hides; and she had to live on miserable fish which the birds brought her. Too soon she discovered that she had thrown her fortune away when, in her foolish pride, she had rejected the Eskimo youth. In her woe she sang:

"Aya! O father, if you knew how wretched I am, you would come to me, and we would hurry away in your boat over the waters. The birds look unkindly upon me, the stranger. The cold winds roar around my bed; they give me miserable food—oh, come and take me back home! Aya."

When a year had passed, and the sea was again stirred with warmer winds, the father left his land to visit Sedna. The daughter greeted him joyfully, and besought him to take her back home. The father pitying his daughter took her in his boat while the birds were out hunting, and they quickly left the country which had brought so much sorrow to Sedna. When the fulmar came home in the evening and found his wife not there, he got very angry. He called his fellows around him, and they all flew away in search of the fugitives. They soon discerned them and stirred up a great storm. The sea rose in immense waves, that threatened the pair with destruction. In his mortal peril the father determined to offer Sedna up to the birds, and threw her overboard. She clung with a death-grip to the edge of the boat. The cruel father then took a knife and cut off the first joints of her fingers. Falling into the sea they were trans-formed into seals. Sedna clung to the boat more tightly, the second finger-joints fell under the sharp knife, and swam away as ground-seals; when the father cut off the stumps of the fingers, they became whales.

In the meantime the storm had subsided, for the fulmars thought Sedna was drowned. The father then allowed her to come into the boat again. But she from that time cherished a deadly hatred against him, and swore bitter revenge. After they got ashore, she commanded her dogs to gnaw off the feet and hands of her father while he was asleep. Upon this he cursed himself, his daughter, and the dogs who had maimed him; then the earth opened and swallowed hut, father, daughter, and dogs. They have since lived in the land of Adlivun, of which Sedna is the mistress.

The seals, ground-seals, and whales, which grew from Sedna's fingers, increased rapidly, and soon filled all the waters, affording choice food to the Eskimo. But since then Sedna hates them as they hunt and kill the creatures which have arisen from her flesh and blood. Her father, who can only move by creeping, appears to the dying; and the wizards often see his crippled hand seizing and taking away the dead. The dead have to stay a year in Sedna's dismal abode. Two large dogs lie on the threshold, and only move aside to let the dead enter. It is dark and cold inside. No bed of reindeer-skins invites to rest, but the new-comer has to lie on hard walrus-hides. Only those who have been good and brave on the earth escape Sedna, and lead happy lives in the upper land of Kudlivun. This land is full of reindeer; it is never cold there, and snow and ice never visit it. Those, also, who have died a violent death, may go into the fields of the blessed. But whoever has been with Sedna must always stay in the land of Adlivun, and hunt whales and walrus. With all the other evil spirits, Sedna lingers in the fall among the Eskimo. But while the others fill the air and the water, she rises from under the ground. It is then a busy season for the wizards. In every hut we may hear singing and praying, and conjuring the spirits is going on in every house. The lamps burn low. The wizard sits in a mystic gloom in the rear of the hut. He has thrown off his outer coat, and drawn the hood of his inner garment over his head. Muttering indistinguishable words, he shakes his hands feverishly. He utters sounds which it is hard to ascribe to a human voice. At last his guardian spirit responds to the invocation. The priest lies in a trance, and when he comes to himself he promises, in incoherent phrases, the help of the good spirits.

The hardest task, that of driving away Sedna, is reserved for the most powerful wizards. A rope is coiled on the floor of a large hut, in such a manner as to leave a small opening at the top, which represents the breathing-hole of a seal. Two wizards stand by the side of it, one of them holding the seal spear in his hand as if he were watching at the seal hole in the winter, the other holding the harpoon-line. Another priest sits in the rear of the hut, whose office it is to lure Sedna up with magic song. At last she comes up through the hard rocks, and the men hear her heavy breathing; now she emerges from the ground, and meets the wizards waiting at the hole. She is harpooned, and sinks away in angry haste, drawing after her the harpoon, to which the two men hold with all their strength. Only by a desperate effort does she tear herself away from it and return to her dwelling in Adlivun. Nothing is left with the two men but the blood-sprinkled harpoon, which they proudly show.

Sedna and the other evil spirits are at last driven away, and a great festival for young and old is celebrated on the next day in honor of the event. But they must still be careful, for the wounded Sedna is greatly enraged, and will seize any one whom she can find outside of his hut. So, on that day, they all wear protecting amulets on the tops of their hoods.

The men assemble early in the middle of the settlement. As soon as they have all got together, they run screaming and jumping around the houses, following the course of the sun. The circuit made, they visit every hut, where the woman must be waiting for them. When she hears the noise of the band, she comes out and throws a dish of little gifts of meat, ivory trinkets, and articles of seal-skin into the yelling crowd, of which each one helps himself to what he can get. No hut is spared in this round.

The men next divide into two parties: the ptarmigans, those who were born in the winter; and the ducks, or the children of summer. A large thong of seal-skin is stretched out. Each party takes hold of one end and tries with all its might to drag the opposite party over to its side. If the ptarmigans give way, then the summer has won the game, and fine weather may be expected to prevail during the coming months.

The contest of the seasons having been decided, the women bring out a large kettle of water and each person gets his drinking cup. The company stand close around the kettle, while the oldest man steps out first among them. He dips a cup of water from the vessel, sprinkles a few drops on the ground, turns his face towards the home of his youth, and states his name and that of the place where he was born. He is followed by all the other inhabitants of the village, down to the youngest children, who are represented by their mothers. As the words of the old are listened to respectfully, those of distinguished hunters are received with demonstrative applause.

Now arises a cry of surprise, and all eyes are turned toward a hut out of which stalk two gigantic figures. They wear heavy boots: their legs are swelled out to a wonderful thickness by several pairs of breeches, their shoulders are covered with a woman's jacket, and their faces with a hideous mask of seal-skin. In their right hands they carry the harpoon, on their backs inflated buoys of seal-skin, and in their left the scraper with which skins are prepared. Silently, with long strides, the Kailertetang approach the assembly, who, screaming, press back from before them. The pair solemnly lead the men to a suitable spot, and set them in a row, against which they set the women in an opposite row. They match the men and women in pairs, and these run, pursued by the Kailertetang, to the hut of the woman, where they stay for the following day. Having performed this duty the Kailertetang go down to the shore and invoke the north wind which brings fair weather, while they warn off the unfavorable south wind.

As soon as the incantation is over, all the men attack the Kailertetang with a great noise. They act as if they had weapons in their hands and would kill both the spirits. One pretends to probe them with the spear, another to stab them with a knife; one to cut off their arms and legs, another to beat them unmercifully on the head. The buoy which they carry on their backs is ripped open and collapses, and soon they both lie as if dead beside their broken weapons. The Eskimo leave them to get their drinking-cups, and the Kailertetang awake to new life. Each man pours some water into their buoys, passes a cup to them, and inquires about the future, about the fortunes of hunt and the events of life. The Kailertetang answer in murmurs, which the questioner must interpret for himself.

I told before a tradition of the Eskimo. They are very fond of telling such tales and have an enormous stock of folk-lore, of which I succeeded in collecting a considerable amount. The scene when traditions are told is extremely interesting, and I welcomed such occasions, as nothing can be more instructive to the traveller than to listen to the songs and legends of the people he studies. The man who relates the tradition strips off his outer jacket and sits down in the rear of the hut facing the wall. He pulls up his hood, puts on his mittens, and prepares himself by a brief song. The audience stand or squat on the floor of the huts, and now the lamps are lowered, a dim light only filling the small room. I shall tell here one of the most characteristic of these stories, as I heard it in a village on Davis Strait.

The Tale of Qaudjaqdjuq

A long time ago there was a poor little orphan boy who had no protector and was maltreated by all the inhabitants of the village. He was not even allowed to sleep in the hut, but lay outside in the cold passage among the dogs, who were his pillows and his quilt. Neither did they give him any meat, but flung old, tough walrus-hide at him, which he was compelled to eat without a knife. Thus he led a miserable life and did not grow at all, but remained poor little Qaudjaqdjuq. He did not even dare to join the play of the other children, as they also maltreated him on account of his weakness.

When the inhabitants of the village assembled for dancing and feasting Qaudjaqdjuq used to lie in the passage and to peep over the threshold. Now and then a man would lift him by the nostrils into the hut and tease him. As he was thus frequently lifted by the nostrils they grew to be very large, though he remained small and weak.

At last the man in the moon, who had seen how badly the men behaved towards Qaudjaqdjuq, came down to help him. He harnessed his dogs to his sledge and drove down. When near the hut he stopped and cried: "Qaudjaqdjuq, come out!" Qaudjaqdjuq answered: "I will not come, go away!" But when he was asked a second and third time to come out he complied, though he was much frightened. Then the man in the moon went with him to a place where some large boulders were lying about, and, having whipped him, asked: "Do you feel stronger now?" Qaudjaqdjuq answered: "Yes, I feel stronger." "Then lift yon boulder," said he.

As Qaudjaqdjuq was not yet able to lift it, he gave him another whipping, and now all of a sudden he began to grow, the feet first becoming of an extraordinary size. Again the man in the moon asked him: "Do you feel stronger now?" Qaudjaqdjuq answered: "Yes, I feel stronger," but as he could not yet lift the stone he was whipped once more, after which he had attained a very great strength and lifted the boulder as though it were a small pebble. The man in the moon said: "That will do. To-morrow morning I shall send three bears; then you may show your strength."

He returned to the moon, but Qaudjaqdjuq, who had now become Qaudjuqdjuaq (i.e., the big Qaudjaqdjuq), returned home, tossing the stones with his feet, and making them fly to the right and to the left. At night he lay down again among the dogs to sleep. Next morning he awaited the bears, and, indeed, three large animals soon made their appearance, frightening all the men, who did not dare to leave the huts.

Then Qaudjuqdjuaq put on his boots and ran down to the ice. The men who looked out of the window said: "Look here, is not that Qaudjaqdjuq? The bears will soon make way with him." But he seized the first by its hind legs and smashed its head on an iceberg, near which it happened to stand; the other one fared no better; the third, however, he carried up to the village, and slew some of his persecutors with it. Others he pressed to death with his hands, or tore off their heads, crying: "That is for your abusing me! that is for your maltreating me!" Those whom he did not kill ran away, never to return. Only a few who had been kind to him while he was poor little Qaudjaqdjuq were spared. He lived to be a great hunter, and travelled all over the country, accomplishing many exploits.

In this story the man in the moon appears as the protector of orphans. He is one of the mighty spirits in the Eskimo mythology. But besides him, a great number of minor spirits are known. They are called Tornait, and appear in the shape of men, bears, or stones. By their help a man may become what is called angakoq, a kind of priest or wizard. The spirits help him to discover the causes of sickness and death, and therefore he is the medicine-man. In their incantations they use a peculiar language, which consists to a great extent of archaic roots, and it is remarkable that some of these words which I collected on the coast of Baffin Bay are found in the language of Alaskan tribes. This shows that a close connection existed in olden times between the Eskimo of Northeastern America and the inhabitants of Alaska. The angakoq, or the priest, exercises a great power over the minds of the Eskimo. His commands are strictly obeyed, and his prescriptions regarding the abstaining of certain kinds of work or food are rigidly observed. It is strange that the Eskimo, who have a very limited supply of food animals, should restrict themselves in regard to food. Still their regulations on this subject are numerous. For instance, it is absolutely impossible to induce them to eat walrus meat during the deer-hunting season, or *vice versa*. Seal and deer must not be brought into contact, and, although they are not at all cleanly, they wash themselves every time before changing from one food to the other. It is generally believed that the Eskimo are extremely filthy, but I can assure you that this is not so everywhere. In a few huts in Cumberland Sound I found the inhabitants cleanly and good-looking in every respect, while in other places it was quite the reverse. I remember one village, which I visited in winter. Every thing looked so filthy and full of walrus oil that I was really disgusted. When I returned to the tribe in Cumberland Sound I told of my observation. Then all the Eskimo laughed, and a woman said to me: "Did not you know that? They are like the fulmars—when they see blubber they will sit down in it and eat away. They do not mind it when they soil their white coats. But we are like the gulls. We also have to take our food from the blubber and oil, but, like those birds, we keep clear of it, and carefully pick out whatever we want."

The trip to the tribe I mentioned just now was remarkable in several respects. In Eskimoland the arrival of strangers is an event, and great ceremonies are connected with it. The natives of the village stand up in a row, playing with small balls and singing. A strong man stands in front of the row and awaits the stranger. The latter approaches, his arms folded over his breast, his head inclined to the right side. Then the native strikes him a terrible blow on the cheek, and then in his turn awaits the blow of the stranger. Thus they continue a long while, until one of the men is vanquished. At the end of the performance the stranger is invited into the huts, and henceforth he is the friend and companion of the natives. When I arrived the men did not know who was coming, and arranged themselves in a row. But as soon as they discovered the white man, the first to visit their settlement, they set up a terrific howling, which induced the women and children to pour forth from the low huts, and then all began a dancing and crying and singing that still rings in my ears. The news: "*Qodlunaq! qodlunaq!*" i.e., "A white man! a white man!" had spread with incredible rapidity over the village. Everybody was eager to see the new-comer; the children hid timidly behind the long frock-like tails of their mothers' jackets, and cried with fear and excitement. In short, it was a scene that will always stand foremost in my recollections of Eskimo life.

After all the many little adventures, and after a long and intimate intercourse with the Eskimo, it was with feelings of sorrow and regret that I parted from my Arctic friends. I had seen that they enjoyed life, and a hard life, as we do; that nature is also beautiful to them; that feelings of friendship also root in the Eskimo heart; that, although the character of their life is so rude as compared to civilized life, the Eskimo is a man as we are; that his feelings, his virtues, and his shortcomings are based in human nature, like ours.

 *PART II*

BASIC
ANTHROPOLOGICAL
VIEWPOINTS

Boas had explored job possibilities in America during a visit in the winter of 1884 on his return from Baffinland, but it was only after another eighteen months in Germany that he finally came to this country to stay. In the interim, he worked under Adolf Bastian, Germany's leading ethnologist, setting up exhibits of Alaskan and Northwest Canadian material at the Royal Ethnographic Museum in Berlin, while simultaneously writing up the results of his own Eskimo research (Boas 1885, 1888). It was during this interval that he moved away from geographical determinism toward a psychological and historical view of human cultural differences. The shift is evident in the first selection included here, a letter written in 1887 to John Wesley Powell, director of the Bureau of American Ethnology, a few months after Boas had completed his first field trip to British Columbia and settled in New York City as geographical editor of the journal *Science*.

Boas had no sooner taken up permanent residence in America than he launched the first thrust in what was eventually to become a frontal assault on the prevailing evolutionist orientation of American anthropology. Perhaps to avoid a direct confrontation with Powell, who controlled a major portion of the resources for anthropological research in this country, Boas directed his attack against Otis T. Mason, curator of ethnology at the United States National Museum; and when Powell himself later entered the fray, Boas rather quickly withdrew. Boas had consulted the National Museum's collections on his way back from Baffinland in 1884, and again on his way to the Northwest Coast in 1886, and had complained then that they were "unintelligible." As Mason pointed out, this was largely due to the fact that they had been collected in 1840 by Horatio Hale and were still not classified. But the principles of their classification were also at issue, and these had serious theoretical implications in a period when museums were much more important to anthropology than they are today—as the second selection (no. 7) suggests.

Although much of his later critique of the comparative method was implicit in the debate with Mason, Boas' attitude toward cultural evolutionism was not at this point so systematically critical as it was later to become. He was after all still in many respects a novice in a discipline most of whose major figures were evolutionists. As a result, it is hardly surprising that he accepted the prevailing evolutionary arguments on some issues, especially in areas where his own background was weak (as in sociology). This is particularly evident in a lecture he gave in New York in March 1888 to a German-language scientific society which he also served as secretary. When he finally published the lecture in English fifty years later, Boas felt it necessary to delete a considerable section in which he had accepted "the current view of a necessary precedence of matrilineal forms of family organization" (Boas 1940, p. 635), as well a to make a number of unacknowledged minor modifications. I have included here the relevant section of the original version, with annotations to suggest some of the more important changes.

When economic cutbacks ended his full-time editorial job at *Science* early in 1889, Boas succeeded in bringing himself to the attention of G. Stanley Hall, who was then in the process of recruiting a faculty for the recently opened Clark University in Worcester, Massachusetts. That fall Boas accepted a position as Docent in the Department of Psychology at Clark, where he trained this country's first Ph.D. in anthropology, A. F. Chamberlain. Although his job ended under acrimonious circumstances in the faculty revolt of 1892, by that time Boas had been relatively free for several years to follow his interests where they might lead, as well as to carry on fieldwork in the Northwest during the summers. It was in this period that he accomplished what has been described as his "systematic self-professionalization" in anthropology (Lowie 1943a, p. 183). This was especially the case in linguistics and physical anthropology, each of which involved the mastery of specialized techniques not immediately accessible to the layman, and which formed the core of the instruction Boas gave to his own graduate students.

From an early point, however, Boas took a critical and innovative approach toward problems of method. His very autodidacticism freed him from "the prejudices and antiquated survivals which weighed heavily on linguistics" (Jakobson 1944, p. 188; cf. Stocking 1968c). We see one of the most significant results in the piece on "alternating sounds," which contains in germ much of the argument of the later introduction to the

Handbook of American Indian Languages (Boas 1911a)—and of his later approach to cultural phenomena in general (Stocking 1968a, p. 159). Similarly, the fact that he began without the training in medicine or zoology that was virtually a *sine qua non* for serious work in physical anthropology led Boas to draw instead on his background in mathematics to develop, under the influence of the English biometrician Francis Galton, a dynamic statistical approach to problems of human variation. At Clark, where Hall's interests in child psychology helped set the tone of research, Boas applied this statistical approach to the systematic study of the growth of Worcester school children (Boas 1891a, 1892). The last selection (no. 10) provides a general statement, in terms comprehensible to the nonmathematician, of Boas' statistical orientation—which in the period prior to 1911 was probably as sophisticated as that of any scientist in America (Tanner 1959, p. 78; cf. Howells 1959).

 SELECTION 6

From Geographical

Surroundings to

Historical Facts

NEW YORK
196 THIRD AVENUE.
June 12th, 1887.

MAJOR J. W. POWELL,
Director, Bureau of Ethnology,
Washington, D.C.

DEAR SIR:

I beg to submit to you the enclosed plan of publication and hope it will enable you to form an opinion of the character of my work.

I wish to add a few remarks which do not belong to the plan. About six

Letter preserved in the Bureau of American Ethnology Archives, in the National Anthropological Archives, Smithsonian Institution, Washington, D.C.

years ago, after I had finished my studies I laid out a plan for my future work. The leading question for this plan was: Is it possible to apply the methods of natural science, more particularly of physics to psychology. This led me to researches on psychophysics and induced me to follow a certain method of ethnological researches. I believe the fundamental question is: How far does an influence of the surroundings exist? In studying this question I found it necessary to limit my inquiry to a study of the influence of geographical surroundings upon migrations and certain classes of ideas. Even these I found to be extremely complex, and began to inquire into their psychological elements. Studying the literature from this standpoint I found, that I could not understand the questions and facts without practical experience; I considered it necessary to study on the spot a people living in a wide area of uniform character.

I considered the Eskimos the best race for these studies and consequently went there. After my return I carried on my researches from the same point of view. The longer I studied the more I became convinced that the phenomena such as customs, traditions and migrations are far too complex in their origin, as to enable us to study their psychological causes without a thorough knowledge of their history. I concluded it necessary to see a people, among which historical facts are of greater influence than the surroundings and selected for this purpose Northwest America.

I write this in order to explain to you the special line of study which I pursue, and to show you, that my explorations were not made at random. This will also explain to you the foundation of my criticism of Prof. Mason's method, which will be set forth more fully in the next issue of "Science." In connection with these remarks it may be of interest to you to see some of my psychological papers, which I send along with this letter.

Yours, very truly,
DR. FRANZ BOAS

SELECTION 7

The Principles of
Ethnological Classification ~ /887

The leading idea of Otis T. Mason's writings on ethnology is
his attempt to classify human inventions and other ethnological phenomena in the light of biological specimens. "They may be divided into
families, genera, and species. They may be studied in their several ontog-
enies (that is, we may watch the unfolding of each individual thing
from its raw material to its finished production). They may be regarded
as the products of specific evolution out of natural objects serving human
wants and up to the most delicate machine performing the same function.
They may be modified by their relationship, one to another, in sets, out-
fits, apparatus, just as the insect and flower are co-ordinately transformed.
They observe the law of change under environment and geographical
distribution." This method of research is founded on the hypothesis that
a connection of some kind exists between ethnological phenomena of
people widely apart. Professor Mason is of this opinion, and expresses it
as follows: "Anthropologists assign similar inventions observed in different
parts of the world to one of the following causes: 1. The migration of a
certain race of people who made the invention. 2. The migration of ideas
—that is, an invention may be made by a certain race of people and
taught or loaned to peoples far removed in time and place. 3. In human
culture, as in nature elsewhere, like causes produce like effects. Under
the same stress and resources the same inventions will arise." From this
stand-point Professor Mason has arranged the ethnological collections of
the national museum according to objects, not according to the tribes to
whom they belong, in order to show the different species of throwing-
sticks, basketry, bows, etc.

We cannot agree with the leading principles of Professor Mason's
ethnological researches. In his enumeration of causes of similar inventions, one is omitted, which overthrows the whole system: unlike causes
produce like effects. It is of very rare occurrence that the existence of
like causes for similar inventions can be proved, as the elements affecting
the human mind are so complicated; and their influence is so utterly

"The Occurrence of Similar Inventions in Areas Widely Apart," and "Museums of
Ethnology and Their Classification," *Science* 9 (1887): 485–486, 587–589.

unknown, that an attempt to find like causes must fail, or will be a vague hypothesis. On the contrary, the development of similar ethnological phenomena from unlike causes is far more probable, and due to the intricacy of the acting causes. As far as inventions are concerned, the disposition of men to act suitably is the only general cause; but this is so general, that it cannot be made the foundation of a system of inventions.

But from still another point of view we cannot consider Professor Mason's method a progress of ethnological researches. In regarding the ethnological phenomenon as a biological specimen, and trying to classify it, he introduces the rigid abstractions species, genus, and family into ethnology, the true meaning of which it took so long to understand. It is only since the development of the evolutional theory that it became clear that the object of study is the individual, not abstractions from the individual under observation. We have to study each ethnological specimen individually in its history and in its medium, and this is the important meaning of the 'geographical province' which is so frequently emphasized by A. Bastian. By regarding a single implement outside of its surroundings, outside of other inventions of the people to whom it belongs, and outside of other phenomena affecting that people and its productions, we cannot understand its meaning. The only fact that a collection of implements used for the same purpose, or made of the same material, teaches, is, that man in different parts of the earth has made similar inventions, while, on the other hand, a collection representing the life of one tribe enables us to understand the single specimen far better. Our objection to Mason's idea is, that classification is not explanation.

His method, as far as applied to objects which have a close connection with each other, is very good. The collection of moon-shaped Eskimo knives or labrets from North-west America has given us great pleasure, and enables us to trace the distribution of those implements; but even they do not fully answer the purpose of ethnological collections. Besides these, we want a collection arranged according to tribes, in order to teach the peculiar style of each group. The art and characteristic style of a people can be understood only by studying its productions as a whole. In the collections of the national museum the marked character of the North-west American tribes is almost lost, because the objects are scattered in different parts of the building, and are exhibited among those from other tribes.

Another instance will show that the arrangement of similar implements does not serve the purpose of ethnological collections. From a collection of string instruments, flutes, or drums of 'savage' tribes and the modern orchestra, we cannot derive any conclusion but that similar means have been applied by all peoples to make music. The character of their music, the only object worth studying, which determines the form of the instruments, cannot be understood from the single instrument, but requires a complete collection of the single tribe. Here, however, it can be seen that each ethnological collection affords only very fragmentary instruction; that its real use is only to illustrate descriptions of the tribes. For a study of native art and its development, they are indispensable. For this purpose, duplicates, of which the superficial visitor of ethnological museums frequently complains, are absolutely necessary. They are the only means of determining what is characteristic of a tribe, and what is merely incidental.

Mason's method takes a place in ethnology similar to the former 'comparing method' in geography. A mere comparison of forms cannot lead to useful results, though it may be a successful method of *finding* problems that will further the progress of science. The thorough study must refer to the history and development of the individual form, and hence proceed to more general phenomena.

Prof. Otis T. Mason's reply to my remarks on his views of the methods of ethnology is mainly a justification of his plan of arranging the collections of the national museum. As this plan is the outcome of his philosophical view of the problems of ethnology, we must scrutinize these in order to judge as to the merits of his system.

His principle object is the study of each and every invention among peoples of all races and countries. I am well aware that this idea was and is shared by many scientists; and at this very moment I read with interest Mantegazza's proposal of erecting a 'psychological museum,' i.e., a museum of ethnological objects arranged according to the ideas to which they belong. Professor Mason's rank among American ethnologists, however, and the weight he can give to his opinions by the arrangement of the large collections of the national museum according to his theories, induce me to criticise his views more particularly.

My view of the study of ethnology is this: the object of our science is to understand the phenomena called ethnological and anthropological, in the widest sense of those words,—in their historical development and geographical distribution, and in their physiological and psychological foundation. These two branches are opposed to each other in the same way as are biology and the so-called systematic 'organology,' or, as I have called it in another place (*Science*, ix. No. 210), when treating on the study of geography, 'physical science and cosmography'; the former trying to deduce laws from phenomena, the latter having for its aim a description and explanation of phenomena. I tried to show that both branches are of equal scientific value.

Let us inquire which method must be applied to carry on ethnological researches of either kind. Ethnological phenomena are the result of the physical and psychical character of men, and of its development under the influence of the surroundings: therefore two problems must be studied for attaining scientific results. The preliminary study is that of the surroundings: the final aim of the researches is the knowledge of the laws and history of the development of the physiological and psychological character of mankind. 'Surroundings' are the physical conditions of the country, and the sociological phenomena, i.e., the relation of man to man. Furthermore, the study of the present surroundings is insufficient: the history of the people, the influence of the regions through which it passed on its migrations, and the people with whom it came into contact, must be considered. All of these are phenomena which may directly be observed by a well-trained observer, or may be traced with greater or less accuracy by historical researches.

The second part of ethnological researches is far more difficult. The physical and psychical character of a people is in itself the result of the action of the surroundings, and of the way in which the present character was attained. Each stage in the development of a people leaves its stamp, which cannot be destroyed by future events. Thus it appears that the elements of the character of a people are extremely complex. There are two ways of treating this problem.

One of the remarkable features of such problems is the occurrence of similar inventions in regions widely apart, and without having a common origin. One method of studying them—and this is Professor Mason's method—is to compare the phenomena, and to draw conclusions by analogy. It is the deductive method. The other method is to study phenomena arising from a common psychical cause among all tribes and as influenced by their surroundings; i.e., by tracing the full history of the single phenomenon. This is the inductive method. For this method of study, the tribal arrangement of museum specimens is the only satisfactory one, as it represents the physical and ethnical surroundings.

I will explain these ideas by giving an example. It has frequently been proposed to establish a museum illustrating the adaptation of organisms to surroundings. The aim of this study is to find the physiological laws or the combination of causes which have the effect of causing these adaptations. The classification and arrangement must, of course, be made according to surroundings, in order to show their influence on different kinds of organisms.

An ethnological collection is analogous to this. The objects of study are researches on psychology. The method of researches is a study of the surroundings. The surroundings are physical and ethnical: therefore the arrangement must also be physical and ethnical, as this is the only way to show the single phenomenon in its peculiar character and surroundings.

It has been the tendency of science to confine the domain of deductive methods more and more, and not to be content with arguments from analogy, which are the foundation of most errors of the human mind, and to which may be traced the religious and other ideas of man in a primitive state of culture, and, to a certain degree, even in a state of advanced civilization. Science is constantly encroaching upon the domain of the argument from analogy, and demands inductive methods.

Nevertheless the psychological and scientific value of the argument from analogy cannot be overrated: it is the most effective method of finding problems. The active part it plays in the origin of philosophical systems and grand ideas which sometimes burst upon scientists is proof of this. But, as far as inductive methods can be applied,—and we believe that their domain will continue to increase,—induction must scrutinize the ideas found by deduction. Therefore I shall call Professor Mason's system a suggestive one, but not fit for scientific researches, as it does not allow the application of the inductive method.

But even this acknowledgment must be limited. The technological idea, which Professor Mason has made the leading one in the arrangement of the collection of the national museum, is only one side, and a very limited one, of the wide field of ideas which must be leading in a 'psychological museum,' as Mantegazza calls it.

The rattle, for instance, is not merely the outcome of the idea of making noise, and of the technical methods applied to reach this end: it is, besides this, the outcome of religious conceptions, as any noise may be applied to invoke or drive away spirits; or it may be the outcome of the pleasure children have in noise of any kind; and its form may be characteristic of the art of the people. Thus the same implement belongs to very different departments of a psychological museum.

Furthermore, let us inquire what is the psychological principle upon which Mason's system is founded. The leading idea is technology. The foundation of technics is the faculty of acting suitably: consequently the purpose of the implement must be made the principle of division. For instance, all kinds of cooking-pots and other arrangements for cooking would belong to one class. The mere fact that certain pots are made of clay would not justify the establishment of a pottery department. This quality of being made of clay is incidental, and does not agree with the psychological basis.

There is one point of view which justifies a classification according to inventions in a psychological museum. This is the extent to which each invention is used by a people: for instance, in what branches of life pottery is made use of, which may be limited in one tribe, very wide in another. But in this case the purpose of the object will not be the principle of division, but the principal invention applied in its manufacture; and thus the specimens would not be arranged according to Professor Mason's system, objects serving widely differing purposes belonging to one class. Therefore I cannot consider it justifiable to make technology, in the sense Professor Mason does, the basis of arranging ethnological collections.

One reason ought to make us very cautious in applying the argument from analogy in ethnology as well as in other sciences of similar character; biology, for instance. Former events, as I have already said, leave their stamp on the present character of a people. I consider it one of the greatest achievements of Darwinism to have brought to light this fact, and thus to have made a physical treatment of biology and psychology possible. The fact may be expressed by the words, "the physiological and psychological state of an organism at a certain moment is a function of its whole history"; that is, the character and future development of a biological or ethnological phenomenon is not expressed by its appearance, by the state in which it *is*, but by its whole history. Physicists will understand the important meaning of this fact. The outward appearance of two phenomena may be identical, yet their immanent qualities may be altogether different: therefore arguments from analogies of the outward appearance, such as shown in Professor Mason's collections, are deceptive. These remarks show how the same phenomena may originate from unlike causes, and that my opinion does not at all strive against the axiom, 'Like effects spring from like causes,' which belongs to that class of axioms which cannot be converted. Though like causes have like effects, like effects have not like causes.

From my statement it will be understood that I cannot content myself with Mr. Dall's remark, in the letter contained in to-day's issue, that both standpoints contain part of the truth. I have expressed in another place (*Verh. Ges. für Erdkunde*, Berlin, 1886, No. 7) my opinion on Dall's ethnological method, and emphasized, as I have here also, the necessity of studying eac. ethnological phenomenon individually.

In conclusion I have to add a few words on the practical side of the question upon which Professor Mason and Mr. Dall touch. In regard to this question, I concur with Mr. Dall, and believe that the public will be much more benefited by the tribal arrangement of ethnological collections.

I cannot agree with Professor Mason's proposal of arranging the cases like a checker-board. In ethnology all is individuality. We should be compelled to leave long rows of cases empty, as certain phenomena occur but in very few tribes. It would be almost impossible to show in this way all important ethnological phenomena, the historical development of tribes, the influence of neighbors and surroundings, etc. It is my opinion that the main object of ethnological collections should be the dissemination of the fact that civilization is not something absolute, but that it is relative, and that our ideas and conceptions are true only so far as our civilization goes. I believe that this object can be accomplished only by the tribal arrangement of collections. The second object, which is subordinate to the other, is to show how far each and every civilization is the outcome of its geographical and historical surroundings. Here the line of tribal arrangement may sometimes be broken, in order to show an historical series of specimens; but I consider this latter point of view subordinate to the former, and should choose to arrange collections of duplicates for illustrating those ideas, as it were, as an explanation of the facts contained in the tribal series. Of course, it is generally impossible to do this, on account of the lack of specimens, or, more frequently, on account of the lack of our knowledge; but it is my ideal of an ethnological museum. I wish to state here again that I am not at all opposed to Mantegazza's psychological museum, which will be very suggestive and important for the development of science, but I consider the ethnological museum indispensable for controlling the ideas suggested by the analogies shown in the psychological collection, and as the only means of showing the state of culture of man.

     SELECTION 8

The Aims of Ethnology ~ 1889

The development of our science itself has only become possible due to the general recognition the principle of the theory of evolution has attained in recent decades. It is a common characteristic of all forms of evolutionary theory that every living being is considered as the product of an historical development. The fate of an individual influences not only the individual himself, but his successors as well; and in order to understand an organism it is therefore necessary not only to know its own history but also that of its forebears. This perspective opens the whole vast field of the natural sciences to the historical method, and has contributed fundamentally to its rapid advance. Ethnology has existed only since this perspective has found common acceptance, for it has taught us to understand that no occurrence in the life of a people disappears without a trace, but affects even the most distant generations. The myths which our ancestors told to each other and in which they believed, have left their impress upon the ways of thinking of their descendants who came under the spiritual domination of a foreign culture. Even the most brilliant genius is influenced by his age and his environment, which is itself a product of the past. Thus culture-history teaches the continuity of inventions and ideas from the levels at which we find primitive peoples today up to our own time. The history of the sciences, the history of

Die Ziele der Ethnologie (New York: Hermann Bartsch, 1889), pp. 17–24. For this translation (which dates from my tenure at the University of California, Berkeley) I am indebted to two research assistants, John Gillingham (who did the major work on the present version) and David Nicholas (who did an earlier version), and to Professor Reginald Zelnik, who checked the final version with me.

inventions, and above all the history of religions point to the study of their germinal forms among primitive peoples.[1]

I have used throughout the expression "primitive people" without further clarification. I hope that in so doing I have not created the impression that we are dealing with peoples living in an original state of simplicity and naturalness as Rousseau conceived of them. On the contrary, we must keep in mind that even a primitive people has had a long history behind it. It may have gone through states of higher civilization and then, due to the gradual loss of inventions and ideas, have sunk down again to a lower state; or it may have climbed more slowly but surely up to its present level. None of these peoples is, however, free from conventional proscriptions and rules. On the contrary: the poorer in cultural achievements, the greater the number of ingrained rules and proscriptions which work to determine every action.

If, however, ethnology viewed as a purely historical science is already inextricably linked with culture-history, this connection stands out even more clearly when we turn to a consideration of the second great task of our science. A comparison of the phenomena of the lives of peoples shows that the foundations of their development are very similar to each other. From this we must conclude that human development follows certain laws, and to establish these is the second and indeed the more important goal of ethnology.

It must nonetheless be kept in mind that there is no basic distinction between the two purposes, since the general law is expressed just as clearly in the individual phenomenon as the individual phenomenon is expressed in the general law. However, the method used in discovering these laws is distinct from the historical method and casts an altogether new light on the individual case under consideration, since it shows which of its features are accidental or individual and which are of general applicability. For this reason the purely historical approach must always be considered incomplete without the illumination which derives from the comparative method. The detailed study of the individual phenomenon leads us directly to the comparative method, since the ways and means at our disposal for studying the history of peoples[2] soon fail us. Written records do not reach back into the distant past and relate only to peoples of a few culture-regions.[3] Even the other methods which we have discussed often leave us in the lurch. In such cases we have no other choice but to compare the life phenomena of the peoples being studied in order to draw our conclusions from existing similarities and dissimilarities. In the pursuit of these studies we often encounter cases in which the same custom or the same idea is found among peoples so

[1] Cf. 1940, p. 633, where this paragraph is modified in a number of subtle ways, and its last phrase is simply "the study of the lives of primitive tribes."

[2] Cf. 1940, p. 634, "the actual history of cultures."

[3] Cf. *ibid.*, "a few cultures." (The original German was *Kulturkreise.*)

widely separated that a common origin is completely precluded.[4] It
therefore becomes necessary for us to determine whether there are laws
from which follow time and again the appearance of the same phenomenon independently in the lives of different peoples—in other words,
whether the development of the human mind follows definite laws. Thus
emerges the second great task of ethnology: the discovery of the laws of
the lives of peoples—or, as it is usually called, the study of folk-psychology.

The first and most important question that must be clarified is whether
there are any fixed laws at all according to which the development of
peoples progresses, or whether this is just a matter of chance. We have
already cited various examples of the occurrence of similar phenomena
in widely separated areas. In these cases the ethnologist always perceives two contradictory and equally possible explanations: that both
phenomena have sprung from common origins, or that both have developed independently of each other. Only with certain quite general phenomena is one never in doubt. For instance, the facts that there are no
peoples without religion, that art and social organization exist everywhere, and that everywhere with the progress of civilization the individual becomes freer in that the innumerable proscriptions and rules
governing his conduct tend to disappear—all these may from the outset
be correctly derived from the mental capacities of mankind.

Let us through an example elucidate the method by which folk-
psychologists draw their conclusions. It will be seen, then, that the facts
collected by the ethnologist play a large, important role in these studies.

The results of recent researches into the development of the family
offer an excellent example.

According to the results of philological and historical researches dealing exclusively with the peoples of the Indo-European language group, it
appeared as if the family comprises the foundation of society, and that
the tribe, the people, and the state are outgrowths of it. From this point
of view it seemed strange that among many peoples the father was not
the unquestioned head of the family, but that often the higher authority
is invested in the wife. Thus Herodotus says of the Lycians that the
daughters inherited, not the sons. It is said of the Athenians that up to
the time of Cecrops children were named after their mother; and according to Tacitus, the mother's brothers were owed particular respect among
Germans. Above all, the numerous tales of Amazons should also be
mentioned. So long as science sought to solve the question of the development of the family from the standpoint of our culture, these facts could
not be explained. Only when we began to place ourselves in the realm of
the thoughts and customs of foreign peoples whose development has

---

[4] Cf. *ibid.*, "peoples for whom we cannot establish any historical connection, so that
a common historical origin may not be assumed."

proceeded independently from our own or which have remained on more primitive levels did an understanding of the true development of the family begin to dawn.[5] It was found that the development abstracted from our culture was nowhere to be observed. Wherever we looked we found primitive tribal configurations, but nowhere was the family their foundation. We observed everywhere that at the lowest levels of culture the tribes separated into hordes of men and women and that a communal marriage existed. We observe this condition for example in Australia, where both hordes regard each other with hostility, and each has its own sacred animals and plants. In such crass form this social condition has been observed only among a few peoples, but traces of it are widespread. Thus the men and women of the Arawaks in South America have different protective deities, and the inhabitants of the Sierra Leone coast have different secret societies for men and women.

Another frequently observed phenomenon is the division of the tribe according to age classes. In such cases the class of adult males takes possession of the women of the tribe, while the younger class raid the neighboring tribes and abduct their women. A further advance out of this condition is manifest in peoples among whom the wife must be secured from other tribes by purchase. This condition is widespread among the North American Indians. Among them the tribe is divided into a number of clans. No member of one clan may marry a member of the same clan, but instead must look for a wife in another clan. In all such cases children belong to the tribe of the wife. They have nothing to do with the father and just as little with the tribe among whom they live, since it is to the mother's tribe that they belong. In the case of war between the two tribes, therefore, they leave their father in order to fight against him.

Nowhere, however, does this condition seem to have been durable, and we see it superseded almost everywhere by the purchase of the children from the maternal tribe so that they thus become the property of the father. Until this happens they belong completely to the maternal tribe and remain under the protection of their maternal uncle, from whom they also inherit. This is the condition which is frequently called matriarchy. The constitution of the family arises only with the purchase of the children by the paternal tribe. This tendency of a transition from matriarchy to patriarchy manifests itself everywhere.

It is only since these facts have been recognized that the phenomena mentioned above regarding the Indo-European peoples have become comprehensible. They must be conceived as survivals from the far distant past in which the father was not yet the head of the family.

[5] Cf. 1940, p. 635, where Boas made subtle modifications in the preceding sentences, substituted for the rest of this paragraph and the four succeeding paragraphs a parenthesis which bears at best a tenuous relationship to the material deleted, and added a footnote indicating he had done so because they contained the no longer tenable view "of a necessary precedence of matrilineal forms of family organization."

The phenomena just described recur in endless variations over the entire globe, so we must assume that this development is basically the same everywhere. Of course, this does not mean that the process of development has been exactly the same everywhere, but rather that its fundamental features have been similar everywhere.

Thus we see from this example that the facts ethnology teaches us imply an important advance for our knowledge of the development of human culture. One fact derived from these studies cannot be emphasized enough, namely, the _relative_ correctness of emotions which seem so natural to us.[6] It is difficult for us to conceive that the feeling the father bears toward his child should be altogether different among primitive peoples from what it is among ourselves. We learn from the data of ethnology that not only our ability and knowledge but also the manner and ways of our feeling and thinking is the result of our upbringing as individuals and our history as a people. To draw conclusions about the development of mankind as a whole we must try to divest ourselves of these influences, and this is only possible by immersing ourselves in the spirit of primitive peoples whose perspectives and development have almost nothing in common with our own. If we use our own feelings in an effort to establish how our ancestors behaved, we should not expect to achieve truthful results, since their feeling and thinking were different from our own. We must reject many presuppositions that seem self-evident to us because precisely such mental states were not self-evident in earlier times. It is indeed impossible to recognize *a priori* what in our feelings is common to all mankind and what is only the result of history[7] —except through the teachings of ethnology. It alone opens to us the possibility of judging our own culture objectively, in that it permits us to strip off the presumably self-evident manner of thinking and feeling which determines even the fundamental part of our culture. Only in this way can our intellect, instructed and formed under the influences of our culture, attain a correct judgment of this same culture.

---

[6] Cf. *ibid.*, "It shows that emotional reactions which we feel as natural are in reality culturally determined."

[7] Cf. 1940, p. 636, "is due to the culture in which we live."

SELECTION 9

On Alternating Sounds —1889

Attention has been called recently to an interesting phenomenon, which, in a somewhat misleading way, has been termed "sound-blindness." It was observed that a considerable number of individuals cannot distinguish differences in key and timbre of sounds which are easily discerned by ordinary ears. The similarity of this phenomenon to color-blindness led to the adoption of the name of "sound-blindness." An exact analogue of color-blindness would, of course, be a case of lacking faculty to distinguish the key of sounds, but this, so far as the writer is aware, has never been observed. The characteristic feature of sound-blindness is inability to perceive the essential peculiarities of certain sounds.

Investigation of this subject has been carried on exclusively in regard to the phonology of languages, researches being made on the faculty of individuals to recognize certain consonants and vowels. It is well known that on hearing for the first time a word of which we do not know the derivation we are liable to misunderstand it. This fact may arise from two causes: The word may be so long that we are unable to grasp its phonetic components and their sequence at a single hearing, or we may fail to perceive the peculiar character of each phonetic element.

We have to consider here only the second case. Experiments on this subject have generally been made on children, as it is comparatively easy to find words unknown to them. Such words are dictated, the children try to render them by writing, and the misspelled words are studied. Recently Miss Sara E. Wiltse, at the instance of Prof. G. Stanley Hall, made a very interesting study of this phenomenon, the results of which have been published in the "American Journal of Psychology," i, p. 702. She discovered very soon that long words, as *ultramarine, altruistic, frustrate, ultimatum,* etc., gave unsatisfactory results, as the children failed to grasp the sequence of the component sounds. Next a series of monosyllabic words, suggested by Dr. Clarence J. Blake, was experimented with, which gave very interesting results. In the word *fan,* for instance, the *f* was understood as *kl* once, *s* once, *th* surd three times, *th* sonant five times, the following words being substituted for fan: Clams (1), ram (1), fang (1), fell (2), fair (4), thank (3), than (5). As will be observed, no senseless combinations of sounds have been substituted for the dictated word, and a glance at Miss Wiltse's list shows that such is very rarely the case.

The results of these experiments are very satisfactory, notwithstanding the unphonetic character of English orthography. They show that sounds are not perceived by the hearer in the way in which they have been pronounced by the speaker.

Let us examine how this misunderstanding of sounds originates. We learn to pronounce the sounds of our language by long usage, and attain great facility in bringing our sound-producing organs into the positions in which these sounds are produced. We also learn by constant and long-continued practice to pronounce certain combinations of sounds. The character of such sounds depends solely upon the position of the sound-producing organs and the force with which the air passes out of the mouth or nose. Although we learn by practice to place our organs in certain positions, it will readily be understood that these positions will not be exactly the same every time we attempt to produce a certain sound, but that they will vary slightly. Preceding and succeeding sounds and many other circumstances will exert a certain influence upon the sound which we intend to produce.

The vibration of the air corresponding to this sound sets into motion the membrane of the tympanum of the hearer, who then perceives the sound. But how does he apperceive it? Only by means of similar sounds he has heard before. We have seen that the vibrations producing the percept vary slightly, about a certain average; besides this, we have to consider that the concept of a sound is still more variable.

It may be well to explain this more fully. If we have two resembling sensations separated by a considerable interval, the probability that we will believe them to be identical, although they are in fact different, will be the greater the more nearly similar both sensations, the longer the interval and the less the attention. For instance, if I am shown a bluish white first and a yellowish white a little later, the probability is that, on being asked, I shall declare both to be of the same color. To use the technical term, the difference between the two stimuli will be so small that it does not exceed the differential threshold. This phenomenon must be clearly distinguished from the differential threshold of two sensations that adjoin one another in space or time. In the latter case the inability to perceive the difference is due to physiological causes, at least to a great extent; it is due to a failure to perceive a phenomenon or a process. If, for instance, two spaces of greater and less intensity adjoin each other, we may be unable to discern the dividing line; if the intensity of a light be suddenly increased, we may fail to discover the change. In the former case, however, when both sensations are separated by an interval, a failure to distinguish both is mainly due to psychical causes.

The inability to distinguish sensations, even if adjoining one another in space or time, proves, however, that what we call one sensation corresponds to certain series of slightly different stimuli. Experiments show that the amplitude of this series is the larger the less the attention bestowed while the sensations were perceived.

On a former occasion the writer made a series of experiments in order to ascertain the influence of the interval between two sensations upon the amplitude of the series of stimuli which cause one sensation, or, as it is generally termed, upon the differential threshold, and it was found that, within certain limits, the amplitude increased rapidly. In other words, the longer the interval the more readily one stimulus is mistaken for another similar one, or the longer the interval the greater the probability that a stimulus considerably differing from the original one is mistaken for the same.

The same series of experiments showed the existence of an unexpectedly great influence of practice. Pairs of parallel horizontal lines, the upper 35 mm. long, the lower from 34 to 39 mm. long, were observed, and the judgment was formed as to which appeared longest. It very soon became evident that the combination 35, 37 mm. assumed the character of a standard, to which all others were compared. Next a similar series of experiments with pairs of lines about 25 mm. long was made, and then I proceeded to form estimates of the absolute length of lines varying from 15 to 40 mm., expressed in whole millimeters. Then I observed that lines approximately 25 and 35 mm. long were generally judged to be 25 and 35 mm. long, while in the case of other lines no such preference for certain figures was found. There was a bias in favor of the two quantities with which I had previously experimented.

This seems to disagree with the established fact that the differential threshold decreases with increasing practice. This disagreement is, however, only apparent. We must remember that our judgment is a classification of the perceptions in classes of 1 mm. extent each. The greater frequency of the judgment "25 mm." and "35 mm." arises from the fact that I recognized these two lines more frequently than others, and that the great similarity of the line of 24 mm. to that of 25 mm. induces me to classify it under this heading, which is better known to me by practice. If the difference between the two lines should materially exceed the differential threshold, the result would, of course, be somewhat different. This phenomenon may be expressed psychologically: a new sensation is apperceived by means of similar sensations that form part of our knowledge.

As this is the most important part of our considerations, we will illustrate it by a few examples. It is well known that many languages lack a term for green. If we show an individual speaking such a language a series of green worsteds, he will call part of them yellow, another part blue, the limit of both divisions being doubtful. Certain colors he will classify to-day as yellow, to-morrow as blue. He apperceives green by means of yellow and blue. We apperceive odors in the same way, and classify new odors with those to which they are similar.

It will be understood that I do not mean to say that such sensations are not recognized in their individuality, but they are classified according to their similarity, and the classification is made according to known sensations. The difficulty and inability to distinguish two sensations is, however, as I indicated above, only an increase and the maximum of their similarity, which depends upon the similarity of the physical stimuli and the degree of attention. In the case discussed on page 3 we found the third factor to be the length of the interval between two sensations. In the present case it is the distinctness of the percept. The clearer the percept of the sensation the less likely it will be that another sensation is mistaken for it, and the less clear it is the more likely it is that such a mistake will take place.

We will apply this theory to the phenomena of mishearing. The speaker pronounces the word *fan*. The *f* will be approximately the average *f*. The hearer perceives a complex of sounds. There may be two causes for his mishearing the spoken word. First, the phonetic elements he hears are similar to other phonetic elements. Fortuitous circumstances may make the sensation somewhat deviate from the average in the direction of another phonetic element, and thus it may happen that, instead of being classified under the proper heading, it is classified under an affiliated one. The classification is made according to the sounds that are known to exist in our language. Thus we find the *f* of *fan* frequently classified under the somewhat similar *th*. Second, the hearer does not know the meaning of the spoken complex of sounds, as there is no context, but he knows that they are intended to represent a certain word. Therefore when he hears the complex of sounds these are at once classified under one of the similar words, and this involuntary assimilation itself may influence the perception of the component sounds.

Far better material than that obtained in schools may be gleaned from the field-notes of philologists, who reduce to writing a language which they hear for the first time and of the structure of which they have no knowledge whatever. In this case men thoroughly trained in the science of phonology attempt to render by writing combinations of sounds to them without any meaning. The study of their misspellings cannot fail to be instructive.

The first phenomenon that strikes us is that the nationality even of well-trained observers may readily be recognized. H. Rink has demonstrated this very clearly in regard to Eskimo vocabularies, and proofs are so abundant that I may well refrain from giving examples. It is found that the vocabularies of collectors, although they may apply diacritical marks or special alphabets, bear evidence of the phonetics of their own languages. This can be explained only by the fact that each apperceives the unknown sounds by the means of the sounds of his own language. Still more instructive are the misspellings of one and the same collector when he endeavors to spell the same word at various times. I will give here some examples gleaned from my own collections of Eskimo texts and words and of languages of British Columbia. The words are spelled in the alphabet of the Bureau of Ethnology:

ESKIMO

Operníving	Upernívik	Uperdnívik
Kikertákdjua	Kekertákdjuak	Kekertáktuak
Nertsédluk	Neqtsédluk	
Kaímut	Kaívun	
Saúmia	Caúmia	

In the first of these examples the change between *o* and *u, n* and *dn, k* and *ng* will be noticed; in the second, the omission of the terminal *k;* in the third, the change between *r* and *q;* in the fourth, between *m* and *v;* in the last, between *s* and *c*. After I had studied the language more thoroughly I noted that the *n* is frequently pronounced the nose being closed. This gives rise to the alternating spelling *n* and *dn*. The *v* is not a dental labial, but a strongly sonant labial, being very similar to both *v* and *m*, and which was apperceived alternately by both these sounds. Finally I observed that there is a sound between *s* and *c*, being neither, which, however, I at first apperceived by means of these sounds. In 1886, when collecting some Tsimshian material, I spelled *päc*, fear. Later on I spelled the same word *bas*. Last summer, when studying this language more closely, I noticed that I had classified the surd-sonant first under *b*, later on under *p*. The *a* sound I found to average between *a* and *ä*; the *c*, similar to the corresponding Eskimo sound, between *s* and *c*.

I think, from this evidence, it is clear that all such misspellings are due to a wrong apperception, which is due to the phonetic system of our native language. For this reason I maintain that there is no such phenomenon as synthetic or alternating sounds, and that their occurrence is in no way a sign of primitiveness of the speech in which they are said to occur; that alternating sounds are in reality alternating apperceptions of one and the same sound. A thorough study of all alleged alternating sounds or synthetic sounds will show that their existence may be explained by alternating apperceptions. It is not necessary that the sounds are always apperceived by means of one's native language, at least not in the case of trained observers. In such cases the first studies of a language may form a strong bias for later researches, or the study of one language may occasion a bias in the study of the phonology of the language taken up immediately after. Every one of these biases tends to induce the collector to classify a sound which does not occur in the phonetic system he bears in mind, and is intermediate to several, alternately under those sounds which it resembles.

There is a crucial test for this theory; if it be correct, it must occur just as frequently that various sounds which resemble one known sound are considered the same, although they are really different. I observed this in Haida and in Kwakiutl, as well as in Eskimo. In the first there occurs a very slight hiatus, which I discovered only with the greatest difficulty when I heard the words for "we" and "you" about twenty times without being able to discover the difference, the one being *d'aléngua*, the other *daléngua*. In Kwakiutl I found frequently the combination *gy*, but finally discovered that there are really two peculiar sounds, which I render by *ky'* and *gy'*. In Eskimo I found the same difficulty in distinguishing the *gdl* of Danish authors from the ordinary *l*.

The second and better crucial test is to attempt to ascertain whether individuals speaking one of these languages with "alternating sounds" hear sounds of our language as alternating sounds. This is, in fact, the case. Last summer I asked a Tlingit to pronounce the English *l*. I found that he alternately pronounced the exploded *l* of the northwest coast and *y*. In the same way he pronounced the German guttural *r* alternately as *r*, *w*, and *g*, and I may add here that a Scotchman whom I asked to pronounce the German word *süd* pronounced alternately *yūd* and *siū'd*. I believe this crucial test is decisive; and it seems to me a sufficient explanation of the phenomena of "sound-blindness," as well as of "alternating sounds," to assume that they originate by "alternating apperception."

 SELECTION 10

Remarks on

the Theory of Anthropometry

The theory of anthropometric statistics is based largely upon Quetelet's investigations, who endeavored to prove that the distribution of anthropometric data follows the law of chance. Some attempts to develop the theory further have been made by Stieda and Ihering and by

Quarterly Publications of the American Statistical Association 3 (1893): 569–575.

Francis Galton. The former emphasized the introduction of the average variation of measurements into the consideration of the subject, the latter developed what has become known as the method of percentile grades. Stieda was also the first to express a doubt as to the general applicability of the law of chance.

The anthropometric characteristics of a group of people are treated in various ways. Some authors consider the average of the measurements the most valuable result; others prefer to compute the mean value, which is, more properly speaking, the probable value, as it is computed as that value above and below which fifty percent of the whole series are found; still others compute the most frequent value. The followers of Francis Galton compute the mean value and the points representing various percentile grades, *i.e.*, points below which ten per cent, twenty per cent, thirty per cent, and so forth, of the total series are found. Anthropologists who study the physical characteristics of races use mostly the method of seriation. They give the percentage of cases of the series which fall between certain limits. Still another method which is frequently applied consists in the comparison of those percentages of the series which lie above or below a certain limit.

We will examine the merits of these methods. Whenever the distribution of measurements follows the laws of chance the average may be considered the type represented by the series. In this case the average, the probable value, and the most frequent value will be identical, provided the series of observations is sufficiently large. In practice they will naturally always show slight differences. In these cases the average must be used, not the probable or the most frequent value, because the first named can be determined with greater accuracy than the others. When a limited number of observations are given, and the mean error of the average, of the probable value, and of the most frequent value are computed, it is found that the mean error of the average is smaller than that of the probable value; the mean error of the latter is, in turn, smaller than that of the most frequent value. For this reason the probable value, or, as it is often called, the mean value, or the fifty percentile grade, must not be used for the purpose of describing the type of a series of measurements which are distributed according to the laws of chance.

When the distribution of cases does not correspond to the laws of chance, neither the average, nor the probable value, nor the most frequent value can be utilized without a previous theoretical treatment of the curve representing the laws of distribution. Based on Quetelet's statements, it has generally been assumed that all anthropometric measurements are distributed according to the laws of chance, and that the curves will approach the theoretical curve the more closely the greater the number of cases that is embodied in the series. I believe that Stieda was the first to intimate that deviations from the law may occur, although he does not follow out this suggestion. A. and J. Bertillon have proved that such deviations occur. Later on, Bowditch has shown that the curves showing the distribution of statures and weights of children do not follow the laws of chance. He shows this by pointing out the fact that during the period of growth a constant difference exists between the average and probable values. Galton also paid some attention to this subject, and Dr. Gulick mentioned it in a recent paper. Glancing over the curves representing large series of measurements, it strikes me that they conform to the laws of chance only in a general way, and that considerable deviations are quite frequent. It is necessary to consider the biological laws underlying the phenomena under consideration. Assuming that there is a uniform ancestral type in a certain district, and that the conditions of life remain stable, we may expect that the people representing its offspring will be grouped around the type according to the laws of chance. Assuming, however, that there were two distinct ancestral types in adjoining districts, and that these types intermingled, we cannot foretell what the distribution of forms among the offspring will be. It may be that they represent an intermediate type between the parental forms. In this case we might expect to find them distributed according to the laws of chance. But it may also be that we find them to have a tendency to reproduce one or the other ancestral type, either pure or slightly modified. In this case the resulting curve would not conform to the laws of chance, and would show an entirely different character. There is considerable evidence that the laws of inheritance are such that there exists a tendency of reproducing ancestral traits, not of producing new intermediate traits. Therefore, we may be prepared to find considerable deviations from the laws of chance. It is clear that, if intermixture does not result in producing an intermediate type, an attempt to express the type by means of an average of the existing forms will have no meaning whatever. The probable value would have just as little meaning. If the two parental forms were entirely distinct and reproduced without change, the most frequent values might have a meaning, as the two forms would occur most frequently. This, however, would depend upon many conditions favorable to such a result; the proportion of the two elements would have to be nearly equal, their difference great, and each form must have a limited amount of variability only. A concrete case of this kind is found in the anthropometry of the half-blood race of Indian and white parentage. Generally speaking, the ancestry of a people will be such that a number of forms which do not differ very much among themselves enter into its composition. The greater the number of forms, the nearer the curve of measurements will conform to a probability curve; but, nevertheless, it must be borne in mind that the mixture may be such that constant deviations from such a curve are found which are not due to accident. Our conclusion from these considerations is that anthropometric measurements do not, as a rule, follow the laws of chance, and that a careful examination of the curves is necessary in each case. We cannot expect that in all cases a classification of the material will lead to curves which follow the laws of chance more closely, as the laws of heredity are such that they do not necessitate an arrangement of this character. These facts must make us very careful in the use of the average considered as the type of a series. It will be necessary to investigate each series in order to ascertain if there are any deviations from the law of chance which seem to be due to constant causes, not to accident.

Besides these biological considerations, we must consider a number of other factors which may cause deviations from the probability curve. If a series of measurements is distributed according to the laws of chance, and the measurements of the whole series are changing, deviations will occur whenever the rate of change is not uniform. Such changes occur during the period of growth, and this is the cause of the asymmetry of distribution of measurements of children to which Dr. Bowditch called attention. Similar changes may occur when the conditions of life of a community are changing, or when one form is gaining preponderance over another form. In all such cases the computation of the average, of the mean, and of the most frequent value have no meaning. The cause and character of the asymmetry of the curve must be determined, and a mathematical treatment must be applied which takes the asymmetry into consideration. It is not necessary to elaborate the theory of treatment of such curves, as the treatment depends upon the character of the asymmetry. It will be sufficient to say that during a period of acceleration in the increase of the measurement the average will always be too great as compared to the typical value for the period under consideration, while for a period of retardation in the increase of the measurement the reverse is the case. For this reason the values for average statures at a certain age which have been computed so often have no biological value as typical statures for the respective age.

I believe I have shown that we must exercise great care in the application of the method of averages, particularly that we cannot assume the average to be the type of a series without a careful scrutiny of its character.

This is still more true if we consider correlations of measurements. It is generally assumed that when a group of measurements of a series of individuals is taken the combination of the average of the measurements will represent the typical individual. Dr. Sargent's statues of the typical American are based on this assumption. The first objection to this assumption is based on the well-known fact that, if a variable is given and a function of the same, then the average of the function is not identical with the function of the average of the variable.

Furthermore, the general distribution of the measurement may apparently correspond to the law of chance, although a number of distinct types are represented in the series whose presence may be revealed by a classification of the whole series. For example: If the measurements of the

Indians around the Great Lakes were tabulated without a subdivision into tribes, it would be found that their length of head and breadth of head are distributed according to the laws of chance. The average length of head would be 193 mm., the average breadth of head 155 mm. According to the method under consideration, this would be the typical combination. When the tribes are properly subdivided in an eastern and a western group, it will be found that the length of head is 195 mm. in the west, 191 in the east, and that 193 does not represent the type of any one tribe. These people speak the same language, and might be gathered on one reservation. In that case a subdivision would be impossible, and an erroneous result would be obtained. Therefore, a critical study of distributions must precede the establishment of the type. The theory of statistics points to a clear way for this study, but unfortunately it has never been applied up to this time. The study must be based on a comparison of the variabilities of measurements. Whenever the variability of a measurement that is correlated to another one is abnormally increased we must suppose that there is an intermixture of types.

I must add a few words regarding the subject of correlations.

The admirable investigations of Mr. Alphonse Bertillon and those of Sören-Hansen, Bischoff, and others have proved that with increasing height all other measurements increase not proportionally, but at a slower rate. This law may be given a wider meaning by saying that whenever a group of people are arranged according to one measurement, with the increase of this measurement all others increase at a slower rate, the rate being the slower the slighter the correlation. This law leads us to establish the fact that we must consider each measurement as a function of a number of variable factors which represent the laws of heredity and environment. The correlation of two measurements will be close when they depend largely upon the same factor, slight when they depend largely upon distinct factors. This difference in the degree of correlation, which is a well-established fact, proves that the system which is applied in many of our gymnasia is faulty. If the teacher of the gymnasium is given a pupil whose stature is, for instance, such that twenty per cent of all the individuals of his age are taller than he, then it is his ideal to train the pupil to that point that all his other measurements come up to the same standard. If all the men who have this particular stature were plotted alone, it would be seen at once that their measurements would be quite different from this assumed standard. This fundamental objection has already been raised by Dr. L. Gulick.

This assumption is one of the developments of the method of percentile grades. While this method has certain advantages in bringing home to the untrained public some of the valuable results to be gained from anthropometric inquiries, it is highly objectionable for theoretical studies. It does not explain any fact that cannot be explained just as well and with the tenth part of labor and with greater satisfaction by the method of mean variations, and whenever it has been applied it has proved to be misleading in so far as it suggests always that a certain percentile grade represents certain groups of individuals. For instance, during the period of growth, the average eighty per cent child has been assumed to represent, "on the average," the same child, which is most assuredly not the case. This method ought, therefore, to be applied with much greater care and for much more limited purposes than has been done heretofore.

I hope my remarks have served to point out some of the directions in which the theory of anthropometric statistics needs further treatment, and what defects remain to be remedied. I have in my full paper given a number of examples and elaborated the theories and methods which here I could indicate only with a few words.

PART III

THE PATTERN
OF BOAS'
FIELDWORK

Boas' fieldwork and ethnographic writing have been the subject of more recent controversy than any other aspect of his career (Ray 1955; Smith 1959; Codere 1959; White 1963; Harris 1968). Partly as a result, a great deal of material relating to these topics has been recently reprinted or published for the first time (Rohner 1966, 1969). I have eschewed duplication, even though this has meant omitting material dealing specifically with the tribe that was the focus of most of Boas' ethnography: the Kwakiutl of Vancouver Island (cf. Boas 1966). I have also refrained in this short note from trying to resolve the major issues of controversy—many of which are outside my competence. But I cannot help noting that although Boas outlived Malinowski, he began his ethnographic work in the year of Malinowski's birth; and though he made seven trips to the field after he was sixty (Rohner 1969, p. 312), he finished the bulk of his fieldwork over a decade before Malinowski went to the Trobriands. In short, he worked in a rather different intellectual and ethnographic context. This is not to say that Malinowski has been used as an explicit standard of comparison by Boas' critics, but merely to suggests that Boas' ethnography has been evaluated somewhat ahistorically. The selections that follow attempt simply to sketch the overall pattern of Boas' fieldwork, and to indicate something of its concrete character, with a due regard for context.

The first (no. 11) offers a link between Boas' Eskimo experience and his later fieldwork on the Northwest Coast. By implication, it serves also to suggest Boas' ties to the pre-evolutionary "ethnological" tradition, which in Germany overlapped somewhat with geography as conceived by the followers of Karl Ritter, of whom Boas was one (Stocking 1968a, p. 141; cf. 1971 and 1973). The older ethnology attempted to trace the migrations and define the ethnic relationships of the various "races" of man, most often on the basis of linguistic or physical criteria. What Boas was proposing to Bastian early in 1886 was the study of a long-mooted question in American ethnology: the ethnic relationship of the Eskimo and the American Indian. Although Bastian liked Boas' proposal, there was no money forthcoming, and when in September of the same year Boas arrived on Vancouver Island to carry out a general ethnographic survey, it was largely on his own funds (Benison 1949).

By early 1888, Boas' articles on Northwest Coast Indians in *Science* and elsewhere (1887a, b) had brought him to the attention of the Committee set up by the British Association for the Advancement of Science in 1884 to study the Northwest tribes of Canada. Between 1888 and 1894 he spent a total of twelve months in the Northwest on five field trips for the Committee. Although chaired by E. B. Tylor, its local direction was in the hands of Horatio Hale, who fifty years before had worked in the area as ethnologist for the U.S. Exploring Expedition, and who provided another link with the pre-evolutionary "ethnological" tradition (cf. Gruber 1967). Boas, however, chafed under Hale's minutely detailed interpretations of the Committee's instructions, which emphasized the need for an areal ethnographic synopsis. From an early point he wanted to focus more intensively on specific tribal groups, and even proposed moving his family to Victoria in order to facilitate this. But although he was able to do some intensive work (particularly in 1889 and 1894 among the Kwakiutl), on the whole Boas' fieldwork for the Committee did have a survey character, as the second selection (no. 12) suggests.

For several reasons, that selection requires brief additional comment. Conscious of the inadequacies of his early work on the Kwakiutl, Boas later suggested that it was "superseded" by subsequent studies (Boas 1909, p. 309; 1897). Nevertheless, the summary of his work for the British Association retains a considerable historical interest, especially in suggesting some of the ways in which his general anthropological orientation was rooted in a specific ethnographic context. This point has been made by other writers (for example, Harris 1968, p. 301). But it is usually argued in negative terms, focusing on the difficulties Boas had interpreting the complex and changing Kwakiutl social structure. There are, however, other broader aspects of Boas' point of view, aspects which we now take so much for granted as to forget how much we owe them to him, which also reflected the ethnographic complexities of the Northwest Coast: among them, the characteristic insistence on the conceptual separation of race, language, and culture and the notion of "secondary explanations," which played such an important role in Boas' later thinking on the cultural determination of behavior. Finally, it is at least worth noting—since the passage has been the subject of some controversy (White 1963, p. 56)—that Boas' discussion of the potlatch in the last two pages of this report is almost word for word the same as a letter he had written a year previously to the Vancouver *Daily Province* at a time when the enforcement of the Canadian antipotlatch laws was a matter of considerable public debate (LaViolette 1961, pp. 67–75).

Once his appointment at the American Museum of Natural History late in 1895 ended a decade of professional wandering, Boas soon found a way to extend his researches on the Northwest Coast. At his suggestion the Museum's president, Morris Jesup, underwrote an expedition which over the next six years involved a total of fourteen investigators in a wide range of anthropological researches on two continents (Boas 1905, p. 93). The expedition's purposes and early activities are recounted in the third selection (no. 13). Again, it is worth noting the continuity with the older ethnological tradition: the questions at issue were closely related to the time-honored ethnological problem of the peopling of the New World. Indeed, there is evidence to suggest that Boas himself saw his early ethnographic work as a whole in this context (Boas 1912a).

The last half of the Jesup report begins to get us to the actual process of fieldwork. Although Boas' fieldwork included a certain amount of "participant observation," his primary research technique was the collection of "texts"—that is to say, of traditional material from individual Indian informants recorded in their native tongues. Although he emphasized the importance of a "practical" knowledge of the native language, and over time became fairly fluent in the difficult Kwakiutl tongue (Codere 1966, p. xxvii; cf. Rohner 1967), fluency was not necessary to record texts. As the fourth selection (no. 14) suggests, these were taken down phonetically and then interlineally translated with the assistance of the informant or some other bilingual person. In several cases where he came across a particularly capable informant, Boas taught him to record texts himself. Both George Hunt (son of a Scotsman and a Tlingit, who had grown up among the Kwakiutl) and Henry W. Tate (a full-blooded Tsimshian) in this way transmitted large bodies of material to Boas in New York (White 1963, pp. 30–34).

Others before Boas had recorded texts (Boas 1917, p. 1), but he was the one who made them the keystone of an ethnographic style. That style was at once the reflection of the exigencies of his early fieldwork and of his characteristic ethnological assumptions. He had gone to the Northwest Coast in 1886 with the idea that mythology—like language and physical characteristics—might be a "useful tool for differentiating and judging the relationships of tribes," and from the beginning he spent much of his time collecting myths (Rohner 1969, p. 29). When this emphasis was called into question by Hale, Boas argued that the collection of "traditions" was especially suitable for the "flying visits" of his early fieldtrips, because they revealed with special clarity "the peculiar customs and character of a people" (Boas 1889a, pp. 811–812). Following Bastian, he felt that folktale and myth were the most characteristic expression of the *Völkergedanken*. Furthermore, the individual informant (sometimes, as in the case of Charles Cultee, the last surviving spokesman of a group) and the recorded text were well suited to the study of language, which was a major focus of his work. Finally, the text was a way of getting at the meaning cultural material had for the Indian himself, since "the points that seem important to him are emphasized, and the almost unavoidable distortion contained in the descriptions given by the casual visitor and student is eliminated" (Boas 1909, p. 309).

But beyond these reasons, there was another rationale, rooted in the basic historical orientation of Boas' ethnology. Like most of the anthropologists of this period, Boas directed his study to the past rather than the present. One might reject the evolutionary assumption that the savage was the living fossil of a prior cultural stage, but even so, it seemed clear that the "ethnological character" of the Indians was rapidly disappearing in the face of advancing white civilization. In its true form, that character existed only in the past, and survived into the present only in memory, or as embodied in oral tradition. In this context, the function of the text (as the fifth selection [no. 15] suggests) was to provide, for a people without written history, a body of documentary material equivalent to those that were the basis of the traditional forms of European historical scholarship: documents deriving from the Indians themselves, uncontaminated by the categories of the European observer, which—like Sanskrit texts or medieval codices—could be analyzed long after their "authors" had died out or become completely acculturated (cf. Jacobs 1959, p. 125; Hymes 1965, p. 334). Needless to say, there were problems in such an approach, some of which are evident, along with an attempt to cope with them, in the sixth selection (no. 16).

Finally, I have included a letter to George Hunt that casts an interesting anecdotal light on the human character of Boas' relationship with the Kwakiutl—and perhaps also on the tensions implicit generically in the always ambiguous relationship between an anthropologist and "his" people.

SELECTION 11

From the Eskimo
to Vancouver Island

Jan. 5, 1886

MOST HONORED HERR PROFESSOR!

You may remember that some time ago I offered to undertake travels in North America. At that time you answered that I would have to come to you with well formulated and financially assured plans before you would be interested. As a result, through the good offices of Dr. Reiss, I applied to the Ethnological Aid Committee, from whom I received the enclosed answer.

At that time you did not allow me to explain my plans, and I now take the liberty to give you a short resume. The objects of my investigation were to be the little known Indian and Eskimo tribes of the British Northwest. I wished to spend a season (i.e., Winter) among the Naskopi and Eskimos of Labrador, collecting and working with them. There is always much work to be done among them. A second season I wished to spend among the completely unknown Eskimos of Chesterfield Inlet and the western Indians, and then [in a third season] to visit the Alaskan tribes. In the fourth year I should like to end with the Indians of Vancouver. My chief idea in [all] this is that these tribes must be studied in relation to one another and that only someone who understands the East will be able to thoroughly understand the West. I also mentioned to the Committee that Jacobsen's collections needed to be supplemented; for example that all the masks could not be understood, because we have no knowledge of [two words illegible]. And it remains impossible to understand without a knowledge of the peoples west of Hudson Bay, who can so easily be reached. It is high time that collections be made there, for example [among] the important Airillik, [who] consist of only about 80 Indians, of whom *nothing* is known. I have not a moment's doubt that such studies would yield splendid results for the Museum.

In my opinion I would have to spend the winter in Washington and search through the surprisingly great treasures of the museums, so that in

Draft of a letter to A. Bastian, preserved in the Boas Papers, American Philosophical Society, along with a translation by Helene Boas Yampolsky, which is slightly modified in the present version.

the summer I shall be well equipped to enter those regions. I am also certain that because of my personal connections in Washington and other places in the states I could be of use to the Museum.

I am giving you this information because the communication from the Committee is not a direct refusal, but rather [indicates] that on your request the matter might be favorably received.

Your warning to [word illegible] as long as there is time has my full agreement. I have tried and am trying to make my knowledge of value for science, but I can find no opportunity. That is why I turn again to you, father of all ethnographic studies, and ask for your assistance. If this attempt should fail, I think I shall have done my duty, and will give up all further research activity without travel. I would not again make one isolated trip, but can only consider it worthwhile if the whole thing can be done as a related unit, as I have sketched out above. The necessary sum of money would not exceed 9,000 Marks per year.

    S E L E C T I O N   1 2

Fieldwork for

the British Association,

1888-1897

At the time when the Committee instituted their investigations, the inhabitants of the Pacific coast of Canada were less known than those of any other part of the North American Continent, with the exception, perhaps, of the tribes of California. What little we knew was based on the brief descriptions of early travellers, or on indirect information obtained from investigators who had been working in the regions to the north and to the south. The only noteworthy work done in recent times

"Summary of the Work of the Committee in British Columbia," *Report of the British Association for the Advancement of Science for 1898* (London, 1899), pp. 667–682. Also printed in separate *Twelfth and Final Report on the North-Western Tribes of Canada*.

was that by Dr. G. M. Dawson during his frequent geological expeditions to British Columbia. But three important problems remained to be solved: the numerous languages of the coast were still unclassified, and the number of their dialects was not definitely known; the physical characteristics of the tribes had never been investigated; it was not known if they represented one homogeneous type, or if several types were found in the Province. Finally, the study of the customs of the various tribes offered a number of difficult problems in regard to the origin and significance of several phenomena.

Material advance has been made by the efforts of the Committee in all these directions. The number of languages and dialects is now known, and it does not seem likely that additional ones will be discovered. The following languages are spoken in British Columbia:—Athapaskan or Tinneh in eight dialects; Tsimshian in three dialects; Haida in two dialects; Wakashan in two divisions, the Kwakiutl with three dialects, and the Nootka with two dialects; the Salish in four main divisions with eleven dialects, and the Kootenay. In this enumeration, dialects which may be classed as well developed and pronounced provincialisms have not been counted, but only such dialects as show distinct differences in vocabulary and grammar, so that intercommunication between the tribes speaking them is, even in the case of the most closely affiliated dialects, not easy. We count, therefore, in all, thirty dialects, which have been here classed, according to their affinities, under six linguistic stocks. Grammatical sketches of all these dialects have been obtained; but a few only are known tolerably well. These are the Kwakiutl and the Tsimshian. All the others require much fuller investigation than they have heretofore received.

While the present state of our knowledge of these languages does not permit us to assume that the number of stocks to which they belong is smaller than the number given above, we may call attention at this place to the morphological relations of some of these languages, which suggest the desirability of further inquiries into their early history.

Haida and Tlingit—which later is spoken in southern Alaska—have a number of morphological traits in common. While all the other languages of the North Pacific coast use reduplication for grammatical purposes, no trace of reduplication is found in these two languages. There is no gender, and no well-defined form for a plural or distributive. Compound nouns are very numerous, the composition being effected by juxtaposition. Words of two, three, and more components, which do not modify each other, occur. Local adverbs, which always retain their independent forms, frequently enter into compound words of this kind. In both languages there are four forms of the personal pronoun. In the independent pronoun, the selective and the ordinary forms may be distinguished. The pronoun of the transitive verb differs from that of intransitive verbs, the latter being identical with the objective form of the former. In this respect there is a close analogy between the Haida and Tlingit, and the Siouan languages.

The Tsimshian presents an entirely different type of language. We find a plural based largely on reduplication. The pronouns are suffixed to the verb. Words are formed almost exclusively by means of prefixes. The system of numerals is very complex, as there are different sets of numerals for various classes of objects.

The southern group of languages—the Kwakiutl, Salish, and Chemakum (which last is spoken in the northern part of the State of Washington)—have a series of very peculiar traits in common. Most prominent among these is the occurrence of what Trumbull has called 'substantivals,' which play so important a part in the Algonkin languages. Such are, primarily, parts of the body; furthermore, designations of localities, of fire, water, road, blanket, domesticated animals (*i.e.*, in olden times, the dog), and many others. These substantivals do not occur in any other northern language, and must be considered one of the most important characteristics of the languages in question. All these languages use reduplication and diæresis for forming collective forms and plurals of verbs. The demonstrative pronoun is used very extensively, and serves for distinguishing locations of object or action according to the three forms of the personal pronoun; namely, such as are located near the first, second, or third person. Besides these, a great many locative suffixes are used. Whenever an adverb accompanies the verb, the former is inflected, while the verb remains unchanged. When a transitive verb is accompanied by an adverb, the latter always takes the suffix of the pronominal subject, while the verb takes that of the pronominal object.

The Kootenay presents still another type of language. It incorporates the object in the same way as the Mexican does, the noun itself being embodied in the verb. It has very few substantivals, if any, but forms compounds by verbal composition, like the Tinneh (Athapascan) and Siouan. While in the preceding class we find, for instance, compounds expressing states of the hand, of water, fire, &c., we find here compounds expressing actions done with the hand, the foot, or other instrumentalities; and in the water, the fire, or in other localities. It seems that there is no reduplication.

It is worth remarking that these types of language are characterised by a few very general features that they have in common, and that distinguish them from the other groups that are found in contiguous areas. The Haida and Tsimshian are spoken in the extreme north; the Kwakiutl, Salish, Chemakum, in the whole southern portion of the Province, and they adjoin the Algonkin, with whom they have a few peculiarities in common. The Kootenay is not far separated from the Shoshonean languages, which resemble it in several particulars. We may therefore well say that the languages of the North Pacific coast belong to several morphological groups, each of which occupies a continuous area.

The investigation of the physical characteristics of the Indians of British Columbia has resulted in establishing the fact that the people are by no means homogeneous. As compared to the Indians east of the Rocky Mountains and farther south, they have in common a lighter complexion and lighter hair; but the shapes of their heads and faces differ considerably. Three types may easily be distinguished—the northern type, represented by the Haida, the Indians of Nass River, and the Tsimshian; the Kwakiutl type; and the Thompson River type.

These types may be characterised by the following measurements:—

	Northern Type		Kwakiutl Type		Thompson River Type	
	Average (mm.)	Mean Error	Average (mm.)	Mean Error	Average (mm.)	Mean Error
I. Men.						
Stature	1675	±7.40	1645	±5.90	1634	±7.90
Length of head	194.6	±0.80	188.7	±1.19	186.5	±0.55
Breadth of head	160.6	±0.67	159.0	±1.00	155.9	±0.52
Breadth of face	153.7	±0.85	151.4	±0.54	147.4	±0.41
Height of face	121.6	±0.87	128.0	±0.67	120.3	±0.71
II. Women.						
Stature	1542	±5.70	1537	±5.90	1540	±5.00
Length of head	185.6	±0.88	186.9	±1.64	179.5	±0.53
Breadth of head	153.2	±0.90	154.3	±1.44	150.0	±0.41
Breadth of face	143.9	±0.80	144.3	±0.64	138.8	±0.40
Height of face	114.3	±0.93	119.3	±0.82	112.5	±0.54

They may be described as follows: All these types are of medium stature, and their arms are relatively long, their bodies short. Among the northern type we find a very large head. The transversal diameter is very great. The same may be said of the face, which has an enormous breadth. The height of the face is moderate, and therefore its form appears decidedly low. The nose is often concave or straight, seldom convex. The noses of the women are decidedly concave. Its elevation over the face is slight. The point of the nose is short.

The dimensions of the head of the Kwakiutl are similar to those of the northern types, but the head seems to be slightly smaller. The face shows a remarkably different type, which distinguishes it fundamentally from the faces of all the other groups. The breadth of face is nearly the same as that of the northern type, but its height is enormous. The same may be said of the nose, which is very high and comparatively narrow. The point of the nose is short: its elevation is also very great. The nasal bones are strongly developed, and form a steep arch, their lower ends rising high above the face. For this reason convex noses are found very frequently among this type. Convex noses also prevail among the women, and for this reason the difference between the female form of the Kwakiutl and the female form of the northern type is very great.

The Thompson River type is characterised by a very small head, both diameters being much shorter than those found on the coast, while the proportions are nearly the same. The transversal diameter of the face is much shorter than that of the coast Indians, being nearly the same as that found among the Indians on the plains. The face is much lower than that of the Kwakiutl type, and also slightly lower than that of the northern type. The nose is convex and heavy. Its point is much longer and heavier than the point of the noses of the coast types.

There are good indications of the existence of a few other types, but they cannot be distinguished with certainty from the types enumerated here. It is probable that further measurements will show that the tribes of Harrison Lake and the Gulf of Georgia represent a fourth type.

The distribution of the types of man in British Columbia has an important bearing upon the much discussed question of the classification of mankind; while some anthropologists have maintained that all classification must be based upon considerations of language, others maintain as rigorously that the main consideration must be that of physical type. The data collected by the Committee show clearly that neither of these contentions is entirely correct. We have seen that certain tribes—such as the Bilqula, who linguistically belong to the Salish group—physically belong to another group. This shows that the two phenomena do not go hand in hand, but that they constantly overlap. The classification of mankind according to physical characteristics takes into consideration only the effects of heredity and environment upon the physical type of man. Race mixture, isolation, and effect of environment will be reflected in the results of these classifications. But there are evidently cases in which a slow infiltration of foreign blood takes place, while language and customs remain unaltered or changed to but a slight extent. The Bilqula branched off from the Coast Salish at an early time, and retain the Salish language; but there has been an infiltration of Kwakiutl blood and of Athapaskan blood, which has entirely changed the physical features of the tribe. With this infiltration of foreign blood came foreign words and foreign cultural elements, but they were not sufficiently powerful to change the original speech of the people.

It is clear, from these considerations, that the three methods of classifying mankind—that according to physical characters, according to language, and according to culture—all reflect the historical development of races from different standpoints; and that the results of the three classifications are not comparable, because the historical facts do not affect the three classes of phenomena equally. A consideration of all these classes of facts is needed when we endeavour to reconstruct the early history of the races of mankind.

It will be sufficient to point out in this place a few of the more general results of the studies conducted by the Committee on the cultures of the primitive people of British Columbia. In the Reports of the Committee only brief abstracts were given of the mythologies and traditions of the tribes, but full collections were made; and a comparison of these has led to the following results:—The culture of the coast tribes of the Province is quite uniform. It has reached its highest development in the district extending from Queen Charlotte Islands to northern Vancouver Island. As we depart from this region, a gradual change in arts and customs takes place, and together with it we find a gradual diminution in the number of myths which the distant tribes have in common with the people of British Columbia. At the same time a gradual change in the incidents and general character of the legends takes place.

We can in this manner trace what we might call a dwindling-down of an elaborate cyclus of myths to mere adventures, or even to incidents of adventures, and we can follow the process step by step. Wherever this distribution can be traced, we have a clear and undoubted example of the gradual dissemination of a myth over neighbouring tribes. The phenomena of distribution can be explained only by the theory that the tales have been carried from one tribe to its neighbours, and by the tribe which has newly acquired them in turn to its own neighbours. It is not necessary that this dissemination should always follow one direction; it may have proceeded either way. In this manner a complex tale may dwindle down by gradual dissemination, but new elements may also be embodied in it.

It may be well to give an example of this phenomenon. The most popular tradition of the North Pacific coast is that of the raven. Its most characteristic form is found among the Tlingit, Tsimshian, and Haida. As we go southward, the connection between the adventures becomes looser, and their number less. It appears that the traditions are preserved quite fully as far south as the north end of Vancouver Island. Farther south the number of raven-tales which are known to the Indians diminishes very much. At Nahwitti, near the north point of Vancouver Island, thirteen tales out of a whole of eighteen exist. The Comox have only eight, the Nootka six, and the Coast Salish only three. Furthermore, the traditions are found at Nahwitti in the same connection as farther north, while farther south they are very much modified. The tale of the origin of daylight, which was liberated by the raven, may serve as an instance. He had taken the shape of the leaf of a cedar, was swallowed by the daughter of the owner of the daylight, and then born again; afterwards he broke the box in which the daylight was kept. Among the Nootka, only the transformation into the leaf of a cedar, which is swallowed by a girl and then born again, remains. Among the Coast Salish the more important passages survive, telling how the raven by a ruse compelled the owner of the daylight to let it out of the box in which he kept it. The same story is found as far south as Grey's Harbour in Washington. The adventure of the pitch, which the raven kills by exposing it to the sunshine, intending to use it for calking his canoe, is found far south, but in an entirely new connection, embodied in the tradition of the origin of sun and moon.

But there are also certain adventures embodied in the raven myths of the north, which probably had their origin in other parts of America. Among these may be mentioned the tale of how the raven was invited and reciprocated. The seal puts his hands near the fire, and grease drips out of them into a dish, which he gives to the raven. Then the latter tries to imitate him, but burns his hands, &c. This tale is found, in one or the other form, all over North America, and there is no proof that it originally belonged to the raven myth of Alaska. Other examples may be found in the collection of traditions published by F. Boas. [Boas 1895]

The proposition that dissemination has taken place among neighbouring tribes will probably not encounter any opposition. Starting from this point of view, we may advance the following considerations:—

If we have a full collection of the tales and myths of all the tribes of a certain region, and then tabulate the number of incidents which all the collections from each tribe have in common with any selected tribe, the number of common incidents will be the larger the more intimate the relation of the two tribes, and the nearer they live together. This is what we observe in a tabulation of the material collected on the North Pacific coast. On the whole, the nearer the people, the greater the number of common elements of traditions; the farther apart, the less their number.

But it is not the geographical location alone which influences the distribution of tales. In some cases, numerous tales which are common to a certain territory stop short at a certain point, and are found beyond it in slight fragments only. These limits do not by any means coincide with the linguistic divisions. An example of this kind is the raven legend, to which reference has been made. It is found in substantially the same form from Alaska to northern Vancouver Island; then it suddenly disappears almost entirely, and is not found among the southern tribes of Kwakiutl lineage, nor on the west coast of Vancouver Island, although the northern tribes, who speak the Kwakiutl language, have it. Only fragments of these legends have strayed farther south, and their number diminishes with increasing distance. There must be a cause for such a remarkable break. A statistical inquiry shows that the northern traditions are in close accord with the tales of the tribes as far south as the central part of Vancouver Island, where a tribe of Salish lineage is found; but farther they do not go. The closely allied tribes immediately south do not possess them. Only one explanation of this fact is possible, viz., lack of assimilation, which may be due to a difference of character, to continued hostilities, or to recent changes in the location of the tribes, which has not allowed the slow process of assimilation to exert its deep-acting influence. The last may be considered the most probable cause. The reason for this opinion is, that the Bilqula, another Salish tribe, who have become separated from the people speaking related languages, and who live in the far north, still show in their mythologies close relations to the southern Salish tribes, with whom they have many more traits in common than their neighbours to the north and to the south. If their removal had taken place very long ago, this similarity in mythologies would probably not have persisted, but they would have been quite amalgamated with their new neighbours.

We may also extend our comparisons beyond the immediate neighbours of the tribes under consideration by comparing the mythologies of the tribes of the plateaus in the interior, and even of those farther to the east, with those of the coast. Unfortunately, the available material from these regions is very scanty. Fairly good collections exist from the Athapaskan tribes, from the tribes of Columbia River, and—east of the mountains— from the Omaha, and from some Algonkin tribes. When comparing the mythologies and traditions which belong to far-distant regions, we find that the number of incidents which they have in common is greater than might have been expected; but some of these incidents are so general that we may assume that they have no connection, and may have arisen independently. There is, however, one very characteristic feature which proves beyond cavil that this is not the sole cause of the similarity of tales and incidents. We know that in the region under discussion two important trade routes reached the Pacific coast—one along the Columbia River, which connected the region inhabited by Shoshonean tribes with the coast, and indirectly led to territories occupied by Siouan and Algonkin tribes; another one which led from Athapaskan territory to the country of the Bilqula. A route of minor importance led down Fraser River. A study of the traditions shows that along these routes the points of contact of mythologies are strongest, and rapidly diminish with increasing distances from these routes. On Columbia River the points of contact are with the Algonkin and Sioux; among the Bilqula they are with the Athapaskan. This phenomenon can hardly be explained in any other way than by assuming that the myths followed the line of travel of the tribes, and that there has been dissemination of tales all over the continent. The tabulations which have been made include the Micmac of Nova Scotia, the Eskimo of Greenland, the Ponca of the Mississippi Basin, and the Athapaskan of Mackenzie River; and the results give the clearest evidence of extensive borrowing.

The identity of a great many tales in geographically contiguous areas has led to the assumption that, wherever a great similarity between two tales is found in North America, it is more likely that it is due to dissemination than to independent origin.

But without extending these theories beyond the clearly demonstrated truths of transmission of tales between neighbouring tribes, we may reach some further conclusions. When we compare, for instance, the legend of the culture hero of the Chinook, and that of the origin of the whole religious ceremonial of the Kwakiutl Indians, we find a very far-reaching resemblance in certain parts of the legends, which makes it certain that these parts are derived from the same source. The grandmother of the divinity of the Chinook, when a child, was carried away by a monster. Their child became the mother of the culture-hero, and by her help the monster was slain. In a legend from Vancouver Island a monster, the cannibal spirit, carries away a girl, and is finally slain by her help. Their child becomes later on the new cannibal spirit. There are certain intermediate stages of these stories which prove their identity beyond doubt. The important point in this case is that the myths in question are perhaps the most fundamental ones in the mythologies of these two tribes. Nevertheless, they are not of native growth, but—partly at least—borrowed. A great many other important legends prove to be of foreign origin, being grafted upon mythologies of various tribes. This being the case, it follows that the mythologies of the various tribes as we find them now are not organic growths, but have gradually developed and obtained their present form by accretion of foreign material. Much of this material must have been adopted ready made, and has been adapted and changed in form according to the genius of the people who borrowed it. The proofs of this process are so ample that there is no reason to doubt the fact. We are therefore led to the opinion that, from mythologies in their present form, it is impossible to derive the conclusion that they are mythological explanations of phenomena of nature observed by the people to whom the myths belong, but that many of them, at the places where we find them now, never had such a meaning. If we acknowledge this conclusion as correct, we must give up the attempts at offhand explanation of myths as fanciful, and we must admit that also explanations given by the Indians themselves are often secondary, and do not reflect the true origin of the myths.

It may be well to explain this point of view a little more fully. Certainly the phenomena of nature are the foundation of numerous myths, else we should not find that the sun, moon, clouds, thunderstorm, the sea, and the land play so important a part in all mythologies. But it seems that the specific myth cannot be simply interpreted as the result of observation of natural phenomena. Its growth is much too complex. In most cases the present form has undergone material change by disintegration and by accretion of foreign material, so that the original idea is at best much obscured.

Perhaps the objection might be raised to this argument that the similarities of mythologies are due, not only to borrowing, but also to the fact that, under similar conditions which prevail in a limited area, the human mind creates similar products. While there is a certain truth in this argument, so far as elementary forms of human thought are concerned, it seems quite incredible that the same complex product should originate twice in a limited territory. The very complexity of the tales and their gradual dwindling down, to which reference has already been made, cannot possibly be explained by any other theory than by that of dissemination. Wherever geographical continuity of the area of distribution of a complex ethnographical phenomenon is found, the laws of probability exclude the theory that in this continuous area the complex phenomenon has arisen independently in various places; but they compel us to assume that the distribution of this phenomenon in its present complex form is due to dissemination, while its composing elements may have originated here and there.

In the Old World, wherever investigations on mythologies of neighbouring tribes have been made, the philological proof has been considered the weightiest; that is to say, the proof of borrowing has been considered the most satisfactory whenever, together with the stories, the names of the actors have also been borrowed. We cannot expect to find such borrowing of names to prevail to a great extent in America. Even in Asia the borrowed names are often translated from one language into the other, so that their phonetic resemblance is entirely destroyed. The same phenomenon is observed in America. In many cases the heroes of myths are animals, whose names are introduced in the myths. In other cases, names are translated, or so much changed, according to the phonetic laws of various languages, that they can hardly be recognised. Cases of transmission of names are, however, by no means rare. We will give only a few examples from the North Pacific coast.

Almost all the names of the Bilqula mythology are borrowed from the Kwakiutl language. A portion of the great religious ceremony of the Kwakiutl has the name 'tlōkoa'la.' This name, which is also closely connected with a certain series of myths, has spread northward and southward over a considerable distance. Southward we find it as far as the Columbia River, while to the north it ceases with the Tsimshian; but still farther north another name of a part of the ceremonial of the Kwakiutl is substituted, viz., 'nō'ntlɛm.' This name, as designating the ceremonial, is found far into Alaska. But these are exceptions; on the whole, the custom of translating names and of introducing names of animals excludes the application of the linguistic method of investigating the borrowing of myths and customs.

We will next consider the social organisations of the coast tribes in connection with certain peculiar customs which have been described in the Reports of the Committee, viz., the secret societies.

The northern tribes have maternal institutions, and are divided into a number of clans, which have animal totems. The clans are not considered descendants of the totem animal, but claim that the ancestor of each clan had a meeting with the totem animal, in which the latter became his friend and helper. The Kwakiutl are divided into a number of clans, most of which have animals for their totems. Most of these totems are explained in the same manner as those of the northern tribes, while others are considered direct descendants of the totem animal. Among the Kwakiutl we find a mixture of paternal and maternal institutions, but the son is not allowed to use his father's totem; he acquires the right to his totem by marriage, receiving at that time the totem of his wife's father. When, later on, his daughter marries, the right to the totem descends upon her husband. In this manner the totem descends in the maternal line, although indirectly. Each clan has a certain limited number of names. Each individual has only one name at a time. The bearers of these names form the nobility of the tribe. When a man receives the totem of his father-in-law, he at the same time receives his name, while the father-in-law gives up the name, and takes what is called 'an old man's name,' which does not belong to the names constituting the nobility of the tribe.

Among the Kwakiutl and Bilqula this social organisation holds good during the summer, while during the winter ceremonials it is suspended. During this time the secret societies take the place of the clans. According to tradition, these societies have originated in the same manner as the clan originated. One of the ancestors of the clan met the presiding spirit of one of the societies, and was initiated by him. This seems to be the general form of tradition explaining the origin of secret societies among all North American tribes. All those who have been initiated by the same spirit, and who have received from him the name, privileges, and secrets of the ceremonial, form a secret society. The most important among the societies on the North Pacific coast are those of the cannibals, the bears, the fools, and the warriors. The number of names composing a secret society is limited in the same manner as the number of names composing the clan. Membership in a secret society may be obtained in two ways: by marriage, in the same way as the acquisition of the totem; and by killing the owner of a certain name. Totem and secret society are not connected inseparably; but the one may be transferred to one person, the other to another.

In order to understand this curious system clearly we must remember that the Salish tribes which are found south of the Kwakiutl are divided into village communities; while their northern neighbours—the Tsimshian, the Haida, and the Tlingit—are divided into maternal clans. The Kwakiutl have been strongly influenced from both sides.

The traditions explaining the totems and the secret societies refer, as stated before, to the initiation of the ancestor of the clan. They are analogous to the traditions of the acquisition of the Manitou. All the tales referring to this subject have approximately the following incident: A youth undergoes a ceremonial fasting and purification, and thus acquires the faculty of seeing a spirit, who becomes his protector. The traditions of the coast tribes explaining the origin of clans have the same contents.

There is only one difference: the protecting spirit has appeared to the ancestor of the clan, and is now inherited by their descendants without personal initiation. In this respect the similarity between the traditions of the secret societies and those referring to the Manitous is much closer, since it is necessary that each new member be initiated by the presiding spirit of the society. Therefore every new member has to undergo the same ceremonies which other Indians undergo at the time of reaching puberty. The beliefs of the Chinooks of Columbia River are similar to those of the northern tribes, although among them the idea of the acquisition of the totem has been more clearly preserved. They believe that a man can acquire only that spirit who belonged to his ancestors in the paternal line, but the relation of this spirit to the individual is identical with that of the Manitou to the eastern Indian.

It can be clearly shown that the development of the family Manitou into the family totem has taken place owing to the influence of the northern tribes. In order to make this clear, it is necessary to consider for a moment the clans of the Kwakiutl somewhat closely. In examining the names of the tribes, it will be seen that very often the name of the tribe is the collective form of the name of its ancestor. At the same time a subdivision of the tribe, one of its clans, may have the name 'The Family of the Ancestor,' while the other clans have different names. It seems that this proves that the first clan formed the original stock of the tribe, and that the other clans joined it later on. This theory is strengthened by two considerations: first, it is stated that each clan originally had its village at a certain place, which it left later on in order to join others. Almost all these places can be proved to be ancient village sites. Secondly, many clans have names which may be translated, as 'Inhabitants of such and such a place,' while nowadays they live with the rest of the tribe in the same village, and have no distinct claims to the territory the name of which they bear. This seems to prove that the present social organisation of the tribe is a late development, and that originally the Kwakiutl were in the same stage of development as their southern neighbours, among whom the social unit is the village community, and who have no crests.

The northern tribes have clearly defined totems, which are inherited in the maternal line, and which have animal names and animal crests. While among these tribes the totem of the whole clan is founded on the tradition belonging to the whole clan, the subdivisions of the latter are explained in exactly the same manner as those of the Kwakiutl clans. The artistic bent of these people has taken hold of these traditions, and has thus formed the crest for the clan and for its subdivisions. There is little doubt that the plastic art of the northern tribes was a most important factor in developing their social system. In the south, where this art begins to disappear, the village community takes the place of the clan with animal totem, while among the tribes located between these two groups, among whom the plastic art is well developed, although not as highly as in the north, there is an intermediate form of social system. It is therefore likely that the development of the social system discussed here has taken place in the northern part of British Columbia.

The northern tribes of Kwakiutl lineage show clearly that their ideas have been influenced by the animal totem of the northern tribes. They have adopted to a great extent the maternal descent and the division into animal totems of the northern tribes. The social organisation of the Hē'iltsuk·, one of the most northern tribes of Kwatkiutl lineage, is similar to that of the Tsimshian, while their southern neighbours, the inhabitants of Rivers Inlet, who speak the same dialect, retain the more complex organisation of the Kwakiutl; but they have mainly maternal descent.

It is an interesting fact that a great many of the clan legends of the Kwakiutl are very insignificant, while others have important mythical bearings by which they are closely connected with the mythological concepts of the people. It seems probable that clan legends first found their way to the Kwakiutl by marriages with women of northern tribes, whose traditions, according to the customs of the northern region, were inherited by the woman's children. This must have given an important impulse to acquiring or inventing similar traditions on the part of other clans, since their possession was undoubtedly considered a prestige. Probably the fastings of young men and the subsequent hallucinations have furnished the greater part of the material for these legends.

It is necessary to consider at this place a few characteristic traditions which belong to the cannibal society of the tribes of the northern and central parts of the coast. The most widely diffused tradition on this subject seems to have originated among the Hē'iltsuk· but it has spread southward to the Kwakiutl. It is told that a young girl was carried away by the cannibal spirit. Her four brothers searched for her, and with difficulty escaped the pursuing cannibal spirit. Finally, they succeeded in killing him, and his ashes were transformed into mosquitoes. In the course of their visit to their sister the brothers learned the songs and secrets of the cannibal society. This tradition is given in most cases as the origin of the secret society. A number of other members were initiated in other ways, one by stealing the cedar-bark ornaments of the bathing cannibal spirit, another one by ascending the sky and obtaining the secrets of the society.

These customs have also spread to the northern neighbours of the Hē'iltsuk·, the Tsimshian. They have the following tradition in regard to the origin of the society:—A hunter pursued a bear, which finally led him into the interior of a rock. Inside he saw people performing the ceremonies of the society, and he was instructed by their chief to repeat the same ceremonies at home. In all the traditions of the Kwakiutl the cannibal spirit presides over the society, while he does not appear in the Tsimshian tradition. This shows that different traditions are used for explaining the same ceremonial.

In connection with these facts we will consider the conclusions which were drawn from a consideration of the mythologies of the tribes of British Columbia. We saw that none of these could be considered as the product of a single tribe. All the traditions were full of foreign elements, which it was possible to trace over wide areas. If, therefore, the same ritual is explained by different traditions, we may conclude that the ritual preceded the tradition; that the former is the primary phenomenon, the latter the secondary.

It seems that the development of the ritual, as well as of the traditions connected with it, is founded in the prestige given by membership in a secret society. There must have developed a desire to become a member of a society, which led, wherever the number of societies was insufficient for the tribe, to the establishment of new ones. It is not meant, of course, that the Indians intentionally invented new traditions, but that the desire stimulated their fancy and excited their mind, and that in this manner, after proper fastings, occasion was given for hallucinations, the material of which was naturally taken from the ideas found among the tribe and its neighbours. Similar phenomena have been treated, from a systematic point of view, by Stoll in his book on Suggestion, and by Tarde in his book on the Laws of Imitation.

It is easily understood how the exciting ceremonial of the cannibal society may have given rise to hallucinations in which a young man thought to see the same spirit under new conditions, and that after his return from the solitude he told his visions. Since the opinion prevailed that the spirit which appeared in this manner had a tendency to reappear to the descendants of the person to whom it once appeared, opportunity was given for the formation of a new place in the secret societies. We may assume, therefore, that, psychologically, the development of the complex system of membership in the secret societies must be explained as due to the combined action of the social system and the method of acquiring guardian spirits.

While these considerations may explain the variety of form of the secret societies, and show that the myths on which a ritual is founded are probably secondary, they do not explain the origin of the societies themselves and of the peculiar customs connected with them. There are, however, indications which lead to the opinion that these societies developed from methods of warfare. First of all, it is important to note that the deity Winā'lagyilis of the Kwakiutl presides over the whole ceremonial. This name means 'the one who makes war upon the whole world,' and his spirit controls the mind of the Indians also during the time of war. For this reason the secret societies are in action also on war expeditions, no matter at what season of the year they may occur. All the oldest songs of the secret societies refer to war. The cannibal, as well as the bear dancers and the fool dancers of the Kwakiutl, are considered warriors, and go into ecstasies as soon as an enemy has been killed. All this indicates that originally the secret societies were closely connected with war expeditions.

One thing more must be considered. The customs which we observe to-day are evidently the modern development of ancient forms. It is known that the ceremonial cannibalism, which nowadays is the principal part of the whole ceremonial, has been introduced very recently among all the tribes. The Kwakiutl state that this custom was introduced among them not longer than sixty years ago, and that it originated among the Hē'iltsuk·. We also know that the custom spread from the Hē'iltsuk· to the Tsimshian not longer than a hundred and fifty years ago. Therefore there is no doubt that the custom was originally confined to the small territory of the Hē'iltsuk·. Among the southern tribes the cannibals originally confined themselves to holding with their teeth the heads of enemies which had been cut off.

The form in which the cannibalism spread from the Hē'iltsuk· is mainly the following:—A slave was killed by his owner, then he was torn to pieces and eaten by the cannibals; or pieces of flesh were bitten out of the arms and the chest of people; or, finally, corpses which had been prepared in a particular way were devoured by the cannibals. The first of these customs clearly bears some relation to war. A slave was obtained in war by the relative of a cannibal, and by killing him the owner celebrated the victory before the assembled tribe. It is not possible to prove definitely that the secret societies developed in this manner from customs related to war expeditions, but the close relationship of the two cannot be doubted.

We may say, therefore, that the investigations of the Committee have proved that dissemination of cultural elements has taken place all along the North Pacific coast, and also that the most distant parts of the American continent, and probably even parts of the Old World, have contributed to the growth of the culture of the Indians of British Columbia. This fact shows that we cannot accept the sweeping assertion that sameness of ethical phenomena is *always* due to the sameness of the working of the human mind, but that it is necessary to consider in all anthropological investigations the important element of dissemination of cultural elements.

The decorative art of the Indians of the North Pacific coast differs from the arts of other primitive people in that the process of conventionalisation has not led to the development of geometric designs, but that the ornaments mostly represent animals. It is generally assumed that all the animal representations found on totem poles or on decorations of household utensils and of wearing apparel represent the totems of the various clans. While it is certainly true that in most cases the artists decorate the objects with the totem of the owner, there are a number of cases in which the reason for applying certain animal designs is founded on other considerations. This is very evident in the case of the fish-club, which is used in despatching halibut and other fish before they are hauled into the canoe. Almost all the clubs that I have seen represent the sea-lion or the killer-whale—the two sea animals which are most feared by the Indians, and which kill those animals that are to be killed by means of the club. The idea of giving the club the design of the sea-lion or killer-whale is therefore rather to give it a form appropriate to its function, and perhaps, secondarily, to give it by means of its form great efficiency.

Another instance in which a close relation exists between the function of the object and its design is that of the grease dish. Small grease dishes have almost invariably the shape of the seal, or sometimes that of the sea-lion; that is, of those animals which furnish a vast amount of blubber. Grease of sea animals is considered a sign of wealth. In many cases abundance of food is described by saying that the sea near the houses was covered with the grease of the seal, the sea-lion, and whales. Thus the form of the seal seems to symbolise affluence.

Other grease dishes and food dishes have the form of canoes, and here, I believe, a similar idea has given rise to the form. The canoe symbolises that a canoe load of food is presented to the guests, and that this view is probably correct is indicated by the fact that in his speeches the host often refers to the canoe filled with food which he gives to his guests. The canoe form is often modified, and a whole series of types can be established forming the transition between canoe dishes and ordinary trays. Dishes of this sort always bear a conventionalised face at each short end, while the middle part is not decorated. This is analogous to the style of the decoration of the canoe. The design represents almost always the hawk. I am not certain what has given origin to the prevalence of this design. On the whole, the decoration of the canoe is totemistic. It may be that it is only the peculiar manner in which the beak of the hawk is represented which has given rise to the prevalence of this decoration. The upper jaw of the hawk is always shown so that its point reaches the lower jaw and turns back into the mouth. When painted or carved in front view, the beak is indicated by a narrow wedge-shaped strip in the middle of the face, the point of which touches the lower margin of the chin. The sharp bow and stern of a canoe with a profile of a face on each side, when represented on a level or slightly rounded surface, would assume the same shape. Therefore it may be that originally the middle line was not the beak of the hawk, but the foreshortened bow or stern of the canoe. This decoration is so uniform that the explanation given here seems to be very probable.

On halibut hooks we find very often decorations representing the squid. The reason for selecting this motive must be looked for in the fact that the squid is used for baiting the hooks.

I am not quite certain if the decoration of armour and weapons is totemistic or symbolic. Remarkably many helmets represent the sea-lion, many daggers the bear, eagle, wolf, and raven, while I have not seen one that represents the killer-whale, although it is one of the ornaments that are most frequently shown on totemistic designs.

I presume this phenomenon may be accounted for by a consideration of the ease with which the conventionalised forms lend themselves to decorating certain parts of implements. It is difficult to imagine how the killer-whale could be represented on the handle of a dagger without impairing its usefulness. On the other hand, the long thin handles of ladles made of the horn of the big horn sheep generally terminate with the head of a raven or of a crane, the beak being the end of the handle. This form was evidently suggested by the slender tip of the horn, which is easily carved in this shape. The same seems to be true in the cases of lances or knives, the blades of which are represented as the long, protruding tongues of animals; but it may be that in this case there is a complex action of a belief in the supernatural power of the tongue, and in the suggestions which the decorator received from the shape of the object he desired to decorate.

To sum up, it seems that there are a great number of cases of decoration which cannot be considered totemistic, but which are either symbolic or suggested by the shape of the object to be decorated. It seems likely that totemism was the most powerful incentive in developing the art of the natives of the North Pacific coast; but the desire to decorate in certain conventional forms once established, these forms were applied in cases in which there was no reason and no intention of using the totemistic mark. The thoughts of the artists were influenced by considerations foreign to the idea of totemism. This is one of the numerous ethnological phenomena which, although apparently simple, cannot be explained psychologically from a single cause, but are due to several factors.

The treatment of the animal design is very peculiar. We may distinguish two principles which govern the form of representation: First, the animal is characterised by a number of symbols; secondly, the artist does not endeavour to render a perspective view of the animal, but rather to show the whole animal.

The first of these principles is probably founded largely on the difficulty encountered in designing realistic representations of various animals which would be clearly recognised as specific animals. For this reason the most characteristic peculiarities of each species become the symbols by which it is recognised. Thus the beaver is always symbolised by two large incisors and a scaly tail; the dog-fish, by an elongated forehead, a mouth with depressed corners, and five curved lines (the gills) on each cheek; the killer-whale, by its tail, flippers, and its large dorsal fin; the sculpin, by two spines which rise over the forehead; the hawk, by a large beak, which is turned backward so that it touches the chin. Probably all these symbols were originally applied to characterise a portion of a quadruped, bird, or fish; but in course of time they came to be considered as sufficient to call to mind the form of the whole animal. We find, therefore, that gradually the symbols were to a great extent substituted for representations of the whole animal. A dorsal fin worn on the blanket of a dancer, or painted on his face, indicates that the person so decorated personates the killer-whale. A strongly curved beak painted on a gambling-stick symbolises that the stick is meant to represent the thunder-bird. A protruding tongue painted on the chin symbolises the bear.

The second principle seems to be quite opposed to the first one. When the artist decorates any object with the representation of an animal, he distorts and dissects the animal in such a way as to show the whole body on the decorative field; but a closer examination of this tendency proves that it originates mainly in the necessity felt by the artist of introducing all the symbols, which are distributed over the whole body of the animal, in the decoration. To give a few instances, bracelets are decorated in such a way that the animal is split along its back, and then represented in such a manner as to make it appear as though the arm were pushed through the opening. On tattooings the animals are shown as split through along their backs or along their chests, and then flattened out, so that a symmetrical design results. Carvings on totem poles must be interpreted in the same way, the animal being represented as bisected along the rear side of the totem pole, and extended so that the two margins of the cut appear on the borders of the carved portion of the pole. The distortion and section of animals is nowhere carried further than in representations on boxes, on slate dishes, and on Chilcat blankets; but in all these decorations we recognise the endeavour to bring such forms of the animal into view as are essential for an understanding of the design—that is to say, all those parts of the animal are represented which serve as its symbols.

So far as I am aware, the process of conventionalising has not led to the formation of geometrical designs, which are exceedingly rare on decorated objects from the North Pacific coast. They are found only in certain kinds of basket work and in mattings.

Finally, it may be well to add a brief explanation of the economic system prevailing among these Indians, which was fully set forth in the Fifth Report of the Committee. This system finds its expression in the so-called 'potlatch.' The meaning of this custom has been much misunderstood, and the recent enactment of a law making the potlatch a criminal offence is probably in great measure due to a misconception in regard to its meaning.

The economic system of the Indians of British Columbia is largely based on credit, just as much as that of civilised communities. In all his undertakings the Indian relies on the help of his friends. He promises to pay them for this help at a later date. If the help furnished consisted in valuables, which are measured by the Indians by blankets as we measure them by money, he promises to repay the amount so loaned with interest. The Indian has no system of writing, and therefore, in order to give security to the transaction, it is performed publicly. The contracting of debts, on the one hand, and the paying of debts, on the other, is the potlatch. This economic system has developed to such an extent that the capital possessed by all the individuals of the tribe combined exceeds many times the actual amount of cash that exists; that is to say, the conditions are quite analogous to those prevailing in our community: if we want to call in all our outstanding debts, it is found that there is not by any means money enough in existence to pay them, and the result of an attempt of all the creditors to call in their loans results in disastrous panic, from which it takes the community a long time to recover.

It must be clearly understood that an Indian who invites all his friends and neighbours to a great potlatch, and apparently squanders all the accumulated results of long years of labour, has two things in his mind which we cannot but acknowledge as wise and worthy of praise. His first object is to pay his debts. This is done publicly and with much ceremony, as a matter of record. His second object is to invest the fruits of his labour so that the greatest benefit will accrue from them for himself as well as for his children. The recipients of gifts at this festival receive these as loans, which they utilise in their present undertakings, but after the lapse of several years they must repay them with interest to the giver or to his heir. Thus the potlatch comes to be considered by the Indians as a means of insuring the well-being of their children if they should be left orphans while still young. It is, we might say, their life insurance.

The sudden abolition of this system—which in all its intricacies is very difficult to understand, but the main points of which were set forth in the preceding remarks—destroys therefore all the accumulated capital of the Indians. It undoes the carefully planned life-work of the present generation, exposes them to need in their old age, and leaves the orphans unprovided for. What wonder that it should be resisted with vigour by the best class of Indians, and that only the lazy should support it, because it relieves them of the duty of paying their debts?

But it will be said that the cruel ceremonies connected with some of the festivals make their discontinuance necessary. An intimate knowledge of the Indian character leads me to consider that any interference with these very ceremonials is unadvisable. They are so intimately connected with all that is sacred to the Indian that their forced discontinuance will tend to destroy what moral steadiness is left to him. It was during these ceremonies that I heard the old men of the tribe exhort the young to mend their ways; that they held up to reprobation the young women who had gone to Victoria to lead a life of shame; and that they earnestly discussed the question of requesting the Indian Agents to help them in their endeavour to bring the young back to the good, moral life of old.

And the cruelty of the ceremonial exists alone in the fancy of those who know of it only by the exaggerated descriptions of travellers. In olden times it was a war ceremony, and captives were killed and even devoured; but with the encroachment of civilisation the horrors of the old ceremonies have died out. An old chief has been heard addressing his people thus: 'How lovely is our time! No longer do we go in fear of each other; peace is everywhere. No longer is there the strife of battle; we only try to outdo each other in the potlatch,' meaning that each tries to invest his property in the most profitable manner, and particularly that they vie with each other in honourably repaying their debts.

The ceremony of the present day is no more and no less than a time of general amusement, which is expected with much pleasure by young and old. But enough of its old sacredness remains to give the Indian, during the time of its celebration, an aspect of dignity which he lacks at other times. The lingering survivals of the old ceremonies will die out quickly, and the remainder is a harmless amusement that we should be slow to take away from the native, who is struggling against the overpowerful influence of civilisation.

  S E L E C T I O N   1 3

The Jesup
North Pacific Expedition

It is only a few years since anthropology has begun to take its rank among other sciences, and it would seem that it is already approaching the solution of its problem,—that it is laying down the laws governing the growth of culture.

This history of anthropology is but a repetition of that of other sciences. When the facts begin to array themselves in seeming order, the ultimate goal of inquiry appears to be near at hand. The fundamental laws which governed the growth of culture and civilization seem to manifest themselves conspicuously, and the chaos of beliefs and customs appears to fall into beautiful order. But investigation goes on incessantly. New

Publications of the Jesup North Pacific Expedition 1 (1898): 1–11.

facts are disclosed, and shake the foundation of theories that seemed firmly established. The beautiful, simple order is broken, and the student stands aghast before the multitude and complexity of facts that belie the symmetry of the edifice that he had laboriously erected. Such was the history of geology, such the history of biology. The phenomena, as long as imperfectly known, lend themselves to grand and simple theories that explain all being. But when painstaking and laborious inquiry discloses the complexity of the phenomena, new foundations must be laid, and the new edifice is erected more slowly. Its outlines are not less grand, although less simple. They do not disclose themselves at once, but appear gradually, as the laborious construction proceeds.

Anthropology has reached that point of development where the careful investigation of facts shakes our firm belief in the far-reaching theories that have been built up. The complexity of each phenomenon dawns on our minds, and makes us desirous of proceeding more cautiously. Heretofore we have seen the features common to all human thought. Now we begin to see their differences. We recognize that these are no less important than their similarities, and the value of detailed studies becomes apparent. Our aim has not changed, but our method must change. We are still searching for the laws that govern the growth of human culture, of human thought; but we recognize the fact that before we seek for what is common to all culture, we must analyze each culture by careful and exact methods as the geologist analyzes the succession and order of deposits, as the biologist examines the forms of living matter. We see that the growth of human culture manifests itself in the growth of each special culture. Thus we have come to understand that before we can build up the theory of the growth of all human culture, we must know the growth of cultures that we find here and there among the most primitive tribes of the Arctic, of the deserts of Australia, and of the impenetrable forests of South America; and the progress of the civilization of antiquity and of our own times. We must, so far as we can, reconstruct the actual history of mankind, before we can hope to discover the laws underlying that history.

These thoughts underlie the conception of the Jesup North Pacific Expedition. Its aim is the investigation of the history of man in a well-defined area, in which problems of great importance await solution. The expedition has for its object the investigation of the tribes, present and past, of the coasts of the North Pacific Ocean, beginning at the Amoor River in Asia, and extending northeastward to Bering Sea, thence southeastward along the American coast as far as Columbia River.

The peculiar interest that attaches to this region is founded on the fact that here the Old World and the New come into close contact. The geographical conditions favor migration along the coast-line, and exchange of culture. Have such migrations, has such exchange of culture, taken place?

This question is of great interest theoretically. The American continent is widely separated from the land area of the Old World, so that the geographical conditions are in favor of the presumption that in the New World culture developed uninfluenced by causes acting in the Old World. Throughout the Old World migrations have brought the peoples of the most distant areas into hostile or peaceful contact, so that there is hardly a tribe that might be considered as uninfluenced by others. If the development of culture in the New World has been quite independent of the advances made in the Old World, its culture will be of the greatest value for purposes of comparison. Therefore, it is necessary to investigate with thoroughness all possible lines and areas of contact, and among these the North Pacific coast is probably the most important.

The problem of the investigation may be stated in the following manner: There is little doubt that the American race has inhabited our continent for a very long time. Although no finds have been made that establish its geological antiquity beyond cavil, we have good reason to believe that man inhabited this continent at a very early time. The principal foundation for this belief is the existence of well-marked varieties of the American race, the establishment of which must have occupied a long period. The general characteristics of the race are fairly uniform. The smooth, dark hair; broad, heavy face; large nose; and rather full mouth,—are common to all the natives of America. But nevertheless a number of distinct types have developed, differing in color of skin, in form of head and of face, and in proportions of the body. The differences in these types show that a long period was necessary for their development. They cannot be explained as due to the mixture of different races, because they all partake of the general characteristics of the American race, and because the members of each type show a remarkable degree of uniformity. The variability of each type is slight as compared to variabilities which we find in Europe, among the tribes of Asia or of the Polynesian Islands. The small variability is an indication of lack of mixture, and therefore of long-continued development by differentiation.

The long period of occupancy of our continent, which thus seems probable, implies that American culture passed through a long period of development. It is likely that the distinct types of the race developed in isolated spots, and therefore culture must also have followed distinct lines of growth.

But this period has long since passed. At the time when American tribes entered the field of our knowledge, and even in periods of which archæology alone gives evidence, contact was established between the tribes of the north and of the south, of the east and of the west, so that it is no longer possible to consider as the product of isolation the cultural possessions of each tribe. Archæological evidence also shows that distinct types followed each other in the occupancy of each area. In short, historical changes of far-reaching importance took place long before the tribes became known to history. They imply mixture of blood, as well as exchange of cultural achievement.

The condition in which we find the tribes of the North Pacific coast of both continents, gives evidence of manifold changes. The multiplicity of languages spoken along both coasts, and their division into numerous dialects; the great variety of types of the area, their irregular distribution, and their affiliations to types of distant regions; the peculiar types of culture,—all intimate that the primitive tribes of the coast have passed through a long and varied history. The types of man which we find on the North Pacific coast of America, while distinctly American, show a great affinity to North Asiatic forms; and the question arises, whether this affinity is due to mixture, to migration, or to gradual differentiation. The culture of the area shows many traits that suggest a common origin, while others indicate diverse lines of development.

What relation these tribes bear to each other, and particularly what influence the inhabitants of one continent may have exerted on those of the other, are problems of great magnitude. Their solution must be attempted by a careful study of the natives of the coast, past and present, with a view of discovering so much of their history as may be possible.

These were the problems that attracted the attention of Mr. Morris K. Jesup, President of the American Museum of Natural History in New York, and induced him to provide personally with great liberality the means for carrying on investigations. The execution of the work was intrusted to the Anthropological Department of the Museum, of which Prof. F. W. Putnam is the curator. The plans for the work, and the general management, were placed in charge of Franz Boas, assistant curator in the Department of Anthropology, who is responsible for the method and execution of the inquiry so generously provided for by Mr. Jesup.

Operations of the Expedition in 1897

The Jesup North Pacific Expedition was organized early in the year 1897. The area in which its investigations are carried on is little known. Although the literature relating to the North Pacific coast is quite extensive, very few thorough anthropological researches dealing with it have been published. On the Asiatic side the description of Kamtchatka, by Steller, is worthy of note, and the reports of Leopold von Schrenck, on the tribes of the Amoor region, are of fundamental importance. In America the Russian missionary Vemiaminof gave descriptions of the languages of Alaska, which are of permanent value. Later on, Horatio Hale's work as a member of the Wilkes Expedition brought clearness into the confusion of languages of the southern part of the coast. Still later

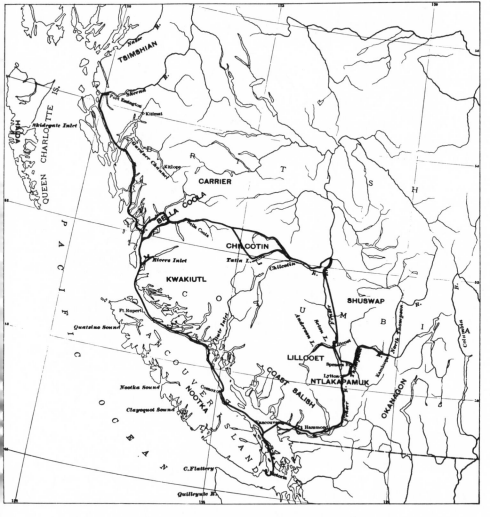

Map of the Northwest Coast Operations

important work was done by George Gibbs and Myron Eells in Washington and southern British Columbia; by George M. Dawson in British Columbia; and by William H. Dall in Alaska. A systematic investigation of the tribes of British Columbia was inaugurated by the British Association for the Advancement of Science, which in 1883 appointed a committee charged with this work. The operations of the committee extended over a period of fourteen years, and field-work was conducted under the auspices of the committee from 1888 to 1897. The Jesup Expedition continues the systematic work of this committee over a wider area, and expands it on lines that were not touched upon before.

The committee directed its attention mainly to the languages, customs, and physical characteristics of the tribes of British Columbia, and its work was nearly completed in 1896. It only remained to study the physical types of the northern interior of British Columbia. The plan for this final work had been elaborated prior to the organization of the Jesup Expedition. Since the plan of the latter expedition made it necessary to supplement the work of the committee of the British Association, particularly in regard to archæological and somatological research, it was deemed best to combine the two expeditions. The committee of the British Association and Mr. Jesup agreed to pursue a common plan. It is due to this enlightened policy that unnecessary duplication of work was avoided, and that the new work can be taken up where the old work ceased. During the year 1897 anthropometric work in northern British Columbia, and linguistic work on the tribes of southern British Columbia, was carried on for the British Association for the Advancement of Science, while all the remaining work was done for the Jesup North Pacific Expedition.

The party which carried on operations during the year 1897 consisted of Mr. Franz Boas, of the American Museum of Natural History; Mr. Livingston Farrand, of Columbia University, New York; and Mr. Harlan I. Smith, of the American Museum of Natural History. This party was assisted by Mr. James Teit, of Spences Bridge, B. C.; Mr. George Hunt, of Fort Rupert, B. C., and Mr. Fillip Jacobsen, of Clayoquot, B. C. The party travelled westward by way of the Northern Pacific Railroad, through the courtesy of whose officials the journey was rendered most pleasant. After having made the necessary preparations in Victoria, B. C., they proceeded to Spences Bridge, where they arrived on the 2d of June, and were met by Mr. James Teit. The great familiarity with the language of this area which Mr. Teit has acquired during a long period of residence there, and the deep interest which he is taking in the Indians, make him a most valuable assistant in the investigations. Early in the year 1897 he collected notes on the Thompson River Indians, for the use of the Jesup Expedition; and with his help a number of additional data were obtained, mainly bearing upon the art of the Indians, their language and physical characteristics. While these investigations were being carried on, Mr. Smith made preparations for archæological investigations in the valley of

Thompson River. It was soon found that Spences Bridge was not the most favorable place for excavations; and for this reason Mr. Smith moved his base of operations first to Kamloops, and later on to Lytton, which is situated at the confluence of Fraser River and Thompson River. At the latter place Mr. Smith was ably assisted by Mr. Charles Hill-Tout of Vancouver, B. C., well known for his researches on the archæology of British Columbia. The Expedition is under great obligations to Mr. Hill-Tout for the deep interest that he manifested in its work, and for the kindly assistance rendered by him. At Kamloops and Lytton Mr. Smith conducted extensive excavations on the hillsides and in the valley, discovering numerous remains of previous habitations, some of which are without doubt of considerable antiquity. Almost all his finds antedate the advent of the whites, and give us an excellent insight into the culture of the people of that period. Beautiful carvings in bone illustrate the high development of plastic art that had been attained by the Indians; shells from the seacoast indicate the existence of early intertribal trade; and numerous implements made of stone, bone, and shell, give a good insight into the general state of culture of the tribe.

While Mr. Smith was conducting his investigations at Kamloops, Mr. Boas and Mr. Farrand, accompanied by Mr. Teit, started on a lengthy trip northward, which was intended to serve two purposes. It was necessary to investigate the physical characteristics of the Indians inhabiting the banks of Fraser River north of Lytton. Furthermore, it was desirable to study the customs and physical characteristics of the Chilcotin, the most southern Athapascan tribe of British Columbia. From here it was intended to continue the journey over the mountains to the coast, in order to study the Bella Coola, an interesting tribe, whose customs and beliefs had never been subjected to systematic inquiry. The party started with a train of ten horses from Spences Bridge. The mountains between Spences Bridge and Lillooet were crossed on narrow trails. It was hoped that a considerable number of Indians would be met with in the high valley of Botani, where the tribes of Fraser River and Thompson River assemble every spring; but only comparatively few were met with, and for this reason the journey was continued after a short delay. At Lillooet Mr. Farrand separated from the main party, and visited the villages of the Upper Lillooet on Seton and Anderson Lakes. Meanwhile the pack-train slowly proceeded along the wagon-road leading to Caribou. All the Indian villages that are situated on or near this wagon-road were visited, and a considerable number of anthropometric measurements were collected. After about a week Mr. Farrand, who had completed his work among the Lillooet tribe, rejoined the party. On the 3d of July they reached Soda Creek, on Fraser River, the most northern village inhabited by the Shuswap tribe. Then they crossed the river and proceeded westward, in order to visit the territory of the Chilcotin. After a few days the first village of this tribe was reached. The party proceeded slowly from village to village until the most western Chilcotin village of any considerable size was reached. Now the further investigation of the interesting tribe was left to Mr. Farrand, while Mr. Boas proceeded on his journey across the mountains to Bella Coola.

The Chilcotin have been brought into contact with the whites comparatively recently; and, although they live in log-cabins at the present time, raise cattle and horses, and till the soil, they are probably the most primitive among the tribes of British Columbia. A number of families still roam in the mountains between Lillooet and Chilcotin River, and have not been induced to settle on reservations; consequently the field of investigation was a most interesting one, and the results of Mr. Farrand's ethnological inquiries are of great value. He spent most of his time in the larger villages of the Chilcotin; but during the month of August he visited the isolated families which live on the shores of Tatla Lake and in the mountains. From here he proceeded northward until the pass which leads to Bella Coola was reached. Mr. Boas followed the more northern route towards this pass, crossing the wild plateau north of Tatla Lake. On this journey a few of the Chilcotin who make their home near Lake Nakoontloon were met with. At this place the Coast Range, seen from the east, seems to form an enormous gap, and a trail leads westward, following a small river that takes its rise in the high mountains of the range. Gradually the valley narrows, and the beautiful peaks and glaciers of the Coast Range come into view. The trail ascends higher and higher, until, at a height of five thousand feet, the summit is reached. Here a few small snow-fields have to be crossed, and the trail suddenly emerges on the north side of Bella Coola River. The river is seen almost five thousand feet below; and on the opposite side of its deep and narrow valley rises the high peak Nuskulst, which plays a most important part in the mythology of the Bella Coola. Enormous glaciers flank its sides, and a little farther down the river appear other snow-clad mountains of beautiful form. In early times the villages of the Bella Coola were found all along the river, up to a place about twenty miles above Nuskulst; but the tribe has so diminished in numbers, that all the villages on the banks of the river have been abandoned. The trail descends the steep mountain-side until the river is reached, at a point about twenty-five miles above its mouth. Here the deep and rapid river had to be crossed. The party built a raft, on which an Indian embarked in order to fetch a canoe that was seen on the other side. In this the men crossed the river, while the horses swam over. From here a day's journey brought the travellers to the village of the Bella Coola Indians. The road passes through a Norwegian settlement that has recently been established in this valley. At Bella Coola Mr. Boas was met by Mr. George Hunt, who, under special instructions, had collected valuable specimens among the Indians. The pack-train returned over the mountains to Fraser River, while Mr. Boas stayed among the Bella Coola Indians.

Here interesting information on the customs and beliefs of the tribe was collected. After this work had been completed, Mr. Boas started down Bentinck Arm. Then he went by steamer northward to Skeena River, where he joined Mr. Smith, who had finished his work in the interior of British Columbia by the beginning of August. Some time was spent near the mouth of Skeena River in making investigations on the graphic art of the Haida Indians, and in studying the physical appearance of the Tsimshian and Haida. Mr. Smith collected a valuable series of photographs, while Mr. Boas was engaged in collecting measurements. By this time Mr. Farrand had completed his work among the Chilcotin. Accompanied by an Indian, he crossed the mountains, and at Bella Coola met Mr. Hunt, who was completing his work among this tribe. Towards the end of August both left Bella Coola, intending to pay a visit to the village of Bella Bella, which is situated just outside the mouth of Bentinck Arm. Mr. Farrand spent here the remainder of the summer, studying the social organization and arts of this tribe. The plan was that Mr. Smith should meet him at Bella Bella in order to assist him in the study of the physical appearance of the Bella Bella Indians. This plan was carried out, both travellers reaching Bella Bella at nearly the same time.

After Mr. Boas had completed his work on Skeena River, he journeyed southward on a coast steamer, and was joined at Bella Bella by Mr. Smith and Mr. Hunt, while Mr. Farrand stayed behind, continuing his investigations. The party landed in Rivers Inlet, where a stay of several weeks was made. Mr. Smith again assisted in the study of the physical appearance of the Indians, and after this work had been completed continued his journey to Vancouver, in order to resume his archæological investigations. Mr. Boas and Mr. Hunt, who stayed in Rivers Inlet, succeeded in collecting much interesting material on the language and customs of this little-known tribe. In the middle of September Mr. Farrand reached Rivers Inlet, having completed his work in Bella Bella. Here he was joined by Mr. Boas and Mr. Hunt. The latter returned to his home in Fort Rupert, while Mr. Boas and Mr. Farrand returned to New York.

Mr. Smith, after his return to Vancouver, took up the investigation of the shell-mounds at the mouth of Fraser River, which yielded important results, clearing up interesting points in the history of the Indians. It seems that the physical appearance of the Indians during the period of deposit of the shell-mounds on lower Fraser River had undergone material changes. The results that were here obtained are so important, that it will be necessary to continue the researches during the coming year. When the rainy season set in, Mr. Smith moved his camp to southeastern Vancouver Island, where he spent some time in the investigation of prehistoric stone monuments. Finally, in the middle of November, the winter rains set in, which compelled him to conclude his operations.

During the summer Mr. Fillip Jacobsen undertook to make a collection

illustrating the culture of the tribes of the west coast of Vancouver
Island. His intimate acquaintance with the Indians, and his varied
experience in ethnological work, have made his assistance of great value.

The Expedition is also under great obligations to Dr. Charles F. New-
combe, who contributed an interesting collection from Queen Charlotte
Islands.

The collections of the Expedition are extensive. They embrace specimens illustrating the archæology of the interior and of the coast of
British Columbia. They illustrate the ethnology of the Thompson River
Indians, of the Chilcotin, of the Bella Coola, of the Kwakiutl, and of the
Nootka. A very material body of facts has thus been added to our
knowledge of the North Pacific coast, and the collections of the Museum
have been enriched by many interesting specimens.

    S E L E C T I O N   1 4

Kathlamet Texts

The following texts were collected in the summers of 1890
and 1891 and in December, 1894. So far as I have been able to ascertain,
the Kathlamet dialect is spoken by three persons only—Charles Cultee
and Samson, both living at Bay Center, Washington, and Mrs. Wilson,
who lives at Nemah, on Shoalwater bay. Unfortunately neither Samson
nor Mrs. Wilson were able to give me any connected texts, so that
Charles Cultee was my only informant. This is unfortunate, as he told
me also Chinook texts, and is, therefore, the only source for two dialects
of the Chinookan stock. In order to ascertain the accuracy of his mode
of telling, I had two stories which he had told in the summer of 1891
repeated three and a half years later, in December, 1894. They show
great similarity and corroborate the opinion which I formed from internal
evidence that the language of the texts is fairly good and represents the
dialect in a comparatively pure state. Cultee lived for a considerable
number of years at Cathlamet, on the south side of Columbia river, a few
miles above Astoria, where he acquired this dialect. His mother's mother

Kathlamet Texts, Bulletin No. 26, Bureau of American Ethnology (Washington:
Government Printing Office, 1901), pp. 5–7, 34–38.

was a Kathlamet, his mother's father a Xuilā'paX; his father's mother
was a Klatsop, and his father's father a TkulXiyogoā'ike, which is the
Chinook name of the Tinneh tribe on upper Willapa river. His wife is a
Chehalis, and at present he speaks Chehalis almost exclusively, this
being also the language of his children.

Cultee (or more properly QiEltē') has proved a veritable storehouse of
information. I obtained from him the texts which were published in an
earlier bulletin of the Bureau of American Ethnology [Boas 1894b], as
well as the material embodied in the present paper. The work of translating and explaining the texts was greatly facilitated by Cultee's remarkable intelligence. After he had once grasped what was wanted, he
explained to me the grammatical structure of sentences by means of
examples, and elucidated the sense of difficult periods. This work was
the more difficult as we conversed only by means of the Chinook jargon.
It will be noticed that the periods of the later dictations are much more
complex than those of his earlier dictations.

The following pages contain nothing but the texts and translations.
These collections of texts will, it is expected, be followed by a grammar
and dictionary of the language, which will contain a comparison of all
the known dialects of the Chinookan stock.

The Kathlamet is that dialect of the Upper Chinook which was spoken
farthest down the river. Its territory extended from Astoria on the south
side and Grey's Harbor on the north side of the river to Rainier. Cultee
stated that above Kalama the pronunciation was slightly different. He
mentioned the following tribes as speaking the Kathlamet dialect: The
Wā'qa-iqam of Grey's Harbor; the Lā'cgENEmaxîx· about opposite
Cathlamet (on the north side); the KLā'ecaLxîx·, at the present town of
Cathlamet; the Lā'qaLala, about three miles above Oak point on the
north side of the river; the Lctā'mēctîx·, half a mile below the mouth
of Cowlitz river; the Lā'kialama, at Kalama; the Tē'iaqiōtcoē, three miles
above Oak point, on the south side of the river; the KLā'gulaq, two miles
below Rainier; and the KLā'môîx·, at Rainier.

ALPHABET

a, e, i, o, u	have their continental sounds (short).
ā, ē, i, ō, u	long vowels.
ᵃ, ᵉ, ⁱ, ᵒ, ᵘ	vowels not articulated, but indicated by position of the mouth.
A, E, I, O, U	obscure vowels.
ä	in German Bär.
â	aw in law.
ô	o in German voll.
ê	e in bell.
î	i in hill.
-	separates vowels which do not form diphthongs.

ai	i in island.
au	ow in how.
l	as in English.
ll	very long, slightly palatized by allowing a greater portion of the back of the tongue to touch the palate.
ʟ	posterior palatal l; the tip of the tongue touches the alveoli of the lower jaw, the back of the tongue is pressed against the hard palate; sonant.
L	the same, short and exploded, surd (Lepsius's t).
Lᵢ	the same with very great stress of explosion.
q	velar k.
k	English k.
k·	palatized k (Lepsius's k'), almost ky.
kX	a posterior palatal k, between k and k·.
x	ch in German Bach.
X	x pronounced at posterior border of hard palate.
x·	palatal x as German ich.
s, c	are evidently the same sound, and might be written s· or c·, both being palatized; c (English sh) is pronounced with open teeth, the tongue almost touching the palate immediately behind the alveoli; s is modified in the same manner.
d, t ⎫ b, p ⎬ g, k ⎭	as in English, but surd and sonant are difficult to distinguish.
h	as in English.
y	as in year.
w	as in English.
m	is pronounced with semiclosure of the nose and with very slight compression of the lips; it partakes, therefore, of the character of b and w.
n	is pronounced with semiclosure of the nose; it partakes, therefore, of the character of d.
ᵢ	designates increased stress of articulation.
2, 4	designate excessive length of vowels, representing approximately the double and fourfold mora.
,	indicates a pause.

Words ending with a short vowel are contracted with the first vowel of the next word. The last consonant of a word is united with the first vowel of the next word to one syllable.

Myth of the Swan (Told 1894)

The people tried to buy a maiden, but her father did not give her away. Then the chief of the Swans bought her. They gave her to him. It became winter. Now the people had eaten all their provisions, and they became hungry. The Swan had a double dish. His mother gave him food. Dry broken salmon was in one dish, and pounded salmon bones were in the other. Then the Swan ate the dry salmon, and his wife ate the salmon bones. Every evening they received food in this way. His wife did not know what her husband was eating. She thought all the food might be salmon bones. For a whole year they ate in this manner. When she chewed, there was a noise of breaking bones. When he ate, there was a noise of meat being munched. Then she began to notice it. After some nights she took her husband's dish, and she saw that he was eating dry salmon. "Oh," she thought, "he has treated me ill. He gave me bones to eat, and, behold, my husband is eating dried salmon! I will go home to my people."

Early the next morning she made herself ready and went home. She arrived at her father's and her mother's house. She said: "Oh, they treated me ill. They gave me pounded salmon bones to eat, while my husband was eating dried salmon." Then she lay down; she was ashamed. For five nights she lay on one side. After five nights she turned over and laid her head on the other side. Then she arose. She was quite white, and no hair was on either side of her head. Then she sang her conjurer's song. Now snow began to fall. It fell for five days. Then she said to the young men of the village: "Take that dip-net down to the water and move it five times up and down there at sea." Then she sang a song conjuring the smelt, and the young men went. Five times they went up and down in their canoe; then it was full of smelt. They went ashore, and the people gathered the smelt. Their houses were full. Now the water began to freeze, and the canoes could not go out, because the water was all frozen. Then the Swans died of hunger. Now their chief heard: "Oh, your wife conjured the smelts." Thus he was told: "Their houses are full of smelts." Then the Swan said: "We will go and I will take my wife back." Thus he spoke to his relatives.

Early in the morning the Swans made themselves ready. They had two canoes. They went. The people said: "Canoes are coming." Then the Swans landed. The woman was told: "Maybe your husband comes to fetch you." She said: "Lock the house. Do not let them enter." Then indeed they locked it, and the Swans were standing outside. The woman said: "Quick! Roast five smelts; I want to eat them." Five smelts were roasted. Then the woman said: "The heads of my smelts are roasted." The Swan replied: "The heads of our smelts are roasted." "The bellies of my smelts are turned over." The Swan said: "The bellies of our smelts are turned over." "The backs of my smelts are turned over." The Swan said: "The backs of our smelts are turned over." "The tails of my smelts are turned over." The Swan said: "The tails of our smelts are turned over."

Then the Swans who were staying outside became cold. They were shut out. Now the smelts were done. Then the woman ate. She said: "Now roast a smelt on five single spits." A smelt was roasted on five single

Original Field Notes (1894) for the Opening Lines of the Swan Myth
(Reproduced from a notebook preserved in the
American Philosophical Society)

IQ̂ÊLŌ'Q IꞀ'KꞀANÊ

SWAN HIS MYTH

1 Êwa' kē'nuwa qomɛlä'lɛmx wuXi ahä'tꞽau. Nȧct qaqō'tx. Ꞓ'qa
   Thus intending she was bought that virgin. Not she was Then
                                                      given away.

2 Ꞁqelō'q iꞀä'XakꞽEmana qatcumɛlä'lɛmx. Aqa qa-ilō'tx. Aqa
   the swans their chief bought her. Then she was given Then
                                              to him.

3 tcä'xElqꞀîX ninō'xoaxîx. QatktūꞀxō'mx tgä'ꞀxalEmaēmax tê'lXam;
   winter it became. They finished their food the people;

4 aqa walō' aktō'xax. Aqa sx·umtꞽē't sqꞽu'nam, sī'aqꞽunam iqelō'q.
   then hunger acted on them. Then two fastened wooden his wooden the swan.
                                       together dishes, dishes

5 Aqa agē'lqoēmx ayä'qō iqelō'q. Tkꞽē'lak aē'Xꞓ aqꞽu'nam, tkꞽanä'ꞀkꞀîX
   Then she gave him his the swan. Dried one dish, dried and broken
                      food mother salmon salmon bones

6 aē'Xt aqꞽu'nam. QatiXElEmō'xumx taXi tkꞽē'lak iqelō'q. Wu'Xi
   one dish. He ate it that dried salmon the swan. That

7 ayä'kikala tkꞽanä'ꞀkꞀîX qataxalEmō'xumx. Ka'nauwē tsō'yustîX
   his wife dried and broken she ate them. Every evening
             salmon bones

8 kꞽoaꞀqē' aqcîlquē'muX. Nîct alō'XuîX wuXi ayä'kikala. AxꞀō'Xuan
   thus they two were Not she knew it that his wife. She thought
         given food.

9 ka'nauwē tkꞽanä'ꞀkꞀîX taXi aqcîlquē'muX. Ê4Xt iqē'taq,
   all dried and broken that they two were One year,
        salmon bones given food.

10 ataxalEmō'xumx, sxōp, sxōp, sxōp, sxōp yaXi itcä'kcXapa. YaXi
   they ate it, noise of eating hard food that her mouth in. That

11 iqelō'q nîxꞀxE'lEmux, tcꞽkuä'k, tcꞽkuä'k iä'kcXa. Aqa xä'xꞺ
   swan he ate noise of eating soft food his mouth. Then notice

12 igiō'xoax yaXi itcä'kikala. Qantcî'xꞀx qanä'pōl aqa agigElgä'x
   she did him that her husband. Several nights then she took it

34

Opening Lines of Interlineated Swan Myth Text
(Reproduced from Bulletin No. 26, page 34,
Bureau of American Ethnology, 1901)

spits. She said: "Make fire of pitch wood when you roast the smelt." Now the smelt was roasted on five spits. They burned pitch wood. Then the smelt became black with soot. It was done. Then she said: "Now open the door that they may enter." Then the door was opened for the Swans, and they entered. They entered, and they were given the smelt, but it smelled of pitch. While they were eating, wings began to grow on them. Then they began to fly. The woman said: "Swan shall be your name; you shall not eat dry salmon. When you smell smelts, you shall fly away. You shall eat only roots and rushes; never shall you eat dry salmon; you shall not make people unhappy. When smelts are caught in the evening, you shall fly away on the following morning. You shall go inland."

    SELECTION 15

The Documentary Function
of the Text

BOLTON LANDING,
WARREN CO., N. Y.,
July 24, 1905.

DEAR PROFESSOR HOLMES:

I had a letter from Swanton a few days ago, in which he tells me, that you propose to print his traditions as Bulletin 29 of the Bureau, and that you propose to print also 14 original texts. Swanton feels, of course, very glad, that this is to be done. I should like, however, to urge upon you the advisability of printing all the texts. I do so entirely from my own convictions. Swanton did not mention the subject in his letter.

I do not think that anyone would advocate the study of antique civilizations or, let me say, of the Turks or the Russians, without a thorough knowledge of their languages and of the literary documents in these languages; and contributions not based on such material would not be considered as adequate. In regard to our American Indians we are in the position that practically no such literary material is available for study,

Letter preserved in the Bureau of American Ethnology Archives, in the National Anthropological Archives, Smithsonian Institution, Washington, D.C.

and it appears to me as one of the essential things that we have to do, to make such material accessible. My own published work shows, that I let this kind of work take precedence over practically everything else, knowing it is the foundation of all future researches. Without it a control of our results and deeper studies based on material collected by us will be all but impossible. Besides this we must furnish in this way the indispensable material for future linguistic studies. What would Indo-European philology be, if we had only grammars made by one or two students and not the live material from which these grammars have been built up, which is, at the same time, the material on which philosophic study of language must be based. This fact is nowhere more apparent than in our studies based on the old missionary grammars. In these the characteristic features of the languages treated are so entirely obscured by the mode of treatment, that without new and ample texts our understanding of the languages will always remain inadequate. As we require a new point of view now, so future times will require new points of view and for these the texts, and ample texts, must be made available.

It seems to my mind, that we can accept undigested collections of translated traditions only in cases, where for one reason or other the collection of the originals was impossible. I have permitted collections of this kind, for instance the Koryak, because on account of the remoteness of the tribe, a full collection of traditions in the original would have required years and more money than I had. I think, however, that in our own country a collection of translated traditions is not up to the standard of excellency that we must demand for the publications of our best institutions. In the work that I have conducted, I have prepared for the publication of such texts of Algonquin, Maidu, Shasta, Tsimshian, Kwakiutl, Haida, and I have accepted translations only when they happen to elucidate a general ethnological point or when, on account of lack of funds, the collection could not be made in a more satisfactory manner.

I trust you will believe, that this letter is dictated only by my deep conviction that the publication of the full text material is necessary and is the right thing to do.

Yours very truly,
FRANZ BOAS

SELECTION 16

A Truthful Picture
for Future Times

March 28, 1907.
Mr. HENRY W. TATE,
Port Simpson, B.C.

MY DEAR MR. TATE,—

I was very glad to receive the 75 pages of the Tkamsum story, which you had the kindness to send me. I enclose in this letter a money-order for $15. As you will see, I have raised the pay to twenty cents a page instead of 15 cents, and I hope that this will be agreeable to you. I trust now that you will be willing to go on, and that I may look forward to some more matter in the near future.

I was very much interested in reading what you have written, but you must allow me to say one thing. You write in your letter that you have omitted some of the stories which to you and to me seem very improper; but if we want to preserve for future times a truthful picture of what the people were before they advanced to their present condition, we ought not to leave out anything that shows their ways of thinking, even though it should be quite distasteful to us.

It is just the same as with some of the horrid customs of olden times, like dog-eating and man-eating. You have no reason to be ashamed of what the people did in olden times, before they knew better: but if we want to give a truthful account of what there was, we ought not to be ashamed or afraid to write it down. I hope, therefore, that you may be willing to overcome your reluctance to write nasty things, since they belong to the tales that were told by your old people. For our purpose it is all-essential that whatever we write should be true, and that we should not conceal anything.

You will recall that you promised also the story of Sucking-Intestines (Namomhat). I hope you will find time to write it to me, and to let me know how it is related to the Tkamsum story.

Yours very sincerely,
[FRANZ BOAS]

Copy preserved in the Boas Papers, American Philosophical Society.

SELECTION 17

"That Book
Contains My Speech"

[This selection was written in answer to a moving complaint from George Hunt—the more moving for its misspellings and fractured grammar. Only recently recovered from a six-week illness, Hunt was beset with troubles occasioned by his relationship with Boas. At Hunt's request, his sister had taken into her home Harlan Smith, who was working for the Jesup Expedition. After Smith and his wife had left, a story derogatory to the Indians had appeared in the Victoria newspapers. Hunt and his relatives attributed it to Mrs. Smith, and they were further upset by the fact that a canoe Smith had used was returned damaged. In her anger, Hunt's sister had told the Kwakiutl that Smith had robbed Indian graves; and to make matters worse, Chief Hemasaka had gone down to Victoria, where he had been told that Boas had made a speech alleging that things were getting better all over the world, except among the Kwakiutl, who were still "living on the Daid People." Hunt was called before the Kwakiutl at a feast and informed that neither he nor Boas would again be allowed to attend ceremonials. Fearing even for his life, Hunt nonetheless promised to continue collecting material for Boas.]

NEW YORK,
Feb. 3, 1899

Mr. GEORGE HUNT,
Fort Rupert,
P.O. Alert Bay,
British Columbia.

MY DEAR GEORGE:—

I just received your letter, of the 10th of January, which worries me very much indeed. I am sorry that you have been sick, and that your family were not well, but I hope that every thing is going smoothly now. There are so many things to answer in your letter, that I must take them up one by one. First of all about Hemasaka. I enclose in this letter

Copies preserved in the Boas Papers, American Philosophical Society.

a letter to Hemasaka, which I want you to read to him. You will find what I refer to on pages 54 and 55 of the book that I am sending to Hemasaka, because I think it will please him. I am sending you a copy too. You must read to him particularly the two paragraphs which I marked with double lines on page 55.[1]

I will ask you to invite the chiefs to a feast at my expense, for which you can charge in your bill, and read my letter at the feast, and read also what is in the book. I am sending the book to Hemasaka himself, so that he may ask any one to translate what I said. I hope that that will end the trouble so far as I am concerned. You can then easily fix up your own affair by telling them that this is the way in which your friend whom you are helping speaks of the Indians.

Now about the Smiths. I simply cannot understand the things you are talking about. All the letters that I received from Smith and Mrs. Smith while they were in British Columbia were just full of praise of your sisters and your mother, and every time they talk about British Columbia, they say how kindly all of you treated them; in fact, they are taking every opportunity to express how much they are indebted to all of you. I am quite certain that neither he nor she would willingly hurt the feelings of any of your people. I suppose the whole trouble lies with the meddlesome and nasty newspaper writers. You do not know how they are bothering us all the time, and how every thing they learn is twisted about in the papers so as to make it look exciting to the people. I suppose you remember the nasty figures and the horrible description of the dance that was in one of the newspapers, said to be written by me, but which was simply made up, and stolen out of my book. You may be quite sure that the same thing happened to the Smiths.

I am going to give him your letter, and I presume both he and Mrs. Smith will feel very badly about it, and they will certainly write to your sisters. As a matter of fact we are just getting ready a brief report on the work done last summer, which is written by Smith and Farrand and one man who has been working in Asia. You will see in that report what Smith has to say about the hospitality of your sisters. I wish you would show this letter to Mrs. Spencer and to Sarah and Jane, and I hope they will see from it that it is quite impossible that Mr. and Mrs. Smith should have had any intention of hurting their feelings.

I have not received the stories yet, but hope they will come soon. I notice what you say about the seventeen generations naming the oldest sons and daughters. I hope you will take time to write all this out in full. I hope you have my letter of Jan 13, in which I wrote about the work for the present year.

---

[1] The book referred to is presumably the separate *Twelfth and Final Report on the North-Western Tribes of Canada*, and the passages indicated would seem to be the last portion of Boas' "Summary," reproduced above as Selection 12.

I expect that the trouble about which you wrote in your letter will be satisfactorily settled by this letter and by what you are going to hear from Smith, and I do not think it is right that on account of this matter you should be on unfriendly terms with Spencer or your sisters, even for a short time. And I believe it would be better for you to keep in touch with Spencer's work in the cannery, because you are sure that it will go on all the time, while there may be times during which I cannot do any work; at least I think that will be best for you and for your family.

We are not going to quarrel about David's canoe. When I wrote to you in October, I said that if you did not think that the provisions and so forth that you received from Smith were sufficient to pay for the canoe, then you must charge me with what you think he owes you. Of course I understand that there was some wear and tear of the canoe, and that is the reason why Smith pays for the hire. You can make that up with David, and I will be satisfied with any arrangement that you think just to David and to myself.

Yours very truly,
[FRANZ BOAS]

NEW YORK,
Feb. 3, 1899

CHIEF HEMASAKA,
Fort Rupert, British Columbia.

Franz Boas, whom you called Heiltsakuls sends this letter to Chief Hemasaka:

I have learned that somebody told you of a speech that I made: that I have been all around the world, and seen every thing changed for the best, except the Kwakiutl tribe; that they are still living on dead people. I think, Chief, that you do not believe this. I never make a speech of that kind. I do not say what is not true. I want to tell you what I said. I send you as a present a book that I made. That book contains my speech. Let one of the young chiefs, or one of your friends, read it to you, and you will see that what I say is true. The Kwakiutl have no better friend than I. Whenever I can, I speak for you. You see in this book that what I say is true, therefore you will not believe the foolish talk that you may hear about me. I have told to the chiefs in Ottawa and to the chiefs in England many times, that the potlatch and that the dance are not bad. You will see my speech in the book. I wait for a letter from you, Chief, in which you will say that I am the best friend of your great tribe,—the four great tribes of Tsaxis.

PART IV

FOLKLORE AND THE CRITIQUE OF EVOLUTIONISM

Boas' critique of the assumptions of nineteenth-century cultural evolutionism was elaborated over a ten-year period, culminating in 1896 with his essay on "The Limitations of the Comparative Method of Anthropology." Much of the argument was developed in relation to the study of folklore, and particularly through a statistical study of the distribution of folktale elements. In the two letters to E. B. Tylor that make up the first selection (no. 18), we get a glimpse of the early development of this approach. Tylor had just sent Boas an abstract of his paper "On a Method of Investigating the Development of Institutions; Applied to Laws of Marriage and Descent," in which, on the basis of a tabulation of data from some 350 peoples, he had studied the "adhesions" of different customs: the tendency for clusters of customs to occur together (Tylor 1889). At this point Boas had completed one field trip for the British Association, and Tylor, apparently worried that he had spent too much time on mythology, sent his paper in part to suggest alternative lines of inquiry. Boas, however, was less interested in the subject matter of Tylor's paper than in its method, which fitted very well with the approach he was already developing. But where Tylor's inquiry had reinforced the traditional evolutionist sequence of development from maternal to paternal forms, Boas used the method of adhesions to approach problems of diffusion (cf. Lowie 1947, p. 305; Stocking 1968a, p. 207). Indeed, in several lines scribbled in the margins of the original draft of this letter, Boas put his finger on a paradox at the root of cultural evolutionism: whereas biological evolutionism assumed that related forms had *one* origin, cultural evolutionism assumed that they had *many*. At this point, however, Boas apparently thought it best not to confront Tylor on this issue, and in the copy Tylor received, the next to last paragraph was omitted.

Most of Boas' essays on the diffusion of folktale elements are either still in print (1891b, 1896b, 1914, 1916a; cf. 1940) or still in German (1895), but in 1905 he published an extended popular statement on American Indian mythology that has since been lost to view. It appeared in two parts. The first, which is not reprinted here, was an essentially descriptive piece in which Boas offered a rough regional typology, emphasizing the contrast between the disconnected hero tales of the Northwest and the more systematic origin myths of the eastern and southern tribes. The second, however, offers an excellent nontechnical summary of Boas' diffusionary approach (no. 19). The opening tale provides an unusual but apt illustration of Boas' general historical viewpoint. Here we are actually able to watch the very process of myth construction, which for Boas provided a model of the development of culture in general. The point, of course, was that human culture developed always in specific historical context, as men in a particular cultural situation remolded and rearranged the materials bequeathed to them by tradition or presented to them by others with whom they came in contact (cf. Spier 1931, 1959).

The last selection of this section (no. 20) offers an example of Boas' interpretation of the cultural development of a particular tribal group. Treating the interrelationship of social organization, ceremonialism, and mythology among the Bella Coola, Boas attempted to unravel the historically complex "psychological motives for the development of certain traditions and myths." But it will be noted that he did not reject entirely the evolutionist concern with universal psychological processes. Although it must be preceded by historical analysis, comparative study was still, at least in principle, an essential component of anthropological inquiry. Finally, this selection offers evidence to show that although Boas' characteristic method of historical inquiry was based on an analysis of discrete cultural elements, it did not treat them in isolation: on the contrary, individual cultural traits could only be understood "in connection with the whole culture of a tribe."

SELECTION 18

Tylor's "Adhesions" and the Distribution of Myth-Elements

NEW YORK.
47 LAFAYETTE PLACE.
October 4th 1888.

DR. E. B. TYLOR.
Oxford.

DEAR SIR:

I received your letter of Sept. 11 in due time and read with great interest the enclosed abstract of your paper, which you were so kind to send me. I delayed my answer, as I concluded from your letter that I should hear from Canada very soon. Yesterday I received a letter from Professor Hale in which he informs me that the British Association intended to apply to the Canadian Government for continuing ethnological work in British Columbia. I hardly need to say that I should be very glad to continue my work in that province.

The social institutions of the Indians in that region are very complicated and difficult to understand. Accurate work in that line requires first of all much time. A long residence among each tribe is almost indispensable and, as during my recent trip, I was not able to devote more than a fortnight to any tribe, the results in this line are necessarily fragmentary. During my first visit I took great pains to ascertain the social institutions of the Kwakiutl, but unfortunately these are the most complicated among the institutions of British Columbia. How difficult the problem is, you will see from the following facts. The Kwakiutl proper are the first in rank among a group of four tribes. They are divided into four septs of different rank. These septs are divided into gentes. Each gens has its own prerogatives and carvings that are connected with some myth. As a rule children follow the father, but there are exceptions, the

Originals preserved in the E. B. Tylor Papers, Pitt Rivers Museum, University of Oxford; bracketed passage from an earlier draft in the American Philosophical Society.

reason for which I did not ascertain. When a man comes to be grownup he acquires by marriage his father-in-law's prerogatives and carvings. He has first to pay to his father-in-law about fifty blankets; three months later about 100 blankets. Then the girl is given to him, but he has to live for three months in the house of her parents and then pay 100 blankets more, to be allowed to take her to his own house. Then the girl's father has to return the whole number of blankets he has received from his son-in-law and must give up all his prerogatives. This must first be permitted by the council. If the young man is not considered worthy of having these rights, his father-in-law is not allowed to transfer them upon him. As these prerogatives must be kept in the tribe and can be transferred *only* by marriage, a sham marriage of one young man to another is sometimes practiced [sic].

You can easily imagine, how difficult it is to find out the truth on all these points during a brief visit.—I am very much interested in your statistical method of studying social institutions. Last winter I had begun a work of similar character. I have a card catalogue of elements of American myths, which are arranged systematically. Then the occurrence and co-occurrence of such elements is ascertained and I hope thus to reach an understanding of the growth of myths and their migrations. My catalogue so far embraces several thousand cards referring to Eskimo, British Columbia and Athapascan myths. I intend to continue the work, as soon as I find sufficient leisure.

I am, Dear Sir,
Yours very respectfully,
Dr. Franz Boas

New York
196 Third Avenue.
March 6th 1889

Dr. Edward B. Tylor.
Oxford.

Dear Sir,

At last I have concluded my report on my last summer's trip to British Columbia, and I should be much gratified, if it would meet the expectations of the Committee. Nobody can be better aware than myself of its shortcomings, but I beg to ask you kindly to bear in mind the shortness of my visit to the coast, during which I had to collect material among an overwhelmingly large number of tribes. As my instructions were first of all to ascertain the number of linguistic stocks and languages of the province, in order to furnish material for an ethnological map, the subjects: enumeration of tribes and linguistics naturally take up a considerable part of [the] report. I consider the Tlingit and Haida as branches of one linguistic stock, but their affinity is so remote, that further evidence seems desirable. I have endeavored to show on the map the range of a number of important customs and institutions: the extent of the practice of tattooing, of ceremonial cannibalism, the use of certain types of houses, the limits of maternal institutions.

I wish to say a few words in regard to the chapters [on] shamanism, art and social organization. The first of these ought to include a full report of the secret societies. I have learned more of these on my first trip in 1886, than is contained in the present report, but the information is so vague and indefinite, being mostly obtained from persons not initiated, that I prefer to keep it back, until I obtain better material. So much, however, has been ascertained, that no doubt can obtain regarding the origin of these institutions among the Kwakiutl. I have written a paper on the ornaments used in their dances for the 'Internationales Archiv' about a year ago, which will probably appear this spring. For a satisfactory study of this difficult subject it would be necessary to learn the Kwakiutl language and then to visit that region in December and January when the festivals of the secret societies are celebrated. I collected the songs of about 12 of these societies, but they do not convey much information.

I have not even touched the subject of art in my report. To say anything new and valuable, it would be necessary to study the conventionalism of NW America patiently, and I have had no time for such an undertaking. As all my ethnological work is done after office hours, I cannot do as much, as I should like to do.

My notes on the social organization of these tribes, although containing a considerable amount of new material, are the most fragmentary part of the report. The totems of the Tlingit, Haida [,] Tsimshian and Heiltsuk are comparatively simple, but farther south it would be necessary to visit every single tribe and village. This study would undoubtedly be of the greatest value and interest, but it requires enough time and money for travelling in canoe. The secret societies and carvings are most intimately connected with the gentes of these tribes. The main principles might of course be ascertained by the study of a single tribe; but it is necessary not only to ask and to hear, but to see and observe. Even among the northern, maternal group of tribes the totem is not the only subdivision of the tribes. Each totem of each village has a certain crest, derived from a myth referring to its ancestor, while that of another village has another crest. The chief is in many cases entitled to an additional crest. This explains the alleged existence of the gentes: gull, halibut, squid, etc.; which in fact are *only* crests. I mention these difficulties, as they will explain the fragmentary character of this chapter. The peculiar laws regarding the naming of children, which are closely connected with the social organisation of the tribes may be of interest to you.

I have sent you from time to time some articles on NW Am. mythology; I hope to publish this summer a summary statement of the results of my comparison of these myths which throws some light upon the history of these peoples. By [a method similar to] your method of adhesions I have endeavored to exclude incidental parts from the original myths and thus so far as possible to reconstruct the original myths of each people, and to trace the migration of myths. Besides the historical point I try to approach a psych[ological] question by this study: how is foreign material when taken up by a people, modified by preexisting ideas and customs? A question all consider one of the most import in the study of anthropology and which bears upon the independent origin of ideas and inventions far apart. I consider it a most characteristic sign of the diversity of our present methods of thinking in physiol[ogical] and psychol[ogical] science that in the former we are inclined to derive genetically similar forms from *one* source; while in psychol[ogical] science we are inclined to believe that an idea can develop independently in different communities or individuals.

I intend to visit Europe for a few weeks this spring, and shall be in Berlin from the middle of May to the middle of June. I shall avail myself of the opportunity to look over the ethnological collections, particularly their new accessions. The old ones I know pretty well having been assistant to Professor Bastian before my first visit to the North West Coast. My principal object is to look after some geographical publications.

> I am, Dear Sir,
> Very truly yours,
> FRANZ BOAS

SELECTION 19 — /905

The Mythologies
of the Indians

The fundamental traits of the mythologies of various tribal groups of North America were described in a previous essay. They were found to differ in type, and to be expressions of different philosophical concepts. In one region we found disconnected, fragmentary accounts of the origin of the present state of things, while in other districts the myths formed one connected historical and philosophical cycle. Before attempting an investigation of the psychological significance of Indian mythologies, we must discuss their historical development.

Generally these two questions are considered one and the same. The psychological and more or less rationalistic explanation of the myth is believed to be also the history of its origin. If the Corn in many mythologies is considered the offspring of a deity personifying Mother Earth, this interpretation is assumed to express the historical origin of the legend. It will be recognized at once that this is not a necessary inference; it might happen as well that a story of different origin would be associated with natural phenomena of special importance to man, and that—to use our literary terminology—the purely anecdotal myth would become secondarily an allegory.

The question is evidently one difficult to decide, because we are unfamiliar with the actual history of Indian mythologies. We know only their present status, not their earlier forms and interpretations. Any observation of the origin of a new myth is therefore of the greatest value for our study, and deserves the most careful attention.

Perhaps the best cases of this kind are the mythification of historical events, examples of which are not unknown, and which illustrate the process of development of a new legend. On account of the importance of these observations we may be allowed to give an example of this kind in some detail.

In 1781 the Siberian Trading Company was formed in Russia and took possession of Kodiak, laying the foundation of the Russian colonies on the

Part II of an essay in *The International Quarterly* 12 (1905): 157–173.

continent of America. In 1790 Alexander Baranoff was appointed manager of the company, and through his energy Russian influence spread rapidly along the coast of Alaska.

Baranoff made a treaty in 1799 with the Sitka Indians, a tribe of southern Alaska, and was permitted to establish a factory in their territory. He selected Sitka for the site of this station, and proceeded at once to erect a stockade for the protection of the buildings. When all was completed, he invited the Tlingit to attend the dedication of the factory, which was to be called Fort Michael. They, however, had become afraid of the Russians, and wished they had not permitted the establishment of the fort; therefore they considered the invitation an insult, and mocked and derided the messenger. Baranoff at once gathered a few soldiers and entered the village, in which about three hundred warriors were assembled, to demand satisfaction. The Sitka were so much impressed by his courage that they did not make any attempt to thwart the undertakings of the Russians while Baranoff was present. They seemed to be once more peaceful and content.

In 1801, after the station was organized, Baranoff returned to Kodiak, leaving a small garrison at the fort, with Medwiednikoff in command. For a short time the natives seemed to be on the best of terms with the Russians; but one day, when the greater part of the Russians were hunting sea-otters, about six hundred Tlingit made an attack upon the fort. The Russians, who numbered about fifteen, defended the fort to the last; but, when the Indians succeeded in setting fire to the stockade, they were compelled to surrender. All were brutally massacred. The struggle lasted only a few hours. The Russians and Aleutian hunters, when they heard of what was going on, hastened back, but they were too late: the fort had been taken, and they were killed one by one, as they arrived. About twenty Russians, Medwiednikoff among them, and a hundred and thirty Aleutians, were killed in this struggle; three thousand sea-otter skins were seized by the Indians, and a vessel belonging to the station was burned.

When Baranoff heard of these events, he prepared an expedition against the Sitka, and in the spring of 1804 he left Kodiak. In September he arrived at Sitka, where the Indians had erected a strong stockade at the mouth of what is now called Indian River. Baranoff landed, and, meeting no resistance, occupied a hill which he named New Arkhangelsk. The Sitka first offered to make peace and to give hostage; but, as they were unwilling to allow the establishment of a fort on the hill which the Russians had occupied, Baranoff attacked their stockade, which, after a long and severe struggle in which Baranoff himself was wounded, was vacated by the Tlingit, who made their escape during the night unnoticed.

These are the historical facts which form the basis of an Indian

Odyssey relating to the adventures of Nanak, as Baranoff is called by the natives. Here is their tale:

"A long time ago Nanak came into our country, accompanied by many Aleuts, who were his slaves. They landed at Sitka, and he ordered the Aleuts to build a fort. They made a stockade which surrounded their houses. When all was completed, Nanak went home again, leaving his son in command of the fort. The latter had his wife with him, who wore a beautiful dress. After a while our grandfathers got angry with Nanak's son and with the Aleuts. They seized one of the latter, painted his face, and sent him back to the young commander, thus mocking him. When Nanak's son saw what our grandfathers had done to his slave, he became very angry. He gathered his slaves around him, and they all went to fight against our grandfathers. These put on their armor, took their bows and arrows, their lances and daggers, and a severe battle ensued. It did not last long, for our grandfathers killed many Aleuts, and those who were not killed were made slaves. Then they set fire to some shavings which they had heaped around the stockade, and soon the fort was all ablaze. Nanak's son and his wife were almost the sole survivors. Our grandfathers had spared them. He felt downcast, and, holding his wife in his arms, slowly went around the burning town. When he saw the houses transformed into ashes, his heart was full of despair, and he flung himself and his wife into the flames. Thus they perished.

"Then our grandfathers asked the Aleuts, 'Where do the Russians build their forts?' They answered, 'They build their forts wherever they find a good landing.' Upon hearing this, our people went to the landing at Sitka and built a stockade. After a few months Nanak arrived, and on hearing what had happened, he made an attack upon our stockade, but he was defeated.

"Then he gathered all the young men who had come with him, went on board his ship, and sailed in search of his son. He had a book which spoke to him and always advised him what to do. It said, 'Tell your men that they must not take their wives on board the ship, else you will not find your son.' Nanak did as he was told by the book. His followers obeyed except one, who loved his wife dearly, and concealed her in his trunk.

"After they had sailed a long while, they approached an unknown coast. Here they found a village, and went ashore. They entered the houses, and found that they were inhabited by women, and that not a single man lived in this country. Nanak's men asked the women to become their wives; but they pointed to a great log lying on the beach, and said, 'Do you see yon log? He is our husband.' The Russians were at first incredulous, but, on examining the log more closely, they saw that its limbs were set with teeth. One of the sailors, however, tried to take hold of a woman; but they attacked him, and almost killed him.

"Nanak called his men back to the ship, and they reached her in safety. They set sail at once, and continued their search. After having sailed many days and nights, they descried another coast, and saw a village in a small opening. They landed and looked around, but they did not see a living being. After a while, they discovered shadows moving about, and feathers flying to and fro.

They were frightened, but soon one and the other mustered courage and entered the houses. Then they discovered boxes full of sea-otter and sealskins, and plenty of fish and deer-tallow. They called their friends, and, as they did not see anybody except the shadows and feathers, they resolved to carry the treasures away. They took bundles of skins out of the boxes, and were going to carry them to the beach, when invisible hands arrested them before they reached the door, and took the bundles from them. Thus they discovered that the shadows and feathers were the owners of this place, and that they would not allow them to take anything away. But their greediness got the better of their caution, and they attempted to rob the shadows and feathers of their treasures. When they tried to do so, invisible hands clubbed them, and it was only with difficulty that they escaped to their ship.

"They set sail, and after many days and nights they arrived in the country where people eat toads. The people whom they met there caught toads that were more than a span long. They sucked them out, and threw the skins away. The Russians, however, disliked this custom, and, as they had nothing else to eat, they fried the toads before eating them.

They proceeded on their search, and soon came to that part of the earth where it is always dark. For ten days they sailed in the dark. Heavy gales made the waves rise to tremendous heights, and the foam struck the top of their masts. Nanak was afraid lest his ship might be lost and he himself and his men might perish. He asked his book, and it said, 'Do not be afraid. Continue your course, and to-morrow you will see your son.' Nanak obeyed, and on the next day he arrived at the edge of the world. Far beyond he saw smoke rising in the land of the dead, but he did not see his son. Then he cried for sorrow. He went to his book, opened it, and asked, 'O book, tell me, why don't I see my son?' The book replied, 'There is a woman on board the ship. That is the reason why you are unable to see your son.' When Nanak heard this his veins swelled with wrath, and he called all his men, and threatened to kill the culprit. He searched in the hold and in all parts of the ship for the woman, and, as he did not find her, he ordered all trunks to be opened. Then he found the unfortunate woman. He cut off her head, and threw the corpse into the sea. Her husband, who had disobeyed Nanak's orders, was also thrown overboard.

"He proceeded along the edge of the world. Nothing was to be seen but sky and water. After a while he heard a terrible noise. He did not know what was the cause of it, but resolved to investigate it. Thus he came to the corner of the earth where the water of the ocean rushes during the ebb-tide in a terrible whirlpool down into the under-world, to return again after a few hours, and thus to make the flood. When the ship approached this dreadful place, she was almost drawn into the whirl; but Nanak cast anchor, and, when the chain became too taut, he cast a second and a third anchor. Having thus secured his ship, he tied a bucket to a long rope, and threw it from the stern of the ship into the whirlpool. He had to pay out many thousand fathoms of rope before the bucket struck the bottom of the sea. Then he pulled it up again, and he found a letter in the bucket, which said, 'We who live here in the under-world are happy that you have come at last! We have no fresh water: please give us some.' Nanak complied with their request, and sent down a bucket of fresh water. When they hauled the line in again, they found the water gone, but the bucket full of money, and a letter in it, which said, 'Please give us some more water, and we will pay you well.' Four times Nanak gave them water, and each time they returned the bucket full of money.

"After Nanak had thus seen where the water goes when it is ebb-tide, he returned to our country. But he had been on his cruise so long that the men who had gone out with him young were gray-haired when they returned."

If this legend were not amalgamated with well-known historic events, and if it did not contain references to European inventions, there would be nothing to indicate its recent origin. Its first part may be considered reasonably accurate, except for the claim of victory in a battle in which the natives were signally defeated; but with the moment of Baranoff's departure—in fact, his departure for Russia—the events become entirely fanciful. The native story-teller has filled out the unknown parts of the life of the admired Baranoff with wonderful exploits. The characteristic and important feature, from our point of view, is that these adventures belong to the common stock of Indian folk-lore. It seems desirable to prove this fact in some detail.

The latter part of the legend refers to the views held by the Tlingit regarding the fate of the soul after death, and regarding the form of the world. There are many stories telling how powerful shamans visited the underworld, or saw the land of the spirits, which is situated just outside the borders of the flat earth. The Tlingit believe that the earth is a square, the corners of which turn toward the four cardinal points. In the beginning, before man was created, it was swinging up and down in space, but eventually a female spirit succeeded in fastening it to an underworld. Since that time she has held the earth, lest it should again lose its hold. In the northern corner is the great whirlpool through which the ebb-tide rushes to the lower world, and from which the flood-tide returns. Outside the borders of the world is the abode of those who died of sickness, while those dying a violent death go to heaven.

The preceding adventure—the visit to the village of the shadows and feathers—occurs as an incident in the raven myth of the Tlingit. According to their beliefs, the Raven created sun, moon, and stars, and man and animals. Later on, he wandered all over the world, and many are the adventures told of him. In these the great creator appears as a cheat and liar throughout; who, however, seldom succeeds in his tricks, and is finally beaten by his enemies. I believe the story of his wanderings, and similar stories of adventures of travelers, have had a great influence upon the Nanak tale, in so far as they encouraged the invention of similar legends of wanderers. The incident of the raven legend, above referred to, is almost identical with that of the Nanak tale. It is told how the raven wished to obtain the skins and the tallow owned by the shadows and feathers, and how he fared at their hands.

The first among the Nanak adventures illustrates another point. The tale of women being married to a log which provides for them is not

common in the folk-lore of the Indians. It appears, however, in the traditions of the Eskimo, who have a tale of a hero who traveled all over the
world, and who in one place had the same adventure that is ascribed in
our legend to Nanak. This, taken together with the reference to a country
of continuous darkness, points to the occurrence of Eskimo elements in
the tale.

It appears, therefore, that the story of Baranoff's adventures is almost
entirely a combination of well-known elements, largely current in the
folk-lore of the tribe, but partly borrowed from a neighboring people.
There is very little in it that is original invention.

It is of importance to inquire whether the historical development of
mythology has been of a similar character, or whether in this case each
myth must be considered a unit in growth and development. If the myths
consist of old elements combined in various ways, it would seem improb-
able, if not impossible, that their interpretation as explanations of phenomena of nature should give us a clew to their historic origin.

This point may also be illustrated by means of a definite example, as
which I will select a sun myth of the North Pacific coast:

"According to the tradition of the Comox, a tribe living on Vancouver
Island, there was a chief who had two sons. Instead of going hunting, the
boys spent their time gathering the roots of bracken, which they ate until roots
began to grow between their fingers. Then their father scolded them, saying,
'You had better go and marry the Sun's daughters rather than spend your time
in this manner.' The boys took their father's words to heart, and went westward. Then they took their bows and arrows, and began to shoot their arrows
toward the sky. The first arrow stuck in the sky. The second arrow hit the nock
of the first arrow, and thus they continued until a chain was formed reaching
down to the ground. They climbed up the chain of arrows, and reached the
sky, a beautiful open prairie. In walking along, they met with two blind women,
whose eyesight they restored. In return, the women pointed out the way to the
Sun's house, and warned them, saying that the Sun tried to kill all the suitors of
his daughters. At the same time the women gave them advice as to how to
escape the attacks of the Sun. They proceeded, and met the Crane, who also
gave them advice. Finally they reached the pond from which the Sun's daughters were wont to draw water. The boys had hidden in the branches of a tree;
and the girls, on seeing their reflection in the water, believed them to be
drowned. On looking up, however, they discovered them in the branches of the
tree, and invited them to come to their father's house. As soon as they had
entered, the Sun spread a mat for them, which was set with long, sharp spikes.
The Crane had made their skin as hard as stone, consequently they were not
harmed by sitting down on the mat; but they crushed the spikes. Next the Sun
heated stones in the fire, and compelled them to swallow the stones. The Crane
had taught them to make stones pass through their bodies rapidly by jumping
up very quickly. They did so, and the hot stones did not harm them. In short,
the Sun was not able to kill them by means of the tests which he had used to

kill the other suitors of his daughters. He was compelled to consent to their marriage; but even then he did not give up his attempts to kill his sons-in-law. "One day he invited them to accompany him when he was going out to cut wood. He split a tree, and intentionally dropped his hand-hammer into the crack of the tree. Then he asked his sons-in-law to get the hammer, and when they had entered the crack, he knocked out the props which kept the tree apart. It closed upon them, and he believed that he had killed them. But the young men flew out of the tree in the shape of birds, and merely squirted some white and red paint out of the crack in order to make the old man believe that they were dead. When the Sun returned home, he was surprised to find his sons-in-law there. Next he tried to kill them by inducing them to catch an artificial seal which he had made, and which he had instructed to drag their canoe far out to sea. The boys escaped this danger by their power over the winds, which drifted them back to shore. Finally, the Sun asked them to catch his playfellows, the wolves, bears, and the grizzly bears. The young men obeyed, but asked the animals to bite and scratch and tear their father-in-law, who was thus killed."

This is a typical example of a certain class of American sun myths, in which the Sun appears as an enemy of mankind, who is finally replaced by some successor.

In analyzing this myth we will not only compare its elements with other myths of the same tribe, but we will consider also the tales of neighboring tribes.

It begins with the disobedience of the sons of the chief, who in consequence orders them to undertake a difficult task. This feature occurs in innumerable tales of Indian tribes, partly, as in the present case, by way of introduction, to explain why a difficult task is undertaken; partly as an important element of the tale itself. Next, the two boys make a chain of arrows reaching to the sky. The same motive is found in many tales referring to visits to the sky. In the interior of the Continent we find a tale of the animals making war upon the inhabitants of the sky. After having gained the victory, they all return along the chain of arrows, which, however, breaks before the fish and the snails have come down. The fallen arrows are the Rocky Mountains. The fish and the snails are compelled to jump down, and thus break their bones. For this reason the snail has no bones at all, while the fish's body is full of small bones.

Another important myth in which the chain of arrows occurs refers to the Mink's visit to his father the Sun, whose place he intends to take.

In the tradition which we are discussing here, the boys reach an open country, and, in search of the Sun's house, meet a number of beings whom they benefit, and who advise them of approaching dangers. This has come to be one of the favorite features in North American tales. Whenever a young man undertakes a difficult task, he meets with the friendly counsel of animals whom he benefits in some way, or whom he causes to believe they have been benefited.

One of the most striking cases of this kind is the story of the attempt of a man to recover his wife, who has been abducted by a whale. He pursues the latter in his canoe, and when the whale dives, he throws out his anchor, descends along the anchor-line, and finds a trail along the bottom of the sea, which he follows. Finally he comes to a giant who is splitting wood by means of wedges and a hammer. The man who hides in the wood breaks off the point of the wedge when the giant drives it in. The giant begins to cry because he fears being punished by his master for having broken the valuable wedge. Then the man appears, asks him why he is crying, and offers to mend the wedge. This pleases the giant, who promises his assistance to the man in obtaining possession of his wife. The same feature is found in a long series of tales referring to the origin of salmon. It is told in these traditions how the hero who obtained the salmon gained the good-will and assistance of various beings whom he helped.

The next step in the development of our tradition of the two boys is their arrival at the house of the Sun. They climb a tree, and are believed by the Sun's daughters to be in the water, because their reflections appear there. The same motive is used in a great variety of traditions. There are tales of monsters living in the woods which descend from the mountains. A person who sees one coming makes his escape by climbing a tree which overhangs the water. The monster stops under the tree, and falls in love with the reflection of the person, mourning at the same time that he is dead at the bottom of the water. Finally the monster discovers his mistake, and the tales then develop in various ways.

Taking up the thread of the sun myth which we are discussing here, we find the entrance into the Sun's house, and a number of severe tests to which the visitors are made to submit. This motive enters into innumerable traditions of the Northwest Indians, only a few of which show any relationship to sun myths. The Chinook tell of the marriage of a young man to the daughter of the Thunder, who lives in the woods, and goes whaling every day. The tests to which the young man is subjected are practically the same as those given to the young men visiting the Sun. Some Indian tribes of northern British Columbia tell the same story of a chief who lived on an island near by, and who disliked his son-in-law; and among another tribe of this region we find a tale of a chief who tries to kill his brothers in various ways. Here the tests vary slightly from those mentioned before, the most interesting difference being the attempt to drown the chief in a box loaded with stones, and by ordering him to bring the giant Clam, which kills everybody between its shells.

Thus we have seen that the elements of a complex myth appear in endless combinations, partly in the tales of the tribe that owns the myth, partly in those of its neighbors. In our case we have taken examples only from tribes that live so near by, and whose culture is so much alike, that

there can be no reasonable doubt of an historic connection between similar tales.

The same method of comparison might, however, be applied the world over, and analogies might be found in the most distant regions. The tale which we selected is a fair instance of this kind. Thus Codrington tells a closely related legend from Banks Island, near New Guinea, of the deity Quat, who makes a chain of arrows in order to recover his wife, that had escaped him and was living in the sky. Of another somewhat complex tale of this region we need give here only a small portion:

"A hero had been vanquished by an enemy, who had shot off his ear with an arrow. The hero borrowed his mother's stone hatchet, and, by striking the root of a tree once, he caused it to break to pieces, and one of the pieces to take the form of a new ear, which he put on. While his enemies were celebrating their victory, he dug a pit, which he covered with a mat made of palm-leaves. Then he made a fire, in which he roasted delicious fruits that attracted the attention of his enemies. They tried to take some of the fruit, and in doing so fell into the pit that had been dug for this purpose. Then the hero took red-hot stones out of his fire and threw them into the pit in order to kill his enemies, who lamented their fate and expected to die. Their leader, however, asked them to stand aside in a small cave that he had prepared. After the hero had gone, the leader took his bow and shot an arrow upward into the branch of a fig-tree which overhung the pit. He shot a second arrow, which hit the nock of the first; and thus he continued until a chain was made which enabled the men to climb up and to make their escape."

The material of which this tale is composed is evidently to a great extent the same as that which we find in the North American sun myth. We have the chain of arrows enabling the hero to ascend to the upper world. We have the attempt to kill by means of red-hot stones in a cave, which is a salient feature of many traditions of this class.

Another part of our myth belongs to the endless variety of tales of tests that are found the world over. This class includes the well-known fairy tales of Europe, telling of persons who, in order to relieve others, have to perform certain tasks, such as finding the golden horse, or bringing up a golden key that has been lost in a pond, or removing a mountain in a single night, or gathering a bagful of pearls that have been scattered over a meadow. In our fairy tales, all these tasks are accomplished by the assistance of animals whom the hero has benefited, or by the kindly help of fairies. The fundamental idea in our American tales is the same. The chief's sons who visit the Sun accomplish their tasks by the gifts that they received from the Crane. They escape the closing tree by transforming themselves into birds. They evade the dangers of the ocean by their power over the wind, and finally overcome their enemy by the assistance of animals.

The incident of the mat set with murderous spikes has a wide distribution in America. It has been found in South America, as well as scattered among tribes here and there in North America.

In all these cases the tribes that possess the same or similar traditions live so far apart that an historical transmission does not seem plausible; and thus it becomes difficult to decide where borrowing must be assumed as a cause of sameness of myths, and where other causes may have been at work. Evidently this question is closely associated with the vexed question of dissemination of cultural elements and their independent origin, here and there, due to the sameness of the organization of the human mind. The similarity of cultural traits in regions as far apart as Africa and Australia, western Asia and South America, seems to be explicable only on the assumption that the human mind must of necessity, under conditions sufficiently alike, develop the same ideas. This theory, carried to its extreme consequences, would lead us to consider the contents of the mind purely as an outcome of the organization of the mind and of sense experience. While our whole knowledge of the historical development of civilization is opposed to this extreme view, showing as it does at all places and in all times the stimulating effect of contact of different peoples and clear evidences of extended borrowing, the burden of proof of historical contact between disconnected regions rests on those who advocate the theory that sameness of ideas or customs can be due to transmission only.

It may be well to illustrate this point by an additional example. The Indians of the Pacific coast believe that the arrow of man is invisible to spirits and animals. This idea is elaborated in a number of traditions. For instance, a monster is stealing provisions from a house every night. It is finally discovered and shot by the owner of the house. It escapes, and he pursues it. Finally he reaches the village in which the monster is living. All the medicine-men belonging to the tribe of the monster are trying in vain to cure it. He is invited to make an attempt, and he withdraws the arrow, which is invisible to the monster's tribe. This idea is, of course, analogous to the idea of material sickness, which is visible only to the shaman.

In Micronesia, more particularly in the Pelew Islands, we find the same idea. It is well expressed in a tradition reported by Kubary. A young man went out fishing. He had a bite, but the fish broke the line and escaped. The young man, desirous of recovering his fish-hook, dived, and reached the bottom of the sea. There he found an open country. He saw a village, and heard moaning in one of the houses. Soon a girl came out of the house, and told him that her mother was sick, and that the shaman was unable to discover the cause of her sickness. He was asked to come in, discovered his hook, and as soon as he had taken out the hook the sick person was cured.

According to the theory of independent origin, we should say offhand that here we have the same idea existing in two widely separated regions, and that its occurrence is fully explained by the organization of the human mind, which develops the idea that sickness is a material object that enters the body, and which must be removed in order to recover health. A second idea is, that all nature is anthropomorphic, but is divided into groups, which differ so much in organization that what is natural to one group is supernatural to any of the other groups.

In the present case, where no connecting links between Micronesia and America are known, it would be rash to say that the sameness of these tales is due to transmission, since we have no clear evidence of contact between these distant regions.

The case is quite different, however, when we confine ourselves to a limited geographical area in which cultural contact has been going on continuously. A mere statistical enumeration of the number of tales that are common to a certain tribe and its neighbors shows very clearly a marked decrease in their numbers as the distances between the tribes increase. At the same time, differences in detail are apt to increase, and the variants from two extreme points of the area of distribution of a tale are apt to be quite distinct. The sun myth which we selected as the starting-point of our discussion furnishes a good illustration. The tradition as a whole is characteristic of a small section of the North Pacific coast. Tales of a visit to the sky are common all over America; but they differ so much in detail from the tradition here recorded that their identity does not appear as certain. The ascent to the sky by means of a chain of arrows belongs to the coast region from central Oregon to Alaska, and inland as far as the Rocky Mountains. The incident of the visible hero's meeting with his advisers has a wider distribution. Thus every incident may be shown to occur over a considerable area. Some are widely known, others spread over a more restricted territory.

In such a case of continuous geographical distribution of complex myths and of numerous elements of myths, and in regions where inter-tribal intercourse has always existed, their sameness must be assumed to be due to historical transmission. While it may be that one or the other single trait originated independently, in the same way as among distant tribes, the increasing divergence with increasing distance, and the great number of complex cultural traits common to neighboring tribes, can be explained only as a result of historical causes.

When we apply this method to the mythologies of America, the complexity of their origin becomes at once apparent. This is the case even if we exclude rigidly all cases of isolated occurrences of myths as possibly due to independent invention, and consider only those of a wide, continuous distribution.

It is also noteworthy that this complexity of origin is not confined to semi-secular tales, but that it is characteristic of the most sacred myths. The incident of the closing of the deluge by animals that bring up from the bottom of the waters some mud from which the new earth is created, belongs to one of the most important myths of the eastern Algonquin. It is distributed over eastern North America, the Mackenzie basin, and appears in a few isolated places on the Pacific coast, sometimes as part of the creation myth, and again as part of an isolated animal tale. Even in the esoteric myths of ritualistic societies these elements may be discovered.

The areas over which legends can thus be proved to have migrated are very large. The incident last mentioned is found over the greater part of our continent. We have also examples of tales that are found in East Greenland, and are known over a continuous area as far south as the southern border of Canada, and westward to the Pacific Ocean. Here belongs, for instance, the tale of a blind boy who was starved by his mother, and whose eyesight was restored by a goose that dived with him; and that of a woman who married a dog and became the ancestress of a tribe. Other tales are common to the Plains and to the Western Plateaus, and seem to extend far into Mexico.

While the details of the geographical distribution of tales are not yet satisfactorily known, it has become evident that there has been liberal exchange all over the northern half of the continent, from the Atlantic to the Pacific Ocean, and also between northern Mexico, the Western Plateaus, and the Plains of the Mississippi. Recent investigations have also shown that quite a number of tales are common to eastern Asia and northwestern America, extending southeastward as far as the Great Plains, so that we must assume a certain amount of interchange between the Old World and the New. To this group belongs the tale of the magic flight, in which is recounted the pursuit of a person who is saved by the transformation into obstacles of a number of objects thrown backward over his shoulder.

The amount of dissemination in the New World seems to be almost the same as that found in the Old World, where we can prove by literary documents that the tales have traveled so far that they occur now in Japan and in Spain, in India and in Siberia. Nothing travels so easily and seems to be absorbed so readily as a tale.

While there is no difficulty in applying this method, as long as the area under consideration is not too large and the similarity of the tales specific, we soon find it difficult, in investigations of this kind, to tell whether the myths are the same, or whether there is only a family resemblance; and we find also that the methodical principles demanding continuity of distribution and identity of contents have become involved in doubt.

This is true, in the case of American mythologies, as soon as we consider the continent as a whole, including both North and South America. The culture-hero myths of both continents, for instance, have much in common. There are the sudden appearance, the migrations, the disappearance of the hero, who is often presented as a bearded man of light color, coming from the east; his actions also are not unlike. Some of these similarities appear sporadically, others occur everywhere in vast areas. There is a general resemblance of style in most American mythologies, which sets them off fairly sharp from those of other continents, and which are nevertheless so vague that they can hardly be ascribed to direct dissemination.

At the same time, the cultural conditions of the tribes to which these mythologies belong are so distinct, embracing the highly advanced Peruvian and Mexican and the poor wanderer of the tropical woods and of the arid plateaus; and their geographical surroundings are so different, ranging from the arid desert and the northern prairie to the tropical forests, and from high mountain-ranges to endless plains, that the similarities cannot be assumed to be due to the influence of analogous conditions. Neither does it seem likely that the peculiar mental characteristics of the American race should have always led to the same forms of thought. This theory is based on an assumption of racial features that can hardly be proved to exist. Even granting differences in the mental traits of different races independent of social conditions, it seems difficult to conceive why members of the same race, provided they are historically entirely independent, should develop ideas that are similar in details. The anatomical differentiation within the American race is so great that we may recognize greater affinity between the natives of eastern Siberia and those of northwestern America than between a Californian and a Botocudo of Brazil; and no good reason can be given why the similarities of mythologies here referred to should belong to the greater part of America, and why they should not appear equally pronounced outside of the New World, among the closely related tribes of Asia.

It seems much more plausible to consider these broad characteristics of American mythology either as survivals of very early cultural forms of the race, which have perished notwithstanding all later modifications, or as an effect of dissemination and acculturation that have been going on for thousands of years, now in one direction, now in another, and which have resulted in a certain resemblance of generalized cultural traits in most parts of America.

The results so far reached are fundamental for the attempt to give a psychological interpretation of Indian mythologies. If it is true that there has been extended borrowing, even in the most sacred myths, then they cannot be simply the result of a rationalistic attempt to explain nature. If we wish to reach a clear understanding of the history of mythology, our first efforts at explanation must therefore be directed toward an interpretation of the reasons leading to borrowing and to the modification of mythological material by assimilation.

It is true, these results seem to make the origin of myths even more obscure than it was before. The facts which we have collected seem to show that the mythologies of the present time are an exceedingly complex growth, and that, besides the question of the origin of myths, another distinct problem, that of its historical development, confronts us; but it may be considered doubtful whether a knowledge of the recent development of mythologies will bring us any nearer to an understanding of the rise of the first anthropomorphic myth.

    S E L E C T I O N   2 0   — 1898

The Mythology of the Bella Coola Indians

We will now discuss the probable origin of the mythology described in the preceding pages. In order to do so, it is necessary to make a brief statement in regard to the social organization of the neighboring tribes. In another paper [Boas 1895] I have fully discussed the considerable amount of borrowing that has taken place among the Coast tribes, and the relation of their mythologies to those of the interior. It is unnecessary to revert to this subject here. The similarity of the Bella Coola legends to those of the other Coast tribes on the one hand, and to the traditions of the Athapascan tribes on the other, is evident.

It is, however, important to compare their social organization with that of the neighboring tribes, in order to gain a clearer understanding of the origin of their peculiar organization. As stated before, the Bella Coola are divided into village communities, which are organized on an endogamic basis. Each village community has its tradition, which is represented in certain ceremonies. The supernatural beings which play a part in these traditions are personified by certain dancers. Other Coast tribes have a much more complex organization. The Tlingit and Haida are divided into two clans, each of which is subdivided into a great many families, which, as it would seem, were originally village communities. This opinion is based on the fact that the names of many of the families must be translated as "inhabitants of such and such a place." The two clans are present in all the villages of the tribe, each family belonging to either one clan or the other. The Tsimshian have the same system, except that the number of clans is four instead of two. Each tribe is divided into families, which embrace the inhabitants of a certain region; but all the families of the whole tribe are classified according to the four clans. Among the Haida, Tlingit, and Tsimshian, descent is purely maternal; among the northern Kwakiutl tribes, conditions are somewhat different, according to observations made by Dr. Livingston Farrand. Here we have village communities which are subdivided according to four clans in the same way as those of the Tsimshian, but descent is not purely maternal. There is a strong preponderance of the latter form of descent, but parents are at liberty to place their children in either the paternal or maternal clan. The preponderance of maternal descent is, however, so strong, that from my previous occasional inquiries I drew the inference that descent was purely maternal.

Among the southern Kwakiutl tribes the families constituting a village community are subdivided into a number of clans, but each clan is confined to one village. We do not find a limited number of clans pervading the whole tribe, as we do among the northern tribes. An analysis of the social organization of this tribe has shown that the present organization has evidently developed from a previous simpler state, in which the tribe was divided into single village communities. The present more complex organization resulted from the amalgamation of various villages. Owing to the influence of the totemism of the northern tribes, each village community adopted a crest, which in course of time became the totem of the clan [Boas 1897]. The Kwakiutl have a peculiar organization, which may be considered a transitional stage between maternal and paternal institutions. Descent is in the paternal line; but a man, at the time of his marriage, receives his father-in-law's crest as a dowry, which he holds in trust for his son, so that actually each individual inherits the crest of his maternal grandfather. The clans are exogamic.

The organization of the Salish tribes of the southern coast, who are linguistically closely related to the Bella Coola, is somewhat similar to that of the Kwakiutl. They are divided into village communities, a few of which have amalgamated, as, for instance, among the Salish tribes of Vancouver Island, among whom the tribe consists of a number of septs, each of which owns a separate village. Here the influence of northern totemism is very much weaker. While most of the village communities have certain crests, these do not play so important a part in the social life of the tribe or in its mythology as they do among the Kwakiutl, and the village communities are not exogamic. The Salish tribes of the interior are organized in very loose village communities without any trace of totem.

The fundamental difference between the northern tribes and the southern tribes consists, therefore, in the fact that the northern tribes have a limited number of clans which are present in all the villages, while among the southern tribes the village community is the only unit of organization.

The organization of the Bella Coola resembles most closely that of the Coast Salish tribes of southern British Columbia. In both cases the tribe is divided into village communities, which possess crests and traditions. This latter feature is, however, very much more strongly developed among the Bella Coola than among the southern tribes. They differ in their laws of intermarriage. While among the southern Coast Salish tribes there is a tendency to exogamy, the Bella Coola have developed a system of endogamy.

The tribes of the Coast Salish of the Gulf of Georgia claim descent from mythical ancestors, who are believed to have originated at the place which the tribe now inhabit. A number of traditions of this kind bear evidence of having been derived from historical events. Some of the tribes in the delta of Fraser River have traditions which refer to the amalgamation of tribes who descended from the mountains, and who are described as the descendants of animals living in the mountains, and of the natives of the delta [Boas 1894a]. I believe that the tribal traditions of the Bella Coola which were told in a previous chapter also bear evidence of the historical fates of the tribe. It is very remarkable that the important tradition of Tōtosō'nx gives Fraser River as the place to which he descended from heaven. In another tradition, Bute Inlet is given as the place at which one of the Bella Coola tribes originated. In still another one, Skeena River is mentioned as the home of one of the tribes. I do not doubt that these allusions to territory inhabited by Salish tribes refer to the early separation of the Bella Coola tribe from the related tribes of the Gulf of Georgia, and that in their traditions they have retained the memory of the emigration of part of the tribe from the southern territory. It seems also probable that the allusion to the origin of one family of the tribe on Skeena River refers to a mixture with the tribes inhabiting northern British Columbia.

The traditions of the tribes also describe the style of house used by the ancestors of certain village communities; and it is interesting to note that some of these houses correspond to the subterranean lodges that were in use among the Chilcotin, while others correspond to the tents that were in use among the Carriers. It is said that the ancestor of the Nullē'ix used the subterranean lodge which is called tsī'pa, while the ancestor of the Nusq!ɛ'lst used the skin lodge which is called sk·ma.

Since the Bella Coola retain the fundamental traits of the social organization of their congeners in the south, and since their traditions bear evidence of an emigration from that region, and since, furthermore, the linguistic evidence proves that the Bella Coola and the Coast Salish at one time inhabited contiguous areas on the coast, we are justified in assuming that the general culture of the Bella Coola at the time of their emigration must have resembled that of the Coast Salish. The question then arises, How did the peculiar endogamic system and the remarkable

mythology of the Bella Coola originate from the much simpler forms that
we find among the Coast Salish?

One of the most remarkable features in the inner life of the tribes of
the northern coast of British Columbia is the great importance of the clan
legend, which is considered one of the most valuable properties of each
clan or family. It is carefully guarded in the same way as material
property, and an attempt on the part of a person not a member of the
clan to tell the tradition as his own is considered one of the gravest
offences against property rights. The possession of a clan tradition is felt
by the Indian to be one of his most important prerogatives. When, therefore, the Bella Coola settled on Bella Coola River, and were thrown into
contact with the northern Coast tribes, the lack of a well-developed clan
tradition must have been felt as a serious drawback. The physical
appearance of the Bella Coola proves that at one time they must have
intermarried to a great extent with the Bella Bella. Through these marriages the peculiar customs of the Coast tribes were first introduced
among them. This is shown by the fact that a great many of the mythological names can be proved to be of Kwakiutl origin, of which stock the
Bella Bella are a branch. Thus the name for their supreme deity,
Smai′yakila, is a Kwakiutl word meaning "the one who must be worshipped." The name O′mq′ōmkilik·a is also of Kwakiutl origin, and may
be translated as "the wealthiest one." The great frequency of words of
Kwakiutl derivation will become clear by a glance at the following list,
which contains words that can be proved to be of Kwakiutl origin:—

a′Lokoala = shaman.
Alk^u = speaker.
E′mask·în (Kwakiutl, Hē′mask·în) = the greatest chief.
Hau′hau = a fabulous bird.
L′ā′qoag·ila = the copper maker.
L′ā′qumêiks = sister of Masmasalā′nîx (the endings, *iks*, designates
    "woman" in Kwakiutl).
Lēqumaii′ = mythological name of deer.
Mā′lak·ilaL.
MEntsī′t.
Mia′ltoa = the country of the salmon (Kwakiutl, mē) = salmon.
Nō′akila.
Ō′′meaLk·as = the real Ō′meāL.
Ō′′meaLmai.
Ōmq′ōmkī′lik·a (Kwakiutl, Q′ō′mq′ōmkilik·a) = the wealthiest one.
Pō′Las.
Qanāatsla′qs.
Q′ōmo′qoa = the wealthy one.
Q′ō′mqūtîs = rich at opposite side of river.
Q′ō′mtsiwa = wealthy at mouth of river.
Smai′yakila = the one who must be worshipped.

sī′siuʟ = a fabulous fish or snake.
Smayalō′oʟla.
T′ō′pewas = the fawn.
Winwī′na = war.
Wa′k·itɛmai = the greatest river.

With these names and customs the clan traditions must have found their way to the Bella Coola, but their social organization differed fundamentally from that of the Bella Bella branch of the Kwakiutl. While the latter, owing to intimate contact with the northern tribes, had adopted the four-clan system with prevalent maternal descent, the Bella Coola were still distinctly divided into village communities that were not exogamic. It seems very likely that the jealousy with which the ownership of a clan tradition was guarded by the Coast tribes was very early introduced among the Bella Coola. Two means were available for preventing outsiders from acquiring the traditions. Among the Coast tribes with prevailing maternal institutions, among whom a limited number of clans existed, the ordinary law of inheritance was sufficient to retain the tradition inside of the clan. Not so among the Bella Coola. If their organization at an early time was similar to that of the Coast Salish, it is likely that the child was counted as well a member of the father's as of the mother's family, although the young woman generally moved to the village occupied by her husband. If the child belonged to the families of both parents, it had the right to use the tradition of either family; and consequently in the course of a few generations, the traditions acquired by each family would have spread practically over the whole tribe. There were only two methods possible to avoid this result. The one was to prevent marriages outside the village community; and this method would seem to have been most natural for a tribe organized in village communities, members of which were allowed to intermarry. The other method would have been to regulate the laws of inheritance in such a way that the child had to follow either father or mother, but that it had not the right to use the property of both parents. It seems to my mind that the former method was more likely to develop under the existing social conditions, and that to this reason we must ascribe the development of an endogamic system among the Bella Coola. The occurrence of endogamic marriage among this tribe is quite isolated on the Pacific coast. All the other tribes have exogamic institutions, and by this means preserve their property rights. It is interesting to note that the southern Kwakiutl, who originally seem to have been organized in village communities, have adopted exogamic institutions; but there is a notable difference, in the organization of the village community, between the Bella Coola and the Kwakiutl. Among the Bella Coola we generally find four ancestors to each village,—usually three men and one woman. It is true that these are generally called brothers and sister, but they were created independently by SENX, and are therefore not necessarily considered as blood relations. Among the Kwakiutl the village community are considered the descendants of one single being; consequently, among the latter tribe they are all relatives, who are forbidden to intermarry; while among the Bella Coola they are not relatives, and may intermarry.

My inference is, therefore, that the curious social system of the Bella Coola developed through the influence of the customs of the Coast tribes upon the loose social unit of the Salish village community. The possession of clan traditions was felt as a great advantage, and consequently the desire developed to possess clan traditions. These were acquired partly by intermarriage with the Coast tribes, as is shown by the fact that many of these traditions are borrowed from these tribes, partly by independent invention. The desire to guard the traditions which were once acquired led to the development of endogamic institutions, in order to prevent the spread of the traditions over the whole tribe.

The jealousy with which the traditions are guarded has had the effect of making each family try to prevent other families from knowing its own clan tradition. For this reason the clan traditions of the whole tribe are remarkably inconsistent. We find, for instance, that the well-known raven legend of the northern Coast tribes has been utilized by many families as a family tradition. But while one family uses one part of the tradition, other families use other parts of the same tradition. Thus it happens that among the Bella Coola we find the most contradictory myths in regard to important events in the world's history. Some families maintain that the Raven liberated the sun, while, according to another one, the Mink was essential in bringing about the present state of affairs. Still others say that Tōtosō'nx, during his travels, caused the sun to appear. The discrepancies in the traditions referring to the visit of the Mink and Wasp to their father, the Sun, are also very remarkable. Although a considerable amount of contradiction is inherent in all the mythologies of the North Pacific coast, they nowhere reach such a degree as among the Bella Coola; and I presume the fact that the traditions are kept secret by the various families accounts for this curious condition.

The prayers of the Bella Coola directed to SENX or Tā'ata bear a remarkable resemblance to the prayers of the Tsimshian addressed to Laxha, the sky. In both tribes we find the idea that when the Sun wipes his face it will be clear weather, and man will be happy; consequently the prayer to the deity "to wipe his face" occurs quite often.

One of the most important customs that the Bella Coola borrowed from the Coast tribes is the kū'siut ceremonial, with which are connected the various secret societies, particularly the custom of ceremonial cannibalism. The ceremonies and the paraphernalia used by the Bella Coola and by the Kwakiutl are practically identical. I told above the legend explaining the origin of cannibalism. Among the Bella Bella and Kwakiutl, another tradition is told to explain the origin of this custom. The tradition tells of a spirit called Baxbakualanuxsī'waē, who lives in the forest, and who initiates the members of the Cannibal Society. The series of traditions clustering around this being differ fundamentally from those referring to the Cannibal Society of the Bella Coola. The custom has also spread to the Tsimshian, who say that the secret societies were introduced by a hunter who was taken into the inside of a cliff by a white bear. Inside he saw a house, in which the various societies were performing their ceremonies. It appears, therefore, that the same ritual which is practised by three distinct tribes is explained by three fundamentally distinct myths; and we must conclude that in this case the ritual is older than the myth, —that the latter has been invented in order to explain customs that were borrowed from foreign tribes, so that the ritual is the primary phenomenon, while the myth is secondary [Boas 1897, p. 660].

These considerations explain some of the psychological motives for the development of certain traditions and myths, as well as the curious inconsistency of the clan traditions of the Bella Coola. They do not, however, explain the most fundamental characteristic of the traditions of the tribe. I pointed out in the third chapter of this paper, that, notwithstanding the numerous contradictions contained in family legends, the conception of the word and the functions of the various deities are so well defined that we must consider the mythology of this tribe vastly superior to that of the neighboring tribes. While the latter believe in a great many spirits which are not co-ordinated, we have here a system of deities. The existence of a systematic mythology among the Bella Coola proves that under favorable conditions the advance from the lower forms of beliefs to higher forms may be a very rapid one.

Our analysis shows that this system cannot be considered as an importation, but that it probably developed among the Bella Coola themselves. After they removed to their new home, a mass of foreign ideas had come into their possession through contact with their new neighbors. While these new ideas were being remodelled and assimilated, they stimulated the minds of the people, or of a few members of the tribe, who were thus led to the formation of an elaborate concept of the world. The concept which they have developed agrees in all its main features with those created by men of other zones and of other races. The mind of the Bella Coola philosopher, operating with the class of knowledge common to the earlier strata of culture, has reached conclusions similar to those that have been formed by man the world over, when operating with the same class of knowledge. On the other hand, the Bella Coola has also adopted readymade the thoughts of his neighbors, and has adapted them to his environment. These two results of our inquiry emphasize the close relation between the comparative and the historic methods of ethnology, which are so often held to be antagonistic. Each is a check upon rash conclusions that might be attained by the application of one alone. It is just as uncritical to see, in an analogy of a single trait of culture that occurs in two distinct regions, undoubted proof of early historical connection as to reject the possibility of such connection, because sometimes the same ideas develop independently in the human mind. Ethnology is rapidly outgrowing the tendency to accept imperfect evidence as proof of historical connection; but the comparative ethnologist is hardly beginning to see that he has no right to scoff at the historical method. Our inquiry shows that safe conclusions can be derived only by a careful analysis of the whole culture. The growth of the myths of the Bella Coola can be understood only when we consider the culture of the tribe as a whole. And so it is with other phenomena. All traits of culture can be fully understood only in connection with the whole culture of a tribe. When we confine ourselves to comparing isolated traits of culture, we open the door to misinterpretations without number.

If, then, the demand is made for a more critical method in the comparative study of ethnology than it has generally been accorded, it does not imply a deprecation of the results of the method. When the human mind evolves an idea, or when it borrows the same idea, we may assume that it has been evolved or accepted because it conforms with the organization of the human mind; else it would not be evolved or accepted. The wider the distribution of an idea, original or borrowed, the closer must be its conformity with the laws governing the activities of the human mind. Historical analysis will furnish the data referring to the growth of ideas among different people; and comparisons of the processes of their growth will give us knowledge of the laws which govern the evolution and selection of ideas.

 *PART V*

THE ANALYTICAL
STUDY OF
LANGUAGE

As a cultural anthropologist, Boas has his detractors, but there are few who would deny his contribution to the study of American Indian languages. His *Handbook of American Indian Languages*, the first volume of which appeared in 1911, marked a transformation in the framework of American linguistic method and assumption, and the starting point of the modern tradition in descriptive linguistics (Emeneau 1943, p. 35; Hymes 1970; Jakobson 1944; Stocking 1968c).

The *Handbook*, however, was the culmination of a quarter-century of linguistic study, whose early stages had a rather different character. At first, the strategy of Boas' linguistic work was much the same as that which produced the linguistic classification we associate with John Wesley Powell (Darnell 1971a). Some of Boas' early field trips to the Northwest were in fact partially subsidized by the Bureau of American Ethnology; and although as early as 1888 he was proposing to Powell a five-year program of research on the Salish languages, his work was in fact carried on largely in terms of regional surveys, vocabulary lists, grammatical "notes," and problems of the classification of stocks—that is, he operated largely within a Powellian framework, and was not yet primarily concerned with the systematic study of grammatical structures. The first selection (no. 21) draws together this early work, but its last paragraph foreshadows a study of a different sort.

From 1893 on, much of Boas' linguistic efforts were devoted to a more intensive "elucidation" of the structure of the branches of the Chinookan stock. Unfortunately, however, Boas' relation to the Bureau of Ethnology was considerably attenuated in 1894, when he was pushed out of a job at the Field Museum as a result of a reorganization of Bureau personnel that sent William Holmes to Chicago; and it was not until later in the 1890s that he began to play a major role in directing the Bureau's linguistic work. As the second selection (no. 22) suggests, Boas' plans for a major program of intensive linguistic study had by 1901 begun to jell, and he was soon appointed honorary philologist to the Bureau in order to direct the work.

Boas exercised a rather tight control over the project, to such an extent that A. L. Kroeber, his first Columbia Ph.D. (1901), preferred not to participate. Those who did were a rather rigorously winnowed and for the most part still dependent group of young scholars he had trained himself. He saw them as "contributors" to an ongoing enterprise that he had singlehandedly initiated—the establishment of American Indian linguistics on a scientific basis—and he took considerable pains to define its methodological assumptions. His own sketch of the Kwakiutl language (the third selection, no. 23) was to be a model, and his letters, as the fourth selection (no. 24) suggests, reiterated the theme that the study was to be purely "analytical." That is to say, grammatical categories were to be formulated as if a native speaker, "without knowledge of any other language, should present the essential notions of his own grammar"— "without reference to the current classifications of Indo-European languages, which have helped to obscure the fundamental traits of American languages for so long a time" (Stocking 1968c; cf. Voegelin 1952).

Work on the *Handbook* progressed rather slowly, and it was not until 1907 and 1908 that it really began to take shape. In some cases (as Selection 25 indicates), Boas exercised a considerable editorial supervision over the final manuscript. This letter to John Swanton is also interesting in showing that Boas had not lost interest in problems of linguistic relationship. The connection he proposed between Tlingit and Athapascan, in the context of his own much-earlier discovery of a relationship between Tlingit and Haida, in effect tied together what were later to be the three major components of Edward Sapir's Na-dene (Sapir 1915; Harrington 1945). Sapir, however, was inclined to go much farther in some matters than Boas' own caution would allow (Darnell 1971b), and in the sixth selection (no. 26) we catch a glimpse of the restraint Boas tried to exercise even over his most brilliant student. Sapir had just reported to Boas on his fieldwork among the Yana, and had casually hypothesized race mixture with a now "extinct" group to explain the presence of distinct male and female speech forms.

When it finally appeared, the *Handbook* was prefaced by a long "Introduction" in which Boas drew together for the guidance of future students the basic principles of his approach to language. Since this has recently been reprinted (Holder 1966), I have incorporated instead as the final selection (no. 27) a brief statement Boas offered in 1905 on the relation of philology and anthropology. Although couched in rather general terms for an audience of nonanthropologists, the essay does suggest in passing two important aspects of the orientation of the *Handbook*. Boas rejected the widespread notion that all American Indian languages were built on a single psychological principle, the incorporative, which stood in evolutionary sequence between the isolative and the inflexive. Instead he emphasized the wide variety in the psychological bases, or "inner forms," of American Indian languages. Following Wilhelm von Humboldt and Heymann Steinthal, he tended to see these as conditioning the *Weltanschauungen* of the people who spoke them, although he viewed this relationship in strictly relativistic terms, rejecting any form of linguistic determinism that might be used to bolster racial determinism or an evolutionary hierarchy (Jakobson 1959; Hymes 1961a).

     S E L E C T I O N   2 1

Classification of the Languages of the North Pacific Coast

The North Pacific Coast is inhabited by a great number of Indian tribes who speak many distinct languages. A comparison of vocabularies of these languages has led to the following grouping in linguistic stocks. In Southern Alaska we find a number of dialects of the Tlingit language. On Queen Charlotte Islands and on a few islands of the Prince of Wales Archipelago the Haida is spoken. In the northern portion of British Columbia, particularly along Naass River and Skeena River, we find the Tsimshian spoken in two dialects. From Northern British Columbia to the central portion of Vancouver Island extend the Kwakiutl, whose language is spoken in three closely allied dialects. Adjoining them

Paper read at International Congress of Anthropology, Chicago, 28 August 1893, as published in *Memoirs of the International Congress of Anthropology* (Chicago: Schulte, 1894), pp. 339–346.

at the west coast of Vancouver Island live the Nootka. South and east of these regions a great number of languages are spoken which are all affiliated, and called the Salish languages. An isolated branch of this stock lives among the Kwakiutl, while the great body is located in the interior of British Columbia, Washington, Northern Idaho and Northwestern Montana. A small isolated branch is found south of Columbia River. On the coast of Washington they enclose a small territory on which the Chemakum language is spoken. Along Columbia River they adjoin the Sahaptin and Chinook languages. The Willamette River valley was occupied by people speaking two distinct languages, the Calapooya and the Molala. In this enumeration I have omitted the Athapascan, which is spoken in the northern interior of British Columbia and in a number of isolated regions along the Pacific coast.

In comparing these languages we are, first of all, struck by a certain similarity of phonetics among most of them. We find an abundance of k sounds, articulated in all positions from the posterior velar to the anterior palatal position; a series of lateral explosives or l sounds articulated at the posterior portion of the palate. On the other hand, the aspirate labials and the lingual r are absent. The only languages which show an entirely different phonetic type are the Calapooya and Molala. As little is known regarding their structure, I must omit them in the following considerations.

The phonetic system of the various languages may best be set forth by the following scheme:

	Labials.	Point of Tongue.	Back of Tongue.	Thrills. R.	Laterals. L.
Tlingit	—	1	1	1	1
Haida	—*	1	1	1	1
Tsimshian	1	1	1	1	1
Kwakiutl	1	1	1	—	1
Nootka	1	1	1	—	1
Salish	1 †	1	1	—	1
Chemakum	1	1	1	—	1
Chinook	1	1	1	—	1

* M occurs sometimes, but pronounced with semi-closure of the lips.
† Except the Tillamook dialect.

This tabulation shows that the Tlingit, Haida and Tsimshian take a peculiar position among the other dialects, as they have an r sound, and as the first two have no labials. The r sound in question is a uvular thrill, the lips assuming at the same time the w position. As the thrill is very light, particularly in Tlingit and Tsimshian, the sound is often mistaken for u. In Bishop Ridley's translation of the Gospel I find, for instance, g̕uel for what I hear as g̕ɛ́rɛl.

In all these languages the difference between surds and sonants is very slight, so much so that I doubt if there is any real difference of this character in Haida and Tlingit. It exists, undoubtedly, in the Kwakiutl and Salish. In the latter language we find the peculiarity that in many dialects *m* and *n* are pronounced with semi-closure of the nose, so that they are difficult to distinguish from *b* and *d*. This peculiarity is also found, although to a less extent, in the Kwakiutl, Nootka, Chemakum and Chinook languages.

When we turn to a consideration of the grammatical form of these languages, we shall find again that Haida and Tlingit stand decidedly by themselves when compared to the rest of the languages. While all the others use reduplication for grammatical purposes, no trace of reduplication is found in these two languages. A closer comparison reveals a number of other traits which they have in common. There is no trace of grammatic gender and no separate forms for singular and plural or distributive. When it is necessary to state expressly that the plural is meant, a word denoting "a number of" is placed after the noun. Compound nouns are very numerous, the compounds being placed side by side without any alteration. Words of two, three and more components which seem to be monosyllabic occur. Local adverbs, which always retain their independence, frequently enter into compound words of this kind. The adjective always follows the noun to which it belongs.

In both languages there are four forms of the personal pronoun. In the independent pronoun the selective and the ordinary form may be distinguished. For instance, in Tlingit, the question: "Who among you is going to go?" requires the answer *xatc*, I; while the question, "Who is there?" requires the answer *xat*, I. The pronoun of transitive verbs differs from that of intransitive verbs, the latter being identical with the objective form of the former. In Tlingit we have *qat* (1) *rᴇ* (2) *nek* (3) I (1) (am) sick (3), the *rᴇ* being a particle, but *at* (1) *qa* (2) *sae'* (3) it (1) I (2) cook (3); in Haida, *de* (1) *sťe'ga* (2) I (1) sick (2); but *tla* (1) *ga* (2) *ta* (3), I (1) it (2) eat (3). The latter example elucidates another point of resemblance between the two languages. When transitive verbs have no object, it is necessary to add a general object, in Tlingit *at* (1) *qa* (2) *qa* (3), It (1) I (2) eat (3); in Haida *tla* (1) *ga* (2) *ta* (3), I (1) it (2) eat (3). The transitive verb is formed in both languages by placing the objective pronoun first, next the subject, and last the verb. The objective pronoun is derived in both languages from the objective form of the personal pronoun. The interrogative is formed in Tlingit by the particle *agᴇ*, in Haida by *gua*. In the former language the particle follows the verb, in the latter the pronoun. In both languages, however, it follows the adverb, if there is one. The enumeration of similarities shows a far-reaching resemblance of structure of the two languages. I will add a short list of compound words which will make the similarity of structure still clearer.

ENGLISH.	TLINGIT	LITERAL TRANSLATION.	HAIDA.	LITERAL TRANSLATION.
ankle	q'os t'aqʟ	leg knuckle	gy'aʟt'amɛ'l	leg knuckle
dancing leggins	} q'os qet	leg dancing apparel	} gy'aʟ gya	{ leg dancing apparel
lycopodium	q'oqan si'ge	deer belt	g'at ʟdsga'wa	deer belt
pipe	ts'eqda ket	smoke around box	} xe'ʟɛn ga'eu da'o	{ mouth smoke box
pregnant	to kat gat'a	her womb child	l taʟ gyit'e'	her womb child
roof	hit ka	house top	na u'na	house top
thief	ta'o s'a'te	stealing master	g'o'ʟta lra'era	stealing master
warrior	g'au s'a'te	fighting master	ra'ʜiʟa lra'era	fighting master

This similarity of structure becomes the more surprising if we take into consideration that not one of the neighboring languages shows any of the peculiarities enumerated here. The structural resemblance of the two languages and their contrast with the neighboring languages can be explained only by the assumption of a common origin. The number of words which may possibly be connected by etymology is small, and the similarities are doubtful. Nevertheless, the structural resemblance must be considered final proof of a historical connection between the two languages. In concluding, I give a brief list of similar words:

ENGLISH.	TLINGIT.	HAIDA.
child	gat	gyit
small	ga'tsko	gɛ'tso
ear	guk	gʋu
thumb	gouc	k'use'
blood	cɛ	g.a'i
knuckle	t'aqʟ	t'amɛ'l
septum	t'aka'	t'a'nri
sinew	t'as	t'a'tse
elbow	t'er	tsɛgui'
heart	tek	tek'o'go
knee	q'ulo'	kyer
people	na	na (house)
to stand	gya	gya
dry	xoq	qa
woman	ca'wat	dja'at
on top of	ki	gi
man	ʟingit	e'ʟinga
"	qa	q'al

The next group of languages embraces the Tsimshian, Kwakiutl and Nootka, Salish and Chemakum. As I have proved at another place

[Boas 1890] that Kwakiutl and Nootka are dialects of the same stock, I do not need to enter on this point here.

All those languages use amplification of the stem for indicating plurality. The plurality may be distributive or frequentative. The amplification of the stem is brought about either by diæresis, by reduplication or by the use of infixes. Time and locality are defined very sharply. In most dialects of these languages presence and absence and past and present are always designated. In other respects the languages show great differences. The Tsimshian has certain characters which mark it out decidedly from all the others. While among the southern languages composition is almost always by means of suffixes, the Tsimshian has almost exclusively prefixes. In counting, a few classifying suffixes are found, but we do not observe the occurrence of suffixes or prefixes denoting nouns that are not class-words, such as: parts of the body, house, fire, water. On the other hand, contractions in which parts of words are suppressed apparently for reasons of euphony appear quite frequently, while they are very rare in the southern group of languages, if they exist at all. Therefore, the analysis of Tsimshian words reveals the fact that the principles of composition are quite distinct from those of the Kwakiutl and other southern languages.

The southern group of languages, the Kwakiutl, Salish and Chemakum, which show hardly any indication of relationship, so far as their vocabulary is concerned, have a series of very peculiar traits in common. First among these I mention the occurrence of suffixes denoting nouns; not class-words, but nouns designating concrete, individual objects. Such are primarily parts of the body, furthermore designations of localities, of fire, water, road, blanket, domestic animal (*i.e.*, in olden times, dog) and many others. These words are so peculiar and, moreover, cover in these languages so nearly the same classes of objects, that I cannot help thinking there must be a common source from which they have sprung. We do not find nouns of this character in the Kutonaxa, which adjoins the Salishan languages, nor in the Athapascan, while similar suffixes are found in the Algonquin languages. It is worth remarking that inside the same linguistic stock, namely, the Salishan, their application varies widely. In the dialects of the interior these suffixes are found very frequently, while they are rarer in the coast dialects. Another very important peculiarity which those three languages have in common, and in which they differ from all the neighboring languages, is that whenever an adverb accompanies the verb the former is inflected, while the verb, at least the intransitive verb, remains unaltered. In the Kwakiutl language the object even is inflected while the verb remains unchanged. When a transitive verb is accompanied by an adverb the latter always takes the suffix of the pronominal subject, while the verb takes that of the pronominal object.

These similarities are so pronounced and so peculiar that they must have originated in a common source.

In judging the differences between the languages of this group, it may be well to dwell briefly on the differences of dialects in two of them, namely, the Salish and the Kwakiutl. The Salish is remarkable for the great number of its dialects and the diversity of forms which they have assumed. These dialects may be grouped in those of the coast, the Lillooet, the Shushwap and the Okanagan. Each of them, except the Shushwap, embraces a number of dialects. The greatest number and greatest diversity are embraced in the coast dialects. All of these have pronominal gender, while the dialects of the interior have no trace of gender. The most northern of this group of dialects, the Bilxula, is remarkable for the extensive elision of vowels. The most southern dialect of the group has lost all the labials, which are frequent in all the other Salishan languages. Most of these dialects also distinguish in the pronoun between presence and absence. The Shushwap dialect is remarkable because it is the only one that has preserved the exclusive and inclusive forms of the first person plural. All the dialects of the interior have many verbs the singular and plural of which is formed from distinct stems. They use suffixes denoting specific nouns much more extensively than the dialects of the coast. They do not distinguish between absence and presence.

The Kwakiutl and Nootka show differences that are still more far-reaching than those between the Salishan dialects. Both localize actions sharply by means of suffixes. The Nootka is satisfied with designating actions as having happened in the house, on the beach, on the water, etc. The Kwakiutl adds always if they took place near the speaker, near the person addressed, absent visible or absent invisible, and also the time, if in the past or in the future. The Kwakiutl has an exclusive and inclusive form of the first person plural which has disappeared in the Nootka. If such differences occur between more closely allied dialects, we do not need to wonder at the greater differences between these languages which show only certain similarities of structure. Each point of similarity gains rather greater weight on account of the divergence of the dialects of each stock among each other.

The differences between the languages may be defined as follows: The Kwakiutl and Nootka have a much sharper localization than any of the other languages. They lack entirely pronominal gender. They have an inclusive and exclusive form of the first person plural. Their use of the negation in compounds deserves special mention. Their negation is a prefix which enters into composition.

The Salishan languages have pronominal gender. They distinguish presence and absence, and have inclusive and exclusive forms of the first person plural.

The Chemakum has also pronominal gender. The amplification of the stem for the purpose of forming distribution takes peculiar forms which are not found in the other languages. An apparent infix—*ts*—is the most peculiar of these forms.

I attribute great weight to the occurrence of pronominal gender in both the Chemakum and Salish, as this is a phenomenon of very rare occurrence in America.

Turning further south, we reach a type of language which is entirely distinct from those treated heretofore. This language is the Chinook. It has none of the peculiar nominal suffixes which characterize the preceding group of languages. In fact, its words are of very simple build, local adverbs only entering into the composition of words. Its most important character is the existence of a real gender. The Chinook has a masculine, feminine and neuter, the last-named gender designating, primarily, small objects. So far as I am able to judge, the classification of nouns according to gender does not follow any rules. The vowel of the stem is always in harmony with the vowel of the prefix, so that *e'-ka-la*, male, becomes *o'-ko-la* in the feminine. There exist a surprisingly large number of onomatopoetic terms. Particularly verbs which designate actions accompanied by a noise belong to this class, as: to laugh, to split, to tear, to dig. The language abounds in abstract terms. Many of our adjectives can be expressed only by such terms. Thus the Chinook says, instead of "the bad man," "the man his badness"; instead of "I am sick," "my sickness is on me." We find a singular, dual and plural. They are not formed by amplification of the stem. The first person dual and plural have an exclusive and inclusive form. The verb is incorporating to a degree. It designates by means of prefixes the subject, direct and indirect object. These characteristics distinguish the Chinook sharply from the other languages which we have considered heretofore.

Our review has shown that the seven languages of this region which show, so far as we can prove at present, no etymological relationships worth considering, may be classed in four groups:

1. The Tlingit and Haida.
2. Tsimshian.
3. The Kwakiutl, Salish and Chemakum.
4. The Chinook.

The similarities of the languages belonging to each group, on the one hand, and on the other hand the differences between the groups, are so striking, that we must assume that some generic connection exists between the languages of each group. The elucidation of the details of this connection must be left to a closer study of the languages, based upon a comparison of their dialects. So far our knowledge of most of the languages of the Pacific Coast is confined to a meager list of vocabularies. Therefore the classification must be considered in its infancy. Etymologies of Indian languages, the histories of which we do not know, is a subject of the greatest difficulty, and must be based on investigations on the structure of the languages, if it shall not sink to the level of mere guessing. In the present state of linguistic science, a classification ought to take into account structure as well as vocabulary. The former will give us valuable clues where the comparison of mere words ceases to be helpful. It is with the desire to call attention to the importance of this method that the imperfect comparison between the languages of the North Pacific Coast has been presented.

     SELECTION 22

A Handbook of
North American Languages

NEW YORK,
April 4, 1901.

PROF. W. J. McGEE,
      Bureau of Ethnology,
         Washington, D.C.

DEAR PROFESSOR McGEE,—

You will remember that we have been discussing now and again the desirability of publishing a handbook of North American languages. I have been giving a good deal of thought to this matter, and my publication of a sketch of the Kwakiutl grammar, in the "American Anthropologist," was partly done with a view of bringing out in a general way what I have in mind. The sketch given in the journal is not quite so full as I should want to see the sketches in such a handbook, but the extent of the paper was limited by the scope of the journal. You will, however, find the fundamental idea incorporated in that paper; namely, to describe the language in an analytical way, giving the fundaments of the phonetics, grammatical processes, and grammatical categories. It would be my wish to follow the sketch of each language with a text of about a thousand words or so, fully annotated, and with references to the corresponding paragraphs of the grammatical sketch.

Copy preserved in Boas Papers, American Philosophical Society.

I think I have trained now a sufficient number of young men to make it possible to take up work of this kind systematically, and I should like to suggest to you that the Bureau take up this work with a plan of bringing out a publication of this sort say in about five or six years. So far as I can judge at the present time, it would be possible to amass the necessary material without very great expense to the Bureau. I am perfectly willing to give my time to this matter without compensation, and much of the funds required for field-work can be covered from outside sources. I wish you would kindly consider this matter. I intend to be in Washington on Monday, the 15th, and I shall set aside the whole day for a discussion of this question, and one or two others closely allied to it.

I believe you agree with me in regard to the importance of a publication of this sort, and I shall be glad to discuss with you and Major Powell the feasibility of the undertaking.

Yours very sincerely,
F. Boas

  SELECTION 23

Sketch of
the Kwakiutl Language

In the course of a series of investigations undertaken for the Jesup North Pacific Expedition, I collected extensive material on the language of the Kwakiutl Indians, who inhabit northeastern Vancouver island and the adjacent coast of British Columbia. A treatise on the grammar of this language, by Rev. Alfred J. Hall, was published in 1889; but the author has not succeeded in elucidating its structural peculiarities. I published a brief sketch of the grammar in the Reports of the Committee on the Northwestern Tribes of Canada, appointed by the British Association for the Advancement of Science [Boas 1890]. While the data given in these sketches are in the main correct, the fundamental traits of the language have hitherto remained unknown.

The phonetic system of the Kwakiutl is very rich. It abounds particu-

American Anthropologist 2 (1900): 708–721.

larly in sounds of the k series and of the l series. The system of consonants includes velars, palatals, anterior palatals, alveolars, and labials. The palatal series (English k) seems to occur only in combination with u articulations. In most of these groups we find a sonans, surd, fortis, and spirans. The sonans is harder than the corresponding English sound. The surd is pronounced with a full breath, while the fortis is a surd with increased stress and suddenness of articulation. The sonans is so strong that it is very easily mistaken for a surd. Besides the groups mentioned before, we have a series of lateral linguals or l sounds; the laryngeal catch; h; y; and w.

This system may be represented as follows:

	Sonans	Surd	Fortis	Spirans	Nasal
Velar	ʒ	q	q!	x	—
Palatal	g(w)	k(w)	k!(w)	X	—
Anterior Palatal	g·	k·	k·!	x·	—
Alveolar	d	t	t!	s	n
Dental	dz	ts	ts!	—	—
Labial	b	p	p!	—	m
Lateral	ʟ	ʟ	ʟ!	ɬ	—
Laryngeal catch	ε				
	h, y, w.				

The velar series are k sounds pronounced with the soft palate. x corresponds to ch in German *Bach*. The palatal series correspond to our g (hard) and k. X is like x, but pronounced farther forward. g· and k· sound almost like gy and ky (with consonantic y); x· is the German ch in *ich*. d, t, and s are almost dental. ʟ, ʟ, and ʟ! are pronounced with tip of tongue touching the lower teeth, the back of the tongue extending transversely across the hard palate, so that the air escapes suddenly near the first molars. In ɬ the tip of the tongue is in the same position, but the back of the tongue is narrower, so that the air escapes near the canine teeth. The sound is at the same time slightly less explosive than ʟ. l is the same as the English sound. ε is a very faint laryngeal intonation. The exclamation mark is used throughout to indicate increased stress of articulation.

The vowels seem to be quite variable. The indistinct E is very frequent. The two pairs i e and o u probably represent each a single intermediate sound. The whole series of vowels may probably be represented as follows:

E

i e, î, ê, a, ô, o u
i ē, – ä, ā, â, ō ū

There are a considerable number of rules of euphony which govern the sequences of sounds. The u vowels do not admit of a following anterior palatal, which is changed into a palatal with following w; for instance, ꞇā'wayō-g·a *this salmon-weir*, becomes ꞇā'wayōgwa. aa is often contracted to ä; for instance, ō^εma-a *that chieftainess*, becomes ō^εmä. oa is contracted to ô; for instance, ꞇa'wayō-a *that salmon-weir*, becomes ꞇā'wayô. It seems that combinations of consonants do not occur in the beginning of words. Extensive clusters of consonants are rare, and even combinations of two consonants are restricted in number. The first sound of such a combination is generally a spirans, nasal, l or ɿ, all of which are produced by stricture, not by closure. k sounds, which in the process of word-composition become first sounds of combinations of consonants, are aspirated; l sounds become ɿ. When, in the process of composition, inadmissible combinations of consonants occur, the second consonant is often dropped. Terminal consonants of words, when followed by words with initial consonants, are often modified in the manner here indicated. From g·ōk^u *house*, is formed g·ōX^udzē *large house; from* ^εnēk· *to say,* ^εnē'x·sō *he is told.* Instead of laa'mʟ mē'x ^ε ēʟ *then he will sleep*, we have laa'mɿ mē'x^εēʟ. Examples of dropping of consonants are the following: qā's-x·^εid *be begins to walk*, becomes qā's^εid; Wā'k!ēqēs-x·ʟa *named Wā'k·!ēqēs*, becomes Wā'k·!ēqēsʟa.

Suffixes influence the terminal sounds of stems, which they often harden or soften. When softened, surd and fortis are transformed into the sonans of the same series; when hardened, sonans and surd are transformed into the fortis. s softened becomes dz or y; hardened, it becomes ts!. x· softened and hardened becomes n; Xw softened and hardened becomes w. ɿ softened and hardened becomes l. n, m, l, y, w, when softened, become sonant by being preceded by the laryngeal catch. The following examples will illustrate these processes:

STEM	SOFTENED	HARDENED
ʟ!aqw-, *red*	ʟ!ā'ʒw-atō, *red-eared*	ʟ!ā'q!w-ôbō, *red-breasted*
hanʟ-, *to shoot*	ha'nꞇ-as, *place of shooting*	ha'nʟ!-āla, *noise of shooting*
qas-, *to walk*	qā'y-as, *place of walking*	qā'ts!-ēnox, *walker*
mîx·-, *to strike*	mEn-a'ts!ē, *drum = striking receptacle*	mE'n^εxst, *to strike hind end*
sēXw-, *to paddle*	sē'w-ayu, *paddle*	sē'^εw-ēnox, *paddler*
ts!ō'ɿ-, *black*	ts!ō'l-is, *black beach*	ts!ō'^εl-a, *black rock*
^εwun-, *to hide*	^ε wu'^εn-îɿ, *to hide in the house*	^εwu^εn-a', *to hide on rock*
dE'nxal-, *to sing*	dE'nxa^εl-as, *place of singing*	

Grammatical relations are expressed by means of suffixes and by reduplication. Suffixes affect the word to which they are attached in different ways. A considerable number are attached to the terminal sound of the word, without causing any modifications of the same, except such as are required by the rules of euphony. To this class belong almost all pronominal, temporal, and conjunctive suffixes. Another group of suffixes is attached to the stem of the word, which loses all its word-forming suffixes. It is probable that all nouns are compounds of a stem and of a number of suffixes. The latter disappear entirely when the noun is combined with one of this class of suffixes, and we observe apparently an apocope of the end of the noun, while actually its stem reappears freed from its suffixes. At the same time, the suffix often modifies the terminal consonant of the stem. Thus we have bɛgwā′nɛm *man*, stem: bɛgw-, and from this bɛk!u′s *man in the woods;* mɛt!ā′nē *clam*, stem: mɛt!-, and from this mɛdā′d *having clams.* This process is analogous to what has been observed in many Indian languages, and has been termed "decapitation" or "apocope." From the instances with which I am familiar, I am inclined to believe that a thorough knowledge of the process will prove that the apparent apocope is due either to laws of euphony, or to the dropping of affixes, as in the case here described.

Other changes of the stem are due to reduplication, the method of which varies according to the grammatical function it performs. Double or even triple reduplication may occur in the same word; for instance, from the stem bɛgw- *man*, we have bā′bagum *boy*, and bā′bɛbagum *boys.*

In discussing the groups of relations expressed by grammatical processes, we will take up first those relating to the person speaking, or the pronominal relations. The language has a strong tendency to define every action and every object in all its relations to the persons conversing. These relations are expressed by the personal, demonstrative, and possessive pronouns. The homology between demonstrative and personal pronouns is here perfect. The personal pronoun indicates the person acting or acted upon, as speaker, person addressed, and person spoken of; the demonstrative indicates the location of an action or of an object as near the speaker, near the person addressed, or near the person spoken of. This strict homology appears in many American languages, but in few is the expression of location so rigidly demanded as in Kwakiutl. The location of object or action in relation to the three persons—speaker, person addressed, and person spoken of—must always be expressed. These three positions are further subdivided into two groups, the one expressing objects and actions visible to the speaker, the other expressing those invisible to the speaker.

LOCATION NEAR	1ST PERSON	2D PERSON	3D PERSON
Visible to speaker	-k·	-x	–
Invisible to speaker	-g·a	-q!	-a

Personal pronouns appear mostly incorporated in the verb. The pronominal form, which we designate as "first person plural," is not a true plural. Plurality implies the presence of several individuals of the same kind. A plurality of speakers is seldom possible; but our "we" expresses either "I and thou," or "I and he." It is therefore not surprising that many languages, and among them the Kwakiutl, use distinct forms for these two ideas. On the other hand, the second and third persons plural are real plurals, and are designated in Kwakiutl by a suffix, -x·da$^\varepsilon$x^u, which precedes the pronominal ending. In the Hē'iltsaq^u dialect this plural is expressed by reduplication.

The personal pronouns have separate forms for expressing their syntactic relation in the sentence; that is to say, there are pronominal cases. These are the subjective (nominative) and objective (accusative).

	1ST PERSON	2D PERSON	3D PERSON	INCLUSIVE	EXCLUSIVE
Subjective	-En	-Es	–	-nts	nu$^\varepsilon$X
Objective	–	-ōL	-q	–	–

A number of secondary cases are derived from these primary forms,— a locative from the objective, an instrumentalis and finalis from the subjective.

	1ST PERSON	2D PERSON	3D PERSON	INCLUSIVE	EXCLUSIVE
Locative	g·ā'xE*n*	lōL	laq	g·ā'xEnts	g·ā'xEnu$^\varepsilon$X
Instrumentalis	(-En ?)	-ōs	-s	(-ents ?)	(-Enu$^\varepsilon$X ?)
Finalis	qa$^\varepsilon$n	qa$^\varepsilon$s	qaē	qa$^\varepsilon$nts	qa$^\varepsilon$nu$^\varepsilon$X

The old objective of the first person, which occurs in the Hē'iltsaq^u dialect, is entirely lost, and replaced by the locative. The instrumentalis of the second and third persons is identical with the possessive. I have not found any unquestionable forms of this case for the first person.

The forms of verbs with incorporated object are derived by combinations of the above forms in the order subject, direct object, indirect object (locative), instrumentalis, finalis. It seems that the first person singular had an older form, -EnL, which is still used in the Koskimo dialect, and which persists in all forms in which the subject first person is followed by another pronominal form. An example of verbal forms with incorporated object and instrument is mìx·$^\varepsilon$ī'daqs *he struck him with it*, from mìx·$^\varepsilon$ī'd *to strike*, -aq *him*, -s *with it*. When substantives are introduced in a sentence of this kind, they are placed following the pronoun which indicates their function. At the same time the pronoun is modified. For instance, mìx·$^\varepsilon$ī'dēda bEgwā'nEmaqs *the man struck him with it;* mìx·$^\varepsilon$ī'dēda bEgwā'nEmaxa g·ìnā'nEms *the man struck the child with it;* mìx·$^\varepsilon$ī'dēda bEgwā'nEmaxa g·ìnā'nEmsa tłē'sEm *the man struck the child with the stone*.

The terminals da, xa, and sa might be interpreted as nominative, accusative, instrumentalis of an article, if it were not for their intimate connection with the preceding verb. The pronominal object and the instrumentalis at the end of the subject in our first example also show that we have here really an incorporation of the noun in the verbal expression. The terminal a, which characterizes the subject followed by an object (like the terminal a in bɛgwā'nɛma of our example), must be explained as the retained a of the compound pronominal ending -aq (as in mîx·ᵋī'daq), and seems to me one of the strongest proofs of our interpretation. The connection between subject of the first person and object elucidates the same point: mîx·ᵋī'dɛnʟaq *I strike him*, where -ʟa- is inserted between the subject first person -ɛn and the pronominal object -q; and mîx·ᵋī'dɛnʟaxa g·înā'nɛm *I strike the child*, which form is strictly analogous to the form with pronominal object. The nouns which form subject, object, indirect object or instrumentalis in the sentence always enter the verbal expression in their full form. They do not lose their word-forming suffixes, as they often do in composition with various other classes of suffixes.

The construction of the sentence is therefore analogous to that found in other American languages, most of which incorporate object and indirect object, although the degree and character of incorporation vary. Mexican and Kootenay embody the object freed of its word-forming affixes, and often replace it by the pronominal object. Chinook, Sioux, and many other languages incorporate only the pronominal representative in the verb, and place the noun as apposition at the end of the sentence. Kwakiutl pursues the same method as Chinook, but, instead of placing the nouns as appositions, it places them immediately following the representative pronoun, thus creating a word-complex held together by pronominal particles.

The phonetic development of the pronoun, when placed before a noun, has two series of forms, a definite and an indefinite. The former are da, xa, laxa, sa, qa; the latter,–, x, lax, s, q. The use of the indefinite is, however, much more restricted than that of the corresponding forms in English. The indefinite forms are also used preceding proper nouns.

The language has a strong tendency to combine the possessive pronoun, which ordinarily appears as a suffix, with the pronominal suffixes just referred to, so that they form a phonetic unit, meaning, he my, he thy, etc. From ɜɛnɛ'm *wife*, we have ɜɛnɛ'mɛn *my wife*; but ᵋnē'k·ɛn ɜɛnɛ'm *said she-my wife*, ᵋnē'k·ēxēs ɜɛnɛ'm *said he-to-his wife*. In the second person the pronoun is repeated as a suffix to the noun; in the third person it is combined with the pronominal suffix when subject and possessor are identical, it is suffixed to the substantive if they are distinct.

ᵋnē'k·ɛn ɜɛnɛ'm *my wife said.*   ᵋnēk·ēxɛn ɜɛnɛ'm *he said to my wife.*

ᵋnē′k·ēs ᴣEnE′mōs *thy wife said.*

ᵋnē′k·ēda ᴣEnE′mas *his wife said.*

ᵋnēk·ēxēs ᴣEnE′mōs *he said to thy wife.*

ᵋnēk·ēxēs ᴣEnE′m *he said to his (own) wife.*

ᵋnēk·ēx ᴣEnE′mas *he said to his (the other man's) wife.*

Our conjunction "and," and interrogative and a number of demonstrative pronouns are treated in the same manner. This phenomenon is evidently closely connected with the tendency of adverbs and auxiliary verbs to take the subjective ending of the verb, while the object remains connected with the verb itself. k·!ē′ ᵋsEn dō′qoaq *not-I see-him,* shows the characteristic arrangement of sentences of this kind. The pronominal elements always take the terminal place in the verb.

Moods, in the proper sense of the term, are very slightly developed. Here might be classed some of the verbals to be discussed later, the imperative, and the conditional. The imperative is indicated by the stem of the verb, or by imperative suffixes, such as -g·a, inchoative; -la, continuative. -x· followed by pronominal endings forms an exhortative. The conditional is expressed by the suffix ō: qaᵋsō lā′lax *if you should go.*

The verb generally consists of a stem and numerous adverbial suffixes, which modify or limit the meaning of the verbal stem. These adverbial expressions may be limitations of time, of cause, of manner, of object. They embrace, therefore, our tenses, conjunctions, adverbs, and even objects or prepositional expressions. The lack of distinction in the method of expressing grammatical relations and material ideas, which is found in most Indian languages, manifests itself in the variety of ideas expressed by these suffixes.

There are four temporal suffixes which are used with verbs as well as with nouns. Words without suffix represent an aorist or historic tense which is indefinite as to time. Three suffixes designate past tenses: -uɭ, -x·ᵋid, -x·dē. -uɭ designates the remote past, -x·ᵋid the recent past, and -x·dē the transition from present to past. The limits between -uɭ and x·ᵋid are not distinct. The usage depends upon the period with which the time elapsed is generally compared. In speaking of last year's salmon-run, it is compared to the period between two fishing seasons, so that half a year is considered remote past. In speaking of the death of a person, the time elapsed since the death is compared with man's life, and therefore -uɭ is not used until five years or more after death. The words for yesterday and day-before-yesterday contain the ending -uɭ, and consequently, when these are used, the verb must take the same ending. The use of -x·dē is quite distinct from the two former tenses. It always implies the transition from existence to non-existence. The future is expressed by the suffix -ʟ. All the temporal suffixes are attached to the full word.

A number of derivational suffixes may be grouped with those expressing tenses. We find, among others, a desiderative expressed by the suffix -ēxst, for instance, nā'qēxst *to desire to drink;* a causative -mas, for instance, qā'samas *to cause to walk;* -ᵋnakula implying a gradual motion, for instance, tē'guᵋnakula *to hang one after the other* (from tē'kwa *to hang*). The most important forms in this group are the inchoative and the "tentative," which latter expresses the attempt to perform an action.

The inchoative is very frequently used, the continuative form being strictly distinguished from it, as is also the case in the allied Nootka. The continuative of most verbs ends in -a, while the inchoative ends in -x·ᵋid, which ending, however, undergoes many changes according to the rules of euphony. From qā'sa *to walk*, we have qā's ᵋid *to begin to walk;* from mō'kwa *to tie*, mō'Xᵋwid. The locative suffixes, which will later be mentioned, have separate forms for inchoative and continuative, which are formed somewhat irregularly.

The "tentative" is formed by reduplication with long ā vowel, and hardened terminal consonant: dā'doq!wa *to endeavor to see*, from dō'qwa, *to see.*

Conjunctional suffixes are numerous. The simple verbal endings described before are used only when the sentence is without inner connection with previous statements—that is to say, when a new idea is introduced in the discourse. That a subject has been referred to before, or that it has been in the mind of the speaker before, is expressed by the suffix -m. g·ā'xɛn ᵋnɛmō'kwē means "my friend of whom I have not been thinking has come unexpectedly"; g·ā'xmɛn ᵋnɛmō'kwē means "my friend who was expected has arrived." -mēs indicates a very weak causal relation, similar to our "and so"; -g·iɪ is causal, signifying "therefore";-ɪa and -t!a signify "but"; -xa, "also."

More or less adverbial are the following: -k·as *really;* -x·ʟä *very;* -x·ɪa *too bad, that!* -x·st! *as usual;* -x·sä *still;* -axōɪ *and I did not know it before*, a mild expression of surprise.

Locative suffixes are very numerous. Many of them have distinctive continuative and inchoative forms:

	CONTINUATIVE	INCHOATIVE
in the house	-iɪ	-liɪ
on the ground	-us	-ls
on rocks	-a	-ala
up	-usta	-ustala

Closely related to the locative suffixes are the objective suffixes, which express either the object acted upon or the subject of an intransitive verb. Suffixes designating parts of the body are particularly numerous in this class: -x·ʟē *head;* -x·ts!ā'ne *hand;* -bôē *chest*, etc. But others are not wanting: -sqwap *fire;* -ᵋsta *water.* Sometimes the suffix may be considered as expressing a local relation rather than an objective one; but it never expresses an instrumental relation, as is the case in Siouan and Athapascan languages.

A number of suffixes express moods; -lax implies the uncertainty of the conditional: -nēᵉsʼɪ the optative "oh, if!" Here we may class the suffix -sō, which expresses the passive.

In this group the series of verbal nouns are particularly remarkable. They are numerous, and in construction always retain their verbal character, governing the pronominal cases that belong to the verb. The most important ones among these are -ēnēᵉ, signifying the abstract noun; for instance, k·!ē′lak·!ēnēᵉ *the clubbing*. This verbal occurs only with the possessive pronoun. It is used very frequently to express the intentional when it is preceded by the particle qa *in order to* or *for*.

The indefinite verbal, which does not differ from the simple form of the third person singular without demonstrative ending, is very frequently used to express subordinate clauses, particularly causal and temporal subordination. The verbal is then expressed in the objective case, takes the possessive suffix, and besides this the demonstrative form peculiar to each person. The following example will make this clear:

ā′ɪᵉɛm yū′Xᵉwidɛxg·in g·ā′xik·   *the wind just began to blow when I came.*

ā′ɪᵉɛm yū′Xᵉwidɛxs g·ā′xaaqōs   *the wind just began to blow when you came.*

ā′ɪᵉɛm yū′Xᵉwidɛxs g·ā′xaē   *the wind just began to blow when he came.*

(ā′ɪ ᵉɛm *lately*, yu′Xᵉwid   *to begin to blow*, g·āx *to come*.)

Other verbal nouns are -kⁿ, a passive participle and noun; as g·ilō′ɪikᵘ *a thing stolen;* -anɛm *obtained by*, as g·ilō′ɪanɛm *obtained by stealing* (from g·ilō′ʟa *to steal*); -ayu *instrument*, as dō′gwayu *trolling-line* (from dō′kwa *to troll*); -ɛm *instrument*, as k·iʟɛ′m *net* (from k·iʟa′ *to fish with net*); -ēnox *nomen actoris*, as g·it!ē′nox *wood-worker* (from g·ita′ *to do work in wood*); and many others.

The suffix -ayu *instrument* sometimes expresses a passive, particularly of intransitive verbs: qā′sᵉidayu *he was the means of walking*, i.e., he was walked away with by somebody.

There are also a considerable number of suffixes which transform nouns into verbs. The possessive verb is used so frequently that it gives the language a peculiar character. It is formed by suffixing -ad to the stem of the noun, which loses all its suffixes. ɜɛnɛ′m *wife* has the stem ɜɛg·- and, therefore, the Kwakiutl form ɜɛg·a′d *having a wife*. nɛXusk·i′n *a berry* has the stem nɛX- and, therefore, nɛwa′d *having berries*.

To eat a certain object is expressed by the reduplicated stem of the noun; from nɛXusk·i′n *berry*, nɛXna′Xᵘ. This derivative, however, is exceedingly irregular. -ōʟ *to obtain*, -sila *to take care of*, -g·ila *to make*, are examples of other derivatives.

Among the categories expressed by grammatical processes we have to mention those of plurality and diminution. The plural seems to have been originally a distributive. It is expressed by reduplication, as bɛgwā'nɛm pl. bē'bɛgwanɛm *man*, g·ōkᵘ pl. g·ig·ō'kᵘ *house*. There is a decided preference for the use of the long ē in the reduplicated syllable. All substantives designating human beings have plural forms, while many other words have no reduplicated plural. Words with local suffixes form their plural with the suffix -ɛm, which probably has a collective meaning, designating a group of individuals: g·î'lg·ilala pl. g·îlɛ'mg·ilala *to walk on rocks*. Diminutives are formed from nouns with *a* vowel in the reduplicated syllable, softened terminal consonant, and the suffix -ɛm: g·ōk *house*, g·ā'g·ogum *small house*; mē'gwat *seal*, mā'megwadɛm *small seal*.

Numerals are formed on the decimal system. They take classifying suffixes, the most important among which are those for designating human beings, round objects, long objects, and flat objects. The classification of nouns and verbs in regard to their form is also found in words denoting existence. These have separate forms for round, long, flat, and soft objects.

In conclusion I will give a few lines of texts with grammatical explanation:

G·ō'kulaᵋlaēda[1]	g·ā'läsa[2]	Dzā'wadɛēnoxwē[3]	lā'xa[4]
The village was it is said the	first of the	Dzā'wadɛēnoxᵘ	at the

ᵋnɛ'ldzäs[5]	wäs[5]	Gwa'ᵋēxa[6] ʇē'ȝadês[7]	Bē'bɛnadē.[8]
upper course of	the river of	Gwa'ᵋē having name of	'Having Phosphorescence.'

Wä,[9] lā'ᵋlaē[10]	â'la pâ'lēda[11]	ᵋwā'latsɛma.[12]	Wä,[9] laɛ'mᵋ laē[13]
Well, then it is said was	really hungry the	great tribe.	Well, then it is said

hē'mɛnaꜞaɛm[14]	ᵋnɛmō'kwēda[15]	pō'sdanäxa[16]	ᵋnēᵋnā'la.[17] Wä,[9]
always	one	died of hunger the	days	Well.

lā'ᵋlaē[10]	yā'q!ēg·aʟēda[18]	ᵋnɛmō'kwē	lax[4] aᵋyi'lkwäs[5]
then it is said	began to speak the	one	among the speakers of

Qa'wadiliȝala	la'xēs[19]	g·ō'kulōtē.[20] Lā'ᵋlaē[10]	ᵋnē'k·a: "ᵋyax·daᵋxᵘ[21]
Qa'wadiliȝala	to his	tribe. Then	he said: "Oh!

wä'ɛntsōs[22]	hō'ʟēla	g·ā'xɛn,[23]	g·ō'kulōt,[20] qaᵋn[24] yā'q!ēg·aʟēsg·a[25]
(do)	listen	to me,	tribe, that I begin to speak of this

ȝwä'ꞁaasg·asg·în[26]	nâ'qēk·.[27]"
this kind of this my	this mind."

---

[1] g·ōkᵘ *house*; -la continuative verbal suffix; -ᵋla quotative; -ē pronominal ending pointing to following noun; -da pronominal subjective ending pointing to following noun.

[2] g·ā'la *first*; g·ā'lä contraction of g·ā'la-a terminal *a* indicating absence; -sa possessive ending indicating following noun.

³ dzā'Xun olachen (a fish); -ad having, requires the dropping of the formative suffix -un in dzā'Xun and softens the terminal X to w; -ēnox^u people of; -ē demonstrative suffix.

⁴ laq at it; with ending indicating following noun, laxa.

⁵ ä contracted from a-a, see ²; -s possessive ending.

⁶ -xa pronominal objective ending pointing to following noun.

⁷ ᴛē'qEm, stem ᴛēq -name; -ad having, see ³; -s possessive.

⁸ bē'x·a to phosphoresce; -ad having, see ³; -ē demonstrative suffix.

⁹ A conjunctional interjection.

¹⁰ la, conjunction 'then,' treated in Kwakiutl as an intransitive verb; -^ɛla quotative; -ē demonstrative suffix.

¹¹ pâla hungry, starving; -ēda see ¹.

¹² ^ɛwā'las great; -sᴣEm a group of individuals.

¹³ laE'm from la then; -m indicates that the subject of the discourse, namely the starvation, has been referred to before; -^ɛla quotative.

¹⁴ -m see ¹³.

¹⁵ ^ɛnEm one, -ōk^u classifying suffix indicating persons; -ēda see ¹.

¹⁶ pō'sdana literally too hungry, from pō'sqa to feel hungry; -xa objective pronominal ending, which form is used for all expressions of time.

¹⁷ ^ɛnā'la day, reduplicated plural.

¹⁸ yā'qant!ala to speak, inchoative yā'q!ēg·aL; these contain the suffixes -k·!āla and -g·aL, noise and beginning of noise.

¹⁹ lax to, -ēs his, the form laxēs means to his own, while lax g·ō'kulōtēs would mean to the other man's tribe.

²⁰ g·ōk^u tribe,-lōt companion.

²¹ ^ɛya oh, -x·da^ɛx^u pronominal plural suffix of second and third persons.

²² Exhortative of wä, see ⁹.

²³ g·ā'xEn locative of first person personal pronoun.

²⁴ qa^ɛn finalis of first person personal pronoun.

²⁵ -s instrumentalis; -g·a demonstrative, signifying this near me invisible.

²⁶ ᴣwä[thus, as referred to; -as place of; hence ᴣwä'[aas the place referred to, the manner referred to; -g·a this near me invisible; -s genitive; g·în this mine near me.

²⁷ nâ'qē mind; -k· this near me visible.

Free translation.—The first Dzā'wadEēnox^u lived on the upper course of the river Gwa'^ɛē at a place named 'Having Phosphorescence.' The people of the great tribe were really hungry. Every day some of them died of hunger. Then one of the speakers of Qa'wadiliᴣala began to speak to his tribe and said: "Listen to me, my tribe; I will say what I am thinking."

SELECTION 24

A Purely Analytical
Study of Language

NEW YORK,
Feb. 15, 1905.
DR. W. THALBITZER,
    25 Amicivej,
        Copenhagen, Denmark.

MY DEAR DOCTOR,—

I feel that I have to apologize for not having thanked you before this for your interesting book, and for not writing in regard to the various questions that we discussed last summer. The reason was that in the course of our arrangements during the end of last year I hoped to see a way of furthering your plans, but nothing definite has occurred up to this time.

I am engaged at present in preparing for the Bureau of Ethnology a "Handbook of American Languages," in which I attempt to present the salient features of various types of American languages, giving to each language about seventy pages of the size of the publications of the Bureau of Ethnology. I write to ask you if you would be willing to contribute to this book a chapter of about seventy pages, giving an analysis of the Eskimo grammar, and containing two or three pages of texts with very detailed analysis, containing, of course, references to the grammatical description. It is my endeavor to have all these sketches of grammar purely analytical; that is to say, to keep out the point of view of Indo-European languages as thoroughly as possible. I try to give a very brief historical introduction, which is followed by a brief description of the phonetics. Then I discuss the grammatical processes which occur in the language, and finally describe the ideas expressed by grammatical process. After these introductory chapters follows a more detailed description, which, however, as I said before, should be purely analytical. Following this description I try to give a characterization of the vocabu-

Copy preserved in the Boas Papers, American Philosophical Society. Thalbitzer was a Danish scholar trained in the classical tradition of Indo-European linguistics, whose work on Eskimo phonetics had recently come to Boas' attention. The fact that, from the Boasian point of view, he was the only "outsider" among the contributors, makes Boas' instructional letter particularly illuminating.

lary of the language. By this I mean a discussion of the groups of ideas expressed by some words. In some American languages there are, for instance, numerous suffixes indicating instrumentality; so that for this reason a word like "to strike" would have a very general significance, while "to strike with the fist," "to strike with the palm of the hand," "to strike with a stick," etc., would all be derivatives. In other languages local ideas corresponding to our prepositions are expressed by verbal elements. Sometimes these elements are so numerous that almost all verbs of motion may be expressed by a very few stems. In Eskimo, on the other hand, we have a very great number of special stems expressing different kinds of motion. I send under separate cover a copy of part of a manuscript describing the Kwakiutl language, which will give you an idea of what I have in mind. I also send you copy of a paper on the Chinook vocabulary, which I have written in order to indicate the character of the description of the vocabulary to which I refer. My manuscript has not been revised, and will require a good many changes; still I think the fundamental idea will appear clearly.

I am authorized to offer you $150 for a manuscript of this kind, which I should like very much to have before the middle of June of this year.

With kindest regards,
Yours very truly,
Franz Boas

☙☙   S E L E C T I O N   2 5

The Relation of
Tlingit and Athapascan

Nov. 25, 1907.

Dr. John R. Swanton,
    Bureau of American Ethnology,
    Washington, D.C.

My dear Swanton,—

During the last few days I have studied your sketch of the Tlingit in some detail, and there are a number of points that occur to me which I think would make your sketch more useful. I find it particularly difficult to translate the examples which you have given without fuller explanations. I wish you would kindly add to all the examples translations of each word, as you have done in the notes to the texts. Otherwise it is very hard to grasp your point without looking at the same time all over your paper.

While this is simply a technical point, there are a number of other matters that seem to be more important. So far as I understand the language from your description, the indefinite demonstrative particle a appears of course very important; but I should rather hesitate to give it as prominent a position as you do by placing its discussion at the head of the whole description of the grammar. In a way the form seems to me analogous to the m and hai in Hupa, and my impression is that it is rather an idiomatic way of speaking by summing up all that precedes than a fundamental formal category of the language.

Closely related to this question is the other one of the interpretation of adverbial prefixes and of post positions. It strikes me that your post positions are quite similar to the adverbial prefixes in Athapascan, and also to the proclitic elements in Tsimshian. The apparent difference between Tsimshian and Tlingit seems to me brought about by the different position of the nominal element, which is repeated following the verb with a very general proposition. Considered in this way, the adverbial prefixes in Athapascan, the adverbial prefixes in Tsimshian, and your post positions would be practically the same thing. It does not appear

Copy preserved in the Boas Papers, American Philosophical Society.

clearly from your sketch whether the Tlingit post positions can be used freely following a pronoun and preceding the verb, or whether all of them can be used entirely adverbially preceding the pronoun.

On the whole, the similarity between Tlingit and Athapascan strikes me even more forcibly than when I first pointed out their similarity. In looking over the material, I also found a small number of words which are very much alike in the two languages:—

	TLINGIT.	ATHAPASCAN.
Name	sa	zi
Song	ci	chen
Fire	xoñ	qon
Salmon	louk	lok
Stone	ta	the

This is not by any means the result of systematic search, so that I consider the indications rather strong. I may of course be prejudiced by the strong impression of morphological relationship between Tlingit and Athapascan: but it seems to me that the form of the language would come out clearer if treated somewhat on the style of Goddard's Hupa; at least, so far as the verb is concerned. In his treatment of the verb I should also suggest a few changes related in a way to the question here discussed. It seems to me that the Hupa verb is clearly built up as follows:—

1. Adverbial proclitics.
2. Deiktic element.
3. Modal elements of the first order (like k, d).
4. Modal elements of the second order (corresponding to Goddard's conjugations).
5. Pronouns.
6. Modal elements of the third order (Goddard's classes).
7. Stem.
8. Suffixes.

I am under the impression that the Tlingit verb could have been advantageously treated in a similar manner.

I am very much obliged to you for the first instalment of the list of Haida stems which I received, and which I am arranging alphabetically.

Yours very sincerely,
[FRANZ BOAS]

SELECTION 26

The Speech Mannerisms
of Social Groups

BOLTON LANDING,
WARREN CO., N.Y.
Aug. 28, 1907.

MR. EDWARD SAPIR,
Montgomery Creek, Cal.

MY DEAR MR. SAPIR,—
Many thanks for your full letter of the 20th of August, which I find extremely interesting. It almost seems that you did not receive my note of [date left blank]. I have not received your thesis, but I presume I shall get it just as soon as I reach New York. I am busy here with some literary work that I want to finish, and I am trying to concentrate myself, so far as feasible, on these subjects. Your letter came only last night, and I have not had time to study it in detail. The characteristics between male and female language are very peculiar. I think, before assuming the origin of the language as due to admixture of tribes, it might be well to consider whether the mannerism of speech of different social groups may not be a sufficient explanation. Take, for instance, our students' slang, which is only used in conversation in college, but which the students readily drop when talking to other people. The same is true of any other professional slang. Whether it is possible to get satisfactory indications as to this or another kind of origin of the division of the language into two forms, I do not know; but if you compare the conditions, for instance, to the peculiar phonetic differentiation in Eskimo, or to the different mannerism in speech between men and women among the Sioux, I think the probability of an inner differentiation should not be disregarded.

Your remarks on the impossibility of adopting our ordinary classification into stems and suffixes seems to me also very important. I presume as our knowledge of American languages progresses, we shall find more

Copy preserved in the Boas Papers, American Philosophical Society.

and more cases where we really ought to speak of co-ordinate stems of different position rather than of stems and modifying elements. I shall always be very glad to hear from you.

With kindest regards,
Yours very sincerely.
[FRANZ BOAS]

    SELECTION 27

Some Philological Aspects
of Anthropological Research

It is, perhaps, partly due to accident that American anthropologists meet to-day, for the first time, jointly with the American Philological Association and with the Archeological Institute of America. Nevertheless, I welcome our joint meeting as a significant fact, because it emphasizes the growing feeling of anthropologists that our science may profit from the methods developed by classical and oriental archeology, and by the well-established methods of philological and linguistic research. We hope that it may also express the growing feeling among philologists and archeologists of the importance of anthropological research for their own studies.

Our cooperation with your societies indicates a radical change in the attitude of students of anthropology. Up to the present time we have affiliated with societies representing the natural sciences and psychology. This is due to the development of modern anthropology under the stimulus of the theory of evolution, and to the important incentives that it has taken from the methods pursued by the natural sciences. It has been the endeavor of anthropologists to discover universal laws, like the laws of physics and of chemistry. This tendency has been somewhat modified by the influence of those historical methods in the biological sciences which

Paper read at the joint meeting of the American Anthropological Association, the Archeological Institute, and the Philological Association, at Ithaca, New York, 28 December 1905; as published in *Science* 23 (1906): 641–645.

endeavor to explain the present types as the result of a long-continued development from previous forms.

Owing to the peculiar conditions under which it has grown up, American anthropology has been devoted almost exclusively to the study of North American problems. As we have penetrated more deeply into these problems we have observed that the general laws for which we have been searching prove elusive, that the forms of primitive culture are infinitely more complex than had been supposed, that a clear understanding of the individual problem can not be reached without taking into consideration its historical and geographical relations.

As this new point of view becomes more and more clearly established, the tendency must increasingly develop of turning away from the comparative methods of the natural sciences, and taking up more and more systematically the methods of history. While the first problem that presented itself to the anthropologist was the puzzling sameness of traits of culture in remote parts of the world, and while his endeavor was directed towards the discovery of the psychological causes that bring about such sameness, we begin to be inclined to view each cultural trait not primarily in comparison with parallel traits found in remote regions, but rather in connection with the direction taken by the whole culture of a tribe or a people. We begin to see that sameness of cultural traits does not always prove genetic relation, but that diverse traits have often tended to converge, so as to develop similar thoughts and activities; while, on the other hand, other traits have tended to diverge, and to assume in different regions different forms.

With the appreciation of this fact, the necessity of a much more thorough and detailed knowledge of primitive culture is recognized. While hitherto we have been satisfied with disconnected fragments of observations on the customs of the various tribes, we begin to see more and more clearly that the student must have a full grasp of all the forms of culture of the people he studies, before he can safely generalize.

It would seem to me that the classical archeologist or the classical philologist must always have an indulgent smile when he hears of serious anthropological studies carried on by investigators, who have neither the time, the inclination, nor the training to familiarize themselves with the language of the people whom they study. According to the canons of philological research, would not the investigator who is not able to read the classics be barred from the number of serious students? Would not the historian who investigates the history of the civilization of the middle ages, and who can not read the literature of that period, be excluded from the number of investigators? Would not the student of Oriental countries, who has to rely for his information on the assistance of interpreters, be considered an unsafe guide in the study of these countries? Still, this is the position which has confronted anthropology up to the present time. There are very few students who have taken the time and who have considered it necessary to familiarize themselves sufficiently with native languages to understand directly what the people whom they study speak about, what they think and what they do. There are fewer still who have deemed it worth while to record the customs and beliefs and the traditions of the people in their own words, thus giving us the objective material which will stand the scrutiny of painstaking investigation. I think it is obvious that in this respect anthropologists have everything to learn from you; that until we acquire the habit of demanding such authenticity of our reports as can be guaranteed only by philological accuracy of the record, can we hope to accumulate material that will be a safe guide to future studies.

The time must come when we must demand that collections of traditions obtained by means of the garbled English of interpreters, descriptions of customs not supported by native evidence, records of industries based only on the objective observation of the student, must be considered inadequate, and that we must demand from the serious student the same degree of philological accuracy which has become the standard in your sciences.

It is true that in many cases this ideal can not be obtained. The general breakdown of native culture, the fewness of numbers of certain tribes, the necessity of rapidly accumulating vanishing material, may sometimes compel the student, much against his will, to adopt methods of collecting which he recognizes as inadequate. Nevertheless, an important step forward will be made if we acknowledge that such collections are makeshifts that should be supplemented as soon as feasible, and wherever feasible, by more painstaking records.

Taking this standard as a guide, we must acknowledge that very little, if any, of our literature is sufficiently authentic. Perhaps the most valuable material that has been collected from this point of view is the long series of texts obtained from the Ponka and Omaha by the late James Owen Dorsey. It is true that they embrace only a limited aspect of the life of the tribe, but so far as they go, they give us a deep insight into the mode of thought of the Indian. In the whole range of American anthropological literature there is hardly anything that may be compared to this publication. We have short series of texts from a few tribes which are highly welcome, but as they stand, they are but fragments of what is required. The tribes thus treated are the Sioux, the Klamath of Oregon, the Kwakiutl, the Chinook and the Haida, and there is also a considerable amount of material available from the Eskimo, although most of the published material in that language is overlaid with Danish culture.

If we consider the whole range of native life that should be treated in the same manner, we see how utterly inadequate the available collections are. To take, as an instance, the best—that of Mr. Dorsey—the contents of the volume are a collection of myths, records of war-expeditions and a long series of personal letters. These topics cover only a narrow range of the life of the Ponka. The whole material culture, their knowledge of the country and of neighboring tribes, their rituals and ritualistic myths, their social organization, their beliefs have not been recorded, and are known to us only by brief notes collected by the author.

If we acknowledge the correctness of the requirements here outlined, the work that is before us is stupendous. Let me remind you that in North America we have probably about fifty-five distinct linguistic stocks and at least three hundred and fifty distinct dialects. If full information on all of these is to be gathered, the most intensive work of a great number of students is immediately required, because the information is rapidly disappearing, and probably almost all of it will be lost inside of fifty years. The demand for thoroughness of method of collection must, therefore, be brought forward with great emphasis.

I have spoken here of the linguistic and historical method only as an adjunct of ethnological research. It is, however, true that the linguistic problem itself is one of intense interest, and one which will gain by a knowledge of the methods applied by Indo-European philology. The forms of the Indian languages differ enormously. It is often assumed that there is one type of American language, but even a superficial knowledge of representative dialects of American stocks shows that much greater than their similarities are their differences, and that the psychological basis of morphology is not by any means the same in the fifty-five stocks that occur on our continent. The scientific problems which are involved in their study have hardly been touched. I must say with regret that the anthropologist of the present day is not the man to solve these problems; that we require not only the stimulating example of philologists, but also their assistance. *You* must give preliminary training to the men who are to take up the problems of American languages; because the centuries of experience and of labor that have been bestowed upon the development of philological methods have given you the advantage of settled lines of approach of linguistic problems. If you are willing to lend us your assistance in this important investigation, I foresee a field of important discoveries which will in their turn be of great benefit to the science of language. The psychological foundation and morphological development of American languages are so peculiar that their study must be a revelation to the student of Indo-European or of Semitic languages. Well-known problems which you have discussed for years appear in new aspects, and broad points of view for discussion of linguistic questions present themselves readily to the student who takes up the types of language peculiar to our continent.

I beg to be allowed to make the direct appeal to you here, asking you to turn the attention of your younger students to this promising field. It is virgin soil, and he who takes up the subject with a fairly adequate equipment is sure to find most ample compensation for his toil in new and valuable discoveries. Without your help we shall never be able to solve this task, which requires the speediest attention and the cooperation of many investigators.

When we once have the equipment such as I have tried to outline, when we have investigators who collect the material in authentic form, and when we have students who will apply themselves to a painstaking analysis of the collected data, our problems will probably appear in entirely new light. The connection between prehistoric archeology and modern ethnology will necessarily become of the same character as the relation between early classical archeology and the study of classical literature. It is true our problems will always remain more obscure and more difficult than yours, because we have no historical documents that carry us back through any considerable length of time, while, by the necessities of the case, we are compelled to use, instead of historical methods, geographical methods. We have to trace historical transmission and historical contact by studies of geographical distribution. Often we find ourselves confronted by contradictory evidence, but, notwithstanding all these difficulties, the little progress that has been made during the last twenty years indicates plainly that, from this point of view, the historical problem of anthropology may be approached with the hope of a certain amount of success and that we may be able to reconstruct important historical facts.

I have given expression here to the growing need of the introduction of sounder philological methods of collection and of historical methods in the treatment of anthropological problems. I do not wish to be understood as advocating a dissociation of anthropology from psychology and the natural sciences. The source from which modern anthropology has grown up, the problems that have presented themselves to us from the point of view of the student of natural sciences, who takes human nature for his subject, are novel and are important. They touch upon the fundamental questions underlying the history of human civilization, and their clear formulation must be recognized as a distinct contribution of anthropology to the scientific development of the day. Most important among these results is, perhaps, the recognition of the fundamental sameness of the traits in human culture the world over and of the psychic unity of mankind. The data on which these conclusions are based have not been without influence upon modern history and modern philology, and I do believe that if we have to learn much from you, we can also offer in return a point of view that will prove fertile in your work. The modification of the theories of the development of mythology, the better appreciation of the earliest development of Greek and Oriental culture, would hardly have come about if anthropological points of view had not made themselves felt in the minds of archeologists and philologists. If it must be *our* endeavor to broaden our methods by learning from *you* the foundations of historical research, we may offer to you also the results of many honest attempts of applying the methods of natural science to the phenomena of human culture.

Let us hope that our first joint meeting may introduce a period of closer contact, of greater readiness on the part of anthropology to learn from her older sisters, and of a better understanding of the aims of anthropology by students of language and of history.

PART VI

THE CRITIQUE OF FORMALISM IN PHYSICAL ANTHROPOLOGY

Boas began his physical anthropological work on a rather small scale, robbing the graves of dead Indians and measuring living ones in a Victoria jail, where the problems of rapport were minimized (Rohner 1969, pp. 88–90). From the beginning, however, he had a model for a much grander inquiry in the work of Rudolf Virchow, who had organized national anthropometric surveys in Germany, and from whom Boas apparently received basic training in anthropometric technique as early as 1883. At Clark, Boas' study of growth in Worcester school children was soon extended to include Oakland, California and Toronto, Canada; and when in 1891 he assumed responsibility (under Professor Frederick W. Putnam of Harvard) for the physical anthropological work connected with the ethnological exhibits at the Chicago World's Fair, the scope of his inquiries was extended to cover the whole of aboriginal North America.

The results of this research, which are presented in the first selection (no. 28), convey quite well the character of Boas' early physical anthropology. In some respects, it was much the same as that of classical European physical anthropology in this period (cf. Boas 1899). Boas spent a good bit of time measuring heads, and his inquiry was directed to such long-mooted issues as the viability of racial hybrids. In other ways, however, the emphases which were to be the hallmark of Boas' later physical anthropology were already very much in evidence. Thus Boas did not conceive racial types in static terms, but as the products of the processes of heredity and growth within specific environmental situations; and he was less interested in describing or classifying types than in understanding the processes that had produced them. Furthermore, he was interested in physical anthropological questions not so much for their own sake as for the light that they might cast on the history of mankind, both in the specific and the evolutionary sense.

Over the next decade and a half, Boas' researches led him to a more fundamental questioning of traditional physical anthropological assumption. The most important of these was the study he carried on between 1908 and 1910 for the U.S. Immigration Commission, which had been set up by Congress to investigate the effects of the so-called "new" immigration from southern and eastern Europe, and ultimately to provide some forty volumes of justification for immigration restriction legislation. If Boas' study of *Changes in Bodily Form of Descendants of Immigrants* seems a bit out of place in this context, it is in part because the initiative came from him rather than the Committee. At this time, major editorial work on the *Handbook of American Indian Languages* was drawing to a close, and Boas—who operated within a rather restricted economy of research—was free to pick up another strand of his varied anthropological interests in order to take advantage of a unique funding opportunity. Working through Jeremiah Jenks, the Cornell economist who was the only academic member of the Commission, he proposed a plan that spoke to the issues of concern to the Commission and at the same time drew together the major lines of his own previous research into racial process. Although some of the Commission's members felt that Boas' study was not germane to their own "sociological" purposes, the project was approved, and by June 1908 a pilot study was begun on Eastern European Jewish boys in New York schools.

Analysis of this preliminary data revealed what Boas described as "very striking and wholly unexpected results." Contrary to accepted physical anthropological belief and practice, which was based on the assumption that the form of the human head was essentially impervious to environmental influence, Boas found that the heads of his immigrant children had apparently grown longer in the American environment. Over the next year, the study was extended to other immigrant groups, and the data showed what Boas described in the introduction to his final report as a "far-reaching change in the type" of each group that could "only be explained as due directly to the influence of environment" (Boas 1911b, pp. 1–7). The four letters to Jenks that I have reproduced here follow the immigrant study through its various stages, ending—as Boas so often did—with proposals for further research, as well as the suggestion that encouraging miscegenation might be the best solution to the problem posed by "an industrially and socially inferior large black population" in the South.

Perhaps the best short presentation of the broader implications of Boas' immigrant study is contained in a short paper he submitted to the First Universal Races Congress held in London in 1911. Here, as in other later statements on the study, he was somewhat more cautious as to the limits of environmental plasticity. But he did carry the argument in an interesting way from the fact of physical to the presumption of mental plasticity, arguing that the "burden of proof" was now shifted to those who believed in the existence of racial mental differences unaffected by environmental change. The quoted phrase suggests the broader impact of Boas' physical anthropological work. The assumptions of classical physical anthropology did not quickly change, but Boas did succeed in shifting somewhat the weight of its influence on matters of racial policy. Immigration restrictionists had appealed to the authority of European science; opponents of restriction could now appeal to that of the dean of American anthropology (Stocking 1968a, pp. 163–194; Cole 1931).

 SELECTION 28

The Anthropology of
the North American Indian—1894

Our knowledge of the anthropology of North America is based mainly upon the discussion of a number of important anthropological collections. First among these must be mentioned the famous Morton collection now in the possession of the Academy of Natural Sciences in Philadelphia, which forms the basis of Morton and Meigs' famous investigations. A large collection relating particularly to prehistoric American peoples has grown up in Cambridge, Mass., and the reports of the Peabody Museum contain much valuable material on our subject. Perhaps the largest collection is that of the U. S. Army Medical Museum in Washington, a published catalogue of which has made accessible a vast amount of anthropological material. But all of these data taken together

Memoirs of the International Congress of Anthropology (Chicago: Schulte, 1894), pp. 37–49.

have not been sufficient to delineate in a satisfactory manner the distribution of types of man in North America.

Investigations on osteological material, particularly on material collected among modern tribes, are always unsatisfactory, in that the identification of the skull, regarding its tribe and sex, often remains doubtful. Neither is it certain if we have to deal with the remains of full-blood Indians or with those of half-breeds. It appears, therefore, that for a more thorough investigation of the anthropology of North American Indians an investigation on living individuals is indispensable.

When the plans for the Department of Ethnology of the World's Columbian Exposition were being formed, Professor Putnam decided to include an investigation of the physical characteristics of the North American Indians in his work, and entrusted me with its organization. A number of young men, principally college students interested in this work, were instructed in the method of taking the observations. The material obtained through their agency has been the basis of the exhibit on the physical characteristics of the North American Indian. The material consists of measurements of about 17,000 full-blood and half-breed Indians which are distributed all over the North American continent with the exception of the Arctic coast and the Mackenzie Basin.

Before I begin to describe the results of this extensive inquiry I may be permitted to dwell briefly upon the leading considerations of the investigations.

The present generation of Indians is mixed to a considerable extent with whites and negroes, so much so that in certain regions it is impossible to find a full-blood individual. Thus the numerous tribes of the Iroquois, Cherokees, Chickasaws and Choctaws contain very few full-blood individuals, if any. Tribes which were once numerous and which inhabited the coast of the Atlantic Ocean have entirely disappeared, or an insignificant rest only survives. It appeared practically impossible to secure adequate data for the whole region embracing New England, the Middle States and the Southern States. On the other hand the great frequency of half-breeds among all these tribes made an investigation on these races very interesting. I decided, therefore, to pay particular attention to the question regarding the anthropology of the half-breeds. In fact, this has proved to be one of the most fruitful fields of the investigation.

In studying the characteristics of various Indian tribes as found by our observers, the question arises how to arrange them. On general principles it seemed best to consider the tribes simply as geographical groups and to treat the results also from a geographical standpoint. Following this principle, a number of tribes have been subdivided according to their present location. Thus the Ojibway, who inhabit a large part of Canada, are divided into an eastern and a western section. On the other hand groups of small tribes which inhabit the same region, and which show no differences in type, have been combined.

In order to define more clearly what is meant by a certain type, I will say that I consider the types as merely representing a series of forms found in a certain district. For convenience sake the names of the tribes among whom these types have been collected have been adopted for designating the types. I do not mean to say that the types which have been established are considered as original types of the respective peoples. The people itself may have become mixed in the course of the centuries with numerous other peoples, so much so that its original type may have disappeared entirely. There is no necessary correlation between the social unit which we call a tribe and the physical unit which constitutes the characteristics of the individuals of a certain region. The physical type is the result of the complex descent of a people and of the effect of the surroundings upon its physical development. It has nothing to do with the political and social organizations which we call tribes or nations. Therefore, if in the following I speak of types of the Sioux, or of Californians, it must be understood that I do not mean the types of the primitive Sioux tribe or the primitive tribes of California, but rather that I mean simply the types of the people inhabiting at present the regions occupied by the Sioux or by the Californian tribes.

It was necessary to confine the series of measurements to the most important ones, and particularly to avoid the necessity of the removal of clothing. Only by this restriction could a sufficient number of measurements be secured. It has been my endeavor to establish differences of types only in such cases where the number of cases was sufficient to show that the differences were real, not accidental. In tracing such differences it was particularly necessary to correct errors and inaccuracies of observation. In order to remedy this I have endeavored to obtain two independent series of observations on each tribe, taken by different observers and at different times. Whenever there was a reason to doubt the accuracy of an observer his returns have been excluded.

I turn now to consider the results obtained by our investigations. It is a well-known fact that the number of Indians is decreasing. This is partly due to the fact that mixed-bloods leave the tribes, but partly also to the actual reduction in numbers. It seemed of importance to know if this fact is due to the small number of births or to other causes, and also to compare the increase among half-breeds with that among full-blood Indians. For this purpose statistics have been collected regarding the number of children of Indian and half-breed women. It appears from these statistics that Indian women of more than forty years have on an average, approximately, six children, while half-breed women have on an average from seven to eight children. When the frequency of cases of women who have no children, or only two, three, four, five children, etc., are plotted, it appears that the smaller numbers of children are very much more frequent among the Indians than among the half-breeds, while the higher numbers of children are much more frequent among the half-breeds than among the Indians; that is to say, we find the rather unexpected result that the fertility among half-breed women is considerably larger than among full-blood women. The average number of children of Indian women is also high, and therefore the decrease in their numbers can only be explained by the fact that there exists a very high infant mortality.

In comparing the measurements of the head and of the face of Indians with those of whites we find the most striking difference to be in the dimensions of the transversal diameters of the face. On an average the breadth of face of the Indian is one centimetre more than that of the American white. It may be remarked that the face of the latter is exceedingly narrow and that in Europe, particularly in its eastern portions, we find faces which are considerably wider.

It is of interest to investigate the breadth of face of the half-breed in order to see if it stands between the measurements of the parental races, and if it is nearer the one than the other. For this purpose I have computed the breadth of face of children of full-blood Indians, half-breeds and whites from year to year, beginning with the fourth year. The tabulation shows that the difference which was noted between the adults exists just as markedly among children. The faces grow in such a way that the relation of the three groups always remains the same. The breadth of face of half-breeds stands always between that of the Indians and that of the whites, but so that it is always nearer the former. This is the case among boys as well as among girls. Thus we find the remarkable fact that at least in this one respect the half-breed is always more alike to the Indian than to the whites.

When we consider the color and structure of the hair the same fact becomes clear: light hair is of very rare occurrence among half-breeds; they have almost always the peculiar dark and coarse Indian hair; the colors of the eyes show also the same phenomenon. Therefore we may safely say that the half-breed resembles his Indian parent more than his white parent. Two reasons may be assigned for this fact. It may be that the dark hair and the wide face are more primitive characteristics of man than the narrow face and light eyes of the whites. Then we might say that the characteristics of the Indian are inherited with great strength because they are older. It must, however, also be considered that half-breeds are almost always descendants of Indian mothers and white fathers, and this may have had an influence, although there is no proof that children resemble their mothers more than their fathers. There is another peculiarity of the measurements of full-bloods and half-breeds which is worth remarking. If we count all the individuals who have a certain breadth of face, say 140, 141, 142 millimetres, etc., it is found that the measurement of 148 millimetres, which is approximately the average measurement, is the one which is most frequent. Among Indians it occurs 16 times among each 100 individuals. Among whites the most frequent measurement for the breadth of face is 138 millimetres, which also occurs about 16 times among each 100 individuals. The average measurement of the half-breeds is about 144 millimetres. This, however, occurs only about 10 times among each 100 individuals. If, on the other hand, we compare the frequency of occurrence of excessively wide faces and excessively narrow faces as compared to the average of each group, we see that they are more frequent among the mixed races than among the pure races. It appears, therefore, that the half-breeds differ among themselves more than do the pure races. But still another phenomenon is of importance. While the average measurement of 144 millimetres occurs only 10 times among each 100 individuals, those of 140 millimetres and 146 millimetres occur each 12 times among each 100 individuals. Thus it appears that the middle form is not as frequent as forms similar to those of the parental races. It may seem that the difference of frequency mentioned here is not very great. It appears, however, that this irregularity occurs in all tabulations of measurements of half-breeds: therefore, it must have some significance. I will call to mind here that the same conclusion has been drawn by Francis Galton from his investigations on heredity; that Dr. von Luschan has also arrived at the same conclusion when considering the forms of skulls of Asia Minor; and that finally the anthropometric investigations on the soldiers enlisted in Baden have given the same results. We may therefore say with a high degree of probability that in the human race the effect of intermixture is not to produce a middle type, but that there is a tendency to reproduce ancestral traits. I shall revert to this matter later on.

The study of the stature of half-breeds reveals biological laws of an entirely different character. The white element which enters into the composition of the half-breeds is very largely of French descent. As the American French are not a very tall race, we may safely say that the white element entering into the composition of the half-breeds is not very tall. Statistics of the stature of Indians show that they may conveniently be classified in three groups: Tall tribes, measuring more than 170 cm.; tribes of middle stature, measuring from 166 to 170 cm., and short tribes, measuring less than 166 cm. When we compare the statures of the tall tribes singly or collectively with those of the half-breeds of the same tribes we find that the latter are always taller than the full-blood Indians. This fact and the increased fertility among half-breed women would tend to show that the mixture of races results in an increased vitality. The difference in favor of the half-breed is so striking that no doubt can be entertained as to its actual existence. I believe the cause of this fact must be considered to be wholly in the effects of intermixture, as the social surroundings of the half-breeds and of the Indians are so much alike that they cannot cause the existing differences.

It is not surprising that the average stature of half-breeds belonging to the tribes of middle stature is still more in excess of that of the pure bloods, as in this case the average stature of the white race is probably greater than that of the Indians. The difference is finally still more sharply marked among the shortest tribes of Indians.

Very peculiar conditions are revealed by the comparison of the laws of growth of full-blood and half-breed children. We have seen that the adult full-blood is shorter than the adult half-breed. Curiously enough the reverse is the case among children. Until the tenth year of boys and until the ninth year of girls the full-blood child is taller than the half-breed child, while beginning at this period the full-blood child lags behind. Thus it is shown that the rate of growth among the half-breeds is throughout greater than among the Indians. It would be interesting to carry out this comparison and to include the whites, but the social conditions of the latter are so different that the comparison cannot be made advantageously. The phenomenon that the half-breed children are shorter than the Indian children of the same age is found not only among the tall tribes, but also among those of middle stature. I am unable to say if it also exists among tribes of shortest stature, as I have not a sufficient number of half-breed children from tribes of the shortest stature at my disposal. The comparison of rate of growth of boys and girls of the same ages is also instructive. It is a well-known fact that for about three years, from the twelfth to the fourteenth year, white girls are taller than white boys. This period of superiority of growth of the former is marked very indistinctly among the North American Indians. It is a little more clearly defined among half-breeds, but not as distinct as among whites.

The results regarding the growth of Indians are not quite satisfactory on account of the difficulty of obtaining information regarding the exact ages of Indian children. Only in comparatively few cases is the actual age of an Indian child known. In most cases it is estimated more or less accurately by the observer and by the help of persons who are acquainted with the Indian families. As this is true of both Indians and half-breeds the same conditions affect both series and make the results of the investigations comparable. One point, however, must be borne in mind. The individuals composing the young classes are not comparable to the individuals composing the older classes, because in the former there are many who die before reaching the age represented by the latter class. We do not know if the measurements of the body are not in some way connected with the probability of death before a certain age. This objection holds good of the results of all investigations referring to growth which are obtained according to what Hertel calls the general method.

I turn to the discussion of the distribution of stature in North America. On the whole, the North American Indians may be called a tall people. In studying the distribution of statures several difficulties are encountered. The tribes have changed their mode of life and their residence often. It is well known that stature depends to a great extent upon surroundings. Therefore the stature which we observe at present cannot be transferred, as it were, to the region inhabited by the tribe under consideration even a short time ago. One of the most striking examples is furnished by the Cherokees. As well known, the bulk of this people was transferred to Indian Territory a number of years ago, while a certain number remained among the mountains of North Carolina. At present the stature of the latter people is decidedly shorter than that of the Cherokee of the plains. Here we may have a good example of the effect of surroundings, but it may also be that the greater admixture of foreign blood among the people of the plains had the effect of raising their average stature. The same may be said of the Iroquois, Choctaws and Creeks, who are among the tallest tribes of North America. Looking at the continent as a whole, the tallest statures may be said to be found on the plains. The mountainous regions of the Southeast and of the West contain the people of the shortest stature. The whole Mississippi Valley is taken up by a very tall people. When we proceed further northward towards North Manitoba and the Saskatchewan, the statures become shorter. Great differences in size are also found north and south of the St. Lawrence River, the Montagnais on the north side being very much shorter than the Micmacs on the south side. The Athapascan tribes of New Mexico are of middle stature only. Scattered among them we find the extremely short Pueblos. The Shoshone, Sahaptin and Salish tribes, of the Rocky Mountains, are of middle stature. As we approach the Pacific coast the distribution of statures becomes more irregular. The most remarkable facts in this region are the increase of exceedingly short statures on the coast of Southern British Columbia, on Puget Sound, in Oregon and in Northern California. With the exception of the Eastern Eskimo these people are decidedly the shortest among all the North Americans. It is very instructive to notice that among these tribes of short statures taller people extend along Columbia River to the Pacific Ocean. As the mode of life of these people is identical, we must consider them the descendants of a taller people.

The distribution of statures in Northern California does not depend alone upon more or less favorable conditions. Thus the considerable difference between the tribes of Hoopa Valley and of Round Valley can hardly be explained by any other means than by assuming that the taller stature of the Hoopa is inherited. From a consideration of the distribution of statures in North America I turn to a discussion of the distribution of head forms. The principal proportion that has been considered in this connection is that between length and breadth of head, generally called the cephalic index. The study of the distribution of the cephalic index in North America is made exceedingly difficult by the prevailing custom of using hard cradle boards. This has the effect of flattening the occiput and thus produces short heads where without the use of the hard cradle board long heads would be found. Besides this the tissues covering the occiput are so extremely thick among the Indians that it is very difficult to discover a moderate degree of flattening. The apparent frequency of short heads among the Winnebagos, Osages and Apaches is entirely due to artificial, although unintentional flattening. The comparison of head forms must therefore be restricted to regions where no deformation is found.

The whole Mississippi Valley is inhabited by people whose cephalic index is approximately 79, that is to say, a mesocephalic people nearly approaching brachycephalism. Around the Great Lakes an increase in this index is found which disappears again further east. The Eastern Arctic coast is characterized by the prevalence of the long heads of the Eskimo. On the North Pacific coast and in isolated spots along the coast we find exceedingly short-headed types, mainly represented by members of the Athapascan stock and extending down the Rio Grande to the Gulf of Mexico. Scattered between these we find another long-headed type, which seems to be most frequent in Southern California, extending north-ward to the boundary of Oregon and probably occupying the Sonora and the pueblos of Queres and Santa Clara. It is not possible to consider these four types as closely related. Each of them is well characterized, and there seems no possibility of combining them with any of the other types. The best known among these types is that of the Eastern Eskimo. Besides the great length of head, they are remarkable for the great height of head and wide face combined with an exceedingly narrow nose. The Indian of the Mississippi Valley is characterized by a large head, meso-cephalic, with long occiput, wide and large face and wide nose. His color is light and assumes the so-called copper hue only after exposure to the sun and air. The brachycephalic type of the Pacific coast is at the same time short of stature, of light skin, with an enormously wide face and narrow nose, which is remarkably flat for an Indian nose. The Californian type is best known through a series of skulls from the Southern Californian islands. It is rather low, with narrow nose and moderately wide face.

The distribution of cephalic indices among a few tribes deserves par-ticular mention. The Micmacs of Nova Scotia show the peculiarity that very low indices occur much more frequently among them than among any other Indian tribe of the eastern part of North America. When we compare the distribution of indices among ancient skulls from New Eng-land with the series of the Micmacs, it becomes clear that both series are very much alike. As I stated before, indices as low as these are not found anywhere else except on the Arctic coast. I consider this conclusive evi-dence of an intermixture with Eskimo blood. It is well known that archæological facts tend to indicate that the Eskimo must have lived along the coast of New England at one time. It is therefore of interest to note that this conclusion is borne out by anthropological evidence. If we grant this point, the irregularity of distribution of the cephalic indices among the Micmacs may also be considered as an argument in favor of the theory advanced above, that the intermixture of tribes does not pro-duce a middle type.

Another series of peculiar interest is that of the Ojibway and of the Menominee. In comparing the variability of the cephalic index of the various tribes from the Rocky Mountains eastward to the Great Lakes, we notice that there is a constant increase from west eastward. This means that among the western tribes most individuals are similar to the average individual, while among the eastern tribes the differences among individuals composing the same tribe are greater. When plotting the cephalic indices of the Eastern Ojibways we find that the same index which is found farther west, namely 79, is the one most frequent, and that the index of 83 is also very frequent, while those indices lying between 79 and 83 are not as frequent. This peculiar fact exists in the series for men, women, boys and girls; therefore, there can be no doubt but that there must be some cause for it. By investigating more closely the distribution of indices among the Western Ojibway, it may be noticed that the index of 83 is still more frequent than it would be if the distribution followed the laws of chance. For this reason I conclude that there must have been among these tribes an intermixture of another tribe having an index of 83. It is difficult to decide who these people may have been, but it is certain that they must have been located around the Great Lakes. An investigation of the prehistoric skulls from this region shows that the index of 83 was very frequent at that time, so that we may be justified in the conclusion that we find here the surviving members of the prehistoric population of the region scattered among the present Indians.

I will call attention here to the peculiar fact, that in several series of measurements of the cephalic index we find two maxima of frequency and a minimum of frequency between the two maxima. As the series at our disposal do not exceed two or three hundred, except in a very few cases, these minima of frequency might be considered accidental. They occur, however, at the same point in the series of women, boys and girls. Therefore, we must conclude that their occurrence is not due to the limited number of observations, but to some actual reason. As mentioned before, this minimum is found markedly in the distribution of the cephalic index of the Eastern Ojibway. It is just as strongly emphasized among the Sioux; but in this case the curve of the men differs considerably from that of women, boys and girls, there being only one maximum in the first curve. We find only a certain irregularity indicating that there are more individuals corresponding to the secondary maximum among women and children than would be expected in a probability curve. I consider these irregularities of the curves of considerable importance, as they show conclusively that anthropometric curves are not always probability curves. This is a matter of great theoretical importance, and must be considered in the statistical investigations of the characteristics of certain races. Wherever we find curves which show two maxima or which are not probability curves, we have no right to consider the average as a type representing the people under consideration. In all such cases, a detailed discussion of their distribution is necessary to obtain satisfactory results. In order to give an instance: It is easily seen that if the biological law which I mentioned several times before in the present remarks is correct,—namely, that the offspring of a mixed race has a tendency to revert to the parental types and not to form middle types—then we must expect that in a mixed race, the composing elements of which show great differences, maxima of frequency of two certain forms must be found which resemble the forms of the ancestors and that one minimum is found representing the mixed form. If then we should interpret the observations in such a way as to say that the average is the typical form of this series we should draw a wrong inference. The average in such a case would have no meaning whatever, while the two maxima would indicate the types composing the mixed race.

If the two parental types do not differ very much, we should not find a distribution of forms showing two maxima, but the intermixture would have the result of producing a more variable race. We might, therefore, expect to find increased variability whenever two distinct types come into contact. There are several good examples of this kind. The Kootenay of the Rocky Mountains, who have intermarried with the Salish of British Columbia and Montana and with the Blackfeet of the Plains, are among the most variable of the North American tribes. I believe the cause of this phenomenon must be looked for in the fact that the Blackfeet are long-headed while the Salish are decidedly shortheaded. The Bella Coola of British Columbia occupy a similar position between the rather long-headed tribes of the coast and the shortheaded tribes of the interior. In this case, also, the effect is an increased variability. The same may be said of the tribes on the coast of Oregon.

The distribution of types upon the Pacific coast deserves particular discussion. Beginning at the Arctic coast we find the longheaded Eskimo. The difference between this group of Eskimo and those of Eastern Arctic America is very remarkable. Their heads are decidedly shorter. As they adjoin all along the coast shortheaded people, it seems that the decrease of their cephalic index is due to the intermixture of Indian blood. While on the eastern coast of America we find the characteristics of the Eskimo type to extend to a considerable distance southward, on the Pacific coast this type ends apparently near the peninsula of Alaska. The Aleutians, although speaking a language allied to the Eskimo, represent an exceedingly shortheaded type. This is true of the prehistoric skulls as well as of recent ones. Continuing down the coast, we find the Tlingit of South-eastern Alaska, who represent the same shortheaded type, which is evidently identical with the Athapascan type of the interior. At the southern boundary of Alaska the type suddenly changes, and we find a much shorter race, characterized by longer heads, exceedingly wide faces and narrow, high noses. This type embraces all the coast tribes of British Columbia as far south as the central portion of Vancouver Island, with the sole exception of Bella Coola, which we mentioned before. In the southern portion of Vancouver Island there is another sudden change of type. Here we find one of the shortest races of North America, which is characterized by the most excessive brachycephalism, very low faces and flat noses. I have not been able to find any type which resembles it anywhere else in North America. The peculiarities of this type extend southward beyond the Columbia River, but at the same time the type represented by the Bella Coola and Tlingit re-appears and occupies the greater part of the coast as far south as Northern California. At this place we find another sudden change of type, brachycephalism changes again to dolichocephalism, the stature decreases, and the faces become narrower. I am rather inclined to believe that the type of the coast of British Columbia is closely related to this longheaded California type. This belief is based principally upon the similarity in the formation of the face. Unfortunately I have no material at my disposal from Nevada and California which would serve to carry on this sketch of the distribution of types on the Pacific coast, but what I have said will be sufficient to show how many problems remain to be solved in this region.

It would be an interesting problem to compare the distribution of types among prehistoric American races with those found among the living Indians. For this purpose the measurement of skulls of a number of collections have been tabulated, but the results of these investigations are very unsatisfactory, as in prehistoric times the custom of using the hard cradle board and the custom of artificial deformation was more extensive than at present. An attempt has been made to distinguish among the prehistoric skulls from Tennessee those which have been deformed and those which have almost their natural shape. The result shows that the least deformed skulls have a very much lower cephalic index than the general average, and I presume that if the exclusion of deformed skulls were carried out rigidly we should find this prehistoric people approximately to have the same index as the present population of the Mississippi Valley. On account of the great deformations the prehistoric skulls have a variability —that is, differences among themselves, which are in excess of anything that is observed at the present time.

I have not been able to glean any important conclusions from the measurement of the face except the one fact, that the facial index becomes lower on the Pacific coast.

I hope the brief presentation of the results of our studies will show that Physical Anthropology offers a promising field of study, and that another of the important biological questions which await an answer—The History of the American Race—will appear in a new light when all the physical characteristics of the various types are taken into consideration.

SELECTION 29

Changes in
Immigrant Body Form

March 23, 1908.

Prof. J. W. Jenks,
Ithaca, N.Y.

Dear Sir,—

During the last ten years attention has been drawn to the change in composition of our immigrant population. Instead of the tall blond northwestern type of Europe, masses of people belonging to the east, central, and south European types are pouring into our country; and the question has justly been raised, whether this change of physical type will influence the marvellous power of amalgamation that our nation has exhibited for so long a time.

The importance of this question can hardly be overestimated, and the development of modern anthropological methods makes it perfectly feasible to give a definite answer to the problem that presents itself to us.

In accordance with our interviews of this month, I beg leave to submit the following plan of an investigation of this kind.

The essential question to be solved seems to be the selection that takes place by immigration, the modifications that develop in the children of the immigrants born abroad, and the further changes which take place in the children of the immigrants born in this country; and the effect of intermarriages in this country. It would be necessary to investigate all these problems, not only by a determination of the adult type, but also particularly by the development of the children of these various classes.

A comparison of the data collected in Europe and America shows that, on the whole, the American develops more rapidly and more favorably than the European, and it should be investigated whether the immigrants become subjected rapidly to the same influences which have determined the physique of the American.

Copies preserved in the Boas Papers, American Philosophical Society.

Furthermore, there are marked distinctions in type between the American and the European of the same nationality. We do not know with what energy the various types that come to our country perpetuate themselves, and whether the power of assimilation of the northwest European type which has brought it about that practically all the nationalities of northern and central Europe have been assimilated will have the same effect upon the more remotely related east European and south European types.

In short, the whole investigation should be directed towards an inquiry into

1. The assimilation or stability of type.
2. Changes in the characteristics of the development of the individual.

If an investigation of this kind were undertaken so as to cover all the divergent racial types that come to this country, the time and money required would be very considerable. But the essential point which will give an answer to the general question may also be determined by selecting the most important types of Europe. These are—

1. North Europeans.
2. East Europeans.
3. Central Europeans.
4. South Europeans (particularly Italians of the region south of Rome).

As a fifth group should be added either Russian Jews or the inhabitants of Asia Minor and Syria.

The method of investigation would have to be directed towards the solution of the two problems mentioned before.

The stability of assimilation of racial type would require the taking of three head-measurements and the taking of observations on color of hair and of eyes.

The characteristics of the rate of development of various races, and an investigation of their physical conditions, would require the taking of the following measurements: stature, weight, circumference of chest, strength of muscles. These would have to be combined with observations on the time of the eruption of the teeth and of the beginning of maturity, in order to gain a standard of the stage of physiological development at different ages. For older individuals, observations will have to be taken upon signs of beginning senility.

The discussion of these data would result in a determination of the following definite points:—

1. How does the immigrant type differ from the home type in regard to physical development and racial character?
2. Is the part of the immigrant population returning to Europe in any way different from that part of the population that stay here?
3. In how far and how much does the development of the children

growing up in the United States differ from the development of the immigrant race, and does it approach the characteristic development of the American child?

4. Is this tendency to assimilation in type of development increased and emphasized in the children of immigrants born in this country?

5. Do the descendants of immigrants differ from the home type, and do they tend to become similar to the American type? Do children of Americans and immigrants form a new type, differing from either, or do they tend to revert to either the American type or the foreign type, and to which? What is the fertility of the mixed marriages?

The problem involved in this last question is similar to the one relating to the mixture of the American Indian and of the white, in regard to which it has been found that in mixtures in which an equal amount of Indian blood and white blood prevails, the Indian influence is on the whole stronger than the white influence. The question to be solved would be whether the American influence exerts itself more markedly than the foreign influence or vice versa; that is to say, the question at issue is, how strong is the power of assimilation of the present American type when intermarrying with types of southern and eastern Europe?

The practical carrying-out of this plan of investigation would require the collection of data among the immigrants on Ellis Island, the collection of data among the outgoing emigrants, and studies among school children and among the resident population. I am inclined to think that all this work could be done to best advantage in New York City. I am reasonably certain that if the powers granted to the Immigration Commission, and with the opportunities that may be granted by the Board of Education of New York, and with the help of the Bureau of Municipal Research and of a number of settlements, this plan could be carried out.

It would be necessary to station a number of male and female observers on Ellis Island to collect data relating to the immigrants, and to make similar arrangements for observations on emigrants leaving this country. At the same time observations should be organized in public and parochial schools, selecting those in which the foreign population is more strongly represented. It seems likely that in these three cases the work may be so organized that data can be collected with a fair degree of rapidity. It would furthermore be necessary to collect data among a number of families of natives of foreign countries who have lived here for a considerable number of years. Since these would presumably require the consent of the individuals measured, the work would undoubtedly progress more slowly.

The important investigation of the change in rapidity and character of development of the individual would require observations on at least fifteen age groups. Considering, furthermore, the two sexes, the five distinct European types to be examined, and the four groups of people to be investigated—namely, immigrants, emigrants, immigrants after their arrival here, and descendants of immigrants,—we obtain in all 15 x 2 x 5 x 4, that is 600 classes. There ought to be at least 200 individuals of each class examined; so that the total investigation would require an examination of 120,000 individuals. Assuming that one observer can measure 40 individuals a day, 3000 days' work would be required. In order to obtain all the data within 150 working days, 20 observers would therefore be needed. This number must be taken with a certain amount of caution, because, in case a considerable amount of explanation should be necessary to get the subjects to consent to be measured, it might be easily necessary to have 30 observers instead of 20.

The work would also require a considerable amount of supervision, as well for the purpose of insuring accuracy of observations as for securing a proper discussion of the material after it has been assembled.

I think the following would be approximately the estimate for the conduct of the work, assuming that the Commission should want the report to be completed by March of next year.

Superintendent, whose duty it would also be to prepare the report	about	$2000
Assistant superintendent	about	1200
20 observers for 6 months @ $90 per month		10800
3 recorders for 6 months @ $75 per month		1350
6 computers for 8 months @ $75 per month		3600
1 stenographer for 4 months @ $90 per month		360
Instruments, etc.		200
TOTAL		$19510

I have assumed in this that the calculating-machines of the office can be used. As pointed out before, the principal uncertainty lies in the rate of work that may be accomplished by the observers, which is to a certain extent an unknown quantity, and will depend largely upon the powers of the Commission. I consider it safer to allow five thousand dollars leeway, in case the work should proceed more slowly than here estimated. Such leeway would make it possible to get larger numbers of residents— a feature of the work which deserves most careful attention.

I believe I can assure you that the practical results of this investigation will be important in so far as they will settle once for all the question whether the immigrants from southern Europe and from eastern Europe are and can be assimilated by our people.

Yours very truly,
[FRANZ BOAS]

BERLIN,
September 3rd, 1908.

PROFESSOR J. W. JENKS,
Commission of Immigration,
Cornell University,
Ithaca, N.Y.

DEAR SIR:—

I beg leave to submit a preliminary report on the results of our investigations carried on during the spring and summer.

In accordance with instructions received from you, we have endeavored to make a preliminary investigation, which would enable us to state definitely what lines of work will have to follow, and to ascertain whether the investigation will give results of importance.

The problem, which we had to ascertain, relates to the immigration of European types in America during the latter part of the 19th century.

The immigrants from Europe came almost exclusively from North Western Europe, and were of the same type as the earlier immigrants. Since that time a fundamental change has taken place, and large numbers of immigrants from Eastern and Southern Europe have come to the United States. Racially these represent at least three distinct elements: the Eastern Race, the Centre European Race, and the South European Race, all of which have physical characters quite different from the type of the North Western European. To these types must be added that of the East European Jews.

The question has justly been raised what the effect socially as well as physically will be of the large influx of these heterogeneous races.

Thus the question which we propose to solve is, whether the assimilation of the foreign types in America takes place, and what the results of the transplantation and intermixture will be.

In order to ascertain the feasibility of this inquiry, it was first of all necessary to investigate in how far the races, as found in the United States, are physically of the same type as those in Europe.

The development of the adult depends largely upon the conditions prevailing during the period of growth, and it seems therefore advisable in a preliminary inquiry to ascertain whether during the period of [growth] an acceleration or retardation, as compared to European conditions, is found, and whether the tendency of such acceleration or retardation will result in a change of type.

Our preliminary inquiries, which were carried on in High Schools of New York City on 14 [year] old boys, have given a positive answer to these questions, and the modifications of the types, which occur, are unexpectedly large.

I have classified the immigrants, according to the idea of the arrival in America, in such:

whose parents arrived before 1880,
those, whose parents arrived between 1880 & 1890, and
those, whose parents immigrated after 1890.

The uniform results for the various groups show that those children, whose parents immigrated earliest, are best developed in height, as well as in weight. Furthermore the rapidity of mental development proceeds in the same way; those whose parents have immigrated earliest, pass through school more rapidly.

Much to my surprise, an important change in type may also be noticed in the East European Jews, which race was particularly the subject of our inquiry; the race is very short headed, but there is a decided tendency to an increase in length of head among the later immigrants.

Although the data, which I briefly mention here, are not absolutely certain, since our inquiry is so far based on limited material only, it may be said with certainty that different changes of considerable magnitude are taking place, and the general directions of the changes may also be taken as certain. The detailed statistic, on which this conclusion was based, will follow in a separate report, which I expect to hand you about October 1st.

So far we have not been able to include in our preliminary work any schools, except the High Schools. It seems, however, indispensable to include in the investigations the poorer classes of children, such as may be found in the schools of Children's Aid Societies, and in the retarded classes of the Elementary Schools. This will presumably give quite different results, and it must be our next aim to compare the retarded classes with the accelerated classes, which we have studied in the High Schools.

While I have no reason to modify materially the plan, as outlined in my previous letters, there are certain points, which may be more definitely stated now. First of all, it seems, that any doubts, which may have been in our minds, before the beginning of the actual investigations, in regard to the results, are dispelled now.

The change that we have observed, is in the direction of a decided assimilation of the foreign types, and it seems likely that we may find that the selected classes represent those individuals, who live in favorable social surroundings, and who are able to give their children a good education, [and who] become gradually similar to the American type, at least in those respects that have been made the subject of our inquiry. This result must not be hastily generalized, and it remains to be seen what the changes are in the development among those classes, who are in less favorable conditions.

Thus the whole inquiry must be directed toward the following points:—

1) What is the development of the classes situated most favorably?
2) What is the development of the medium classes?
3) What is the development of the poorest class?
4) What percentage of the immigrants are liable to pass into the better situated class?

This last inquiry can presumably be answered from the other line of the work that your commission has undertaken, so that it must be considered our principal task to give a definite answer to the three first questions, as here formulated.

It seems highly desirable that the work should be continued without interruption, and the principal task at the present time for us is the investigation in the Elementary Schools, and in the schools of Children's Aid Societies. In October and November I should like to employ at least two observers in Elementary Schools for about six weeks each, & two observers in schools of Children's Aid Societies for about four weeks each, at an average expense of about $25,—a week. This would be an expenditure for the collection of data of $500.—

We have also proceeded, besides the collection of data, with correspondence and discussions bearing upon the organisation of the complete work.

As outlined in my last letters of November last, Doctor C. Ward Crampton has carried on a correspondence with such organisations, as have been engaged in investigations, the results of which may be utilized for our purposes. These are particularly:—

1) Public Schools.
2) Private Schools.
3) Board of Health (School children, vital statistic, labor certificates).
4) State Department of Labor.
5) Settlements.
6) Young Men's Christian Association.
7) Young Women's Christian Association.
8) Young Men's Hebrew Association.
9) Young Women's Hebrew Association.
10) Asylums.
11) Reformatories.
12) Day Nurseries.
13) Hospitals.
14) Other institutions caring for children.

Dr. Crampton's full report on this subject will be submitted about October 1st.

I have made inquiries during the summer relating to the possibility of obtaining the necessary comparative material from South Italy, Eastern Europe and Central Europe. I find that the only comparative material, which could be used, has been collected by the institution of Dental Hygiene in Dresden, under the able direction of Dr. C. Roese. I have had a number of consultations with Dr. Roese in regard to the subject, and I find that it would be best to utilize the impression gained in his institution for the purpose of our inquiry.

The extension of the work would be best carried out in Gallicia, and in the neighborhood of Naples.

In Gallicia I have found Dr. V. Schreiber, a gentleman of considerable experience in anthropological work, but it will be necessary to collect entirely new data. The same conditions prevail in Southern Italy. In regard with this region, I have conferred with Dr. Ridolfo Livi, Chief of the Sanitary Department of the Italian Army, who has written extensively about the anthropology of Italy. In his opinion it will be easy to carry out our work in cooperation with the Italian Immigration Commission in Rome. The principal difficulty in Italy would be the securing of an investigator, who could take sufficiently accurate observations on the teeth of the children, a subject, which is quite important for our work.

The preliminary estimate of the expense of the necessary parallel investigations in Europe is between $5000 and 6000 including all expenses for assistance and transportation, excluding the statistical reduction of the observations. This would include the obtaining of comparative material from Southern Germany, the region of Lemberg, Gallicia, and from Naples, Italy; the observations to be strictly parallel to those taken in America. In this work would be included inquiries at the stations, maintained by the large steamship companies, at which intending immigrants are examined before they are allowed to embark.

I have also paid special attention to the question of obtaining the necessary standards of colors for investigations for the hair and for the eyes, a subject, which requires particular care, on account of the vagueness of descriptive terms, and on account of the necessity of taking into consideration any changes in this important physical feature.

While the standards for colors of eyes are available, it has proved very difficult to secure adequate standards of hair colors, but I have finally succeeded in securing sets from Messrs. C. Bergmann in Laupheim, who very generously offered to furnish samples at cost.

The examination of measuring instruments has shown that the only instruments, which will answer our purposes, are those made at Zurich, Switzerland, and it will be necessary to order these speedily, as a sufficient number of sets will take at least two months.

Based on the present conditions of the work, I recommend that the investigations be continued after the 1st of October, and that an appropriation of $2000 be made, to be available during the period from October

1st to December 31st of the current year, to cover the necessary expenses of the work, as here outlined. The allotment of this appropriation to be as follows:—

For direction of the work, F. Boas	$ 750
Doctor Crampton	$ 375
For observers and incidentals	$ 875
	$2000

The sooner it can be decided where the whole work is to be undertaken, the more economically can the whole be planned out.

Respectfully submitted,
[FRANZ BOAS]

March 11, 1909.

PROF. J. W. JENKS,
U. S. Immigration Commission,
Washington, D.C.

DEAR SIR,—

Following is a brief report of the anthropological work in my charge.

In the spring of last year the Commission made an appropriation of $1000 for preliminary work intended to ascertain the feasibility of conducting successfully anthropological investigations, and to test whether results showing important points could be obtained. With this appropriation in hand, measurements were collected in three of the high schools of this city, and relating to East European Jews. The essential points which appear from this investigation were:—

1. Descendants from the immigrants are better developed and developed earlier than the immigrants themselves.

2. The effect of American surroundings is the stronger, the more time has elapsed since the immigration of the parents before the birth of the child in this country.

3. The changes in the second generation are not confined to changes in the rapidity of development, but we find also a change in type indicating apparently an approach to the American type.

All these results were so definite and promising, that the Commission made an additional appropriation of $1000 in October for the purpose of carrying on the work. With this money in hand, the investigation was extended to grammar schools for the purpose of investigating the effect of social environments upon the development of children here. The results of this inquiry showed that—

1. The children of East European Jews born in America and attending grammar schools are better developed than foreign-born children of the same race.

2. The children attending high school are much better developed physically than the children attending public school.

3. This difference is partly due to an acceleration in development, partly to a general better development.

4. The conclusion in regard to change in type was corroborated.

The investigation of Italian children showed a most marked contrast to the children of East European Jews, in so far as the American-born children who have grown up in the congested districts of New York are much more unfavorably developed than children born abroad. The composition of the Italian types in the schools proved to be so complex that no safe inference could be drawn in regard to the stability of type.

The investigation conducted up to this point in the schools has proved that in order to obtain conclusive results, families, including parents and children, had to be measured, and a plan for further investigations was submitted to the Commission in November, which led to an appropriation of $5000 for the further conduct of the work. This made it possible to appoint two investigators to carry on the proposed work in Italian and in East European Jewish families. In March, authority was given to employ three additional investigators.

The experience heretofore gained shows that the expense of collecting data has been about fifty cents for each card, including the considerable amount of tentative sorting, classifying, and calculating. With the larger number of observers now allowed by the Commission, the expense of collection and supervision will be reduced to thirty cents per card. This includes the current supervision of tabulation and other incidental expenses. The actual expense of collection per card will be reduced approximately to eighteen cents.

An estimate of the amount of material needed for the two types so far selected suggests that by approximately the 1st of July enough material may have accumulated to enable us to draw unassailable conclusions in regard to the influence of American environment upon these two types. It is possible, however, that the difference of type of the region of Naples and Sorrento as compared to Calabria and Sicily may make it necessary to obtain more material than now estimated for Southern Italy. After this, I estimate that the reduction of the observations will take about six months' time; but this estimate is necessarily uncertain. According to this estimate, the expenditure required to finish up what has been undertaken, assuming that the clerical work is paid for out of the general office expenses, not out of the appropriation for anthropological research, will be $4200. According to my understanding, the total amount allowed by the Commission was $7000. This estimate would leave about $200 for unforeseen expenses. According to Mr. Crane's understanding, the total amount appropriated was only $6000. If this is the case, the work of collecting would have to be stopped sooner than here estimated.

It seems to my mind that the results so far obtained are so fundamental and far-reaching, that I feel justified in recommending that the Commission appropriate a sufficient amount of money for this work, so that it could be carried through so far as to show definitely what becomes physically of the immigrants into our country. This would necessitate particularly the inclusion of at least one more racial type and of the third generation of Americans in the investigation. According to the experience gained during the last two months, it would seem to me that an additional appropriation of $5000 might enable us to carry through the work, if not quite on the scale originally suggested, still in a manner which will give results more important than those which we were originally justified in anticipating. It is very important that whatever action is taken should be taken now, because the assistance of the schools, which is essential, cannot be had after June; and if the results of the investigation are to be presented to Congress on the 1st of March of next year, the collection of the material should be completed not later than the 1st of October.

Respectfully submitted.

[Franz Boas]

Dec. 31, 1909.

Professor J. W. Jenks,
    Cornell University,
        Ithaca, N.Y.

My dear Professor Jenks.—

The anthropological investigation conducted under the auspices of the Immigration Commission has resulted in a number of conclusions that seem to be of great practical importance. Some of these conclusions were entirely unforeseen at the time when we started the investigation.

The few data that we have observed have shown conclusively that the change of environment from Europe to America has a decided effect on the bodily form of the immigrants, and that the same surroundings are not equally favorable to different European types. Thus we have found that the Hebrews in New York, notwithstanding unfavorable surroundings, show a more favorable development than in Europe; while the Sicilians, a type small and diminutive at home, lose in physical vigor in New York City. At the same time other physical traits of these two types show a decided tendency to approach an intermediate type.

Two important conclusions may be drawn from our observations: the one that the fundamental change in anatomical traits must be accompanied by corresponding changes in mental make-up; and the preliminary inference seems justifiable that there may be an approximation of distinct types immigrating into America. Quite recently I have had an opportunity to examine extended observations on college students measured in

Ann Arbor, which gave the same result to which I have referred on previous occasions: namely, a greater uniformity of type among Americans than among the European stocks from which they are descended. This corroborates our previous view of the probability of an assimilation of types in each separate American environment.

It seems to my mind that if this point can be proved by more extended investigations and by modified methods in different American surroundings, our fundamental attitude towards immigration must be decided by it. It seems to me perfectly evident that a continuation of this investigation will decide whether the descendants of distinct types of European immigrants become alike, no matter where they come from. If this should be the case, all fear of an unfavorable influence of South European immigration upon the body of our people should be dismissed. I do not think that the investigations, so far as carried on at present, allow us to generalize in regard to this point, although all the evidence that we have points in this direction.

The second point, and one of more immediate practical importance, is the study of the influence of environment upon each racial type. We can now say with great certainty to the Sicilians that they should stay away from New York, because the hygienic influences are bad. If we could supplement this by the positive suggestion to go to one or the other part of the country because it is beneficial to that type, a definite direction could be given to the activities of societies interested in the welfare of immigrants, and presumably strong pressure could be brought to bear upon the people themselves.

Perhaps even more important than these two problems is the problem of mixture of distinct types—a question which we have not taken up at all; and here it is particularly the question of the mixture between negro and white that should receive particular attention. With the large immigration from southern Europe, the time is not distant when the problem of racial intermixture between these two types will become acute; and we ought to know what social and hygienic significance the recent laws of Southern States, forbidding intermarriages between the two races, will have. Broadly speaking, the question before us is that of whether it is better for us to keep an industrially and socially inferior large black population, or whether we should fare better by encouraging the gradual process of lightening up this large body of people by the influx of white blood. Expressing the same question in still other words, we might say the question before us is whether conditions can be so regulated that without a proportionate increase in the black population it will be of advantage to accelerate the infusion of white blood among them.

The whole investigation is a large one, and our former experience in the conduct of this work shows that to push the investigation forward economically and effectively, an annual outlay of approximately $18,000 would be required, covering both field-work and office-work (see enclosure). The one point most urgently needed at the present time to check our results is the investigation of the unselected European groups and of the immigrants immediately before they leave the shores of Europe, and I should like to be able to add to the work already undertaken this important inquiry.

If I were to make a plan for this investigation covering a period of about three years, I should say that I should devote the present year to the investigation of conditions in Europe; the next year, to an investigation parallel to the one of 1909, [but] in rural communities; and the third year, to investigations on mixed types. When this work has been done, a very important step forward in our knowledge of the biological conditions of immigration will have been made.

Yours very sincerely,

[Franz Boas]

 S E L E C T I O N   3 0

Instability of Human Types

When we try to judge the ability of races of man, we make the silent assumption that ability is something permanent and stationary, that it depends upon heredity, and that, as compared to it, environmental, modifying influences are, comparatively speaking, of slight importance. While in a comparative study of the physical characteristics of races that are as distinct as the white and the negro, or the negro and the Mongol, this assumption might be accepted as a basis for further studies, its validity is not so clear in a comparison of the mental characteristics of branches of the same race. When, for instance, it is claimed that certain types of Europe show better mental endowment than other types of Europe, the assumption is made that these types are stable, and cannot undergo far-reaching differences when placed in a new social or geographical environment.

It would seem, therefore, that a study of the stability of race-types has

Papers on Interracial Problems Communicated to the First Universal Races Congress Held at the University of London, July 26–29, 1911, ed. Gustav Spiller (Boston: Ginn and Co., 1912), pp. 99–103.

not only a fundamental biological importance, but that it will also determine our views of the relative mental endowment of different types of man.

A theoretical investigation of this problem will show that the assumption of an absolute stability of human types is not plausible. Observations on growth have shown that the amount of growth of the whole body depends upon more or less favourable conditions which prevail during the period of development. Unfavourable conditions retard growth; exceptionally favourable conditions accelerate it. A more detailed study of the phenomena of growth has shown that the development of different parts of the body does not proceed by any means at the same rate at a given period. Thus at the time of birth the bulk of the body and stature are very small, and increase with great rapidity until about the fourteenth year in girls, and the sixteenth year in boys. On the other hand, the size of the head increases rapidly only for one or two years; and from this time on the increment is, comparatively speaking, slight. Similar conditions prevail in regard to the growth of the face, which grows rapidly for a few years only, and later on increases, comparatively speaking, slowly. The amount of water contained in the brain also changes with a fair amount of rapidity during the early years of life, and remains about the same later on. It follows from this observation that if an individual is retarded by unfavourable conditions after a certain organ has obtained nearly its full development, while other organs are still in the process of rapid evolution, the former cannot be much influenced, while the latter may bear evidence of the unfavourable conditions which were controlling during a certain period of life. This must necessarily have the result that the proportions of the body of the adult will depend upon the general conditions of life prevailing during youth, and the effects of these conditions will be most noticeable in those organs which have the longest period of development.

It is a well-known fact that the central nervous system continues to develop in structure longer perhaps than any other part of the body, and it may therefore be inferred that it will be apt to show the most far-reaching influences of environment.

It follows from this consideration that social and geographical environment must have an influence upon the form of the body of the adult, and upon the development of his central nervous system.

This theoretical consideration is borne out by observation. The investigations of Bolk have shown clearly that an increase in stature has occurred in Europe during the last decades, due evidently to a change of environment; and the numerous investigations which have been made on the proportions of the body of the well-to-do and of the poor, of able students and poor students—all show characteristic differences, which may be explained in great part as effects of the retardation and acceleration to which we have referred.

It would seem, however, that besides the influences of more or less favourable environment which affect the form of the body during the period of growth, a number of other causes may modify the form of the body. Professor Ridgeway goes so far as to think that the stability of human types in definite areas and for long periods is an expression, not of the influence of heredity, but of the influence of environment; and that, on the other hand, the modifications of the human form which are found in the Mediterranean area, in Central Europe, and in North-western Europe, are due to the differences of climate, soil, and natural products. It does not seem to me that adequate proof can be given for modifications of the human form as far-reaching as those claimed by Professor Ridgeway, although we must grant the possibility of such influences. We have, however, good evidence which shows that the various European types undergo certain changes in a new environment. The observations on which this conclusion is based were made by me on emigrants from various European countries who live in the city of New York, and on their descendants.

The investigation of a large number of families has shown that every single measurement that has been studied has one value among individuals born in Europe, another one among individuals of the same families born in America. Thus, among the East European Jews the head of the European-born is shorter than the head of the American-born. It is wider among the European-born than it is among the American-born. At the same time the American-born is taller. As a result of the increase in the growth of head, and decrease of the width of head, the length-breadth index is considerably less than the corresponding index in the European-born. All these differences seem to increase with the time elapsed between the emigration of the parents and the birth of the child, and are much more marked in the second generation of American-born individuals.

Among the long-headed Sicilians similar observations have been made, but the changes are in a different direction. The stature does not change much; if anything, it is shorter among the American-born than among the European-born. The head is shorter among the American-born, and at the same time wider, than among the European-born. Thus a certain approach of the two distinct types may be observed.

It would of course be saying too much to claim that this approach expresses a tendency of diverse European types to assume the same form in America. Our studies prove only a modification of the type; but we are not able to determine what the ultimate amount of these modifications will be, and whether there is any real tendency of modifying diverse types in such a way that one particular American type should develop, rather than a limited modification of each particular European type.

The people of Bohemia and Hungary show also the effect of the changed environment. Among them both width of head and length of head decrease. The face becomes much narrower, the stature taller.

It is most remarkable that the change in head-form of American-born individuals occurs almost immediately after the arrival of their parents in America. A comparison of individuals born in Europe with those born in America shows that the change of head-form is almost abrupt at the time of immigration. The child born abroad, even if it is less than one year old at the time of arrival, has the head-form of the European-born. The child born in America, even if born only a few months after the arrival of the parents, has the head-form of the American-born. The failure of American environment to influence the foreign-born might be expected, because the total change of the head-index from early youth to adult life is very small. On the other hand, those measurements of the body which continue to change during the period of growth show a marked influence of American environment upon European-born individuals who arrive in America as young children. Thus the stature of European-born individuals increases the more the younger they were at the time of their arrival in America. The width of the faces decreases the more the younger the child that came to America.

These observations are of importance, because it might be claimed that the changes in head-form develop because the mechanical treatment of children in America differs from their treatment in Europe. The European child is swaddled, while the American child is allowed to lie free in the cradle. The change in the face diameters and in stature show, however, that such mechanical considerations alone cannot explain the changes that actually take place.

The results obtained by a rough comparison of European-born and American-born have been corroborated by a direct comparison of European-born parents and their own American-born children, and also by a comparison of the European immigrants who came to America in one particular year, and of their descendants born in America. In all these cases the same types of differences were found.

These observations seem to indicate a decided plasticity of human types; but I wish to repeat that the limits of this plasticity are not known to us. It follows, however, directly, that if the bodily form undergoes far-reaching changes under a new environment, concomitant changes of the mind may be expected. The same reasons which led us to the conclusion that more or less favourable conditions during the period of growth will have the greater influence the longer the period of development of a particular part of the body, make it plausible that a change of environment will influence those parts of the body most thoroughly which have the longest period of growth and development. I believe, therefore, that the American observations compel us to assume that the mental make-up of a certain type of man may be considerably influenced by his social and geographical environment. It is, of course, exceedingly difficult to give an actual proof of this conclusion by observation, because we know that the mental manifestations depend to a great extent upon the social group in which each individual grows up; but it is evident that the burden of proof is shifted upon those who claim absolute stability of mental characteristics of the same type under all possible conditions under which it may be found.

It may be pointed out here that the change of type which has been observed in America is in a way analogous to the difference of type that has been observed in Europe in a comparison between the urban population and the rural population. In all those cases in which thorough investigations have been made in regard to this problem, a difference in type has been found. The interpretation given in this phenomenon is, however, entirely different from the one attempted here. One group of observers, particularly Ridolfo Livi, believe that the type found in urban communities is largely due to the greater mixture of local types found in cities when compared to the open country. Others, notably Otto Ammon and Röse, believe that we have here evidence of natural selection, and that the better type survives. It seems to my mind that the latter theory cannot be substantiated, but that both mixture and change of type are sufficient to explain what is taking place in the transition from rural life to urban life.

It will naturally be asked, what produces changes in human types? Can these changes be so directed as to bring about an improvement of the race? I do not believe that these questions can be answered in the present state of our knowledge. The structural changes which must necessarily accompany the modifications of gross form are entirely unknown, and the physiological functions which are affected by the new environment cannot even be surmised. It seems, therefore, a vain endeavour to give a satisfactory explanation of the phenomenon at the present time. The investigation should be extended over numerous types, and carried on in different climates and different social environments, before we can hope to understand the correlation between bodily form and function and outward influences. The old idea of absolute stability of human types must, however, evidently be given up, and with it the belief of the hereditary superiority of certain types over others.

 *PART VII*

RACIAL CAPACITY
AND CULTURAL
DETERMINISM

Boas is remembered today above all else as a critic of racism, and this is quite appropriate. But the context and character of this contribution—the extent to which his early argument was conditioned by the racist milieu in which he wrote, the way in which it drew together the various aspects of his anthropological thought, and the conception of culture implicit in his critique of racial determinism—are somewhat less well understood. This may be in part because the only available version of *The Mind of Primitive Man* is a reprint of the second edition (Boas 1938; cf. 1911c). The revisions Boas made after twenty-five years no doubt reflected the development of his thinking in the interim; but they also helped to obscure large changes in intellectual milieu. Furthermore, they did not help particularly to clarify his contribution to the anthropological concept of culture, which by that time had undergone considerable elaboration in the work of other anthropologists. The present selections are an attempt to recapture both context and contribution —although limits of space make it impossible fully to explicate either (cf. Stocking 1968a, pp. 198–233; Gossett 1963; Haller 1971).

The first piece (no. 31) was written in July 1894, at a critical point in Boas' career. His job at the Field Museum supervising the transfer of ethnological material from the Chicago Fair had just ended in bitterness; and the alternative possibility of a professorship at the University of Chicago had not been realized, at least in part because President Harper felt Boas did not "take direction" well. Boas' employment crisis was not to be resolved for eighteen months, and he was already feeling a severe financial pinch. On the other hand, the first eight years of his work in this country had just won him recognition as the presiding officer of what was then the only national organization in his profession—Section H of the American Association for the Advancement of Science—an honor that pleased Boas all the more because some still thought of him as a "foreigner." As topic for the customary annual address, Boas chose "Human Faculty as Determined by Race."

Much of the argument of *The Mind of Primitive Man* is contained here (and indeed, considerable portions of this essay were later incorporated into the latter volume). There is the same emphasis on the historical conditions of diffusion as a basis for rejecting traditional assumptions about racial achievement; on the overlapping of variations that made it impossible to draw sharp lines between racial groups; on the functional, environmental factors affecting presumably racial characters; and on the explanation of apparent racial mental differences in terms of differences in motivation. On the other hand, one is struck by the limits of Boas' critique in 1894. He expected that some mental differences between races would be found to exist; he accepted the inference his friend, the neurologist Henry Donaldson, made from apparent differences in "the capacity for education" to the cessation of brain growth in the "lower races"; and he was rather naïvely optimistic about the possibilities of psychological testing in the public schools. In short, he had not achieved a fully developed notion of the cultural determination of behavior as an alternative to the prevailing racial determinism. As I have argued elsewhere, this is reflected in his usage of the terms "culture" and "civilization," which changed in subtle ways between 1894 and 1911 (Stocking 1968a, p. 202).

Boas' thinking on cultural determinism was developed in three articles published in the first decade of this century, the last of which is reprinted here (no. 32 [cf. Boas 1901, 1904a]). It was given as a lecture in 1909 at the celebration of the twentieth anniversary of the founding of Clark University—an occasion attended by a number of international luminaries in the behavioral sciences, including Sigmund Freud. Drawing rather heavily on ideas developed in the course of his studies of language, Boas here offered a much more sophisticated view of the cultural determination of behavior, in which the "classification of concepts, the types of association, and the resistance to change of automatic acts" characteristic of different social groups were seen as developing unconsciously, only to be given rationalistic "secondary explanations" when they were somehow called into question. Boas developed this argument to explain the mental differences between primitive and civilized men, and he did not here speak specifically of different "cultures" determining different forms of behavior. But the clear implication was that the behavior of human beings everywhere, primitive or civilized, was determined, in ways that never came fully to their consciousness, by the particular cultural tradition in which they experienced their "early bringing up." Boas always remained critical of Freudian theory, and his usage of "unconscious" was a far cry from the Freudian unconscious, but there is still a sense in which it was appropriate that they shared the same platform in 1909. In a way that has not always been adequately appreciated, Boas, too, was a major contributor to the intellectual revolution that destroyed the rationalistic Victorian conception of man.

 SELECTION 31

Human Faculty
as Determined by Race

Proud of his wonderful achievements, civilized man looks down upon the humbler members of mankind. He has conquered the forces of nature and compelled them to serve him. He has transformed inhospitable forests into fertile fields. The mountain fastnesses are yielding their treasures to his demands. The fierce animals which are obstructing his progress are being exterminated, while others which are useful to him are made to increase a thousand fold. The waves of the ocean carry him from land to land and towering mountain ranges set him no bounds. His genius has moulded inert matter into powerful machines which wait a touch of his hand to serve his manifold demands.

What wonder when he pities a people that has not succeeded in subduing nature; who labor to eke a meagre existence out of the products of the wilderness; who hear with trembling the roar of the wild animals and see the products of their toils destroyed by them; who remain restricted by ocean, river or mountains; who strive to obtain the necessities of life with the help of few and simple instruments.

Such is the contrast that presents itself to the observer. What wonder if civilized man considers himself a being of higher order as compared to

Address as Vice-President of Section H before the Section of Anthropology of the American Association for the Advancement of Science at the Brooklyn Meeting, August 1894; as published in the Association's *Proceedings* 43 (1894): 301–327; later reworked and incorporated in Boas 1911c.

primitive man; if it is claimed that the white race represents a higher type than all others.

When we analyze this assumption, it will soon be found that the superiority of the civilization of the white race alone is not a sufficient basis for this inference. As the civilization is higher, we assume that the aptitude for civilization is also higher; and as the aptitude for civilization presumably depends upon the perfection of the mechanism of body and mind, the inference is drawn that the white race represents the highest type of perfection. In this conclusion, which is reached through a comparison of the social status of civilized man and of primitive man, the achievement and the aptitude for an achievement have been confounded. Furthermore, as the white race is the civilized race, every deviation from the white type is considered a characteristic feature of a lower type. That these two errors underlie our judgments of races can be easily shown by the fact that, other conditions being equal, a race is always described as the lower the more fundamentally it differs from the white race. This becomes clearest by the tendency on the part of many anthropologists to look for anatomical peculiarities of primitive man which would characterize him as a being of lower order, and also by the endeavors of recent writers to prove that there exist hardly any anatomical features of the so-called lowest races which would stamp them as lower types of organisms. Both these facts show that the idea dwells in the minds of investigators that we should expect to find in the white race the highest type of man.

In judging social distinctions the same error is frequently committed. As the mental development of the white race is the highest, it is also supposed to have the highest aptitude in this direction, and therefore its mind is supposed to have the most subtle organization. As the ultimate psychical causes are not so apparent as anatomical characters, the judgment of the mental status of a people is generally guided by the difference between its social status and our own; the greater the difference between their intellectual, emotional and moral processes and those which are found in our civilization the harsher the judgment on the people. It is only when a Tacitus finds the virtues of past stages of the culture of his own people among foreign tribes, that their example is held up to the gaze of his fellow-citizens, who probably had a pitying smile for the dreamer who clung to the ideas of a time which they had left far behind.

It might be objected that although achievement is not necessarily a measure of aptitude, it seems admissible to judge the one by the other. Have not most races had the same chances for development? Why, then, did the white race alone develop a civilization which is sweeping the whole world and compared to which all other civilizations appear as feeble beginnings cut short in early childhood, or arrested and petrified in an early stage of development? Is it not, to say the least, probable that the race which attained the highest stage of civilization was the most gifted one, and that those races which remained at the bottom of the scale were not capable of rising to higher levels?

It seems desirable to enter into these questions somewhat fully. Let our mind go back a few thousand years until it reaches the time when the civilizations of eastern and of western Asia were in their infancy. As time passed on, these civilizations were transferred from one people to another, some of those who had represented the highest type of culture sinking back into obscurity, while others took their places. During the dawn of history we see civilization clinging to certain districts, in which it is taken up now by one people, now by the other. In the numerous conflicts of these times the more civilized people were often vanquished. The conqueror, however, learned the arts of life from the conquered and carried on the work of civilization. Thus the centres of civilization were shifting to and fro over a limited area and progress was slow and often interrupted. At the same period the ancestors of the races, who are now among the most highly civilized, were in no way superior to primitive man as we find him now in regions that have not come into contact with modern civilization.

Was the culture attained by the ancient civilized people of such character as to allow us to claim for them a genius superior to that of any other race? First of all, we must bear in mind that none of these civilizations was the product of the genius of a single people. Ideas and inventions were carried from one to the other; and, although intercommunication was slow, each people which participated in the ancient civilization added to the culture of the others. Proofs without number have been forthcoming which show that ideas have been disseminated as long as people have come into contact with each other and that neither race nor language nor distance limits their diffusion. As all have worked together in the development of the ancient civilizations, we must bow to the genius of all, whatever race they may represent: Hamitic, Semitic, Aryan or Mongol.

We may now ask, Did no other races develop a culture of equal value? It would seem that the civilizations of ancient Peru and of Central America may well be compared with the ancient civilization of the Old World. In both we find a high stage of political organization; we find division of labor and an elaborate ecclesiastical organization. Great architectural works were undertaken requiring the coöperation of many individuals. Animals and plants were domesticated and the art of writing had been invented. The inventions and knowledge of the peoples of the Old World seem to have been somewhat more numerous and extended than those of the races of the New World, but there can be no doubt that the general status of their culture was nearly equally high. This will suffice for our consideration and I will not enter upon the fact that a greater variety of peoples had contributed to the progress of civilization in the Old World, and that nature had endowed their homes more abundantly with useful animals and plants than the homes of the peoples of the New World.

What then is the difference between the civilization of the Old World and that of the New World? It is only a difference in time. The one reached a certain stage three thousand or four thousand years sooner than the other. This difference in period does not justify us to assume that the race which developed more slowly was less gifted. Certainly the difference of a few thousand years is insignificant as compared to the age of the human race. The time required to develop the existing races is entirely a matter of conjecture, but we may be sure that it was long. We also know that man existed in the eastern and western hemispheres at a time which can be measured by geological standards only; and, if we assume arbitrarily no more than 20,000 years as the age of man, what would it mean that one group of mankind reached the same stage at the age of 20,000 years which was reached by the other at the age of 24,000 years? Would not the life history of the people and the vicissitudes of its history be fully sufficient to explain a delay of this character, without necessitating us to assume a difference in their aptitude to social development?

When admiring the high achievements of the white race we also ought to bear in mind that civilization originated among few of its members and by the help of other races, and that there is no evidence that the cognate tribes which have all developed under the influence of this ancient civilization would not, without its help, have required a much longer time to reach the high level which they now occupy.

But why did these tribes so easily assimilate the culture that was offered them, while at present we see primitive people dwindle away and become degraded before the approach of civilization, instead of being elevated by it? Is not this a proof of a higher organization of the inhabitants of Europe? I believe the reasons for this fact are not far to seek and do not necessarily lie in a greater ability of the races of Europe and Asia. First of all, these people were alike in appearance to civilized man of their times. Therefore the fundamental difficulty for the rise of primitive people, namely, that an individual which has risen to the level of the higher civilization is still looked upon as belonging to an inferior race, did not prevail. Thus it was possible that, in the colonies of ancient times, society could grow by accretion from among the more primitive people. Furthermore, the devastating influences of diseases which nowadays begin to ravage the inhabitants of territories newly opened to the whites were not so strong on account of the permanent contiguity of the people of the Old World who were always in contact with each other and therefore subject to the same influences. The invasion of America and Polynesia, on the other hand, was accompanied by the introduction of new diseases among the natives of these countries. The suffering and devastation wrought by epidemics which followed the discovery are too well known to be described in full.

In addition to this it may be said that the contrast between the culture represented by the modern white and that of primitive man is far more fundamental than that between the ancients and the people with whom they come in contact. Particularly, the methods of manufacture have developed so enormously that the industries of the primitive people of our times are exterminated by the cheapness and large quantity of the products imported by the white trader; because primitive man is unable to compete with the power of production of the machines of the whites, while in olden times the superior hand product rivalled with a hand product of a lower type. It must also be considered that in several regions, particularly in America and in parts of Siberia, the primitive tribes are swamped by the numbers of the immigrating race which is crowding them so rapidly out of their old haunts that no time for gradual assimilation is given. In olden times there was certainly no such immense inequality in numbers, as we observe in many regions nowadays.

We conclude, therefore, that the conditions for assimilation in ancient Europe were much more favorable than in those countries, where in our times primitive people come into contact with civilization. Therefore we do not need to assume that the ancient Europeans were more gifted than other races which have not become exposed to the influences of civilization until recent times.

This conclusion may be corroborated by other facts. In the middle ages, the civilization of the Arabs had reached a stage which was undoubtedly superior to that of many European nations of that period. Both civilizations had sprung largely from the same sources and must be considered branches of one tree. The Arabs who were the carriers of civilization were by no means members of the same race as the Europeans, but nobody will dispute their high merits. It is of interest to see in what manner they influenced the negro races of the Soudan. At an early time, principally between the second half of the eighth century and the eleventh century of our era, the Soudan was invaded by Hamitic tribes and Mohammedanism was spreading rapidly through the Sahara and the western Soudan. We see that, since that time, large empires were formed and disappeared again in struggles with neighboring states and that a relatively high degree of culture has been attained. The invaders intermarried with the natives, and the mixed races, some of which are almost purely negro, have risen high above the level of other African negroes. The history of Bornu is perhaps one of the best examples of this kind. Barth and Nachtigal have made us acquainted with the history of this state, which has played a most important part in the history of north Africa.

Why, then, have the Mohammedans been able to civilize these tribes and to raise them to nearly the same standard which they had attained, while the whites have not been capable of influencing the negro in Africa to any considerable extent? Evidently on account of the different method of introduction of culture. While the Mohammedans influence the people in the same manner in which the ancients civilized the tribes of Europe, the whites send only the products of their manufactures and a few of their representatives into the negro country. A real amalgamation between the higher types of the whites and the negroes has never taken place. The amalgamation of the negroes by the Mohammedans is facilitated particularly by the institution of polygamy, the conquerors taking native wives and raising their children as members of their own family.

The spread of the Chinese civilization in eastern Asia may be likened to that of the ancient civilization in Europe. Colonization and amalgamation of kindred tribes and, eventually, extermination of rebellious subjects with subsequent colonization, have led to a remarkable uniformity of culture over a large area.

When, finally, we consider the inferior position held by the negro race of the United States, who are in the closest contact with modern civilization, we must not forget that the old race-feeling of the inferiority of the colored race is as potent as ever and is a formidable obstacle to its advance and progress, notwithstanding that schools and universities are open to them. We might rather wonder how much has been accomplished in a short period against heavy odds. It is hardly possible to say what would become of the negro if he were able to live with the whites on absolutely equal terms.

Our conclusion drawn from the foregoing considerations is the following: Several races have developed a civilization of a type similar to the one from which our own had its origin. A number of favorable conditions facilitated the rapid spread of this civilization in Europe. Among these, common physical appearance, contiguity of habitat and moderate difference in the modes of manufacture were the most potent. When, later on, civilization began to spread over other continents the races with which modern civilization came into contact were not equally favorably situated. Striking differences of racial types, the preceding isolation which caused devastating epidemics in the newly discovered countries and the greater advance in civilization made assimilation much more difficult. The rapid dissemination of Europeans over the whole world cut short all promising beginnings which had arisen in various regions. Thus no race except that of eastern Asia was given a chance to develop an independent civilization. The spread of the European race cut short the growth of the existing independent germs without regard to the mental aptitude of the people among whom it was developing. On the other hand, we have seen that no great weight can be attributed to the earlier rise of civilization in the Old World, which is satisfactorily explained as a chance. In

short, historical events appear to have been much more potent in leading
races to civilization than their faculty, and it follows that achievements
of races do not warrant us to assume that one race is more highly gifted
than the other.]

We will next compare the physical and psychical characteristics of the
various races with a view to the question of their mental ability.

There is no doubt that great differences exist in the physical characteristics of the races of man. But the question is not if differences exist,
but if any one race is anatomically considered superior to others. It is
clear that our answer cannot be based upon vague descriptions of travellers who remark upon the enormous digestive organs of primitive man, or
on his small size, or on the lack of development of his limbs, or even upon
his resemblance to apes, but upon serious studies of anatomical characteristics. A number of these differences are sufficiently fundamental to
distinguish certain races clearly from others, although we must bear in
mind that innumerable transitions exist between the races of man. The
color of the skin, the form of the hair and the configuration of the lips
and nose distinguish the African negro clearly from most other races.
Nevertheless, it would be easy to find among members of the American
race, for instance, lips and nose which might be mistaken for those of a
negro. The same may be said of color, while no negro hair will be found
among American aborigines. When studying any single anatomical characteristics of races, we find the same phenomenon which was observed in
the cases here quoted: the variations inside any single race are such
that they overlap the variations in another race so that a number of
characteristics may be common to individuals of both races. Still, the
single feature does not characterize the race and the differences are
sufficiently numerous to permit a satisfactory definition of the characters
of races.

The overlapping of variations is significant in so far as it shows that
the existing differences are not fundamental. I will describe these phenomena somewhat more fully and enumerate at the same time a number
of variations between races. In treating first the anthropometric characteristics I must call to mind the important fact, which is frequently
overlooked in comparisons of races, that the proportions of the body show
certain correlations which must be taken into consideration. The most
obvious of these is the correlation between stature and sizes of parts of
the body. For this reason tribes of different stature cannot be compared
without a proper reduction of the observed figures. In our comparison it
will be well to pay particular attention to those races which we are
inclined to consider the lowest; to wit, the negroid races and the oldest
prehistoric races.

The proportions of the body as found among various races show very
slight differences only. We may say that the trunks of the Mongoloid
races as compared to their statures are longer than those of Europeans

whose trunks in turn are longer than those of the negroes; that the lower limbs of the last-named race are longer than those of the white and Mongoloid races, and that the same is true in regard to the upper limbs. The head of the Mongoloid race is highest when compared to the stature; that of the negro is smallest. All these differences are slight and not in such a direction as to make one race more ape-like than the other. On the contrary, we find that the characteristic differences between man and ape are often more pronounced in the negro race than in the white race, and we may say with Ranke that many proportions of the lower races are to a higher degree human than those of the white.

In judging the value of these differences we must remember that the proportions of the body do not depend entirely upon descent, but just as much upon mode of life. Fritsch was the first to make it clear that between primitive man and civilized man differences are found which are quite in accord with the differences between wild animals and domesticated animals, and we all know how far-reaching the influence of domestication may become. He found that the skeletons of primitive races remain lighter while the bones are thinner and denser than those of civilized man. The secondary sexual characters are not clearly marked and effects of malnutrition or irregular nutrition are always present. The necessity of physical effort which applies to all the muscles of the body causes a different development from that observed in civilized man, in whom muscular effort is slighter or more specialized. These conclusions are borne out by the striking differences in the proportions of the body which develop among different occupations inside the same population.

The best authenticated fact, because it is based on the greatest number of observations, is the difference in type between sailors and soldiers who were measured during the war of the Rebellion. It was found that sailors had legs as long as those of the negroes and correspondingly a shorter trunk, while their arms were equally long as those of the soldiers of the army. We may also call to mind the investigations carried on in the gymnasia of our colleges which show that a series of measurements which depend largely upon the functions of groups of muscles change very rapidly under the influence of practice. It will be acknowledged at once that differences in the use of muscles during childhood and continued in later life must result in differences of structure. Such differences must, therefore, not be considered racial but cultural features. The differences which cannot be explained by functional causes are few in number and they are not of such a character as to stamp one race as lower than the other.

We will next consider a number of formations which have often been described as characterizing lower races or as theromorphisms. One of these is a variation in the form of the temporal bone which, in man, is ordinarily separated from the frontal bone by the sphenoid and parietal bones. It has been found that in some individuals the temporal bone encroaches upon the sphenoid and parietal and comes into contact with the frontal bone. This formation is the prevalent one among the apes. It has been proved that this variation is found among all races but with unequal frequency, and that it is probably connected with disturbances in the formation of the temporal region which depend upon malnutrition in early infancy. We must therefore not wonder that the phenomenon is found more frequently among primitive people than among civilized people.

The peculiar formation of the tibia known as platycnemism, which has been observed on skeletons of the oldest remains of man in Europe and which was considered a proof of his lower stage of development, and the peculiar formation of the articular surfaces of tibia and femur, have been recognized as purely functional and as occurring among all races of the present times.

Certain other variations which were at one time considered as characteristics of races are also found to occur all over the world. Such are the *Os Incæ* which occurs among all races but most frequently among the Peruvians and the inhabitants of the ancient pueblos; the smallness of the nasal bones and their synostosis with the maxilla; the so-called prenasal fossæ; the variations in the arrangement of arteries and of muscles. All these variable features are found to vary among all races, but the degree of variability is not everywhere the same. Presumably such variations may be considered human characteristics which have not yet had time to become stable and which in this sense may be considered as still in process of evolution. If this interpretation be correct, it might seem that we can consider those races in which the various features are more stable as those which are more highly organized.

This would refer, however, only to such features as are not caused by the influence of environment. But even this conclusion is subject to an important restriction. Numerous primitive tribes are very small in numbers or have had for long periods, during which they increased in numbers, little intercourse with foreign people. If, in such a group, any of the original families showed a certain peculiarity, it must now be found more frequently than in other tribes. A case of this kind is the frequency of supernumerary vertebræ among the Indians of Vancouver Island, and probably also the frequency of the *torus palatinus* among the Lapps. It may be left an open question, if the frequent occurrence of the *Os Incæ* among the Pueblo Indians may be explained by the same consideration. Therefore, it may be that the greater variability of certain races, in regard to these phenomena, is not an expression of a lower degree of development of the whole group, but of the presence of a great number of members of a family which possessed the peculiar character. That is to say, in order to admit the conclusion that greater variability means lower stage of development, it would be necessary first to prove that the variations appear spontaneously among any number of the group and do not belong to certain families in which the feature is hereditary.

While the consideration of the characters treated heretofore has not given any conclusive evidence of the superiority of certain races, the study of the form and size of the head seems to promise better results. We find that the face of the negro as compared to the skull is larger than that of the American, whose face is in turn larger than that of the white. The lower portion of the face assumes larger dimensions. The alveolar arch is pushed forward and thus gains an appearance which reminds us of the higher apes. There is no denying that this feature is a most constant character of the black races and that it represents a type slightly nearer the animal than the European type. The same may be said of the broadness and flatness of the nose of the negro and of the Mongol; but here again we must call to mind that prognathism and low, broad noses are not entirely absent among the white races, although the more strongly developed forms which are found among the negroes do not occur. The variations belonging to both races overlap. We find here at least a few indications which tend to show that the white race differs more from the higher apes than the negro. But does this anatomical difference prove that their mental capacity is lower than that of the white? The probability that this may be the case is suggested by the anatomical facts, but they by themselves are no proof that such is the case. I shall revert to this subject later on.

It has been stated that the individuals of certain races are arrested in their development earlier than others and that the latter races must therefore be considered as more highly developed. Among these phenomena I will mention the fact that the noses of children of various races are more alike than those of adults. The nose of the Mongols does not change so much during adolescence as that of the whites. According to Quatrefages the basin of the negro does not differ so much from the foetal forms as that of other races and resembles at the same time more that of higher apes than the basins of other races. On the other hand, the face of the negro child is less prognathous than that of the adult. In this case we find that the more energetic development tends to produce a type which is apparently lower than that of the white. We may even go a step farther and say that the ontogenetic development of the higher apes and of man is such that the young forms are more alike than the old ones. While in man the face develops moderately only, it grows considerably among the apes. The earlier arrest in this case is therefore an indication of higher type. Thus it will be seen that it is not the earlier arrest alone which determines the place of a race, but the direction of this development. For this reason we cannot assume that the earlier arrest of development of that portion of the face situated between the eyes, as is observed in the Mongol race, is an indication of a lower type, while the marked increase of breadth and elevation of nose, as found among the whites indicates a higher type.

In a general review of these phenomena we find that the peculiarities of the various races develop in such a manner that some remain in one respect on earlier stages than others, while other features develop more strongly. Among instances of such development carried on to a higher degree may be mentioned the large size of the frontal sinuses among the Melanesians, the prognathism of the Negroes, the greater length of the limbs of the same race, the high and narrow nose of the whites. In judging the value of these facts we must also not forget that the female sex is in all the proportions and forms of its body more like the child than the male, and that the most specialized types appear among the male sex. But who would explain this earlier arrest of development of women as mark of a lower type?

In comparing human races in regard to the periods over which the development of certain parts of the bodies extend, we must always consider the functions of the organs in question. If we could prove that the brain of certain races ceases to develop at an earlier period than that of others, the inference of the inferiority of race would seem highly probable. At the present time no satisfactory basis for such comparisons exists. Growth during adolescence is always small, and extensive and accurate series of observations are required in order to establish any characteristic differences between races. It has been shown that among the white race growth of the whole body continues until after the thirty-fifth year. The same phenomenon has been observed among the negroes, while the Indians appear to have reached their highest stature before the thirtieth year. The growth of the head of Indians and whites seems to extend over an approximately equal period. It would be of great interest, if we could ascertain the growth of the head of other races with accuracy. Since it has been proved that the most gifted students of our colleges show a longer period of growth than those who form the average class, the period of head-growth has become of great importance in connection with our inquiry.

Unfortunately, data are lacking entirely at least for a comparison between the white race and those races which are considered the lowest. As we know that the laws of the general growth of the body of the Indian and of the white differ considerably, the inference is justified that such differences may be found in the growth of certain organs and that they will prevail among different races. It is true that in such comparisons mortality, nutrition, occupation, play an important part; but, nevertheless, racial differences may be expected to exist. In fact, the similarity of children of various races and the dissimilarity of the adult make it certain that they will be found and we anticipate that they will give us a better idea of the relation of the races than comparison of the adult stage alone can do.

We will now turn to the important subject of the size of the brain, which seems to be the one anatomical feature which bears directly upon the question at issue. It would seem that the greater the central nervous system, the higher the faculty of the race and the greater its aptitude to mental achievements. Let us review the known facts. Two methods are open for ascertaining the size of the central nervous system: the determination of the weight of the brain and that of the capacity of the cranial cavity. The first of these methods is the one which promises the most accurate results. Naturally, the number of Europeans whose brain-weights have been taken is much larger than that of individuals of other races. There are, however, sufficient data available to establish beyond a doubt the fact that the brain-weight of the whites is larger than that of most other races, particularly larger than that of the negroes. That of the white male is about 1370 grammes. The investigations of cranial capacities are quite in accord with these results. According to Topinard, the capacity of the skull of males of the neolithic period of Europe is about 1560 cc.; that of modern Europeans is the same; of the Mongoloid race 1510 cc.; of African negroes 1405 cc., and of negroes of the Pacific ocean 1460 cc. Here we have, therefore, a decided difference in favor of the white race. These differences cannot be explained as the effect of difference in stature, the negroes being at least as tall as the Europeans.

In interpreting these facts we must ask, Does the increase in the size of the brain prove an increase in faculty? This would seem highly probable and facts may be adduced which speak in favor of this assumption. First among these is the increase of the relative size of the brain among higher animals, thence to man. Furthermore Manouvrier has measured the capacity of the skulls of thirty-two eminent men. He found that they averaged 1663 cc. as compared to 1560 cc. general average. On the other hand he found that the cranial capacity of forty-one murderers was 1593 cc., also superior to the general average. The same result has been obtained through weighings of brains of eminent men. The brains of thirty-four of these showed an average increase of 163 grammes over the average brain-weight of 1370 grammes. The force of the arguments furnished by these observations must, however, not be overestimated. Most brain-weights are obtained in anatomical institutes, and the individuals which find their way there are poorly developed on account of malnutrition and life under unfavorable circumstances, while the eminent men represent a much better nourished class. As poor nourishment reduces the weight and size of the whole body it will also reduce the size and weight of the brain. It is not certain, therefore, that the observed difference is entirely due to the higher ability of the eminent men. The difference between the cranial capacities of eminent men and of the general population is increased beyond its actual size by the difficulties encountered in determining the sex of skulls. Skulls of a number of men are always mistaken for those of women and *vice versa*, which tends to reduce the capacity for males, while it increases that of the females. As, in the case of eminent people, the sex is known accurately, it may be expected that the average capacity of the skulls of eminent men will be higher than that of skulls the sex of which is not known. It must be said, however, that Broca's measurements, the results of which are given above, show that he determined the sex of a skull with considerable accuracy. Another fact which may be adduced in favor of the theory that greater brains are accompanied by higher faculty, is, that the city population show higher capacities than those of the country; also that the observation that the heads of the best English students continue to grow longer than those of the average class of students.

While the force of these arguments must be admitted, a number of restricting facts must be enumerated. The most important among these is the difference in the brain-weight between men and women. When men and women of the same stature are compared it is found that the brain of the woman is much lighter than that of the man. Nevertheless, the faculty of woman is undoubtedly just as high as that of man. This is therefore a case in which smaller brain-weight is accompanied throughout by equal faculty. We conclude from this fact that it is not impossible that the smaller brains of males of other races should not do the same work that is done by the larger brain of the white race. But this comparison is not quite on equal terms, as we may assume that there is a certain structural difference between male and female which causes the difference in size between the sexes, so that comparison between male and female is not the same as a comparison between male and male. We will also remember that, although the brains of eminent men are, on the average, larger than those of the average individual, there are some small brains included in their number.

Notwithstanding these restrictions, the increase of the size of the brain in the higher animals and the lack of development in microcephalic individuals are fundamental facts which make it more than probable that increased size of the brain causes increased faculty, although the relation is not quite as immediate as is often assumed.

Assuming that capacity is nearly proportional to the size of the brain, we must remember that the average sizes of the brain of the white are numerously represented among other races. Middle-sized brains of whites may be represented by the group of individuals having capacities of from 1450 to 1650 cc. This group encloses 55 per cent of the Europeans, 58 per cent of the African negroes and 58 per cent of the Melanesians. The same result appears when we compare the number of individuals having great capacities. We find that 50 per cent of all whites have a capacity of the skull greater than 1550 cc., while 27 per cent of the negroes and 32 per cent of the Melanesians have capacities above this value. We might, therefore, anticipate a lack of men of high genius, but should not anticipate any great lack of faculty among the great mass of negroes living among whites and enjoying the advantages of the leadership of the best men of that race.

This, however, is hardly the correct standpoint, as mental ability certainly does not depend upon the size of the brain alone. The proper point of view of this question is brought out most clearly by Dr. H. H. Donaldson whose opinion I will quote. He says, "I consider the significance of the encephalon to depend upon the number and size of the cells composing it. In the negroes and lower races generally, the number of cells is probably less than in the white. This is mainly an inference from the total weight of the encephalon. Equally important are the final stages in the enlargement of the structural elements, stages which apparently have the result of bringing a larger number of elements into physiological connections by means of a very slight quantitative extension of their branches. Changes, which moreover can be followed, say in the cortex of the brain of the white in individuals thirty or more years of age. When we compare the capacity for education between the lower and higher races, we find that the great point of divergence is at adolescence and the inference is fairly good that we shall not find in the brains of the lower races the post-pubertal growth in the cortex to which I have just alluded. As to the sculpturing of the brain surface by gyri and sulci we still lack any good racial characters."

We have now gone over the field of anatomical differences between races so far as they have a bearing upon our question. Our conclusion is, that there are differences between the physical characters of races which make it probable that there may be differences in faculty. No unquestionable fact, however, has been found yet which would prove beyond a doubt that it will be impossible for certain races to attain a higher civilization.

We must next examine the psychological characteristics of primitive people in order to discover if there are any which assign them a lower place among mankind. This investigation is exceedingly difficult and unpromising because it appears doubtful throughout which of these characteristics are causes of the low stage of culture and which are caused by it, or which of the psychological characteristics are hereditary and would not be wiped out by the effects of civilization. The fundamental difficulty of collecting satisfactory observations lies in the fact that no large groups of primitive man are brought nowadays into conditions of real equality with whites. The gap between our society and theirs always remains open and for this reason their mind cannot be expected to work in the same manner as ours. The same phenomenon which led us to the conclusion that primitive races of our times are not given an opportunity to develop their abilities prevents us from judging their innate faculty. On account of this insurmountable difficulty which seems to make all attempts at a satisfactory solution of this problem impossible, I will confine myself to a few fundamental points and suggestions as to the method by which this important question may be solved.

Numerous attempts have been made to describe the peculiar psychological characteristics of primitive man. Among these I mention those of Wuttke, Klemm, Eichthal, de Gobineau, Nott and Gliddon, Waitz, Spencer and Tylor. Their investigations are of merit as descriptions of the characteristics of primitive people, but we cannot claim for any of them that they describe the psychological characters of races independent of their social surroundings. Klemm and Wuttke designate the civilized races as active, all others as passive, and assume that all elements and beginnings of civilization found among primitive people—in America or on the islands of the Pacific ocean—were due to an early contact with civilization. Eichthal considers human society as an organism and assumes that the white race represents the male, the negro the female principle. De Gobineau calls the yellow race the male element, the black race the female element and calls only the whites the noble and gifted race. Nott and Gliddon ascribe animal instincts only to their lower races, while they declare that the white race has a higher instinct which incites and directs its development. All such views are generalizations which either do not sufficiently take into account the social conditions of races, and thus confound cause and effect, or were dictated by scientific or humanitarian bias or by the desire to justify the institution of slavery. Tylor and Spencer, who give an ingenious analysis of the psychological faculty of primitive man, do not assume that these are racial characteristics, although the evolutionary standpoint of Spencer's work often seems to convey this impression. I think the true point of view has been expressed most happily by Waitz. He says, "According to the current opinion the stage of culture of a people or of an individual is largely or exclusively a product of his faculty. We maintain that the reverse is at least just as true. The faculty of man does not designate anything but how much and what he is able to achieve in the immediate future and depends upon the stages of culture through which he has passed and the one he has reached."

The descriptions of the state of mind of primitive people, such as are given by most travellers, are too superficial to be used for psychological investigation. Very few travellers understand the language of the people they visit, and how is it possible to judge a tribe solely by the descriptions of interpreters, or by observations of disconnected actions the incentive of which remains unknown? But even when the language is known to the visitor, he is generally an unappreciative listener of their tales. The missionary has his strong bias against the religious ideas and customs of primitive people, and the trader has no interest in their beliefs and in their barbarous arts. The observers who really entered into the inner life of a people, the Cushings, Callaways and Greys, are few in number and may be counted at one's finger's ends. Nevertheless, the bulk of the argument is always based on the statement of hasty and superficial observers.

I will now select a few of the mental qualities which are most persistently claimed as racial characteristics of the lower groups of mankind. Among the emotional characters impulsiveness is considered the most fundamental. Most of the proofs for this alleged peculiarity are based on the fickleness and uncertainty of the disposition of primitive man and on the strength of his passions aroused by seemingly trifling causes. I will say right here, that the traveller or student measures the fickleness of the people by the importance which he attributes to the actions or purposes in which they do not persevere, and he weighs the impulse for outbursts of passion by his standard. Let me give an example. The traveller, desirous to reach his goal as soon as possible, engages men to start on a journey at a certain time. To him time is exceedingly valuable. But what is time to primitive man who does not feel the compulsion of completing a definite work at a definite time? While the traveller is fuming and raging over the delay, his men keep up their merry chatter and laughter and cannot be induced to exert themselves except to please their master. Would not they be right in stigmatizing the impulsiveness and lack of control of many a traveller when irritated by a trifling cause like loss of time? Instead of this the traveller complains of the fickleness of the natives who quickly lose interest in the objects which the traveller has at heart. The proper way to compare the fickleness of the savage and that of the white is to compare their behavior in undertakings which are equally important to each. Does not primitive man persevere wonderfully in the manufacture of his utensils and weapons? Does he shrink from privations and hardships which promise to fill his ambition of obtaining higher rank among his fellows? The Indian, fasting in the mountains, awaiting the appearance of his guardian spirit, the youth who must give a proof of his bravery and endurance before being accepted in the ranks of the men of his tribe may be adduced as examples. The alleged fickleness may always be explained by a difference of the valuation of motives and is not a specific characteristic of primitive man. Primitive man perseveres in certain pursuits which differ from those in which civilized man perseveres.

The same may be said of the outbursts of passion occasioned by slight provocations. What would a primitive man say to the noble passion which preceded and accompanied the War of the Rebellion? Would not the rights of slaves seem to him a most irrelevant question? On the other hand, we have ample proof that his passions are just as much controlled as ours, only in different directions. The numerous customs and restrictions regulating the relations of the sexes or the use of the food supply may serve as examples. The difference in impulsiveness may be fully explained by the different weight of motives in both cases. In short, perseverance and control of passion are demanded of primitive man as well as of civilized man but at different occasions. If they are not demanded as often, the cause must be looked for not in the inherent inability to produce them, but in the social status which does not demand them to the same extent.

Spencer mentions as a particular case of this impulsiveness the improvidence of primitive man. I believe it would be more proper to say instead of providence, optimism. "Why should I not be as successful to-morrow as I was to-day?" is the guiding thought of primitive man. This thought is, I think, not less powerful in civilized man. What builds up business activity but the belief in the stability of existing conditions? Why do the poor not hesitate to found families without being able to lay in store beforehand? We must not forget that starvation among most primitive people is an exceptional case the same as financial crisis among civilized people, and that for times of need, such as occur regularly, provision is always made. Our social status is more stable so far as the acquiring of the barest necessities of life is concerned, so that exceptional conditions do not prevail often; but nobody would maintain that the majority of civilized men is always prepared to meet emergencies. We may recognize a difference in the degree of improvidence caused by the difference of social status but not a specific difference between lower and higher types of man.

Another trait which has been ascribed to primitive man is his inability of concentration when any demand is made upon the more complex faculties of the intellect. I will mention an example which seems to make clear the error committed in this assumption. In his description of the natives of the west coast of Vancouver Island, Sproat says: "The native mind, to an educated man, seems generally to be asleep. . . . On his attention being fully aroused, he often shows much quickness in reply and ingenuity in argument. But a short conversation wearies him, particularly if questions are asked that require efforts of thought or memory on his part. The mind of the savage then appears to rock to and fro out of mere weakness." Spencer, who quotes this passage, adds a number of others corroborating this point. I happen to know the tribes mentioned by Sproat through personal contact. The questions put by the traveller seem mostly trifling to the Indian and he naturally soon tires of a conversation carried on in a foreign language and one in which he finds nothing to interest him. I can assure you that the interest of those natives can easily be raised to a high pitch and that I have often been the one who was wearied out first. Neither does the management of their intricate system of exchange prove mental inertness in matters which concern the natives. Without mnemonic aids they plan the systematic distribution of their property in such a manner as to increase their wealth and social position. These plans require great foresight and constant application.

I will select one more trait which has often been adduced as the primary reason why certain races cannot rise to higher levels of culture, namely, their lack of originality. It is said that the conservatism of primitive man is so strong that the individual never deviates from the traditional customs and beliefs. While there is certainly truth in this statement in so far as customs are more binding than in civilized society, at least in its most highly developed types, originality is a trait which is by no means lacking in the life of primitive people. I will call to mind the great frequency of the appearance of prophets among newly converted tribes as well as among pagan tribes. Among the latter we learn quite frequently of new dogmas which have been introduced by such individuals. It is true that these may often be traced to the influence of the ideas of neighboring tribes, but they are modified by the individuality of the person and grafted upon the current beliefs of the people. It is a well-known fact that myths and beliefs have been disseminated and undergo changes in the process of dissemination. Undoubtedly this has often been accomplished by the independent thought of individuals. I believe one of the best examples of such independent thought is furnished by the history of the ghost-dance ceremonies in North America. I am indebted to Mr. James Mooney, a close student of this subject, for the following opinion: "Briefly and broadly it may be stated that the more primitive a people, the more original their thought. Indian prophets are usually original as to their main doctrine, but are quick to borrow anything that may serve to make it more impressive. Heathenism is usually tolerant and the Indian sees no inconsistency in adding to his heathenism anything that he can borrow from Christianity." A few cases which have come under my own observation are entirely in accord with this opinion; that is to say, the doctrine of the Indian prophet is new, but based upon the ideas of his own people, their neighbors, and the teachings of missionaries. The notion of future life of the Kwakiutl of Vancouver Island has undergone a change in this manner, in so far as the idea of the return of the dead in children of their own family has arisen. The same independent attitude may be observed in the replies of the Nicaraguan Indians to the questions regarding their religion which were put to them by Bobadilla and which were reported by Oviedo.

To my mind the mental attitude of individuals who thus develop the beliefs of a tribe is exactly that of the civilized philosopher. The student of the history of philosophy is well aware how strongly the mind of even the greatest genius is influenced by the current thought of his time. This has been well expressed by my friend Rudolph Lehmann in his work on Schopenhauer. "The character of a system of philosophy is, just as that of any other literary work, determined first of all by the personality of its originator. Every true philosophy reflects the life of the philosopher as well as every true poem that of the poet. Secondly, it bears the general marks of the period to which it belongs, and the more powerful the ideas which it proclaims, the more strongly it will be permeated by the currents of thought which fluctuate in the life of the period. Thirdly, it is influenced by the particular bent of philosophical thought of the period."

If such is the case among the greatest minds of all times, why should we wonder that the thinker in primitive society is strongly influenced by the current thought of his time? Unconscious and conscious imitation are factors influencing civilized society, not less than primitive society, as has been shown by G. Tarde, who has proved that primitive man and civilized man as well, imitates not such actions only as are useful, and for the imitation of which logical causes may be given, but also others for the adoption or preservation of which no logical reason can be assigned.

Based on these considerations we believe that in the more complicated psychological phenomena no specific differences between lower and higher races can be found. By this, however, we do not mean to say that no such differences exist or can be found, only that the method of investigation must be different. It does not seem probable that the minds of races which show variations in their anatomical structure should act in exactly the same manner. Differences of structure must be accompanied by differences of function, physiological as well as psychological; and, as we found clear evidence of difference in structure between the races, so we must anticipate that differences in mental characteristics will be found. Thus, a smaller size or lesser number of nervous elements would probably entail loss of mental energy, and paucity of connections in the central nervous system would produce sluggishness of the mind. As stated before, it seems probable that some differences of this character will be found between the white and negro, for instance, but they have not been proved yet. As all structural differences are quantitative, we must expect to find mental differences to be of the same description, and as we found the variations in structure to overlap, so that many forms are common to individuals of all races, so we may expect that many individuals will not differ in regard to their faculty, while a statistical inquiry embracing the whole races would reveal certain differences. Furthermore, as certain anatomical traits are found to be hereditary in certain families and hence in tribes and perhaps even in peoples, in the same manner mental traits characterize certain families and may prevail among tribes. It seems, however, an impossible undertaking to separate in a satisfactory manner the social and the hereditary features. Galton's attempt to establish the laws of hereditary genius points out a way of treatment for these questions which will prove useful in so far as it opens a method of determining the influence of heredity upon mental qualities.

On account of this difficulty I do not enter upon a discussion of the characters of nations. Much has been said about the hereditary characteristics of the Jews, of the gypsies, of the French and Irish, but I do not see that the social causes which have moulded the character of members of these people have ever been eliminated satisfactorily; and, moreover, I do not see how this can be accomplished without previous investigations into the question as to which groups of mental qualities are hereditary. A number of external factors may easily be named: climate, nutrition, occupation; but, as soon as we enter into a consideration of social factors, we are unable to separate cause and effect or external and internal factors. The first-named groups affect the physiological functions of the body and through them the mind. An excellent discussion of these influences upon the character of a people is given by A. Wernich in his description of the character of the Japanese. He finds some of their peculiarities caused by the lack of vigor of the muscular and alimentary systems which in their turn are due to improper nutrition, while he recognizes other physiological traits which influence the mind as hereditary. We may expect to find still more far-reaching effects of malnutrition which was continued through long generations among the Bushmen and the Lapps.

We know some of the correlations between physiological and psychological functions. It is clear, therefore, that where such correlation is known, the physiological phenomena which accompany the psychical traits ought to be made a subject of special study in reference to the question, whether the mental traits under consideration are hereditary or not.

The only feasible way of attacking the psychological problem while excluding social factors seems to be to investigate the psychical processes of great numbers of individuals of different races who live under similar conditions. This can be accomplished but has not been done yet to such an extent as to allow us to draw far-reaching conclusions. I mention that Professor Barnes and Miss Hicks found differences of favorite colors between children of different races and different ages; that attempts have been made to show that the minds of negro children cease to develop sooner than those of white children, although the results are not conclusive. Modest investigations of the senses and of simpler mental activities of children will give the first satisfactory answer to the important question of the extent of racial differences of faculty. The schools of our country, particularly those of large cities, open a vast field for researches of this character.

We have now one more point to consider, namely, the question if the faculty of man has been improved by civilization, and particularly, if that of primitive races may be improved by this agency. We must consider both the anatomical and psychological aspects of this question. I have already pointed out that civilization causes anatomical changes of the same description as those accompanying the domestication of animals. It is likely that changes of mental character go hand in hand with them. The observed anatomical changes are, however, limited to this group of phenomena. We cannot prove that any progressive changes of the human organism have taken place, and particularly no advance in the size or complexity of the structure of the central nervous system caused by the cumulative effects of civilization can be proved.

There seems to be no doubt that the anatomical characters of the races have in all their main points remained constant. Kollmann has proved that the oldest remains of man found in Europe represent the types which are still found among the modern civilized populations. As our knowledge of the older types of Europeans is confined to their osseous remains, it cannot be expected that finer differences, even if they existed, would be found. The difficulty of proving a progress of faculty is still greater. It seems to me that the probable effect of civilization upon an evolution of human faculty has been much overestimated. The psychical changes which are the immediate consequence of the domestication or civilization may be considerable. They are changes due to the influence of environment. It is doubtful, however, if any progressive changes or such as are transmitted by heredity have taken place. The number of generations subjected to this influence seems altogether too small. For large portions of Europe we cannot assume more than forty or fifty generations, and even this number is probably considerably too high, in so far as in the middle ages the bulk of the population lived on very low stages of civilization.

Besides this, the tendency of human multiplication is such that the most highly cultured families tend to disappear, while others which have been less subjected to the influences regulating the life of the most cultured class take their place. Therefore, it is much less likely that advance is hereditary than that it is transmitted by means of education. I believe, furthermore, that educational influences, which include the general educating influence of social surroundings, are superficial as compared to hereditary causes.

In illustrating the improving effects of civilization through transmission, much weight is generally laid upon cases of relapse of individuals belonging to primitive races who have been educated. These relapses are interpreted as proofs of the inability of the child of a lower race to adapt itself to our high civilization, even if the best advantages are given to it. It is true that a considerable number of such cases are on record. Among these I will mention Darwin's Fuegian who was educated in England and returned to his home where he fell back into the ways of his primitive countrymen; and the West Australian girl who was married, but suddenly fled to the bush after killing her husband and resumed life with the natives. These cases are true, but not one of them has been described with sufficient detail. The social and mental conditions of the individual have never been subjected to a searching analysis. I should judge that, notwithstanding their better education, their social position was always one of isolation, while the ties of consanguinity formed a connecting link with their uncivilized brethren. The power with which society holds us and does not give us a chance to step out of its limits cannot have acted as strongly upon them as upon us. On the other hand, the station obtained by many negroes in our civilization seems to me to have just as much weight as the few cases of relapse which have been collected with much care and diligence. I should place side by side with them the cases of white men who live alone among native tribes and who sink almost invariably to a semi-barbarous position, and the members of well-to-do families who prefer unbounded freedom to the fetters of society, and flee to the wilderness where many lead a life in no way superior to that of primitive man.

We have now considered the question in how far human faculty is determined by race from three points of view. We have shown that the anatomical evidence is such, that we may expect to find the races not equally gifted. While we have no right to consider one more ape-like than the other, the differences are such that some have probably greater mental vigor than others. The variations are, however, such that we may expect many individuals of all races to be equally gifted, while the number of men and women of higher ability will differ. When considering the psychological evidence, we found that most of it is not a safe guide for our inquiry, because causes and effects are so closely interwoven that it is impossible to separate them in a satisfactory manner, and as we are always liable to interpret as racial character what is only an effect of social surroundings. We saw, however, that investigations based on physiological psychology and experimental psychology will allow us to treat the problem in a satisfactory manner. In these and in detailed studies of the anatomy of the central nervous system of the races we must look for a final solution of our problem.

Finally, we found that there is no satisfactory evidence that the effects of civilization are inherited beyond those which are incident to that domestication to which civilization corresponds. We know that these are hereditary to a limited degree only and that domestication requires only few generations. We did not find proof of cumulative increase of faculty caused by civilization.

Although, as I have tried to show, the distribution of faculty among the races of man is far from being known, we can say this much: the average faculty of the white race is found to the same degree in a large proportion of individuals of all other races, and although it is probable that some of these races may not produce as large a proportion of great men as our own race, there is no reason to suppose that they are unable to reach the level of civilization represented by the bulk of our own people.

SELECTION 32

Psychological Problems in Anthropology

The science of anthropology deals with the biological and mental manifestations of human life as they appear in different races and in different societies. The phenomena with which we are dealing are therefore, from one point of view, historical. We are endeavoring to elucidate the events which have led to the formation of human types, past and present, and which have determined the course of cultural development of any given group of men. From another point of view the same phenomena are the objects of biological and psychological investigations. We are endeavoring to ascertain what are the laws of hereditary stability and of environmental variability of the human body. These may be recognized in the historical changes that the bodily appearance of man has undergone in the course of time, and in his displacement from one geographical or social environment to another. We are also trying to determine the psychological laws which control the mind of man everywhere, and that may differ in various racial and social groups. In so far as our inquiries relate to the last-named subject, their problems are problems of psychology, though based upon anthropological material. I intend to speak of this aspect of anthropology to-day.

The fundamental problem on which all anthropological inquiry must be founded relates to the mental equipment of the various races of man. Are all the races of mankind mentally equally endowed, or do material differences exist? The final answer to this question has not been given, but anatomical observations on the various races suggest that differences in the form of the nervous system are presumably accompanied by differences in function, or, psychologically speaking, that the mental traits which characterize different individuals are distributed in varying manner among different races; so that the composite picture of the mental characteristics of one race would presumably not coincide with the composite picture of the mental characteristics of another race. The evidence that has been brought forward does not justify us, however, in claiming that

Lecture delivered at the celebration of the twentieth anniversary of the opening of Clark University, September 1909; as published in *American Journal of Psychology* 21 (1910): 371–384; subsequently incorporated in Boas 1911c.

the characteristics of one race would be an advance over those of another, although they would be different.

This question has also been approached from the standpoint of racial achievement. It has been pointed out that only the white race and the Mongolian race have reached any high grade of cultural development, and on this basis it has been assumed that the other races of man have not the ability to reach the same grade of civilization. It has been shown, however, that the retardation of the other races is not necessarily significant, because the amount of retardation is small as compared to the time consumed in reaching the present stages. It would seem, therefore, that the weight of evidence is, on the whole, in favor of an essential similarity of mental endowment in different races, with the probability of variations in the type of mental characteristics. Further inquiries into this subject must be based not only on sociological studies, but also on anatomical, physiological, and psychological inquiries among individuals belonging to the distinct races of mankind.

While the problem that I have just outlined relates to hereditary racial differences, a second fundamental problem of anthropology relates to the mental characteristics of social groups regardless of their racial descent. Even a superficial observation demonstrates that groups of man belonging to distinct social strata do not behave in the same manner. The Russian peasant does not react to his sense experiences in the same way as does the native Australian; and entirely different from theirs are the reactions of the educated Chinaman and of the educated American. In all these cases the form of reaction may depend to a slight extent upon hereditary individual and racial ability, but it will to a much greater extent be determined by the habitual reactions of the society to which the individual in question belongs.

The reaction of a member of a society to the outer world may be twofold. He may act as a member of a crowd, in which case his activities are immediately determined by imitation of the activities of his fellows; or he may act as an individual; then the influence of the society of which he is a member will make itself felt by the habits of action and thought of the individual.

I have discussed the racial question repeatedly at other places. The problem of the psychology of the crowd is a peculiarly intricate one, based largely upon the data of social psychology in a wider sense of the term, and upon data of individual psychology. I may be allowed for these reasons to confine myself to-day to the third of the problems which I have outlined, that of the psychological laws which govern man as an individual member of society.

This problem has been the object of intensive study by the great minds that have laid the foundation of modern anthropology. The ultimate aim of Waitz's great work is the inquiry into the question whether there are any fundamental differences between the mental make-up of mankind the world over, racially as well as socially. Tylor, in his brilliant investigations on the development of civilization, showed the common occurrence of similar types of ideas the world over, and demonstrated the possibility of conceiving of the scattered phenomena as proof of certain tendencies of evolution of civilization. The many investigators who have studied the evolution of marriage relations, the evolution of law, of art, of religion, all start from the same basis—the assumption of a general similarity of mental reaction in societies of similar structure. Bastian has tried to prove by the use of anthropological data that man the world over develops the same elementary ideas, on which the fabric of his mental activities is based; and that these elementary ideas may be modified by geographical and social environment, but that they remain essentially the same everywhere.

It may be well to illustrate the facts here referred to by a few examples. In the domain of industrial activity we find that mankind is everywhere in possession of the art of producing fire by friction, that everywhere food is prepared by cooking, that shelters are built, that tools are used for breaking and cutting. We do not know mankind in any stage where any of these inventions are absent. In regard to social structure we find that man nowhere lives alone; that even the cases in which the social group consists of members of one family only, are exceedingly rare and of temporary occurrence. We furthermore find that the social units are subdivided into groups, which are kept apart by customary laws forbidding intermarriages in one group, and prescribing intermarriages in another.

In the domain of religion an idea of this type is that of life after death. There is probably no people that believes in the complete extinction of existence with death, but some belief in the continuity of life seems to exist everywhere. To the same domain belongs that type of concepts of the world, in which the surface of our earth is considered as forming a central level, above and below which other worlds are located.

An examination of the types of ideas represented by the few examples that I have here given shows that their subject-matter is highly complex, and that in a strict sense the occurrence of these ideas by itself does not explain clearly the psychological processes that produce them and that cause their stability. Attempts at a psychological interpretation of these concepts have often been made by means of a comparative treatment of similar ideas, and by endeavors to arrange these ideas in such a way as to show a more or less rationalistic development of one from the other. While this may be feasible in some cases, it does not seem likely that this method of treatment will lead us to the most generalized laws governing the forms of thought in human societies.

The principal obstacle in the way of progress of these lines seems to my mind to be founded on the lack of comparability of the data with which we are dealing. When, for instance, we speak of the idea of life after death as one of the ideas which develop in human society as a psychological necessity, we are dealing with a most complex group of data. One people believes that the soul continues to exist in the form that the person had at the time of death, without any possibility of change; another one believes that the soul will be reborn in a child of the same family; a third one believes that the souls will enter the bodies of animals; and still others that the shadows continue our human pursuits, waiting to be led back to our world in a distant future. The emotional and rationalistic elements which enter into these various concepts are entirely distinct; and we can readily perceive how the various forms of the idea of a future life may have come into existence by psychological processes that are not at all comparable. If I may be allowed to speculate on this question, I might imagine that in one case the similarities between children and their deceased relatives, in other cases the memory of the deceased as he lived during the last days of his life, in still other cases the longing for the beloved child or parent, and again the fear of death—may all have contributed to the development of the idea of life after death, the one here, the other there.

Another instance will corroborate this point of view. One of the striking forms of social organization, which occurs in many regions wide apart, is what we call totemism,—a form of society in which certain social groups consider themselves as related in a supernatural way to a certain species of animals or to a certain class of objects. I believe this is the generally accepted definition of totemism; but I am convinced that in this form the phenomenon is not a single psychological problem, but embraces the most diverse psychological elements. In some cases the people believe themselves to be descendants of the animal whose protection they enjoy. In other cases an animal or some other object may have appeared to an ancestor of the social group, and may have promised to become his protector, and the friendship between the animal and the ancestor was then transmitted to his descendants. In still other cases a certain social group in a tribe may have the power of securing by magical means and with great ease a certain kind of animal or of increasing its numbers, and the supernatural relation may be established in this way. It will be recognized that here again the anthropological phenomena, which are in outward appearances alike, are, psychologically speaking, entirely distinct, and that consequently psychological laws covering all of them can not be deduced from them.

Another example may not be amiss. In a general review of moral standards we observe, that, with increasing civilization, a gradual change in the valuation of actions takes place. Among primitive man human life has little value, and is sacrificed on the slightest provocation. The social group among whose members any altruistic obligations are binding is exceedingly small; and outside of the group any action that may result in personal gain is not only permitted, but even approved; and from this starting point we find an ever-increasing valuation of human life and an extension of the size of the group among whose members altruistic obligations are binding. The modern relations of nations show that this evolution has not yet reached its final stage. It might seem, therefore, that a study of the social conscience in relation to crimes like murder might be of psychological value, and lead to important results, clearing up the origin of ethical values; but I think here the same objections may be raised as before, namely the lack of comparable motives. The person who slays an enemy in revenge for wrongs done, a youth who kills his father before he gets decrepit in order to enable him to continue a vigorous life in the world to come, a father who kills his child as a sacrifice for the welfare of his people, act from such entirely different motives, that psychologically a comparison of their activities does not seem permissible. It would seem much more proper to compare the murder of an enemy in revenge, with destruction of his property for the same purpose, or to compare the sacrifice of a child on behalf of the tribe with any other action performed on account of strong altruistic motives, than to base our comparison on the common concept of murder.

Similar observations may also be made in the domain of art. The artist who tries to display his skill in handling his material will be led to æsthetic results. Another one, who wishes to imitate certain forms in his work, may be led to similar results. Notwithstanding similarity of results, the psychological processes in these two cases are quite distinct and not comparable.

For these reasons it seems to me that one of the fundamental points to be borne in mind in the development of anthropological psychology is the necessity of looking for the common psychological features, not in the outward similarities of ethnic phenomena, but in the similarity of psychological processes so far as these can be observed or inferred.

Let us next consider in what direction the psychological problems of anthropology have to be looked for. I must confine myself here to a very few examples of what seem to me fundamental psychological facts.

One of the most striking features in the thoughts of primitive people is the peculiar manner in which concepts that appear to us alike and related are separated and re-arranged. According to our views the constituting elements of the heavens and of the weather are all inanimate objects; but to the mind of primitive man they appear to belong to the organic world. The dividing-line between man and animal is not sharply drawn. What seem to us conditions of an object—like health and sickness—are considered by him as independent realities. In short, the whole classification of experience among mankind living in different forms of society follows entirely distinct lines. I believe this subject can be made clear most easily by a comparison with a similar phenomenon in languages.

If the whole mass of concepts, with all their variants, were expressed in language by entirely heterogeneous and unrelated sound complexes, a condition would arise in which closely related ideas would not show their relationship by the corresponding relationship of their phonetic signs. An infinitely large number of distinct sound complexes—in other words, of distinct words—would be required for expression. If this were the case, the association between an idea and its representative sound complex would not become sufficiently stable to be reproduced automatically at any given moment, without reflecting. The automatic and rapid use of language has brought it about that the infinitely large number of ideas have been reduced by classification to a lesser number, which by constant use have established firm associations, and which can be used automatically. It seems important to emphasize the fact that the groups of ideas expressed by specific words show very material differences in different languages, and do not conform by any means to the same principles of classification. To take the example of English. We find that the idea of water is expressed in a great variety of forms. One term serves to express water as a liquid; another one, water in the form of a large expanse, a lake; others, water as running in a large body or in a small body, a river and brook. Still other terms express water in the forms of rain, dew, wave, and foam. It is perfectly conceivable that this variety of ideas, each of which is expressed by a single independent term in English, might be expressed in other languages by derivations from the same term. It seems fairly evident that the selection of simple terms must to a certain extent depend upon the chief interests of a people; and where it is necessary to distinguish a certain phenomenon in many varieties, which in the life of a people play each an entirely independent rôle, many independent words may develop, while in other cases modifications of a single term may suffice. In the same way as concepts are classified and groups of perceptions are expressed by a single term, relations between perceptions are also classified. The behavior of primitive man makes it perfectly clear that all these linguistic classes have never risen into consciousness, and that consequently their origin must be sought not in rational, but in entirely unconscious processes of the mind. They must be due to a grouping of sense impressions and of concepts which is not in any sense of the term voluntary, but which develops from entirely different psychological causes. It is a characteristic of linguistic classifications that they never rise into consciousness, while other classifications, although the same unconscious origin prevails, often do rise into consciousness. It seems very plausible, for instance, that the fundamental religious notions, like the idea of will power immanent in inanimate objects, or the anthropomorphic character of animals, are in their origin just as little conscious as the fundamental ideas of language. While, however, the use of language is so automatic that the opportunity never arises for the fundamental notions to emerge into consciousness, this happens very frequently in all phenomena relating to religion.

I believe that anthropological investigations carried on from this point of view offer a fruitful field of inquiry. The primary object of these researches would be the determination of the fundamental categories under which phenomena are classified by man in various stages of culture. Differences of this kind appear very clearly in the domain of certain simple sense-perceptions. For instance, it has been observed that colors are classified according to their similarities in quite distinct groups without any accompanying difference in the ability to differentiate shades of color. What we call green and blue are often combined under some such term as "gall-like color," or yellow and green are combined into one concept, which may be named "young-leaves color." The importance of the fact that in thought and in speech these color-names convey the impression of quite different groups of sensations can hardly be over-rated.

Another group of categories that promise a field of fruitful investigation are those of object and attribute. The concepts of primitive man make it quite clear that the classes of ideas which we consider as attributes are often considered as independent objects. The best-known case of this kind, one to which I have referred incidentally before, is that of sickness. While we consider sickness as a condition of an organism, it is believed by primitive man, and even by many members of our own society, to be an object which may enter the body, and which may be removed. This is exemplified by the numerous cases in which a disease is extracted from the body by sucking or by other processes, in the belief that it may be thrown into people, or that it may be enclosed in wood in order to prevent its return. Other qualities are treated in the same way. Thus the condition of hunger, exhaustion, and similar bodily feelings, are considered by certain primitive tribes as independent objects which affect the body. Even life is believed to be a material object that may become separated from the body. The luminosity of the sun is considered as an object that the Sun himself may put on or lay aside.

I have indicated before that the concept of anthropomorphism seems to be one of the important categories underlying primitive thought. It would seem that the power of motion of the self and the power of motion of an object have led to the inclusion of man and movable objects in the same category, with the consequent imputation of human qualities to the moving objective world.

While in many cases we can see with a fair degree of clearness the fundamental concepts underlying these categories, in other cases these are not by any means clear. Thus the concept of incest groups—those groups in which intermarriage is strictly forbidden—is omnipresent. But no satisfactory explanation has so far been given for the tendency to combine certain degrees of blood relationship under this view-point.

Much material for this field of inquiry is contained in the works on comparative anthropology, but I believe a more thorough psychological analysis of the accumulated data may reveal important new information.

We will now turn to the consideration of another group of psychological phenomena that seem to me of considerable importance. In all forms of society certain groups of activities and of thoughts appear in certain typical associations. Thus in our modern society the consideration of cosmic phenomena is constantly associated with the efforts to give adequate explanations for them, based on the principle of causality. In primitive society the consideration of the same phenomena leads to a number of typical associations which differ from our own, but which occur with remarkable regularity among tribes living in the most remote parts of the world. An excellent instance of this kind is the regular association of observations relating to cosmic phenomena with purely human happenings; in other words, the occurrence of nature myths. It seems to my mind that the characteristic trait of nature myths is the association between the observed cosmic events and what might be called a novelistic plot based on the form of social life with which people are familiar. The plot as such might as well develop among the peoples themselves; but its association with the heavenly bodies, the thunder-storm, or the wind, makes it a nature myth. The distinction between the folk-tale and the nature myth lies solely in the association of the latter with cosmic phenomena. This association does not naturally develop in modern society. If it is still found every now and then, it is based on the survival of the traditional nature myth. In primitive society, on the other hand, it is found constantly. The investigation of the reason for this association is an attractive problem, the solution of which can only in part be surmised.

A number of other examples will demonstrate that the kind of association here referred to is quite common in primitive life. An excellent instance is furnished by certain characteristics of primitive decorative art. With us almost the sole object of decorative art is æsthetic. We wish to beautify the objects that are decorated. We recognize a certain appropriateness of decorative motives in accordance with the uses to which objects are to be put, and the emotional effect of the decorative motive. In primitive life the conditions are quite different. Extended investigations on decorative art in all continents have proved that practically everywhere the decorative design is associated with a certain symbolic significance. There is hardly a case known where a primitive tribe cannot give some sort of explanation for the designs they use. In some cases the symbolic significance may be exceedingly weak, but ordinarily it is highly developed. The triangular and quadrangular designs of our Plains Indians, for instance, almost always convey definite symbolic meanings. They may be records of warlike deeds, they may be prayers, or they may in some way convey other ideas relating to the supernatural. It would almost seem that among primitive tribes decorative art for its own sake does not exist. The only analogies in modern decorative art are such as the use of the flag, of the cross, or of emblems of secret societies, for decorative purposes; but their frequency is insignificant as compared to the general symbolic tendencies of primitive art. Thus it will be seen that we have here again a type of association in primitive society quite different from the type of association found among ourselves. Among primitive people the æsthetic motive is combined with the symbolic, while in modern life the æsthetic motive is either quite independent, or associated with utilitarian ideas.

I will give still another example of a form of association characteristic of primitive society. In modern society, social organization, including the grouping of families, is essentially based on blood relationship and on the social functions performed by each individual. Except in so far as the Church concerns itself with birth, marriage, and death, there is no connection between social organization and religious belief. These conditions are quite different in primitive society, where we find an inextricable association of ideas and customs relating to society and to religion. I have referred before to the phenomena of totemism, which are perhaps the best example of this type of association. Totemism is found among many American tribes, as well as in Australia, Melanesia, and in Africa. I have described before its characteristic trait, which consists in supernatural connection that is believed to exist between a certain class of objects, generally animals, and a certain social group. Further analysis shows very clearly that one of the underlying ideas of totemism is the existence of definite groups of man that are not allowed to intermarry, and that the limitations of these groups are determined by considerations of blood relationship. The religious ideas found in totemism refer to the personal relation of man to certain classes of supernatural powers, and the typical trait of totemism is the association of certain kinds of supernatural power with certain social groups. Psychologically, therefore, we may compare totemism with those familiar forms of society in which certain social classes claim privileges by the grace of God, or where the patron saint of a community favors its members with his protection. It will be recognized that we have here again a type of association in primitive society which has completely changed with the development of civilization.

We will now turn to the consideration of a third point, to the peculiar importance of automatic actions in the development of the customs and beliefs of mankind. It is a well-known fact that all those actions which we perform with great frequency are liable to become automatic; that is to say, that their performance is ordinarily not combined with any degree of consciousness. Consequently the emotional value of these actions is also very slight. It is, however, remarkable that the more automatic an action, the more difficult it is to perform the opposite action; that it requires a very strong effort to do so; and that ordinarily the opposite action is accompanied by strong feelings of displeasure. It may also be observed that to see the unusual action performed by another person excites the strongest attention and causes feelings of displeasure. An example will make clear what I mean. When we consider our table manners, it will readily be recognized that most of them are purely traditional and cannot be given any adequate explanation. Still the constant performance of the actions which constitute good table manners makes it practically impossible for us to act otherwise. An attempt to act differently would not only be difficult on account of the lack of adjustment of muscular motions, but also on account of the strong emotional resistance that we should have to overcome. To eat with people having table manners different from our own seems to us decidedly objectionable and causes feelings of displeasure which may rise to such intensity as to cause qualmishness. Another good example is the feeling connected with acts that in our society are considered as modest or immodest. Every one will feel instinctively the strong resistance that he would have to overcome, even in a different society, if he were required to perform an action that we are accustomed to consider as immodest, and the feelings that would be excited in his mind if he were thrown into a society in which the standards of modesty differed from our own. It seems to my mind that these feelings of displeasure exert a very strong influence upon the development and conservation of customs. The young child in whom the habitual behavior of his surroundings has not yet developed will acquire much of this behavior by unconscious imitation. In many cases, however, it will act in a way different from the customary behavior, and will be corrected by its elders. This is presumably one of the most important elements that tend to bring customary behavior into the consciousness of the people practising it. When educating their children to conform to the tribal standards, these standards must necessarily become conscious to the educators.

One of the cases in which the development of ideas based on behavior is best traced, is that of the taboo. Although we ourselves have hardly any definite taboos, to an outsider our failure to use certain animals for food might easily appear from this point of view. Supposing an individual accustomed to eating dogs should inquire among us for the reason why we do not eat dogs, we could only reply that it is not customary; and he would be justified in saying that dogs are tabooed among us, just as much as we are justified in speaking of taboos among primitive people. There are a number of cases in which it is at least conceivable that the older customs of a people, under a new surrounding, develop into taboos. I think, for instance, that it is very likely that the Eskimo taboo forbidding the use of caribou and of seal on the same day may be due to the alternating inland and coast life of the people. When they hunt inland, they have no seals, and consequently can eat only caribou. When they hunt on the coast, they have no caribou, and consequently can eat only seal. The simple fact that in one season only caribou can be eaten, and that in another season only seal can be eaten, may have easily led to a resistance to a change of this custom; so that from the simple fact that for a long period the two kinds of meat could not be eaten at the same time developed the law that the two kinds of meat must not be eaten at the same time. I think it is also likely that the fish taboo of some of our Southwestern tribes may be due to the fact that the tribes lived for a long time in a region where no fish was available, and that the impossibility of obtaining fish developed into the custom of not eating fish.

It would seem, therefore, that we may say in a general way that the customary action is the ethical action, that a breach of custom is everywhere considered as essentially unethical.

It is very likely that the same causes have had a strong influence upon the development of local conventional styles of art. It is no less true that the customary form is liable to be considered the beautiful form than that the customary behavior is considered ethical behavior. Therefore the stability of primitive styles of art may ultimately be due to the same causes as the stability of primitive customs.

If the origin of concepts and of distinct types of association is such as I suggested to-day, and if the existence of these concepts and types of association is brought into the consciousness of primitive man by the incidents of his daily life, when customary concepts and customary associations seem to be broken, we recognize that man must in a great many cases find himself confronted with the fact that certain ideas exist in his mind for which he cannot give any explanation except that they are there. The desire to understand one's own actions, and to get a clear insight into the secrets of the world, manifests itself at a very early time, and it is therefore not surprising that man in all stages of culture begins to speculate on the motives of his own actions.

As I have explained before, there can be no conscious motive for many of these, and for this reason the tendency develops to discover the motives that may determine our customary behavior. This is the reason why in all stages of culture customary actions are made the subject of secondary explanations that have nothing to do with their historical origin, but which are inferences based upon the general knowledge possessed by the people. I think the existence of such secondary interpretations of customary actions is one of the most important anthropological phenomena, and one which is hardly less common in our own society than in more primitive societies. It is a common observation that we desire or act first, and then try to justify our desires and our actions. When, on account of our early bringing up, we act with a certain political party, most of us are not prompted by a clear conviction of the justice of the principles of our party, but we do so because we have been taught to respect it as the right party to which to belong. Then only do we justify our standpoint by trying to convince ourselves that these principles are the correct ones. Without reasoning of this kind, the stability and geographical distribution of political parties as well as of church denominations would be entirely unintelligible. A candid examination of our own minds convinces us that the average man in by far the majority of cases does not determine his actions by reasoning, but that he first acts, and then justifies or explains his acts by such secondary considerations as are current among us.

That the same conditions prevail to even a greater extent among primitive people can easily be shown by a number of examples. It has been pointed out before that decorative art among primitive people is almost everywhere symbolic. This does not preclude the possibility of designs, and even of the whole style, of one region being borrowed by the people of another region. This has been the case, for instance, among the tribes of our Northwestern Plains, who have borrowed much of their art from their more southern neighbors; but they have not adopted together with it the symbolical interpretations given by their neighbors, but invented interpretations of their own. I imagine that this is the outcome of a mental process which set in when the designs were found pleasing, and, according to the general character of primitive thought, a symbolic interpretation was expected. This was then secondarily invented in accordance with the ideas current among the tribe.

The same observation may be made in primitive mythology. The same kind of tales are current over enormous areas, but the mythological use to which they are put is locally quite different. Thus an ordinary adventure relating to the exploits of some animal may sometimes be made use of to explain some of its peculiar characteristics. At other times it may be made use of to explain certain customs, or even the origin of certain constellations in the sky. There is not the slightest doubt in my mind that the tale as such is older than its mythological significance. The characteristic feature of the development of the nature myth is, first, that the tale has associated itself with attempts to explain cosmic conditions—this has been referred to before—and, secondly, that when primitive man became conscious of the cosmic problem, he ransacked the entire field of his knowledge until he happened to find something that could be fitted to the problem in question giving an explanation satisfactory to his mind. While the classification of concepts, the types of association, and the resistance to change of automatic acts, developed unconsciously, many of the secondary explanations are due to conscious reasoning.

In the preceding remarks I have tried to point out a direction in which anthropological data may be used to good advantage by the psychologist; that from a psychological point of view, the starting-point of our investigations must not be looked for in anthropological phenomena that happen to be alike in outward appearance, but that in many cases diverse phenomena are based on similar psychic processes, and that these offer to the investigator a promising line of attack.

PART VIII

ANTHROPOLOGICAL OVERVIEWS

It was characteristic of Boas that his most general statements of the positive results of anthropological inquiry—as opposed to criticisms of presumed results, or general methodological orientations—were occasional pieces, offered rather apologetically. Thus in his presidential address to the New York Academy of Sciences in 1911 he reluctantly laid aside "the scruples and doubts of the study" in order from his "dreams" to sketch an "airy picture" of "The History of the American Race" (Boas 1912a, p. 177). That lecture is still in print, but there are two other general statements that seem of sufficient interest to include here: one relating to a specific area of ethnological inquiry; the other presenting an overview of anthropology as a whole.

The first (no. 33) was written in the summer of 1907 for the Bureau of Ethnology's long-awaited *Handbook of American Indians*. When it became evident that the person assigned to do the article on religion would not finish in time, William Holmes, Chief of the Bureau, asked Boas to take on the job. Although he was planning a European trip, and was preoccupied with his own linguistic *Handbook*, Boas agreed somewhat reluctantly to complete an essay by the end of the summer. He actually wrote it in a day or two late in August, apologizing for being unable to do full justice to the subject. To compare in a few words such an occasional piece to Durkheim's *Elementary Forms of the Religious Life* may seem a rather dubious enterprise; but the fact itself that his most general statement on religion was an occasional piece tells us something rather important about Boas' anthropology, and several brief further comments may suggest a good bit more.

Both men began with a definition of religion (cf. Durkheim 1912, p.

62). But whereas Durkheim pursued the issue systematically in order to arrive at a basis for subsequent observation and analysis, Boas simply offered a quick statement, and then immediately went on to argue that in reality matters were not quite so simple. Both spoke of "concepts and acts" (or, in Durkheim, of "beliefs and practices"), but whereas to Durkheim these constituted a "unified system," to Boas they were merely a "group." For Durkheim, religion was based on the *absolute* distinction between the sacred and the profane; for Boas, religion was defined in what were in effect *residual* terms: it had to do with the relations of man and the outer world "so far as these relations are not considered as due to physical forces" that might be accounted for by "purely rationalistic considerations." For Durkheim, religion was fundamentally social: its function, explicit in its definition, was to unite its adherents "into one single moral community." For Boas, religion was in a fundamental sense individual: it had to do with "the relation of the individual to the outer world." True, he discussed its social aspect, but his very formulation suggests that this was accidental and historical rather than essential: "religion has become closely associated with the social structure of the tribes." Both men were reacting against the overly rationalistic views of religion characteristic of the late nineteenth century. But although Boas saw religion as having to do primarily with "imagination and emotion" rather than reason, his conception of it was still conditioned, if only in a negative way, by the rationalistic, individualistic liberal ideals that, as his own ethical norm, he never abandoned. Religion did not play an important part in his personal scheme of things, nor was he forced by the instability of his social milieu to a consideration of its social function. This may have had something to do with the nature of this general statement—perhaps, in its own way, as much as his characteristic reluctance to carry generalization much farther than descriptive summary.

The second selection (no. 34) dates from later in the same year, when Boas gave the talk on anthropology in the "Columbia University Lectures on Science, Philosophy and Art." Characteristically, it is as much a statement of methodological orientation as it is of "the principal results of anthropological research." Nevertheless, it does provide an excellent overview of his anthropological thought, and suggests that despite the tendency to fragmentation implicit in subdisciplinary specialization, there was a unity underlying Boas' anthropology. Similar to that he had found two decades previously in "The Study of Geography," it was a unity of *affect* rather than *effect*, and was "largely due to the fact that everything that concerns our own species is of special interest to us." Although taking as its starting point the *differences* rather than the *similarities* among men, Boasian anthropology nevertheless found a single focus in the study of the historical processes by which these differences, whether physical or mental, had developed. Wherever possible, it sought "to express in the form of laws [the] ever-recurring modes of historical happenings"; but even after this was accomplished—or if it should prove impossible—"a strong interest" would remain "in the actual developments which have occurred among the various peoples of the world." Beyond this, the lecture has the further advantage of treating certain aspects of Boas' anthropological thought that have at best only been touched on in previous selections—most notably, in the discussion of human racial history, and the fairly full statement of his critique of the assumptions of cultural evolutionism. Finally, the lecture is interesting as the most explicit and illuminating statement of the influence of Bastian and Dilthey on Boas' thought, at the same time suggesting the types of generalization that he hoped might emerge from cultural anthropological research. Here, it seems clear, is a major source of Ruth Benedict's psychocultural archetypes (cf. Aberle 1960), although in Boas' case, the emphasis was less on emotional predispositions than on differing "categories of thought" and a typology of cognitive styles (Hymes 1961a).

 S E L E C T I O N   3 3

The Religion of
American Indians

For the purpose of a brief description of the religion of the American Indians we may define religion as that group of concepts and acts which spring from the relation of the individual to the outer world, so far as these relations are not considered as due to physical forces the action of which is accounted for by purely rationalistic considerations. The scope of religious concepts will depend to a certain extent, therefore, on the knowledge of the laws of nature; and, since the border-line of the natural and the supernatural, as conceived in the mind of primitive man, does not coincide with our view of this subject, there will be marked differences between the scope of religion among civilized nations and that among less advanced peoples. For instance, the causal relations determining the movements of the stars are recognized by civilized man;

"Religion," in *Handbook of American Indians North of Mexico*, ed. F. W. Hodge, Bureau of American Ethnology Bulletin No. 30, Part II (Washington: Government Printing Office, 1910), pp. 365–371.

but at an earlier time it was believed that the positions of the stars influenced in a mysterious manner the fates of man and that their movements could be controlled by his will. Among tribes which held to the latter opinion, views relating to the heavenly bodies would form part of the religion of the people; while among those peoples to which the causal relations determining the motions of the stars are known, these motions are no longer subject to religious interpretations.

Owing to the different point of view, it may also happen that certain ideas of primitive man, which from our standpoint would have to be considered as religious in character, are interpreted by the people holding them as purely rationalistic. In our judgment, for instance, sympathetic cures, which are believed in by most primitive tribes and even by uneducated people among ourselves, can not be considered as due to any physical effect, while among primitive tribes they may be so viewed. The same is true of certain mythological concepts. If an Indian tribe explains the markings on the skin of the chipmunk as due to the fact that at an early time the grizzly bear scratched its back, this may be to the mind of the Indian a perfectly rationalistic explanation, while to us it would be entirely mysterious. Thus it appears that the general views of nature—the explanations given for the occurrence of natural phenomena—necessarily enter into a consideration of the religions of primitive tribes, even if these explanations should be based on a purely rationalistic attitude on the part of primitive man. The less clear the line between observation and reasoning on the one hand and imagination and inference due to emotional states on the other, the less sharply drawn will be the line between what may be called science and religion. In accordance with the definition given before, those concepts that spring from the relation of the individual to the outer world, and the form of which depends on imagination and emotion, may be said to form the tenets of religion.

When religious acts are considered in greater detail, it appears that here also acts prompted by rationalistic considerations are not sharply separated from others dictated by imagination and emotion. Thus, when a medicine-man pursues and captures the fleeing soul of a sick man, he may follow out by his acts in a rational way opinions based largely on reasoning, although deeply affected in their origin by such emotions as fear and love. When, on the other hand, he tries to gain greater efficiency by putting himself into a state of emotional excitement, in which he believes his chances of success are enhanced, his acts become religious, in the stricter sense of the term. This lack of sharp division between rationalistic and religious forms of activity is found everywhere. Furthermore, it must be borne in mind that many actions are performed without any conscious reason, except so far as they are required by custom. This is true particularly of actions that are considered as proper, like those determined by rules regulating the behavior of the young to the old, or of the common people to the nobility; or also of actions that are considered as ethical, like those of hospitality and of pity. Here the line of demarcation between religious activities and others not connected with religion becomes even less sharp, because it often happens that actions originally performed without any particular reason or for purely rationalistic purposes are secondarily given religious motives. It thus follows that religious views and actions are not primarily connected with ethical concepts. Only in so far as man in his religious relations to the outer world endeavors to follow certain rules of conduct, in order to avoid evil effects, is a relation between primitive religion and ethics established.

The religious concepts of the Indians may be described in two groups —those that concern the individual, and those that concern the social group, such as tribe and clan. The fundamental concept bearing on the religious life of the individual is the belief in the existence of magic power, which may influence the life of man, and which in turn may be influenced by human activity. In this sense magic power must be understood as the wonderful qualities which are believed to exist in objects, animals, men, spirits, or deities, and which are superior to the natural qualities of man. This idea of magic power is one of the fundamental concepts that occur among all Indian tribes. It is what is called *manito* by the Algonquian tribes; *wakanda,* by the Siouan tribes; *orenda,* by the Iroquois; *sulia,* by the Salish; *naualak,* by the Kwakiutl, and *tamanoas,* by the Chinook. Notwithstanding slight differences in the signification of these terms, the fundamental notion of all of them is that of a power inherent in the objects of nature which is more potent than the natural powers of man. This idea seems adequately expressed by our term "wonderful"; and it is hardly necessary to introduce an Indian term, as has often been attempted. Among the American terms, the word *manito* has been most frequently used to express this idea. The degree to which the magic power of nature is individualized differs considerably among various tribes. Although the belief in the powers of inanimate objects is common, we find in America that, on the whole, animals, particularly the larger ones, are most frequently considered as possessed of such magic power. Strong anthropomorphic individualization also occurs, which justifies us in calling these powers deities. It seems probable that among the majority of tribes, besides the belief in the power of specific objects, a belief in a magic power that is only vaguely localized, exists. In cases where this belief is pronounced, the notion sometimes approaches the concept of a deity, or of a great spirit which is hardly anthropomorphic in its character. This is the case, for instance, among the Tsimshian of British Columbia and among the Algonquian tribes of the Great Lakes, and also in the figure of the Tirawa of the Pawnee.

As stated before, the whole concept of the world—or, in other words, the mythology of each tribe—enters to a very great extent into their religious concepts and activities. The mythologies are highly specialized in different parts of North America; and, although a large number of myths are the common property of many American tribes, the general view of the world appears to be quite distinct in various parts of the continent. Taking into consideration the continent of America as a whole, we find a type of explanation of the world which is psychologically quite different from the familiar Semitic type. In the Semitic religions eternal existence appeared as an unintelligible problem, and the mind preferred to assume a beginning which was accounted for by transferring the existing world, as it was known by observation, into the thought of a creator, and interpreting the creation as a projection of his thoughts by his will-power into objective existence. The Indian mind, on the other hand, accepts the eternal existence of the world, and accounts for its specific form by the assumption that events which once happened in early times settled for once and all the form in which the same kind of event must continue to occur. For instance, when the bear produced the stripes of the chipmunk by scratching its back, this determined that all chipmunks were to have such stripes; or when an ancestor of a clan was taught a certain ceremony, that same ceremony must be performed by all future generations. This idea is not by any means confined to America, but is found among primitive peoples of other continents as well, and occurs even in Semitic cults.

Considering American mythologies in their broadest outlines, the following areas may be distinguished: (1) The Eskimo area, the mythology of which is characterized by an abundance of purely human hero-tales, and a very small number of traditions accounting for the origin of animals, and these generally largely in human setting. (2) The North Pacific Coast area, characterized by a large cycle of transformer myths, in which the origin of many of the arts of man is accounted for, as well as the peculiarities of many animals; the whole forming a very disconnected heterogeneous mass of traditions. (3) Allied to these appear the traditions of the Western plateau and of the Mackenzie basin area, a region in which animal tales abound, many accounting for the present conditions of the world, the whole being very disconnected and contradictory. (4) The Californian area, the mythologies of which are characterized by a stronger emphasis laid on creation by will-power than is found in most other parts of the American continent. (5) The principal characteristic of the mythologies of the area of the Great Plains, the eastern woodlands, and the arid Southwest, is the tendency to systematization of the myths under the influence of a highly developed ritual. This tendency is more sharply defined in the S. than in the N. and N. E., and has perhaps progressed further than anywhere else among the Pueblos, to whom the origin of the clans and societies seems to give the keynote of mythological concepts; and among the Pawnee, whose contemplation of the stars seems to have given the principal tone to their mythology. The religious concepts of the Indians deal largely with the relation of the individual to the magic power mentioned above, and are specialized in accordance with their general mythological concepts, which determine largely the degree to which the powers are personified as animals, spirits, or deities.

Another group of religious concepts, which are not less important than the group heretofore discussed, refers to the relations of the individual to his internal states, so far as these are not controlled by the will, and are therefore considered as subject to the external magic influences. Most important among these are dreams, sickness, and death. These may be produced by obsession, or by external forces which compel the soul to leave the body. In this sense the soul is considered by almost all tribes as not subject to the individual will; it may be abstracted from the body by hostile forces, and it may be damaged and killed. The concept of the soul itself shows a great variety of forms. Very often the soul is identified with life, but we also find commonly the belief in a multiplicity of souls. Thus, among the Eskimo, the name is considered as one of the souls of man, another soul belongs to the body, a third one is independent of the body. The soul is also identified with the blood, the bones, the shadow, the nape of the neck. Based on these ideas is also the belief in the existence of the soul after death. Thus, in the belief of the Algonquian Indians of the Great Lakes, the souls of the deceased are believed to reside in the far west with the brother of the great culture-hero. Among the Kutenai the belief prevails that the souls will return at a later period, accompanying the culture-hero. Sometimes the land from which the ancestors of the tribe have sprung, which in the S. is often conceived of as underground, is of equal importance.

Since the belief in the existence of magic powers is very strong in the Indian mind, all his actions are regulated by the desire to retain the good will of those friendly to him, and to control those that are hostile.

The first means of retaining the good will of the friendly power is the strict observance of a great variety of proscriptions. An important group of these may be combined under the term "taboo." Among these, furthermore, food taboos are particularly common. Every tribe of America, no matter how scanty their means of subsistence may have been, had certain kinds of tabooed food—that is, food forbidden, either permanently or at certain seasons, or on certain occasions. Thus, one division of the Omaha were forbidden to eat the shoulder of the buffalo, while another one was forbidden to eat the elk; the Iroquois were forbidden to eat the animal from which their family name was taken, and the same is true of Pueblo and other clans; the Eskimo must not eat caribou and walrus at the same season; the Navaho must not touch flesh of the bear, nor the Zuñi anything that lives in the water.

Not less numerous are the taboos of work. These are perhaps nowhere so highly developed as among the Eskimo, among whom work on caribou-skins, seal-skins, metals, ice, and heather is forbidden under certain conditions. Here belong, also, the taboos of story-telling, and of playing certain games at certain seasons, which are quite common. Of great importance are the taboos intended to prevent the evil effects of impurity. Thus we find a large number of taboos forbidding menstruating women, murderers, and mourners from performing certain kinds of work. They must not touch fresh food lest the magic powers controlling the food supply may be offended.

Social taboos, which are very common in Polynesia, are not so markedly developed in America, although the strict secrecy with which certain sacred actions are performed by privileged members of a tribe is akin to this institution. Thus it is forbidden, except on certain occasions, for any member of the tribe to touch or even see the contents of sacred bundles, and even then only the keeper of the bundle is allowed to open it to view. While all these taboos are essentially negative in their character, forbidding certain actions in order to avoid giving offense, there are positive acts which are required for the same purpose. Some of these might well be called rules of ethical conduct, although the one reason given for them is the endeavor to retain the good will of the wonderful powers of nature. All the numerous regulations which are found all over the continent, and intended to retain the good will of the food animals, and which are essentially signs of respect shown to them, belong to this class. Dogs must not gnaw the bones of food animals, because this is a sign of disrespect. The bear, after having been killed, receives marks of reverence; and the first game animals obtained at the beginning of the hunting season must be treated with particular care. The complicated customs relating to buffalo hunting, and the salmon ceremonials of the N. W. Indians, as well as the whale ceremonials of the Eskimo, may also be given as examples. Respectful behavior toward old people and generally decent conduct are also often counted among such required acts. Here may also be included the numerous customs of purification that are required in order to avoid the ill will of the powers. These, however, may better be considered as constituting one of the means of controlling magic power, which form a very large part of the religious observances of the American Indians.

The Indian is not satisfied with the attempt to avoid the ill will of the powers, but he tries also to make them subservient to his own needs. This end may be attained in a variety of ways. Perhaps the most characteristic of North American Indian methods of gaining control over supernatural powers is that of the acquisition of one of them as a personal protector. Generally this process is called the acquiring of a manito; and the most common method of acquiring it is for the young man during the period of adolescence to purify himself by fasting, bathing, and vomiting, until his body is perfectly clean and acceptable to the supernatural beings. At the same time the youth works himself by these means, by dancing, and sometimes also by means of drugs, into a trance, in which he has a vision of the guardian spirit which is to protect him throughout life. These means of establishing communication with the spirit world are in very general use, also at other periods of life. The magic power that man thus acquires may give him special abilities; it may make him a successful hunter, warrior, or shaman; or it may give him power to acquire wealth, success in gambling, or the love of women.

While the above is the most common method of acquiring magic power, other means are well known among the American Indians, particularly among those tribes in which strong clan organizations prevail. They believe that wonderful power may be attained by inheritance. There are also numerous cases, as among the Arapaho and Blackfeet (Siksika), where the privilege of acquiring it and the control over it may be purchased. Among the American Eskimo the idea prevails that it may be transmitted by teaching and by bodily contact with a person who controls such powers. Ordinarily its possession is considered so sacred that it must not be divulged except in cases of extreme danger, but among other tribes it may be made known to the whole tribe. In a few cases the opinion prevails that such powers exist in certain localities, but can not be acquired by individuals.

Another means of controlling the powers of nature is by prayer, which may be directed either to the protecting spirit of the individual or to other powers. Objects of prayer may be protection in danger, removal of sickness, the obtaining of food or other material benefits, or a more general and abstract request for the blessing of the powers. Many prayers are addressed in fixed form or contain at least certain old formulas.

Another way of invoking the protection of the powers is through the use of charms (also called fetishes). The charm is either believed to be the seat of magic power, or it may be a symbol of such power, and its action may be based on its symbolic significance. Of the former kind are presumably many objects contained in the sacred bundles of certain Indians, which are believed to be possessed of sacred powers; while symbolic significance seems to prevail in charms like the stones worn by the North Pacific Coast Indians, which are believed to harden the skin against missiles of hostile shamans, or the magic whip of wolf-skin of the Eskimo, which is believed to have the power of driving away spirits.

Symbolic actions are also made use of. Such acts are, for instance, the setting-up of prayer-sticks, which are meant to convey man's wishes to the powers. Often these wishes are indicated by special attachments, expressing in symbolic or pictographic manner the thing wished for. Somewhat related to such symbolic actions are also all processes of divination, in which, by a symbolic act, the propitiousness of the proposed undertaking is ascertained.

Still more potent means of influencing the powers are offerings and sacrifices. On the whole, these are not so strongly developed in North America as they are in other parts of the world. In many regions human sacrifices were common—for instance, in Mexico and Yucatan—while in northern America they are known only in rare instances, as among the

Pawnee. However, many cases of torture, particularly of self-torture, must be reckoned here. Other bloody sacrifices are also rare in North America. We may mention the sacrifice of the dog among the Iroquois. Only to a limited extent do we find the tendency of considering the killing of game as a bloody sacrifice. On the other hand, sacrifices of tobacco smoke, of corn, and of parts of food, of small manufactured objects, and of symbolic objects, are very common. These gifts may be offered to any of the supernatural powers with the intent of gaining their assistance and avoiding their enmity.

Still another way of gaining control over supernatural powers is by incantations, which in a way are related to prayers, but which act rather through the magic influence of the words. Therefore the traditional form of these incantations is rigidly adhered to. They occur frequently among the Arctic tribes of the continent, but are not by any means lacking among others, who believe that the recitation of a short formula may aid in reaching a desired end. In the same way that incantations are related to prayer, certain acts and charms are related to offerings. We find among almost all Indian tribes the custom of performing certain acts, which are neither symbolic nor offerings, nor other attempts to obtain the assistance of superior beings, but which are effective through their own potency. Such acts are the use of lucky objects intended to secure good fortune; or the peculiar treatment of animals, plants, and other objects, in order to bring about a change of weather.

There is also found among most Indian tribes the idea that the supernatural powers, if offended by transgressions of rules of conduct, may be propitiated by punishment. Such punishment may consist in the removal of the offending individual, who may be killed by the members of the tribe, or the propitiation may be accomplished by milder forms of punishment. Of particular interest among these is confession as a means of propitiation, which is found among the Athapascans, the Iroquois, and the Eskimo. Other forms of punishment are based largely on the idea of purification by fasting, bathing, and vomiting. Among the Plains Indians the vow to perform a ceremony or another act agreeable to the powers is considered an efficient means of gaining their good will or of atoning for past offenses.

Protection against disease is also sought by the help of superhuman powers. These practices have two distinct forms, according to the fundamental conception of disease. Disease is conceived of principally in two forms—either as due to the presence of a material object in the body of the patient, or as an effect of the absence of the soul from the body. The cure of disease is intrusted to the shamans or medicine-men, who obtain their powers generally by the assistance of guardian spirits, or who may personally be endowed with magic powers. It is their duty to discover the material disease which is located in the patient's body, and which they extract by sucking or pulling with the hands; or to go in pursuit of the absent soul, to recover it, and to restore it to the patient. Both of these forms of shamanism are found practically all over the continent, but in some regions—for instance, in California—the idea of material bodies that cause sickness is particularly strongly developed; while in other regions the idea of the absence of the soul seems to be more marked. In treating the patient, the shamans almost everywhere use various means to work themselves into a state of excitement, which is produced by singing, by the use of the drum and rattle, and by dancing. The belief also widely prevails that unpropitious conditions may counter-act the work of the shaman, and that for this reason particular care must be taken to remove all disturbing and impure elements from the place where the shamanistic performance is held. When the shaman has to have intercourse with the spirits, whom he visits in their own domain, or when he has to pursue the soul of the patient, we find frequently sleight-of-hand employed, such as the tying of the hands of the shaman, who, when his soul leaves the body, is believed to free himself with the help of the spirits.

The belief that certain individuals can acquire control over the powers has also led to the opinion that they may be used to harm enemies. The possession of such control is not always beneficial, but may be used also for purposes of witchcraft. Hostile shamans may throw disease into the bodies of their enemies or they may abduct their souls. They may do harm by sympathetic means, and control the will-power of others by the help of the supernatural means at their disposal. Witchcraft is every-where considered as a crime, and is so punished.

Besides those manifestations of religious belief that relate to the indi-vidual, religion has become closely associated with the social structure of the tribes; so that the ritualistic side of religion can be understood only in connection with the social organization of the Indian tribes. Even the fundamental traits of their social organization possess a religious import. This is true particularly of the clans, so far as they are characterized by totems. The totem is almost always an object of more or less religious reverence to the clan; and there are many cases in which taboos relating to the totemic animal exist, like those previously referred to among the Omaha. Also in cases where the clans have definite political functions, like those of the Omaha and the Iroquois, these functions are closely asso-ciated with religious concepts, partly in so far as their origin is ascribed to myths, partly in so far as the functions are associated with the per-formance of religious rites. The position of officials is also closely associ-ated with definite religious concepts. Thus, the head of a clan at times is considered as the representative of the mythological ancestor of the clan, and as such is believed to be endowed with superior powers; or the posi-tion as officer in the tribe or clan entails the performance of certain definite religious functions. In this sense many of the political functions among Indian tribes are closely associated with what may be termed "priestly functions." The religious significance of social institutions is most clearly marked in cases where the tribe, or large parts of the tribe, join in the performance of certain ceremonies which are intended to serve partly a political, partly a religious end. Such acts are some of the intertribal ballgames, the busk of the Creeks, the sundance of the Plains Indians, performances of the numerous warrior societies of the Plains, which will be found treated under these headings. Here also belong the secret societies, which are highly developed among the Pueblos, in California, and on the North Pacific coast. It is characteristic of rituals in many parts of the world that they tend to develop into a more or less dramatic representation of the myth from which the ritual is derived. For this reason the use of masks is a common feature of these rituals, in which certain individuals impersonate supernatural beings. In those tribes among which very complex rituals have developed we find the ceremonies frequently in charge of certain officers, who are at the same time the keepers of the sacred objects belonging to the tribe or to the societies; and it would seem that the whole system of religious beliefs and practices has developed the more systematically, the more strictly the religious practices have come to be in charge of a body of priests. This tendency to systematization of religious beliefs may be observed particularly among the Pueblos and the Pawnee, but it also occurs in isolated cases in other parts of the continent; for instance, among the Bellacoola of British Columbia, and those Algonquian tribes that have the Midewiwin ceremonial fully developed. In these cases we find that frequently an elaborate series of esoteric doctrines and practices exists, which are known to only a small portion of the tribe, while the mass of the people are familiar only with part of the ritual and with its exoteric features. For this reason we often find the religious beliefs and practices of the mass of a tribe rather heterogeneous as compared with the beliefs held by the priests. Among many of the tribes in which priests are found, we find distinct esoteric societies, and it is not by any means rare that the doctrines of one society are not in accord with those of another. All this is clearly due to the fact that the religious ideas of the tribe are derived from many different sources, and have been brought into order at a later date by the priests charged with the keeping of the tribal rituals. Esoteric forms of religion in charge of priests are found among the tribes of the arid region in the Southwest, the tribes of the southern Mississippi basin, and to a less extent among the more northerly tribes on the Plains. It would seem that, on the whole, the import of the esoteric teachings decreases among the more northerly and northeasterly tribes of the continent. It is probably least developed among the Eskimo, the tribes of the Mackenzie basin, and the tribes of the great plateau region, in so far as these have remained uninfluenced by the Plains Indians and by those of the Pacific coast.

On the whole, the Indians incline strongly toward all forms of religious excitement. This is demonstrated not only by the exuberant development of ancient religious forms, but also by the frequency with which prophets have appeared among them, who taught new doctrines and new rites, based either on older religious beliefs, or on teaching partly of Christian, partly of Indian origin. Perhaps the best known of these forms of religion is the Ghost-dance, which swept over a large part of the continent during the last decade of the 19th century. But other prophets of similar type and of far-reaching influence were numerous. One of these was Tenskwatawa, the famous brother of Tecumseh; another, the seer Smohalla of the Pacific coast; and even among the Eskimo such prophets have been known, particularly in Greenland.

    S E L E C T I O N   3 4

Anthropology ~ 1907

In attempting to set forth briefly the principal results of anthropological research, I find my task beset with many difficulties. If the clear enunciation of the aims and methods of physical or biological science is not an easy matter, difficulties many times greater are encountered in an attempt to explain the present position of investigation dealing with mankind from the biological, geographical, and psychological points of view,—subjects that seem to lack in unity, and that present a number of most divergent aspects. Owing to the apparent heterogeneity of method, it seems necessary to explain the aims that unify the many lines of anthropological research. I can then proceed to describe what little has been attained, and how we hope to make further progress.

We do not discuss the anatomical, physiological, and mental characteristics of man considered as an individual; but we are interested in the diversity of these traits in groups of men found in different geographical areas and in different social classes. It is our task to inquire into the causes that have brought about the observed differentiation, and to investigate the sequence of events that have led to the establishment of the multifarious forms of human life. In other words, we are interested in anatomical and mental characteristics in so far as they are peculiar to groups of men living under the same biological, geographical, and social

Anthropology: A Lecture Delivered at Columbia University in the Series on Science, Philosophy, and Art, December 18, 1907 (New York: Columbia University Press, 1908).

environment, and as determined by their past. Thus we are concerned with the effects of the climate and products of a country upon human life, with the influence of heat and of cold upon the bodily frame, with modifications in the life of communities brought about by geographical isolation, and with those due to the sufficiency or insufficiency of food-supply. No less interesting to us are the phenomena of dependence of human life upon those social conditions that find expression in the customary mode of nutrition and occupation; in the effects of contact between neighboring groups of people; in modifications brought about by migrations; and in the forms of life as influenced by the density of population. To understand these modifications, we require a knowledge of individual anatomy, physiology, and psychology, because the establishment of a characteristic social group can be brought about only by a parallel development which occurs in all the individuals exposed to similar influences.

Thus it appears that the genesis of the types of man, considered from an anatomical, physiological, and psychological point of view, is the chief object of anthropological research. When our problem is formulated in this manner, we recognize at once that a separation of anthropological methods from the methods of biology and psychology is impossible, and that certain problems of anthropology can be approached only from the point of view of these sciences. It might perhaps even be said that the investigation of the types of man is a purely biological problem, and that the only questions involved are such as can be treated by the application of those biological methods which are gradually clearing up the genesis of the types of animals and plants. A similar claim may be made in regard to the psychological problems. If there are any laws determining the growth and development of the human mind, they can be only laws that act in the individual, and consequently they must be determined by the application of individual psychology.

Thus an examination of our problems suggests that the whole group of anthropological phenomena may be evanescent, that they may be at bottom biological and psychological problems, and that the whole field of anthropology belongs either to the one or to the other of these sciences.

Nevertheless, anthropological phenomena possess a very genuine interest and unity. This is largely due to the fact that everything that concerns our own species is of special interest to us. The feeling of solidarity of mankind, but more particularly of the individual with his people and with the class of society to which he belongs, which finds in our day its strongest expression in the strife of the nations, has brought it about that the minute differences between the physical organization of different races, types, and social groups, have arrested attention much more vigorously than similar differences in the rest of the animal kingdom have done; and points of view have early become important that until recent times have received little attention on the part of biologists, or that have not yet claimed their attention. The distribution of distinct psychological types in man has proved an even more fascinating study, the investigation of which has led to problems that the inductive psychology of modern times is not yet ready to attack.

This centralization of interest in the manifestations of life in social units has determined the course of development of anthropology.

Anthropological research leads us to two fundamental questions: Why are the tribes and nations of the world different, and how have the present differences developed? The first question, if it can be solved adequately, will always lead us to biological and psychological laws that act on man as an individual, in which we see the single event mirrored in one broad generalization. But even if we should have succeeded in reducing to a series of laws the multiplicity of events which manifest themselves in the development of new types and in the growth of new mental activities, a strong interest will remain in the actual developments which have occurred among the various peoples of the world.

This is true not only of anthropology, but also of biology and genetic psychology, and of other sciences describing the sequence of events in the universe; and the intense modern interest in evolution expresses the recognition of the importance of what might be called the historical viewpoint.

In this sense, anthropology is the science that endeavors to reconstruct the early history of mankind, and that tries, wherever possible, to express in the form of laws ever-recurring modes of historical happenings. Since written history covers a brief span of time, and relates in fragmentary records the fates of a few only of the multitude of peoples of the earth, the anthropologist must endeavor by methods of his own to clear up the darkness of past ages and of remote parts of the world.

While, from this theoretical point of view, anthropology must devote itself to the investigation of human types and human activities and thought the world over, its actual field of work is much more restricted. Biology and psychology on the one hand, and history, economics, sociology, and philology on the other, have taken up anthropological problems, each from its own point of view, and each in connection with its own subject of investigation. As a matter of fact, the field of work as theoretically outlined would require such a vast variety of training, that no single person could possibly hope to master it. The special task that is actually assigned at the present time to the anthropologist is the investigation of the primitive tribes of the world that have no written history, that of prehistoric remains and of the types of man inhabiting the world at present and in past times. It will be recognized that this limitation of the field of work of the anthropologist is more or less accidental, and originated because other sciences occupied part of the ground before the development of modern anthropology.

It implies, however, also a point of view fundamentally distinct from that of history in the narrow sense of the term. In history we are, on the whole, concerned with events only that have had an influence upon the development of our own civilization; in anthropology the life of every people of the world is equally important. Therefore, in a wider sense, it is impossible to exclude any part of mankind from the considerations of anthropology. The results of studies carried on by the historian and by the sinologist must not be neglected by the anthropologist in his endeavors to investigate the history of mankind and its controlling forces. It will thus be seen that anthropology differs from history, and resembles the natural sciences in its endeavor to disregard the subjective values of historical happenings; that it tries to consider them objectively, simply as a sequence of events, regardless of their influence upon the course of our own civilization.

In the vastness of the outlook over the unwritten history of past ages, the individual is merged entirely in the social unit of which he forms a part, and we see in the dim distance of time and space only the movements of peoples, the emergence of new types of man, the gradual development of new forms of civilization, and a constant repetition of processes of integration and disintegration of peoples and cultures. Prehistoric remains, characteristics of bodily form, traits of language, industrial and economic achievements, peculiar customs and beliefs, are the only evidence that we can use,—evidence that was little regarded by history until the anthropological standpoint began to develop. Thus it happens that although the anthropologist may not be able, owing to the specialization of the methods of inquiry, to investigate problems like those dealing with the modern history of Europe and China, the historian and the sinologist will be able to view their problems from an anthropological standpoint. With the increase of our knowledge of the peoples of the world, specialization must increase, and anthropology will become more and more *a method* that may be applied by a great number of sciences, rather than a science by itself.

We shall next take up a consideration of the results of the biological and psychological researches carried on by anthropologists. It is somewhat remarkable that these two large branches of investigation have remained quite separate, and that the results of the one throw little light upon the problems of the other. Biological anthropology has concerned itself chiefly with the classification of races, their relations to their predecessors and ultimately to the higher animals; and little progress has been made in the clearing-up of the genealogical relations of distinct types. Diligent search has revealed a number of lower forms which lived during the early quaternary and the late tertiary periods that help a little in bridging the wide gap between man and animal; but we are still entirely in the dark regarding the origin of the fundamental races and of the types of man.

Since observations in different geographical areas showed at an early time the differentiation of local types, which it was difficult to define in words, anthropology was the first of the biological sciences to have recourse to metrical methods; and the whole modern development of biometry takes its origin in the application of methods developed by anthropologists, and by means of which fine distinctions between closely related types can be discovered. Originally the metrical methods of anthropologists were used for purely taxonomic ends, for the description of distinct types; and for years chief attention has been paid to the classification of the types of man according to their similarities, and to speculation on their relationships; but, owing to the influence of Francis Galton and his successors, we are gradually outgrowing this condition, and we see that more and more problems relating to the influence of social and geographical environment, of heredity, of race mixture and selection, are made the subject of study. This development has been closely associated with the growth of biometric methods applied to zoology and botany.

One of the important facts that has been recognized by a study of the morphology of the races is that man must be considered as a domesticated animal, and that even those tribes which are industrially the most primitive are somewhat removed from the anatomical conditions characterizing the wild animals. It appears, however, that the degree of domestication has strongly increased with the growing complexity of industrial organization; and most of the races of the present day are anatomically in the same condition as those types of domesticated animals which are highly modified by regular feeding and by disuse of a considerable portion of the muscular system, without, however, having been subjected to any considerable artificial selection. This seems to be one of the causes of the high degree of variability of the races of man.

While it is not yet possible to express definite views in regard to the relationship of the races of man, a few facts stand out boldly. We recognize that the two extreme types of mankind are represented, on the one hand by the Negro race, on the other hand by the Mongoloid race. The former of these includes the races of Africa and many of those inhabiting the large islands surrounding Australia; the other includes the people of eastern Asia and of America. The other strongly divergent types of man can most readily be classed with these two fundamental types, and may perhaps be considered as mutants which developed at an early period. Thus we find affiliated with the Negro race two divergent types, nevertheless apparently closely related to it,—the dwarfish South African, who is perhaps intimately related to the many isolated dwarfish tribes of other parts of Africa and southern Asia; and the Australian. The Mongoloid type, on the other hand, has also a considerable number of affiliated types, which may perhaps represent mutants of this type. Here belong the Malay of southeastern Asia, the Ainu of northern Japan, and perhaps the European. If we base our conception of the division of mankind on this broad outline, it would appear that two large divisions were established at an early geological period,—the race of the Indian Ocean, which represents all the Negroid types; and the race of the Pacific Ocean, which represents the Mongoloid and affiliated types. The enormous increase in the number of Europeans during the last two or three thousand years, and their rapid spread over the surface of the globe, disturb the clearness of this view; but we must remember that the white race represented originally only a very small part of mankind, and occupied only a small portion of the inhabited world.

What relation the two principal types may have had to the predecessor of mankind which is represented by the early quaternary race of Europe is unknown.

The history of the spread of these large races over the continents remains also, to a great extent, obscure. It seems likely, however, that the race of the Pacific Ocean immigrated into America at a very early time, and that after the retreat of the ice-sheet it swept back into northern Asia and re-established itself in the whole northern part of the Old World, which had been uninhabited for long periods. Much of this, however, remains hypothesis, which may be confirmed or disproved by further studies.

While the divergence of the types of man suggests that the tendency to form mutants has been ever-present, it would seem that the varieties which have survived up to the present time have been exceedingly stable, within the limits of their characteristic ranges of variation. The human remains found in Europe, which undoubtedly date back many thousands of years, and the remains of ancient Egypt, both of which may be compared with the types represented in the modern population of those countries, are much like the modern forms, and apparently no change of type has occurred in these districts for thousands of years. The same stability of race types manifests itself in cases of mixture. It would seem that among the human races there is a strong tendency for hybrids to revert to either parental type without forming an intermediate race. Thus we find that in western Asia the low-headed Semitic type and the high-headed Armenian type persist, although an intermingling of these people has been going on for thousands of years.

Nevertheless an influence of environment must be recognized. It may be observed, for instance, in the development of the European after his immigration into America. It may be recognized in the minute but noticeable differences of types in various parts of Europe and in different occupations, in the acceleration of growth of children of well-to-do classes, and in the stunting and retarding effect of mal-nutrition. Whether, however, these effects can be considered as permanent, is a question that is still entirely open.

Our investigations of the permanence and relationships of human types have also shown that it is exceedingly difficult, if not impossible, to find what might be called a pure type, and the endeavors to find pure races through a mixture of which the present variable types may have originated must be given up. We have recognized that the transitions between types are so gradual, and in so many different directions, that the establishment of any one of the series as a primary type would be quite arbitrary. All the nations of modern times, and those of Europe not less than those of other continents, are equally mixed; and the racial purity on which European nations like to pride themselves does not exist.

In still other directions have the investigations of anthropology rudely shattered some of our cherished illusions. It has been tacitly assumed and loudly proclaimed that one of the effects of advance in civilization has been the improvement of the physical organization of the human body, and particularly of the central nervous system. At the present time we are not so apt to accept this assumption as proved. No progressive development of the nervous system in regard to complexity of connections or in regard to size has so far been proved. A critical examination of the facts leaves the desire to feel ourselves as superiors to our fellow-beings as almost the sole support of this contention. The question involved is, of course, a very important one, and forms an aspect of the general question of the transmission of acquired characters; but our present attitude can only be one for a demand for further investigation.

A word should also be said about the question of the difference of mental ability in different races. Here also the evidence given by anthropology does not sustain the claim of superiority of any race over the others. All the arguments that have been brought forward to prove the superiority of the white race over all others can readily be explained by other anthropological considerations. There *are* differences in form and size of the brains of different races, but the variability within each race is so great that the small average differences between distinct racial types are almost insignificant as compared to the total range of racial variability; and if we base our inferences entirely on the results of anatomical study, it would seem that there is no reason to believe that the bulk of the people constituting two distinct races might not be approximately on the same level. Nevertheless it seems reasonable to assume that the differences in form of the body must be accompanied by differences in function, and we may suppose that there may be certain peculiarities in the general mental tendencies of each race, only we must guard against the inference that divergence from the European type is synonymous with inferiority.

The history of development of the mental side of anthropology has been quite different from the growth of physical anthropology. While in the latter branch of our science the *differences* between human types were the first to attract attention, it was the *similarity* in cultural types found in remote regions which first impressed itself upon ethnologists. A comparison of the descriptions of the customs of primitive peoples the world over brought out analogies in ever-increasing number. These were early correlated with general impressions regarding the degrees of civilization; and thus it happened that one of the most difficult and complex problems of ethnology—namely, the question of the general typical evolution of the history of civilization of mankind—was the first to receive attention. I cannot pass this subject by without mentioning the deep impression made by men like Tylor and Bachofen, Morgan and Spencer, who were among the first to present the data of anthropology as illustrating the history of civilization.

The development of this side of anthropology was stimulated by the work of Darwin and his successors, and its fundamental ideas can be understood only as an application of the theory of biological evolution to mental phenomena. The conception that the manifestations of ethnic life represent a series, which from simple beginnings has progressed to the complex type of modern civilization, has been the underlying thought of this aspect of anthropological science.

The arguments in support of the theory that the development of civilization has followed a similar course everywhere, and that among primitive tribes we may still recognize the stages through which our own civilization has passed, are largely based on the similarities of types of culture found in distinct races the world over, but also on the occurrence of peculiar customs in our own civilization, which can be understood only as survivals of older customs, that had a deeper significance at an earlier time, and which are still found in full vigor among primitive people.

It is necessary to point out at least a few of the aspects of this general problem, in order to make clear the significance of the evolutionary theory of human civilization.

The social organization of primitive tribes shows similar traits in many different parts of the world. Instead of counting descent in the way we do, many tribes consider the child as a member only of its mother's family, and count blood-relationship only in the maternal line; so that cousins on the mother's side are considered as near relatives, while cousins on the father's side are considered as only distantly related. Other tribes have a strict paternal organization, so that the child belongs only to the father's family, not to the mother's, while still others follow the same principles that we adhere to, reckoning relationships in both directions. Connected with these customs is the selection of the domicile of the newly married couple, who sometimes reside with the wife's tribe or family, sometimes with the man's tribe or family. When the couple take up their residence with the social group to which the wife belongs, it is often found that the man is treated as a stranger until his first child is born. These phenomena have been made the subject of thorough studies, and the observation has been made that apparently the customs of residence and of descent are closely associated. As a result of these inquiries the conclusion has been drawn that everywhere maternal institutions precede paternal institutions, and that the social organization of mankind was such that originally perhaps no distinct family organization existed; that later on maternal institutions developed, which in turn were followed by paternal institutions, and again by the system of counting blood-relationship equally in maternal and paternal lines.

Similar results were obtained by the study of human inventions. It has been observed that apes and monkeys sometimes use stones for defence, and in a way the artificial shelters of animals indicate the beginnings of invention. In this sense we may seek for the origin of implements and utensils among animals. In the earliest times when human remains appear on the surface of the earth, we find man using simple stone implements which are formed by rough chipping, but the multiplicity of forms of implements increases quite rapidly. Since many implements may have been made of perishable materials, we are not able to tell whether at a very early time the implements and utensils used were really confined to the few stone objects that may now be recovered; but certainly the implements were few, and comparatively speaking, simple. From this time on, the uses of fire, and of tools for cutting and striking, for scraping and perforating, have increased in number and complexity, and a gradual development may be traced from the simple tools of primitive man to the complex machinery of our times. The inventive genius of all races and of unnumbered individuals has contributed to the state of industrial perfection in which we find ourselves. On the whole, inventions, once made, have been kept with great tenacity, and, owing to incessant additions, the available resources of mankind have constantly been increased and multiplied.

Researches on art have led to similar results. Investigators have endeavored to show, that, since the cave-dwellers of France drew the outlines of the reindeer and mammoth on bone and antler, man has tried to reproduce in pictographic design the animals of the region in which he lived. In the artistic productions of many people, designs have been found which are readily associated with pictographic presentations, which, however, have lost their realism of form, and have become more and more conventional; so that in many cases a purely decorative motive has been interpreted as developed from a realistic pictograph, gradually breaking up under the stress of esthetic motives. The islands of the Pacific Ocean, New Guinea, South America, Central America, prehistoric Europe, have furnished examples for this line of development, which therefore was recognized as one of the important tendencies of the evolution of human decorative art, which was described as beginning with realism, and as leading through symbolic conventionalism to purely esthetic motives.

Religion has furnished another example of typical evolution in human thought. At an early time man began to think and ponder about the phenomena of nature. Everything appeared to him in an anthropomorphic form of thought; and thus the first primitive concepts regarding the world came into being, in which the stone, the mountain, the heavenly orbs, were viewed as animate anthropomorphic beings endowed with will-power, and willing to help man or threatening to endanger him. The observation of the activities of man's own body and of his mind led to the formulation of the idea of a soul independent from the body; and with increasing knowledge and with increasing philosophic thought, religion and science grew out of these simple beginnings.

The sameness of all these phenomena in different parts of the world has been considered as proof not only of the fundamental unity of the mind of all the races of man, but also of the truth of the theory of evolution of civilization; and thus a grand structure has been reared, in which we see our present civilization as the necessary outcome of the activities of all the races of man, that have risen in one grand procession, from the simplest beginnings of culture, through periods of barbarism, to the stage of civilization that they now occupy. The march has not been equally rapid; for some are still lagging behind, while others have forged forward, and occupy the first places in the general advance.

While this evolutionary aspect has occupied the centre of attention for a long time, another view of the field of the phenomena of ethnology was defended by Bastian,—a view which makes its influence felt ever more deeply as time goes on. The sameness of the forms of thought found in regions wide apart appeared to Bastian as a proof of the unity of the human mind, but it also suggested to him that the forms of thought follow certain definite types, no matter in what surroundings man may live, and what may be his social and historical relations. In the varieties of thought found among peoples of distant areas he saw the influence of geographical and social environment upon these fundamental forms of thought, which were called by him elementary ideas. Bastian's theory of the permanence of forms of thought is related to Dilthey's conception of the limitation of possible types of philosophy; and the similarity of the line of thoughts of these two men appears also clearly in Bastian's constant references to the theories of philosophers as compared to the views held by primitive man. From Bastian's viewpoint the question of a single or multiple type of evolution of civilization appeared irrelevant. The important phenomenon in his mind was the fundamental sameness of forms of human thought in all forms of culture, no matter whether they were advanced or primitive.

In the views as propounded by him, a certain kind of mysticism may be recognized, in so far as the elementary ideas are to his mind intangible entities. No further thought can possibly unravel their origin, because we ourselves are compelled to think in the forms of these elementary ideas.

In a way the evolutionists and Bastian represent thus, the former the historical point of view, the latter a psychological point of view, in the field of ethnology. More recent discussions have taken up both threads of investigation, and both views are slowly undergoing a number of radical changes.

With increasing knowledge of the data of anthropology, the forms of society, of religion, of art, and the development of invention, do not seem quite so simple as they appeared to earlier investigators. Attempts were made to fit the hypothetical typical evolution of mankind to the historical development of culture in different parts of the world, so far as it had been reconstructed. Thus an opportunity was given to examine the correctness of the accepted theory. As soon as this was done, peculiar difficulties developed, which showed that the theory was hardly ever applicable to specific cases, and that the actual development, as it was traced by historical reconstruction, differed considerably from the theory. From this investigation has developed an entirely new view regarding the relation of different races. We begin to recognize that in prehistoric times, transmission of cultural elements has been almost unlimited, and that the distances over which inventions and ideas have been carried cover whole continents. As an instance of the rapidity with which cultural achievements are transmitted, may be mentioned the modern history of some cultivated plants. Tobacco was introduced into Africa after the discovery of America, and it took little time for this plant to spread over the whole continent; so that at the present time it enters so deeply into the whole culture of the Negro that nobody would suspect its foreign origin. We find in the same way that the banana has pervaded almost the whole of South America; and the history of Indian-corn is another example of the incredible rapidity with which a useful cultural acquisition may spread over the whole world. The history of the horse, of cattle, of the European grains, illustrates that similar conditions prevailed in prehistoric times. These animals and plants occur over the whole width of the Old World, from the Atlantic Ocean to the shores of the Pacific. The use of milk was probably disseminated in a similar way at an early time; so that when the people of the world enter into our historic knowledge, we find milk used all over Europe, Africa, and the western part of Asia.

Perhaps the best proof of transmission is contained in the folk-lore of the tribes of the world. Nothing seems to travel as readily as fanciful tales. We know of certain complex tales, which cannot possibly have been invented twice, that are told by the Berber in Morocco, by the Italians, the Irish, the Russians, in the jungles of India, in the highlands of Tibet, on the tundras of Siberia, and on the prairies of North America; so that perhaps the only parts of the world not reached by them are South Africa, Australia, Polynesia, and South America. The examples of such transmission are quite numerous, and we begin to see that the early inter-relation of the races of man was almost worldwide.

It follows from this observation that the culture of any given tribe, no matter how primitive it may be, can be fully explained only when we take into consideration its inner growth as well as its relation to the culture of its near and distant neighbors and the effect that they may have exerted.

The sameness of a number of fundamental ideas and inventions has suggested to some investigators the belief that there are old cultural achievements belonging to a period previous to the general dispersion of the human race,—a theory that has some points in its favor, though its correctness cannot be proved.

An important theoretical consideration has also shaken our faith in the correctness of the evolutionary theory as a whole. It is one of the essential traits of this theory that, in general, civilization has developed from simple forms to complex forms, and that extended fields of human culture have developed under more or less rationalistic impulses. Of late years we are beginning to recognize that human culture does not always develop from the simple to the complex, but that in many aspects two tendencies intercross,—one from the complex to the simple, the other from the simple to the complex. It is obvious that the history of industrial development is almost throughout that of increasing complexity. On the other hand, human activities that do not depend upon reasoning do not show a similar type of evolution.

It is perhaps easiest to make this clear by the example of language, which in many respects is one of the most important evidences of the history of human development. Primitive languages are, on the whole, complex. Minute differences in point of view are given expression by means of grammatical forms; and the grammatical categories of Latin, and still more so those of modern English, seem crude when compared to the complexity of psychological or logical forms which primitive languages recognize, but which in our speech are disregarded entirely. On the whole, the development of languages seems to be such that the nicer distinctions are eliminated, and that it begins with complex and ends with simpler forms, although it must be acknowledged that opposite tendencies are not by any means absent.

Similar observations may be made on the art of primitive man. In music as well as in decorative design we find a complexity of rhythmic structure which is unequalled in the popular art of our day. In music, particularly, this complexity is so great that the art of a skilled virtuoso is taxed in the attempt to imitate it. If once it is recognized that simplicity is not always a proof of antiquity, it will readily be seen that the theory of the evolution of civilization rests to a certain extent on a logical error. The classification of the data of anthropology in accordance with their simplicity has been re-interpreted as an historical sequence, without an adequate attempt to prove that the simpler antedated the more complex.

Notwithstanding this serious criticism, much of the older theory seems plausible; but presumably a thorough revision and a more individualized aspect of the development of civilization in different parts of the world will become necessary.

The psychological aspect of anthropology, which was first emphasized by Bastian, is also undergoing rapid development, particularly in so far as the problem of the origin of elementary ideas is concerned, the investigation of which Bastian considered as impossible. Here, again, the study of language promises to point the way in which many of our problems may find their solution. I have stated before that the languages of primitive tribes are, on the whole, complex, and differentiate nicely between categories of thought. It is very remarkable to find that these categories, which can be discovered only by an analytical study of the languages, and which are unknown to the speakers of these languages, although they are constantly used, coincide with categories of thought which have been discovered by philosophers. It would be possible to find in the languages of primitive people grammatical forms corresponding to a variety of philosophical systems; and in this we may perhaps recognize one of the most brilliant proofs of the correctness of Bastian's and Dilthey's theory of the existence of a limited number of types of thought.

We infer from these linguistic facts that the categories of thought, and the forms of action, that we find among a people, do not need to have been developed by conscious thought, but that they have grown up owing to the fundamental organization of the human mind. Linguistic evidence is of such great value, because grammatical categories and forms have never risen into the consciousness of the speaker, while in almost all other ethnological phenomena people have come to observe what they think and what they do. With the moment that activities and thoughts rise into consciousness they become the subject of speculation; and for this reason the peoples of the world, primitive as well as more advanced, are ever ready to give explanations of their customs and beliefs. The importance of the constant occurrence of such secondary explanations cannot be overrated. They are ever present. The investigator who inquires into the history of institutions and of customs will always receive explanations based on such secondary interpretation, which, however, do not represent the history of the custom or belief in question, but only the results of speculation in regard to it.

I will mention one other psychological point that seems of special importance in the discussion of the significance of primitive culture and its relation to more advanced types. In primitive culture certain activities appear closely connected which in more advanced types of civilization have no longer any relation. Thus it is one of the fundamental traits of primitive culture that social organization and religious belief are inextricably related. To a limited extent this tendency persists in our own civilization; but, on the whole, there has been a marked tendency to separate social and political organization, and religion. The same is true of primitive art and religion; and of primitive science, social organization, and religion. So far as we are able to investigate the causes for the peculiar associations between these varied manifestations of ethnic life and the history of their gradual disappearance, we find that in the stream of consciousness of primitive man a sensory stimulus is very liable to release strong emotions, which are in turn connected with certain groups of ideas. Thus the emotions common to both establish associations between groups of ideas that to us appear entirely unrelated. For the same reason it seems impossible for primitive man to establish those purely rationalistic associations between sense-impressions and acts determined by volition which are characteristic of civilized man. A study of primitive life shows that particularly every customary action attains a very strong emotional tone, which increases the stability of the custom. These forces are still acting in our own civilization. In order to make this clear, I only need to remind you of any of those actions which we call good manners, for which no satisfactory reason can be given; which nevertheless have acquired an emotional tone so strong that a breach of good manners is felt as a grave offence. It would, for instance, be impossible to give a reason why a gentleman should not be allowed to keep on his hat indoors, while it is good form for a lady to do so; and the instantaneous judgment by which we characterize an offender against these rules as rude, and the discomfort felt when we unwittingly commit a breach of good manners, show how deep-seated their emotional values are.

There is no doubt that the further pursuit of the psychological investigation, which has hardly been begun, will help us to find a more satisfactory explanation of many anthropological phenomena than those that we have been able to give heretofore.

You will perceive that anthropology is a science that is only beginning to find its own bearings, that many of the fundamental questions are still open to discussion, and that the promising lines of approach are just opening.

Nevertheless, anthropology has been able to teach certain facts that are of importance in our common every-day life. Owing to the breadth of its outlook, anthropology teaches better than any other science the relativity of the values of civilization. It enables us to free ourselves from the prejudices of our civilization, and to apply standards in measuring our achievements that have a greater absolute truth than those derived from a study of our civilization alone. The differences between our civilization and another type in which perhaps less stress is laid upon the rationalistic side of our mental activities and more upon the emotional side, or in which the outer manifestations of culture, as expressed in manner and dress, differ from ours, appear less as differences in *value* than as differences in *kind*. This broader outlook may also help us to recognize the possibility of lines of progress which do not happen to be in accord with the dominant ideas of our times.

Anthropology may also teach a better understanding of our own activities. We pride ourselves on following the dictates of reason and carrying out our carefully weighed convictions. The fact which is taught by anthropology,—that man the world over *believes* that he follows the dictates of reason, no matter how unreasonably he may act,—and the knowledge of the existence of the tendency of the human mind to arrive at a conclusion first and to give the reasons afterwards, will help us to open our eyes; so that we recognize that our philosophic views and our political convictions are to a great extent determined by our emotional inclinations, and that the reasons which we give are not the reasons by which we arrive at our conclusions, but the explanations which we give for our conclusions.

An important lesson is also taught by the course the general development of society has taken. Primitive social units were small, and the members possessed a strong feeling of solidarity among themselves and of hostility against all aliens. The social units have been increasing in size through all ages. Greater individual freedom was allowed to the members of the groups, and the feeling of hostility against strangers weakened. We are still in the middle of this development; and the history of mankind shows that any policy which oversteps the limits of necessary self-protection and seeks advancement of one nation by a policy disregarding the interests of others is bound to lose in the long-run, because it represents an older type of thought that is gradually disappearing.

I cannot leave my subject without saying a word in regard to the help that anthropological methods may render in the investigation of problems of public hygiene, of race-mixture, and of eugenics. The safe methods of biological and psychological anthropometry and anthropology will help us to remove these questions from the sphere of heated political discussion and to make them subjects of calm scientific investigation.

I have tried to outline in this imperfect picture the methods, aims, and hopes of anthropology. The definite facts that I could lay before you are few, and even the ground-work of the science appears hardly laid. Still I hope that the view of our ultimate aims may have engendered the feeling that we are striving for a goal which is bound to enlighten mankind, and which will be helpful in gaining a right attitude in the solution of the problems of life.

 *PART IX*

THE PROPAGATION
OF ANTHROPOLOGY

During many periods of his career, Boas spent as much or more time on administrative and organizational activities connected with the propagation of anthropology as he did in actual anthropological work —and needless to say, the anthropology he was most concerned to propagate was Boasian. He had arrived in the United States at a time when the entrepreneurial style was beginning to play an important role in science and in the academy; and from the beginning of his career he acted on the principle he later attributed to Virchow, working to create and control the institutional framework that would enable his ideas to wield "a far-reaching influence." At that time, the center of anthropological power in this country lay in the Bureau of Ethnology, to which, whether by chance or calculation, Boas remained an outsider throughout his career. Retrospectively, Boas' early career may be seen as a series of attempts to establish or to capitalize on alternative centers of institutional power. Following an unsuccessful attempt to revive the American Ethnological Society in New York after his debate with Mason and Powell in 1887, he established a connection with the New England–based American Folklore Society, contributing regularly to their journal, which he later edited for seventeen years (1908–1925). Boas' ultimate success depended on his connections with certain important subcultural milieux in New York and Boston. His uncle, Abraham Jacobi, was quite prominent in the New York German-Jewish community and had married a daughter of the publisher George Putnam. While at Clark, Boas established a close relationship with one of the New England Putnams, Professor Frederick Ward Putnam of Harvard's Peabody Museum, who was at this point perhaps the most influential American anthropologist outside Washington, and who, significantly, had always remained somewhat skeptical of the assumptions of cultural evolutionism. Though there were moments of strain, this was the one subordinate relationship that Boas was able to maintain over a fairly long period. During the critical decade of the 1890s, his career followed almost literally in Putnam's footsteps, as Putnam moved first to the Chicago Fair and then to the American Museum of Natural History (all the while maintaining his position at Harvard). The turning point, of course, was the appointment Boas received early in 1896 through the combined efforts of Jacobi and Putnam as lecturer in physical anthropology at Columbia University. Together with the position he had just accepted at the American Museum as assistant to Putnam, the Columbia appointment provided Boas with a firm institutional base. Significantly, it was one of a very different sort than the Washington anthropologists', whose lack of ties to any important academic institution would constrict severely the channels of Washington influence in the period after 1900.

Boas' vision of the way he might build upon this institutional base is contained in a letter he wrote in 1901 to Zelia Nuttall, who was advising Phoebe Apperson Hearst on plans to establish an anthropology department at the University of California (cf. Parmenter 1966). Despite Boas' opposition, the California department was of course founded, under the direction of Putnam (Freeman 1966)—one of a number of events that attenuated their relationship at about this time. Over the next few years Boas' plans were to suffer a number of setbacks, but the Nuttall letter demonstrates clearly that it was not for lack of larger vision that Boasian anthropology focused primarily on North American Indians.

In order to cover as wide a range of Boas' activity as possible, the remaining selections are fairly brief, most of them from Boas' unpublished correspondence. There are two letters that illuminate Boas' teaching activity at Columbia, where he was promoted to a full professorship in 1899 (apparently in response to an offer of a chair at the University of Vienna). The letter to President Butler was the first of the annual reports Boas wrote for the Department of Anthropology, which prior to 1901 had been part of the Psychology Department. In general, the proposals Boas made here for the department's development were achieved within the next few years, although the man chosen as professor of archaeology (as it later turned out, at Putnam's suggestion) was bitterly opposed by Boas, who felt that his own prerogative had been violated. The letter to Frank Speck, although very short, is interesting for several reasons. It gives a hint of how Boas ran his seminar, and suggests that his concern for the integration of whole cultures was already manifest in 1905, although by some accounts it did not become a major focus of his teaching until much later (Mead 1959a, p. 11; 1959b). Beyond this, it reminds us that Boas' influence was not restricted to his Columbia Ph.D.'s (who by 1911 numbered seven); others also passed through his seminars, including several who like Speck got their degrees at other institutions.

The fourth and fifth selections (nos. 38 and 39) are both letters to Morris Jesup, the president of the American Museum. The first suggests one facet of Boas' response to the new American imperialism of the late 1890s. Although he later saw this as his own moment of awakening from the American dream, at the time Boas worked rather hard—especially among portions of the business community with whom he had contact— to capitalize on public interest in the Far East in order to expand the horizons of his anthropological activity. The second letter to Jesup was written in the course of an acrimonious dispute with the new director of the Museum, Herman Bumpus, which led to Boas' resignation in the spring of 1905. Although some of the issues are reminiscent of those in the debate with Otis Mason, the selection also illustrates Boas' view on the role of museums in the propagation of anthropology.

In the aftermath of his break with the museum, Boas' extraterritorial research interests were redirected to the southern portions of the New World, as the sixth selection (no. 40) illustrates. Written to the stepson and heir of the railroad magnate Collis Huntington, this is one of a genre of Boas letters: the appeal to wealthy businessmen (among them also Henry Villard, George Peabody, Robert Ogden, and Jacob Schiff) for money to support anthropological research. At this time, Boas was president of the American Anthropological Association, although at its founding in 1902 his attempt to limit its membership to professionals had been defeated by the Washington anthropologists (Stocking 1960). By 1907, however, his influence had grown to the point that he was able to organize the various national leaders of his profession in an appeal, "signed by practically all students of anthropology in the United States," for money to support research in South America along explicitly diffusionist lines (Boas 1907b). Three years later Boas' "southern strategy" achieved partial fulfillment with the formation, in cooperation with German scholars, of the International School of American Archaeology and Ethnology in Mexico City (Boas 1912b). He himself spent the academic year 1911–1912 as director of the school, and while in Mexico supervised the first stratigraphic archaeological investigation in the New World (Adams 1960; Gamio 1959). However, the life of the school was cut short by the outbreak of war, and the areal focus of American anthropological research returned for a time to the North American Indian— who had in the meantime been the subject of a good deal of American Museum research by Boas' students, despite his gloomy forecast of 1905.

Boas' two decades of organizational activity in the propagation of his viewpoint left some residues of bitterness, especially vis-à-vis certain Washington scientists. In 1909, these came to the surface in a dispute with Charles D. Walcott, the secretary of the Smithsonian Institution. The position of chief of the Bureau of Ethnology had recently become vacant, and Boas was piqued that the job had not been offered to him, though in all likelihood he would have refused it. In this context, he heard from another anthropologist that Walcott had said that "financial transactions between the Bureau of Ethnology and myself during the time of Mr. McGee's administration would not bear the light"—specifically, that money had been paid to Boas for manuscripts in order that he might use it to cover the costs of the *American Anthropologist.* In the final selection (no. 41), Boas offers his version of the situation to his uncle, with some interesting sidelights on the history of his relation to the Washington anthropologists (cf. Boas 1910). As we shall see, the bitterness of that history was not dissipated for at least another decade. (On Boas' role in the anthropological profession, cf. Stocking 1968a, pp. 273–307; Darnell 1969, 1971c).

    S E L E C T I O N   3 5

The Boas Plan
for American Anthropology

May 16, 1901.

Mrs. Zelia Nuttall,
  Hotel Brunswick,
    Boston, Mass.

Dear Mrs. Nuttall,—

I received your very kindly note of Tuesday yesterday morning. You know how deeply I am interested in the question of California ethnology, and I feel that your question requires a somewhat full answer in regard to my general plans and the scope of the work which I have laid out for myself.

Since I took hold of the work in New York, I have tried to develop the same in such a way that it will ultimately result in the establishment of a well-organized school of anthropology, including all the different branches of the subject. I consider this one of the fundamental needs of

Copy preserved in the Boas Papers, American Philosophical Society.

our science, because without it we can never hope to thoroughly investigate and explore all the numerous problems of American anthropology. For this reason I am trying to develop the collections of this Museum in such a way that they will ultimately form the basis of university instruction in all lines of anthropological research. This aim of course must be combined with the general educational aims of the Museum, but I find that both are very easily harmonized. I am endeavoring to develop each department to such a point that within a very short time it will demand the care of a specialist, and this will be the opportune moment for introducing instruction in each particular line in Columbia University. My plan in taking up East Asiatic problems at the present time is on a line with this more general plan, and I am hoping to follow this undertaking with others which will lead us also into new lines. I want to see represented anthropology as well in its physical side as in its psychological, comparative side, and also specialists capable of carrying on work in archaeology, in American ethnology, and in the problems found in China, the Malay Archipelago, East Indies, Africa, etc. I am fully aware of the difficulties of really carrying out this undertaking, but I am fairly confident of ultimate success.

You may notice that I have worked somewhat systematically on these lines during the last five years. The Jesup Expedition gave me the first foothold outside of our continent. This is now being followed out by our Chinese enterprise, and plans have been laid for the successive steps also, although they have not matured yet.

I am confident that in this manner we shall be able inside of a very few years to give a young man a thorough all-round schooling, which cannot be had at the present time anywhere. Neither Berlin with its five anthropological professorships, nor Paris with its anthropological school, nor Holland with its colonial school, could give a proper training to the observers whom we need. I believe that the plans which I have in mind, based largely on the co-operation of this Museum and of Columbia University, will ultimately result in obtaining what we want.

Of course this end is still a long ways off, and our work in North America must be carried on now. For this reason we have taken up at Columbia a number of special lines which seem to be most important for carrying on field-work, and here I lay particular stress upon a training in linguistics, a general ethnological training, and knowledge of certain field methods of physical anthropology. By pursuing this method, I have been able to train a small number of young men who are able to do pretty good work.

You might say that to a certain extent the emphasis which I lay upon the necessity of having trained observers is a criticism of our present generations of ethnologists. This is true. I believe you will agree with me that almost every one of us is deficient in certain lines with which he ought to be familiar, and that lack of systematic knowledge may be observed in the writings of even our best men. But besides this, the number of young men is exceedingly limited, and I am very anxious that those who do take up the work should not be as unprepared as most of our generation have been.

I have the conviction that in certain lines at least I know exactly what is needed for furthering our knowledge of American ethnology, and I believe that the method which I am pursuing is more systematic than that followed by many others. It is only for this reason that I have ventured to concentrate in my hands a considerable part of the ethnological work that is being done on our continent. I have laid out the lines of all the ethnological work that has been done by this Museum. This embraces particularly work all along the Pacific coast of North America and work among the Indians of the Plains. It also embraces the archaeological work done on the Pacific coast of our continent.

I have, furthermore, always retained a certain connection with the Bureau of Ethnology, through which I have been enabled to expand our work over lines which do not properly fall in the scope of work in the Museum. I refer particularly to work in linguistics. One of the most important steps that I have taken in this direction is to suggest to the Bureau the publication of a handbook of American languages, which I am to edit. I have been working up this point for several years, and I believe that the plan will now be carried out. Through this undertaking I hope to be put in a position to push the necessary linguistic and ethnological work very considerably. It is self-evident that the Government alone cannot spend enough money on field-work to collect all these data; but, being in charge of this work, I anticipate that I can much more forcibly suggest to other institutions the expenditure of means in this direction.

I think you will understand the drift of this rather lengthy statement of my activity and of my plans. I am committed here in many directions, which centre in my activity in the Museum and in Columbia; and if I were to sever my connection with these institutions, it would practically mean beginning all over again.

At the same time I believe that it will be of advantage to American anthropology if I can retain a certain amount of control in the direction of the various activities which I outlined before for a few years.

I do not believe at all in the policy of a single man retaining longer than is absolutely necessary the direction of such a multitude of plans as I have in my charge at the present time, and it is my strong endeavor to find as soon as possible men upon whose shoulders the carrying-out of certain parts of these plans may be transferred. Thus I hope that three years hence, after the return of our exploring party from China, the whole division of our work will be taken entirely off my hands. I am looking forward to a time when I do not need to trouble myself about the work in comparative ethnology, and when all the various important divisions will be carried on independently; but, owing to the lack of men, that time has not yet come.

If you were to ask me at this moment whom to put in charge of the whole field of Californian ethnology, I should be unable to name any man in this country whom I should consider capable of doing so, while I am very confident that five years hence either Mr. Dixon or Mr. Kroeber will have gained sufficient experience to do so. I do not think that I need to enlarge on this point, because you know personally all the American anthropologists and the scope of their work.

As I stated in my former letter, it is a matter of the greatest importance that the work in California should be taken up with the greatest energy. If the question were asked, how greater funds could be expended advantageously, I would suggest that the following method would give the most satisfactory results: Establish for a period of five years four fellowships in ethnology and two fellowships in archaeology. Let these fellowships be made for the first few years in Columbia for ethnology and in Harvard for archaeology. As soon as one of these fellows is trained far enough to do independent work, let the fellowship be transferred to the University of California, and give the fellow an opportunity to do field-work in that State. I stated in my last letter how much it would cost to carry on field-work and to pay for publication. For the next five years, and not longer, give me the opportunity to direct the operations, in order to establish them on a definite systematic basis, and I am certain that at the close of this time a strong department in the University of California could be formed entirely independently of any further co-operation on our part.

I should like to add, that I consider the large amount of administrative work which I am doing at the present time a necessity, under the present conditions of American anthropology, but that I decidedly look forward with pleasure to a time, which I hope may come about ten years hence, when I can again devote myself entirely to scientific pursuits.

I hardly need to say how much I appreciate your very kindly expressions of confidence in my work, and how sincerely I thank you for your kindly letter.

Yours very truly,
FRANZ BOAS

S E L E C T I O N   3 6

Anthropological Instruction in Columbia University

Nov. 15, 1902.

PRESIDENT NICHOLAS MURRAY BUTLER,
Columbia University,
    New York City.

DEAR SIR,—

In submitting the Budget for the coming year, I beg leave to offer the following remarks regarding the work of the Anthropological Department.

Anthropological instruction in Columbia University was first given by Dr. Farrand and Dr. Ripley in 1893–94. I was appointed lecturer of anthropology in 1896, and held this position until 1899, when I was appointed professor of anthropology. Since 1899 Dr. Farrand has devoted one-half of his time to anthropology by kindly permission of Professor Cattell, Dr. Farrand belonging to the Psychological Department.

Until 1899 instruction in anthropology was given under three faculties —Professor Farrand under the faculty of philosophy, Dr. Ripley under the faculty of social science, and myself under the faculty of pure science. In 1899 anthropology was given its base in the faculty of philosophy.

During the first few years the instruction embraced comparative ethnology and a short course on the races of Europe. To this was added in 1896 a course in physical anthropology and one on American languages. Since 1899 the course on comparative ethnology has been divided into an introductory course given alternately by Professor Farrand and myself, and an advanced course given by Professor Farrand. Furthermore, research work, which is to a great extent done in the American Museum of Natural History, has been added to the courses; and in 1900 a descriptive ethnographical course was added, which covers a period of two years, and is given jointly by Professor Farrand and myself. In 1902 an assistant without salary was appointed in the Department.

During the development of anthropological teaching it has been found useful to place the beginning of our work farther and farther back, and it

Copy preserved in the Boas Papers, American Philosophical Society.

is our desire for the coming year to open the introductory courses to junior students. It seems to us that anthropological teaching may be made very useful in the undergraduate course, and particularly in connection with the teaching of history and social science. It is perhaps the best means of opening the eyes of students to what is valuable in foreign cultures, and thus to develop a juster appreciation of foreign nations and to bring out those elements in our own civilization which are common to all mankind. In this we see the principal educational value of anthropology as an undergraduate course.

In developing this idea it is our desire to open the general introductory course in anthropology to junior students, and to give them also an opportunity to take a descriptive course on the ethnography of primitive tribes. At the present time we do not include the cultures of Asia in this course, but it is our desire so to develop it that ethnography of primitive people is given primarily for junior students, and lectures on the culture of Asia primarily to seniors. For the time being these courses must probably be given by myself and Professor Farrand, who will lecture on the tribes of northeastern Asia, the Malay, Polynesians, and the Africans. I hope, however, that it will be possible in the course of time to have the second year course given by specialists, who would treat the cultures of China, India, and Semitic peoples. I am certain that within a very few years this can be done by co-operation with the Chinese Department and the Department of Oriental Languages.

The graduate work of the Department is of diverse character. I give an introductory course on the statistical study of variation, which is the basis of physical anthropology. This course is open to seniors. It is used at the same time by the Zoological Department, by the Psychological Department, and recently also by the Sociological Department, which require the same kind of preliminary training. The work in physical anthropology has not been, so far, a great success, on account of the difficulty of establishing relations with the Zoological Department and with the Medical School. Some instruction of this kind has been given to students. In this work I have used the anthropological laboratory in the American Museum of Natural History.

Another side of ethnological work requires a thorough linguistic preparation. For this reason it has been necessary for me to give a course of lectures on Indian languages, and I may say that all the younger men who study Indian languages have been trained in this course.

A third part of anthropological training requires studies in comparative and special ethnology. This work has been carried on principally by Professor Farrand, who has also made extensive use of the collections in the American Museum of Natural History. Special research work in this line has been done under the direction of both Professor Farrand and myself.

During the present year I am giving instruction to advanced students in museum administration. This course is so successful that I propose to announce it formally for the coming year.

There is still one very important gap in our teaching, which hampers the development of the Department. The majority of our students must make a living by what they learn at the University. Anthropological positions are not numerous; nevertheless every student who has chosen this field and who has passed through our department has found a position at once. At the present time there is a great need for well-trained students of American archaeology. We have no courses of this kind to offer, and it will be necessary to have a new man for introducing this branch. With archaeology represented, we should be able to train anthropologists in all directions. There are three men in this country who could give instruction in these lines. These are Prof. W. H. Holmes, Dr. M. Uhle, and Dr. J. Walter Fewkes; but I believe it would be more advantageous for Columbia to train a man for the position. Such a man should be sent to Berlin to study under the direction of Prof. E. Seler, and should get a good training in geology, civil engineering, and architecture. If it were feasible to establish a fellowship for such a purpose for four years, a man could be trained who would be fit to fill this place.

Much of the progress that has been made in the Department has been possible only through the thorough method of co-operation between the University and the American Museum of Natural History. During the summer months students of the Department have carried on field-work for the Museum, and have thus enjoyed the advantages of field experience. During the academic year the collections have been used extensively, and the graduate students of the Department have based their researches largely on the collections of the Museum, to the benefit of both the University and the Museum. The experience of foreign universities and museums shows clearly that this co-operation can be carried on only when the officers of the University are at the same time officers of the Museum, and vice versa. For this reason I consider it desirable that the co-operation between the University and the Museum be as close as possible.

It will be remembered that the condition of my appointment in Columbia University is that I am to devote part of my time to the American Museum of Natural History, and part of my time to the University, so that as a matter of fact Columbia University controls at the present time only one-half of one man's time for the development of the Anthropological Department. Through all these years I have devoted a great share of my time to the development of the Department, so much so that I feel unable to carry on much longer, on the same scale as I do at the present time, the work of both the University and the Museum. For this reason I feel that my own work requires readjustment.

With the opening of introductory courses to juniors the courses will be closed to Barnard students, and I believe it would be the desire of the authorities of Barnard College to have these courses given. If this is to be done, it would seem to my mind that the best method would be the appointment of Professor Farrand in the Anthropological Department, with the understanding that he is to give the undergraduate courses in Barnard. In this way he would still give no more than one-half of his time to the University, and in so far no relief would be given to my own work in the Department. I consider it necessary that some form of readjustment be found, either by the increase of my salary to the normal salary of a professor, which would enable me to relieve myself of much routine work by the employment of clerical assistance, or by transferring part of the work in the Department that I am doing now to a new man.

The following Budget would be required to carry out the proposed plan:

Salary of professor	$4000
Salary of Prof. Farrand at Columbia (half time)	1500
Fellowship	600
Expenses of Department	600
Purchase of instruments for laboratory (for one year only)	600
TOTAL	$7300

Respectfully submitted,
[FRANZ BOAS]

    S E L E C T I O N   3 7

Boas' Graduate Seminar

June 12, 1905.

MR. F. G. SPECK,
Hackensack, N.J.

MY DEAR MR. SPECK,—

I have made a tentative plan for the Seminar of next year, and I wish that you would give us in the first hour, which will be about two weeks after the opening of the term, an account of the Uchee and their relation to the neighboring tribes, according to your own studies. I desire, so far

Copy preserved in the Boas Papers, American Philosophical Society.

as feasible, to make the subject-matter of next year's Seminar ethnographical and rather to emphasize the inter-relation between cultural phenomena inside of each tribe.

Yours very truly,

FRANZ BOAS

    S E L E C T I O N   3 8

A Plea for
a Great Oriental School

MORRIS K. JESUP, ESQ.,
    President Committee on Collections from Eastern Asia,
    American Museum of Natural History,
        New York.

DEAR SIR—
    I beg to report on the general work carried on under the direction of the Committee on Collections from Eastern Asia. The work of collecting has been continued by Dr. Berthold Laufer. The general plan of his work has been to bring together collections which illustrate the popular customs and beliefs of the Chinese, their industries and their mode of life. We hope by means of these collections to bring out the complexity of Chinese culture, the high degree of technical development achieved by the people, the love of art, which pervades their whole life, and the strong social ties that bind the people together. In bringing together collections bearing upon these points of view, we desire to illustrate the needs of the Chinese and the products of their industries. These will demonstrate the commercial and social possibilities of more extended intercourse. We also wish to imbue the public with greater respect for the achievements of Chinese civilization. Our object has not been to bring together a collection of Chinese works of art—this matter belongs more properly to the scope of an art museum—but to emphasize the general characteristics of Chinese culture.

Journal of the American Asiatic Association 3 (1903): 7–8.

In pursuit of this work Dr. Laufer made collections in the southern part of China. Early in 1902 he moved to Peking, where he continued work on the lines indicated. During the past year he has made collections illustrating, among other things, cloisonné work, engraving, lacquer work, medicine and carpet weaving. He devoted considerable time to making collections illustrating popular amusements of the people of Peking, and incidentally carried on interesting researches on the early history of Northern China.

The collections received at the end of 1901 were temporarily exhibited in the Museum. Naturally these collections were fragmentary, since they represent only the results of the first few months of Dr. Laufer's work. We are now in receipt of Dr. Laufer's collections made in Peking, but they have not been unpacked yet. During the present year the gallery of the Museum in which the collections are to be permanently installed has been completed, and we are now engaged in rearranging the collections, which, it is hoped, may soon be opened to the public.

It seems important at the present time to refer to the general subject of East Asiatic work which was outlined at the time when the committee was first formed. Under present conditions a more extended knowledge of East Asiatic cultures seems to be a matter of great national importance. Our commerce and political intercourse with Eastern Asia are rapidly expanding, and in order to deal intelligently with the problems arising in this area we require a better knowledge of the people and of the countries with which we are dealing. This is true of China and Japan, and this is true of our Malay possessions. The work of the committee was undertaken with a view of making a beginning with educational work relating to the countries of Eastern Asia. The necessity was recognized of establishing a collection which should form the basis for instruction relating to the cultures of Eastern Asia. It was hoped that the establishment of these collections would give an impetus which might lead the universities of our city, particularly Columbia University, to take up the establishment of an East Asiatic Department. This hope has been fulfilled at an unexpectedly early date. Through the gift of General Carpentier a Department of Chinese was established in Columbia University, and Prof. Friedrich Hirth has been appointed as Professor of Chinese. Professor Hirth will find the collections made under the direction of the committee of much use in his educational work.

It is evident that the establishment of a single professorship of Chinese, and the making of a collection illustrating the popular life of China, are not adequate for reaching the desired results. It can hardly be expected that a single professor of Chinese can create that interest in Oriental matters which the subject requires. It would rather seem that what we have to aim at is the gradual establishment of a department in which all the different cultures of Eastern Asia are represented, and in which information on the products, commercial possibilities and social status of these countries can be imparted. The Oriental schools of Paris, Berlin and St. Petersburg show what can be accomplished through a department of this kind. In these schools are trained officers for the diplomatic and consular service, military and civil officers and business men whose interests centre in Eastern Asia. The number of students in these institutions is considerable. The school of Paris has 402 students and an income of $34,000; that at Berlin, 160 students and an income of $30,000, and the school of St. Petersburg, 212 students. The efficiency of these schools is due to the comprehensive way in which the whole subject of East Asiatic culture is treated.

The next step which might be taken in New York in order to develop the Oriental school that we need consists in the establishment of collections illustrating the cultures of other East Asiatic regions. At the present moment it seems most opportune to take up collections in the Philippine Islands. While the whole subject of Malay culture is a vast one, the number of men who are capable of dealing with this is very small; and at the present time it would be impossible to find, outside of a few men in Holland, anyone sufficiently well trained in Malay ethnology to give adequate instruction on the subject. For this reason it would seem best to train a young man to work up this field. A man with proper preliminary training might fit himself inside of three or four years' field work to begin instruction in this subject. I therefore believe that the next step to be taken in developing the subject of East Asiatic instruction would be the organization of work in the Malay countries, more particularly on the Philippine Islands. An annual expenditure of $5,000 would be sufficient to open this field.

I may be allowed to quote the following passage from a report addressed to President Butler, of Columbia University, dated October 21, 1901, regarding the immediate needs of an East Asiatic Department:

"If the plans outlined above were to be carried out, the establishment of a chair of Chinese would simply mark the first of a number of departments treating the cultures of Asia. The whole domain of Chinese culture is so enormous that a single scientist can master this subject just as little as a single man can master the whole of the culture, language and literature of Europe. In order to attain the objects here outlined, a combination of men of the type of Hirth and De Groot and of a practical man would be required. Furthermore, the scientific foundation of East Asiatic cultures would make it indispensable to have one man representing the whole domain of Tibetan culture, which connects the cultures of India, China and the Turkish people of Siberia. These last are of special importance, because they form the connecting link between East Asiatic and European cultures.

"Most important of all at the present juncture would seem to be that opportunity be given for acquiring knowledge in matters pertaining to the Philippine Islands.

If we are to hope that within a reasonable length of time the instruction on the culture of the Malay people, more particularly of the Philippines, will be given, it would be necessary to prepare a young man for this purpose by giving him opportunities to study in Leyden, in European museums and on the spot, and in this way to prepare himself for the task."

Respectfully submitted,
FRANZ BOAS,
Secretary Committee on Collections from Eastern Asia

 SELECTION 39

The Educational Functions
of Anthropological Museums

April 29, 1905.
MORRIS K. JESUP, ESQ.,
President American Museum of Natural History,

DEAR SIR,—

In reply to your letter of the 28th, I take the liberty to state my opinions regarding installation with perfect frankness.

If I understand your wishes correctly, particularly in view of your praise of the present Peruvian installation, you desire a certain definite scheme adhered to in every anthropological exhibit, so that the visitor will find all collections arranged according to one simple guiding principle.

Permit me to state my views regarding installation in some detail. I am not going to speak of scientific studies, but only of the educational exhibit of the Museum.

It seems to my mind that it is the object of a large anthropological collection to illustrate all the principal features of the history of human civilization, from the earliest forms up to the highest, so far as this can be done by the presentation of material objects belonging to diverse cultures.

Copy preserved in the Boas Papers, American Philosophical Society.

The principal points of view that must be emphasized, therefore, are the relation of man to nature, industrial development, the forms of customs and beliefs. These must be explained by taking into consideration the historical conditions of each people.

Granting these general premises, which, I believe, coincide with your wishes, it seems to me that we must make a fundamental distinction between a small museum and a large museum. In a small museum only the most generalized questions can be treated, and details must be disregarded. In a large museum, where more extended material is available, more special questions, which are at the same time fundamental for an understanding of human history, become important. A large museum will therefore take up the general question of evolution of human culture in some detail. As soon as this is done, the few simple points of view sufficient for a small museum become inadequate, and it is no longer possible to adhere to a systematic plan.

For this reason the installation in a large museum must necessarily cease to be intelligible without particular explanation of the subject-matter of the exhibits, because the points of view are different in each area. There is therefore a conflict between the aims of a simple and small collection, which is to appeal only to the general public, and which should consist of a few specimens only, and those of a collection the object of which is to be instructive to people interested in somewhat more complex questions, like our high-school students, teachers, artists, missionaries, those interested in special trades, in general historical questions, etc.

I have tried to solve this conflict of interests by arranging one series of collections for the general visitor, and by separating out those collections that bear upon more special questions. I have made the suggestion that in course of time these general collections be assembled in one hall, in order to make it easier for the general public to grasp the idea in question. The other collections bear upon special problems. The points of view from which they must be seen and studied vary from case to case. If we try to devise a general scheme for their exhibition, we frustrate our own end. I may illustrate this by some special points. In the West Hall you will find one case devoted to the general type of culture of the Prairie Indians, another to the general culture of the Woodland Indians. The more special collections are arranged to illustrate two points —the importance of the warrior societies in the life of the Prairie Indians and the modification they have undergone, and the history of the development of the art of those Indians. In the North Hall we have also a general group and a number of special groups showing primarily the peculiar development of religious ideas and social organization among various tribes. In the California collection the centre of interest has been made the development of basketry technique, and so on. If, therefore, your criticism is directed to a lack of uniformity of scheme, I must admit there is no such uniformity. It is not there, because every collection bears upon a special question, which it elucidates. By classifying our material under one general scheme, these points would be lost entirely and we should destroy the usefulness of our large collections.

This question hinges, of course, upon our whole conception of the function of the Museum. We have a building containing now twenty-four beautiful large halls. If it is our sole object to instruct the general public, we defeat our own purpose by the magnitude of our building and the beauty and mass of its contents. To *teach* the general public, a building of eight halls would be ample; but a small museum of eight halls would not attract the masses. The magnitude of the Museum is what brings them here. They come to admire, to see, and to be entertained. We instruct them almost against their wish and will. To *teach* anthropology to the general public, I need only one hall: to impress them with the fact that our people are not the only carriers of civilization, but that the human mind has been creative everywhere, I need a large exhibit of impressive specimens. If impressiveness were our only aim, it would perhaps hardly justify the large expenditure of money and energy necessary for upbuilding a large museum. The extended collections serve, however, another purpose.

Just as our school system requires, besides primary and grammar schools, high schools and universities, so a large museum should fulfil the function of a primary objective school for the general public, as well as serve those who strive for higher education and help to train the teacher. The educational methods of university, high school, grammar school, and primary school are different; and thus the methods of exhibition must differ, according to the public to which we appeal. By adapting every exhibit to the level of the needs of the uneducated, we frustrate our object of adding to the knowledge of the educated who come here in search of more special information.

To sum up, I believe it is the educational function of a museum of the size of the American Museum of Natural History to entertain the masses, to instruct the large number of people who come here to get knowledge, to advance the knowledge of those who possess a higher education, and to help those interested in special studies. The adaptation of the *whole* exhibit to the masses would destroy, in my opinion, its usefulness for the purposes of secondary and higher education, which have their own methods.

I do not wish to explain here in detail how I have tried to reach this end, and what practical difficulties are encountered, which make progress of installation very slow. It would be necessary to point out the work done in special cases, in order to bring out these technical points.

I think what I have said before explains why I cannot indorse the exhibit in the Peruvian Hall. The essential traits of Peruvian culture do not appear in the small fragmentary groups, in which a hard and fast scheme has been applied to material that does not fit it. So far as the general public is concerned, it should be shown in the Peruvian Hall what distinguishes that culture from all others. What was the state of agriculture of this region? What animals were domesticated? What was the general style of architecture, the characteristics of the metal industry, spinning and weaving? I do not think that you can find specimens answering these questions assembled in any one case in that hall. On the other hand, you see over and over again that Peruvians worked in stone, wood, clay—a fact that is without significance in relation to their culture.

I may say that the very fact that Professor Bumpus had arranged the Peruvian Hall in this manner made it quite impossible for me to accept his proposition, which he urged over and over again, and from which he receded very reluctantly, that I should accept the scientific direction of the Anthropological Department, and let some one else take the work of installation. I knew that this would mean a re-arrangement on principles with which I could not agree without compromising my convictions.

I hope that I have made my point clear. If I understand you rightly, you criticise the lack of a schematic arrangement. My reply is, that I have never attempted that, because I consider it impossible to arrange an anthropological exhibit on this basis without sacrificing all that is essential for the anthropological work of a large museum devoted to the education of the masses as well as of those who have had the advantage of higher education. If you decide to devote a hall to a special exhibit for the general public, I shall be glad to make it. In fact, I have advocated this for some time.

I fully appreciate all that you have done for the Museum, and I think I should betray the trust that you have placed in me if I did not do my best to defend what I consider sound principles of installation and administration.

Yours very respectfully,
FRANZ BOAS

SELECTION 40

Plans for Research in Central and South America

Jan. 20, 1906.

MR. ARCHER M. HUNTINGTON,
1083 Fifth Avenue,
New York City.

MY DEAR SIR,—

I feel that the whole position in the Museum here is so desperate that I must anticipate seeing my work ended practically any day. As I told you when I had the pleasure of seeing you on Friday, my present policy is to try to make a contract with the Museum by which I can finish and carry on as much of my work as may be, undisturbed by Professor Bumpus, if necessary outside of the institution. I consider it very doubtful how far I may succeed in this. At best, therefore, my work can be considered but a hasty attempt to carry on and complete investigations that ought to be made quietly and with conscientious slowness. I also explained to you that the material I have in hand is going to give out soon.

Notwithstanding my repeated attempts to get a decided answer, which attempts have been continued since last July, I have not been able to secure from the Museum a definite statement as to whether I shall be permitted to carry on scientific work. Under all these conditions, I feel that I am in a most undignified position.

The question therefore arises for me what to do. I have outlined to you several plans which I am considering, and for which I am working. The development of the Anthropological Department in Columbia University is of course a work of some importance, which will always demand more or less of my attention. My success up to this time in this work has been due largely to the opportunities of co-operation with the Museum and with the Smithsonian Institution. During the last seven or eight years I have trained a good many young investigators, who now occupy positions all over the country. Their training has been secured largely by giving them opportunity for field-work through this Museum and through

Copy preserved in the Boas Papers, American Philosophical Society.

the Smithsonian Institution, and letting them work up their results under my supervision. Since, through the change of policy in the American Museum of Natural History, no opportunity for field-work will be given to students, I have found it necessary to search for opportunity in other fields, and this has led me to take up with greater energy a plan that I have pursued for some time. I mentioned to you my endeavors to establish a school for the study of Latin America, the Far East, and the United States dependencies. According to my promise, I enclose a summary which I submitted to President Butler at an early stage of my endeavors, and which will give you an idea as to what was done in these lines a few years ago. I may say that since that time the work in all foreign countries has been expanded, and that a few months ago a similar school was founded in England. I am in hopes that something may be done to make a beginning in this direction.

Another line of approach of which I have thought is a change of my field of work from the Northwest to more Southern parts of our continent. In this connection I have tried to interest the Archaeological Institute of America and some universities in the establishment of an archaeological school in Mexico, Central America, or South America, and the project seems to me promising.

Considering the whole position, I am very much inclined to transfer my own work entirely to the South, and to try to take up particularly the study of languages and cultures of the natives of these regions, using in the same way as I did heretofore my older students for supplementing my own work. I think you have seen the various publications for which I am responsible, which show that this method of work is feasible and yields ample returns. If work of this kind were undertaken, the correct method would be to begin with our pueblos in the north, and work southward systematically, taking, to begin with, at least one representative of each linguistic stock as a sample, and to discuss the language and ethnology thoroughly. I should imagine that work of this kind would fit in very well with the plans of an archaeological school in Mexico, Central America, or South America. Under our present conditions, the first thing required would be the training of men.

Of course this is a work which is quite expensive, and will require, in my judgment, an expenditure for administration, field-work, and publication, of from $10,000 to $12,000 a year to begin with. The results of work of this kind, if continued systematically, would be a compendium of the languages and of the important points of the ethnology of America south of the United States.

It might perhaps seem to you that with all the old missionary grammars that we have, such work would hardly be necessary, but the modern requirements of linguistic study are so entirely different from what the old fathers and also the modern fathers give us, that field-work is necessary to achieve this work.

I told you last week that I am compiling for the Smithsonian Institution a work of this kind on the northern half of North America. This, however, has been possible only through the many different lines of research work that I have conducted partly for this Museum, partly for the Smithsonian Institution, partly for the Carnegie Institution, during the last twenty years.

Your remark that you regretted that I am not working on Spanish America suggests to me to write to you in regard to this matter. Although, of course, I have never done much on the southern countries, the problem is the same as the one with which I have been dealing heretofore, and would not require any particular change in the character of my work. I hardly know whether plans of this kind come under the scope of the Hispanic Society, and whether they are not too extensive, considering the manifold objects which the Society is to serve; but, under present circumstances, I think it may be worth while to bring the matter to your attention.

Yours very truly,
FRANZ BOAS

    SELECTION 41

A Residue of Bitterness

Sept. 2, 1909.

DR. A. JACOBI,
  Bolton Landing,
    Warren County, N.Y.

MY DEAR DOCTOR,—

I want you to see the reply to my letters to Walcott, which I received just before my departure from here to Winnipeg. I enclose copy.

His reply is entirely unsatisfactory to me, particularly since I know that incriminations against McGee of the same sort were made in 1904. At that time Professor Morris Loeb of New York said to me one day, "Is it not too bad that McGee has gone to the bad?" and upon my inquiry, I learned that Dr. Cyrus Adler, who had been conducting an investigation

Copy preserved in the Boas Papers, American Philosophical Society.

of the Bureau of Ethnology under Secretary Langley's direction, had made this statement to Loeb. Later on in the same year Professor Haupt of Baltimore made exactly the same statement to me during the Americanists' Congress in Stuttgart, and upon my inquiry gave me the same source of his information. On my return to America, I went to call on Dr. Rathbun, then acting Secretary of the Smithsonian Institution, and objected to what seemed to me an outrageous abuse of apparently official information, which could neither be substantiated nor disproved. Mr. Rathbun tried to protect Dr. Adler, but finally, as I understood him, agreed that he would see to it that these insinuations should not be continued. For this reason I did not inform McGee, in order to avoid further complications of an already bad situation.

Since I learned from Dorsey what Walcott has said about me, I rather presume that my name has always been involved in this matter, and I shall not rest content until it is completely cleared up.

I do not know what Walcott refers to in speaking of the "American Anthropologist." In 1898 the "Anthropologist," which was owned by the Washington Anthropological Society, was practically dying. At that time I interested a number of people in the Journal, particularly Mr. C. P. Bowditch, the Duke of Loubat, Mr. A. Hemenway of Boston, Mr. Marshall Field, and Mr. E. E. Ayer of Chicago; and, with other financial assistance, I ventured to take the financial responsibility for the Journal. In 1900 I also revived the American Ethnological Society of New York to support the Journal, and in that way have been enabled to put it on its feet. During the first few years I covered the deficit of the Journal myself. I might as well have had the money for this purpose from the gentlemen contributing to the support of the Journal.

In effecting the transfer of the Journal from the Washington Anthropological Society, and in making the contracts with the publishers, McGee and myself acted together. Originally I did not want any one else concerned in the matter, but I finally agreed because it was presented to me by members of the Editorial Committee (I have forgotten now by whom) that in case I should act alone, the financial responsibility would rest on my estate in case of my death. I think in 1902, at the meeting of the American Association for the Advancement of Science in Pittsburgh, an American Ethnological [Anthropological] Association was founded to continue the publication of the "Anthropologist." I was strongly opposed to this move, because I foresaw that the attempt to get a wide circulation would make it more difficult than before to keep up the scientific standard of the Journal. I was, however, out-voted, McGee voting with the other party; and from that time on I have had nothing to do financially with the Journal, except as a member of the Association. I do not know what in the world this matter has to do with my relations to the Bureau.

I do not know whether you know about my personal relations to the various parties concerned in this whole matter. In 1893, at the close of the World's Fair, I was placed in charge of the Anthropological Department of the newly established Field Columbian Museum, and worked hard to enable the Museum to open its doors in May, 1894. While I was at work there, I learned that Mr. Holmes had been engaged behind my back, and under the condition of secrecy from me, to take my place as soon as I should have done the work of installation, which, owing to my knowledge of the material, nobody else could do. This move was, as I understand it, part of the general attempt at re-adjustment in Washington. Major Powell was to be transferred to the Bureau of Ethnology from the Geological Survey, and some one had to get out of the Bureau to make room for Powell. This whole negotiation was largely carried on, as I understand it, by Walcott, who was one of the candidates for the position of Director of the Geological Survey. I was in their way, and, owing to their influence in Chicago, I was simply turned out. When I learned about these moves, I tried to protect my interests. Among the Washington people concerned I heard nothing but prevarication except from McGee, who had the courage to shoulder his part of the responsibility.

Later on, after Major Powell's death, Secretary Langley did not wish to appoint McGee Director of the Bureau—a position which he had practically filled for many years, shouldering the whole responsibility for Major Powell, who, during the last few years of his life, was practically incapacitated. There was only one opinion among competent anthropologists at the time, that this was a great injustice to Mr. McGee; and I took the opportunity, during the meeting of the Americanists' Congress in New York in 1902, to point out to Professor Holmes that if he were to decline the office, nobody would take it, to which he replied that when his superior (that is, the Secretary of the Smithsonian Institution) ordered him to take the office, he had to do so.

About that time Secretary Langley appointed a committee to investigate the Bureau, but, so far as I am aware, nobody has ever seen its report; but the impression was conveyed that gross irregularities in McGee's administration were found. I urged McGee at that time to have the matter followed up with legal advice, but he did not do so. If I remember correctly, he was taken down with typhoid fever, and was not himself for quite a while, but I cannot recall the details without looking them up.

It is perfectly clear to my mind that Walcott's attitude towards me is largely influenced by these two matters. First, I was in his way in Chicago, and then I stood by McGee, who is disliked by a great many of the Washington people. I do not agree myself, by any means, with every thing McGee does; but he gained my esteem and friendship by the courage he showed at the time of my troubles in Chicago, in which I found him the only person who had the courage to speak the truth.

Of course, it is quite immaterial, in connection with the present matter, whether or not I am capable of administering large affairs; but I think my successes in connection with the very work of the Bureau of Ethnology, the expeditions which I have conducted for the American Museum of Natural History, my success in bringing all the American anthropologists together in their request to the Carnegie Institution, which the president of the Institution declared to be the greatest obstacle in the promotion of anthropological work by the Carnegie Institution, are ample proof that he is mistaken.

With kindest regards,
Yours very sincerely,
[FRANZ BOAS]

PART X

ANTHROPOLOGY
AND SOCIETY

Although we think of Boas today as an intellectual activist, it was not until rather late in his career that he became a public spokesman for the anthropological viewpoint on broader social issues. There may be other ephemera like his letters to Canadian newspapers defending the Kwakiutl potlatch, but the first clear expression of this activism was not published until Boas was forty-six and had been full professor at Columbia for five years (Boas 1904b). This is a bit surprising when one considers that his liberal political ideas were well established in his youth; that he had left Germany at least in part because he felt he could not accept in silence the Bismarckian turn to imperialism nor the intolerance that accompanied it; and that he had worked out the substance of his critique of racialism by 1894. It is true that he tended at times to draw a sharp line between science and popularization: one of the recurring themes of his letters after 1905 was that the American Museum and the Bureau of Ethnology were abandoning serious research to cater to public interests. But this certainly did not free the scientist of his obligation to speak out on public issues where his knowledge was relevant and his voice would carry weight. Perhaps there lies a reason for the delay: it was not until his institutional position was secure and his viewpoint no longer that of a young turk that Boas could speak with the authority of America's "leading anthropologist." But whatever the reason for his early silence, it is quite likely that the Columbia milieu was a factor in ending it. A high proportion of the faculty, including various colleagues of Boas, were involved in off-campus "social welfare" and political activity during the progressive period, and it is worth noting that the first popular articles

Boas published on race appeared in journals associated with the social welfare movement (Boas 1904b; 1905b; cf. Levenstein 1963).

By this time he was sufficiently well-known that leaders of the black movement in this country approached him as an authority on racial differences. In September 1905, W. E. B. DuBois wrote asking for references on the physical anthropology of Negroes and inviting Boas to speak to an assembly of black professional men the following May at the Eleventh Atlanta University Conference, whose subject was to be "The Health and Physique of the Negro American." While there, Boas gave the commencement address, which is the first selection included here (no. 42). It is perhaps the most interesting of his early statements on the "Negro problem" because it was directed to an audience of blacks. Its image of the American black, its appeal in terms of traditional European values, and its counsel of infinite patience suggest the limits of his own cultural vision. But the attempt to strengthen American Negro identity by an affirmation of the value of African culture was at this time quite radically innovative for a white American.

To a different end, Boas used essentially the same argument to white audiences. Like many intellectuals of the progressive period, he had great faith in the reformative power of scientific knowledge widely disseminated. As he suggested in 1906 in a letter to Booker T. Washington, the most influential black man of his day, if one could "bring home to the American people" the cultural achievements of blacks in Africa, it would be "of great practical value in modifying the views of our people in regard to the Negro problem." The second selection (no. 43), one of a number of similar letters Boas wrote to various business and social welfare leaders, suggests the kind of program he envisioned to accomplish this goal.

The appeal, however, was not successful, and Boas' research on problems relating to race moved instead toward the issues raised by the "new immigration." While his immigrant study was in process, he gave a talk to Section H of the American Association for the Advancement of Science (his second vice-presidential address) on "Race Problems in America," which I have included here as his most general statement on race problems in this period.

Racial issues were to occupy much of Boas' activity as publicist until the day of his death, but the outbreak of World War I gave a new focus to his polemical energies. Although he had become an American citizen in 1891, he remained in a deep sense culturally German, and the war years were a time of great emotional strain for him—as the fourth selection suggests (no. 45). Ostensibly an explanation of his reasons for sympathizing with Germany, it is actually a fascinating statement of his own changing attitude toward American culture and also a piece of cultural analysis that is not without relevance even today.

Boas' public opposition to the war did not end with American entry. By the election of 1918, he was so disturbed by the repressive atmosphere he felt around him that he announced, in the fifth selection (no. 46), his intention to vote for the Socialist party. Indeed, for a brief period he was actually a member of the Socialist party branch in Grantwood, New Jersey, though his own politics were rather more in the progressive tradition (he had voted for McKinley in 1896, Hughes in 1916, and was later to support LaFollette and Franklin Roosevelt).

There was, however, one matter concerning the war about which Boas remained silent until it was over. In the summer of 1917, he had received information that several anthropologists had been engaged in espionage activities in Mexico while carrying on anthropological research. Two of them had apparently capitalized on contacts they made through Boas while studying at the International School of American Archaeology and Ethnology. After seething for two years, Boas exploded in December 1919 in a letter to the editor of the *Nation*, which I have reprinted here as the sixth selection (no. 47). It precipitated a bitter fight at the American Anthropological Association several weeks later—the final engagement in his controversy with the Washington anthropologists, who were able on this charged issue to marshal enough votes to censure Boas and strip him of office. But if Boas lost the last battle, the outcome of that longer controversy had already been decided by the number and the influence of his students, who had dominated the executive board of the Association since 1910, and who within several years were able to reassert their control (Stocking 1968a, p. 296; cf. Darnell 1969, 1971c).

As a final selection (no. 48), I have included one of a number of essays Boas wrote on another topic that deeply concerned him: the problem of university governance and academic freedom, or the institutional conditions affecting the pursuit of knowledge. Although he had for forty years devoted his intellectual and professional energies to remodeling anthropology according to his own conception, Boas did not lose all sensitivity to the dangers of intellectual monopoly.

SELECTION 42

The Outlook
for the American Negro

I have accepted with pleasure the invitation to address you on this day, because I believe that the broad outlook over the development of mankind which the study of the races of man gives to us, is often helpful to an understanding of our own everyday problems, and may make clear to us our capacity as well as our duty. I shall speak to you from the standpoint of the anthropologist, of one who has devoted his life to the study of the multifarious forms of culture as found in different races.

Modern life makes certain definite demands upon us and requires certain qualities of character. In judging the work of men, it is, however, well to remember that there have been cultures different from ours and that the qualities that are today dominant and most highly esteemed, and the possession of which makes a person a most useful member of society, have not always had the same value; and may at a later period be superseded by others not so highly valued now. In early ages brute force was one of the highest qualities of man. Sagacity counted little. At the present time energetic self-assertion counts for most, while in the age of early Christianity humility won the highest praise. Such differences in the valuation of our activities are also found at the present time in countries that have developed untouched by the influence of modern civilization.

Our gifts, our wishes and our ideals are not alone determined by the demands of the civilization in which we live, but each of us has his own individuality which makes him more or less fit to adapt himself to the demands of life. Therefore it behooves young men and young women to tarry long enough before rushing into the activities of a busy life, to know what powers are given to them, what they are able to achieve and what place their work is to occupy in the conflicting interests of modern life.

On the day when the student leaves the protecting wings of the institution which has nurtured and trained his mind, he naturally halts with a last glimpse backward. Then he looks forward timidly, but at the same

Commencement Address at Atlanta University, May 31, 1906, Atlanta University Leaflet, No. 19; later incorporated in large part into Boas 1945.

time with the exuberant joy of having acquired the right of independent action, and now he is in the midst of the struggle which even to the best, is not all sweetness of success, but bound to bring the bitterness of disappointment. Then will come the test of your strength, of your loyalty to the ideals that your instructors have tried to instil into you.

If these trials are not spared to the youth who enters the struggle of life, a member of a homogeneous people, they will be encountered with even greater certainty in communities where diverse elements live side by side, and have to work for their joint welfare as well as for the protection of their separate interests.

This is to be your future. The more clearly you recognize the tasks it involves, the better you will be fitted to fill your place in the life of the nation.

The fundamental requirement for useful activity on your part is a clear insight into the capabilities of your own race. If you did accept the view that the present weakness of the American Negro, his uncontrolled emotions, his lack of energy, are racially inherent, your work would still be a noble one. You, the more fortunate members of your race, would give your life to a great charitable work, to support the unsteady gait of your weak brother who is too feeble to walk by himself. But you have the full right to view your labor in an entirely different light. The achievements of races are not only what they have done during the short span of two thousand years, when with rapidly increasing numbers the total amount of mental work accumulated at an ever increasing rate. In this the European, the Chinaman, the East Indian, have far outstripped other races. But back of this period lies the time when mankind struggled with the elements, when every small advance that seems to us now insignificant was an achievement of the highest order, as great as the discovery of steam power or of electricity, if not greater. It may well be, that these early inventions were made hardly consciously, certainly not by deliberate effort, yet every one of them represents a giant's stride forward in the development of human culture. To these early advances the Negro race has contributed its liberal share. While much of the history of early invention is shrouded in darkness, it seems likely that at a time when the European was still satisfied with rude stone tools, the African had invented or adopted the art of smelting iron.

Consider for a moment what this invention has meant for the advance of the human race. As long as the hammer, knife, saw, drill, the spade and the hoe had to be chipped out of stone, or had to be made of shell or hard wood, effective industrial work was not impossible, but difficult. A great progress was made when copper found in large nuggets was hammered out into tools and later on shaped by smelting, and when bronze was introduced; but the true advancement of industrial life did not begin until the hard iron was discovered. It seems not unlikely that the people that made the marvelous discovery of reducing iron ores by smelting were the African Negroes. Neither ancient Europe, nor ancient western Asia, nor ancient China knew the iron, and everything points to its introduction from Africa. At the time of the great African discoveries toward the end of the past century, the trade of the blacksmith was found all over Africa, from north to south and from east to west. With his simple bellows and a charcoal fire he reduced the ore that is found in many parts of the continent and forged implements of great usefulness and beauty.

Due to native invention is also the extended early African agriculture, each village being surrounded by its garden patches and fields in which millet is grown. Domesticated animals were also kept; in the agricultural regions chickens and pigs, while in the arid parts of the country where agriculture is not possible, large herds of cattle were raised. It is also important to note that the cattle were milked, an art which in early times was confined to Africa, Europe and northern Asia, while even now it has not been acquired by the Chinese.

The occurrence of all these arts of life points to an early and energetic development of African culture.

Even if we refrain from speculating on the earliest times, conceding that it is difficult to prove the exact locality where so important an invention was made as that of smelting iron, or where the African millet was first cultivated, or where chickens and cattle were domesticated, the evidence of African ethnology is such that it should inspire you with the hope of leading your race from achievement to achievement. Shall I remind you of the power of military organization exhibited by the Zulu, whose kings and whose armies swept southeastern Africa. Shall I remind you of the local chiefs, who by dint of diplomacy, bravery and wisdom united the scattered tribes of wide areas into flourishing kingdoms, of the intricate form of government necessary for holding together the heterogeneous tribes.

If you wish to understand the possibilities of the African under the stimulus of a foreign culture, you may look towards the Soudan, the region south of the Sahara. When we first learn about these countries by the reports of the great Arab traveller Iben Batuta, who lived in the 14th century, we hear that the old Negro kingdoms were early conquered by the Mohammedans. Under the guidance of the Arabs, but later on by their own initiative, the Negro tribes of these countries organized kingdoms which lived for many centuries. They founded flourishing towns in which at annual fairs thousands and thousands of people assembled. Mosques and other public buildings were erected and the execution of the laws was entrusted to judges. The history of the kingdom was recorded by officers and kept in archives. So well organized were these states that about 1850, when they were for the first time visited by a white man, the remains of these archives were still found in existence, notwithstanding all the political upheavals of a millennium and notwithstanding the ravages of the slave trade.

I might also speak to you of the great markets that are found throughout Africa, at which commodities were exchanged or sold for native money. I may perhaps remind you of the system of judicial procedure, of prosecution and defense, which had early developed in Africa, and whose formal development was a great achievement notwithstanding its gruesome application in the persecution of witchcraft. Nothing, perhaps, is more encouraging than a glimpse of the artistic industry of native Africa. I regret that we have no place in this country where the beauty and daintiness of African work can be shown; but a walk through the African museums of Paris, London and Berlin is a revelation. I wish you could see the scepters of African kings, carved of hard wood and representing artistic forms; or the dainty basketry made by the people of the Kongo river and of the region near the great lakes of the Nile, or the grass mats with their beautiful patterns. Even more worthy of our admiration is the work of the blacksmith, who manufactures symmetrical lance heads almost a yard long, or axes inlaid with copper and decorated with filigree. Let me also mention in passing the bronze castings of Benin on the west coast of Africa, which, although perhaps due to Portuguese influences, have so far excelled in technique any European work, that they are even now almost inimitable. In short, wherever you look, you find a thrifty people, full of energy, capable of forming large states. You find men of great energy and ambition who hold sway over their fellows by the weight of their personality. That this culture has, at the same time, the instability and other signs of weakness of primitive culture, goes without saying.

To you, however, this picture of native Africa will inspire strength, for all the alleged faults of your race that you have to conquer here are certainly not prominent there. In place of indolence you find thrift and ingenuity, and application to occupations that require not only industry, but also inventiveness and a high degree of technical skill, and the surplus energy of the people does not spend itself in emotional excesses only.

If, therefore, it is claimed that your race is doomed to economic inferiority, you may confidently look to the home of your ancestors and say, that you have set out to recover for the colored people the strength that was their own before they set foot on the shores of this continent. You may say that you go to work with bright hopes, and that you will not be discouraged by the slowness of your progress; for you have to recover not only what has been lost in transplanting the Negro race from its native soil to this continent, but you must reach higher levels than your ancestors had ever attained.

To those who stoutly maintain a material inferiority of the Negro race and who would dampen your ardor by their claims, you may confidently reply that the burden of proof rests with them, that the past history of your race does not sustain their statement, but rather gives you encouragement. The physical inferiority of the Negro race, if it exists at all, is insignificant when compared to the wide range of individual variability in each race. There is no anatomical evidence available that would sustain the view that the bulk of the Negro race could not become as useful citizens as the members of any other race. That there may be slightly different hereditary traits seems plausible, but it is entirely arbitrary to assume that those of the Negro, because perhaps slightly different, must be of an inferior type.

The arguments for inferiority drawn from the history of civilization are also weak. At the time when the early kingdom of Babylonia flourished the same disparaging remarks that are now made regarding the Negro might have been made regarding the ancestors of the ancient Romans. They were then a barbarous horde that had never made any contribution to the advance of that civilization that was confined to parts of Asia, and still they were destined to develop a culture which has become the foundation and an integral part of our own. Even later the barbarous hordes of northern Europe, who at the time of the ancient Romans were tribal groups without cultural achievements, have become the most advanced nations of our days.

Thus, impartial scientific discussion tells you to take up your work among your race with undaunted courage. Success will crown your endeavors if your work is carried on patiently, quietly and consistently.

But in taking up your position in life you must also be clear in regard to the relation of your work to the general life of the nation, and here again anthropology and history will help you to gain a healthy point of view. It is not the first time in human history that two peoples have been brought into close contact by the force of circumstances, who are dependent upon each other economically but where social customs, ideals and—let me add—bodily form, are so distinct that the line of cleavage remains always open. Every conquest that has led to colonization has produced, at least temporarily, conditions of this kind. The conquest of England by the Normans, the Teutonic invasion of Italy, the Manchoo conquest of China are illustrations of this point. But other instances are more typical. The position of Armenians and Greeks in Turkey, and the relations of the castes of India, bring up the same problem.

The best example, however, is that of the Jews of Europe, a people slightly distinct in type, but originally differing considerably in customs and beliefs from the people among whom they lived. The separation of the Jew and the Gentile was enforced for hundreds of years and very slowly only were the various occupations opened to him; very slowly only began to vanish the difference in customs and ideals. Even now the feeling of inequality persists and to the feeling of many the term Jew assigns to the bearer an exceptional position. And this is so, although the old barriers have fallen, although in the creative work of our times, in industry, commerce, science, and art, the Jew holds a respected place.

Even now there lingers the consciousness of the old, sharper divisions which the ages have not been able to efface, and which is strong enough to find—not only here and there—expression as antipathy to the Jewish type. In France, that let down the barriers more than a hundred years ago, the feeling of antipathy is still strong enough to sustain an anti-Jewish political party. I have dwelt on this example somewhat fully, because it illustrates the conditions that characterize your own position.

Even members of the same people, when divided by social barriers, have often been in similar relations. Thus has the hereditary nobility of Europe—although of the same descent as the people—held itself aloof for centuries and has claimed for itself superior power and a distinct code of honor. In short, you may find innumerable instances of sharp social division of a people into groups that are destined to work out jointly the fate of their country.

You must take to heart the teachings of the past. You observe, that in the case of the Patricians and Plebeians in Rome, of the nobility and the townspeople of more modern times, it has taken centuries for the exclusive groups to admit the ability of the other groups, and that after this had been achieved, it was impossible for long periods to break down the constantly recrudescent feeling of difference in character. You observe, furthermore, that when there is such a slight difference in type as between European and Jew, the feeling of distinction persists strongly, long after the reasons that created it have vanished. You must, therefore, recognize that it is not in your power, as individuals, to modify rapidly the feelings of others toward yourself, no matter how unjust and unfair they may seem to you, but that, with the freedom to improve your economic condition to the best of your ability, your race has to work out its own salvation by raising the standards of your life higher and higher, thus attacking the feeling of contempt of your race at its very roots.

It is an arduous work that is before you. If you will remember the teachings of history, you will find it a task full of joy, for your own people will respond more and more readily to your teachings. When they learn how to live a more cleanly, healthy and comfortable life, they will also begin to appreciate the value of intellectual life, and as their intellectual powers increase, will they work for a life of greater bodily and moral health. The vastness of the field of improvement and the assurance of success should be an ever present stimulus to you, even though it will take a long time to overcome the inertia of the indolent masses. On the other hand, if you carry on your work with side glances on your white neighbor, waiting for his recognition or support of your noble work, you are destined to disappointment. Remember that in every single case in history the process of adaptation has been one of exceeding slowness. Do not look for the impossible, but do not let your path deviate from the quiet and steadfast insistence on full opportunities for your powers.

Your advance depends upon your steadfastness of purpose. While the white man may err from the path of righteousness and, if he falls by the wayside, will have to bear the blame for his weakness individually, any failure of one of your race, and particularly any fault of one of you who have enjoyed the advantages of education, will be interpreted only too readily as a relapse into the old ways of an inferior race. If, therefore, you want to overcome the old antagonism, you have to be on your watch all the time. Your moral standards must be of the highest.

Looking at your life work thus, everything should combine to make you happy idealists. A natural goal has been set before you, which—although it may lie in the dim future—will be attained, if every one of you does his or her duty; in the fulfillment of which you are supported by the consciousness of your responsibility. May happiness and success be the reward of your endeavors!

SELECTION 43

Changing the Racial Attitudes
of White Americans

Nov. 30, 1906.

Mr. Andrew Carnegie,
2 East 91st Street,
New York City.

Dear Sir,—

I beg leave to submit to you the following considerations and plans.

The increasing antagonism between the white and the black races is not only a matter of concern from a humanitarian point of view, but entails serious dangers to the Commonwealth. Notwithstanding all that has been written and said on the subject of racial ability or inability of the Negro, a dispassionate investigation of the data at hand shows neither that his inability has ever been demonstrated, nor that it has been possible to show that the inferiority of the Negro in America is entirely due to social rather than to racial causes.

Copy preserved in the Boas Papers, American Philosophical Society.

All that we can say at the present time is that it seems unfair to judge the Negro by what he has come to be in America, and that the evidence of cultural achievement of the Negro in Africa suggests that his inventiveness, power of political organization, and steadiness of purpose, equal or even excel those of other races of similar stages of culture. Mixture of races in Africa has always been concurrent with the establishment of great and powerful states and the production of strong individualities, who put their stamp upon the culture of large areas and long periods. Those vices and undesirable qualities of the Negro which are generally brought forward do not exist in Africa except where it is ravaged by the slave trade.

It seems plausible that the whole attitude of our people in regard to the Negro might be materially modified if we had a better knowledge of what the Negro has really done and accomplished in his own native country.

It would seem that any endeavor of this kind should be connected with thorough studies of the conditions of the American Negro on such scientific basis that the results could not be challenged. The endless repetition of remarks on the inferiority of the Negro physique, of the early arrest of development of Negro children, of the tendency in the mulatto to inherit all the bad traits of both parental races, seems almost ineradicable, and in the present state of our knowledge can just as little be repudiated as supported by definite evidence.

There seems to be another reason which would make it highly desirable to disseminate knowledge of the achievements of African culture, particularly among the Negroes. In vast portions of our country there is a strong feeling of despondency among the best classes of the Negro, due to the economic, mental, and moral inferiority of the race in America, and the knowledge of the strength of their parental race in their native surroundings must have a wholesome and highly stimulating effect. I have noticed this effect myself in addressing audiences of Southern Negroes, to whom the facts were a complete revelation.

Considering that the future of millions of people is concerned, I believe that no energy should be spared to make the relations of the two races more wholesome, and to decide by unprejudiced scientific investigation what policy should be pursued. I should be inclined to think that an institution which might be called "African Institute" could contribute materially to the solution of these problems. Its purpose ought to be the presentation to the public, by means of exhibits and by means of publications, of the best products of African civilization. This should be accompanied by a scientific study of this civilization—one of the most important means of creating a group of men who will intelligently present the subject.

A second division of such an institution should be devoted to the study of the anatomy of the Negro. The investigations of such a division would be necessarily technical, but they would have the most important bearing upon the question of general policy to be pursued in regard to the Negro. The questions that are obscure in reference to this point are innumerable. We do not know the significance of the slightly different type of organization of the brain; we do not know the laws of growth and of development of the Negro race; and all these, taken together, should be investigated, and the results of a patient investigation of these problems should be of the very greatest help in all practical problems.

A third division of such an institution should be devoted to statistical inquiries of the Negro race in this country; and here, also, I believe most useful work could be done.

A plan of this kind would, of course, be exceedingly expensive. It would require a building devoted to the purpose, with at least one hall for educational exhibits, other more modest halls for students, and workrooms. It would furthermore require a room for anatomical preparations and studies, and the usual outfit for statistical investigation. I do not believe that a building of this kind could be had for less than about $500,000. Besides this, such an institution would have to have an income sufficient to carry on its work; and the current expenses, if it is to be efficient, would hardly be less than $40,000, including exhibits, publications, and investigations.

I am, dear sir,
Yours very sincerely,
[FRANZ BOAS]
Professor of Anthropology

  SELECTION 44

Race Problems in America

The development of the American nation through amalgamation of diverse European nationalities and the ever-increasing heterogeneity of the component elements of four people have called attention to the anthropological and biological problems involved in this process.

Address as Vice-President of Section H, American Association for the Advancement of Science, Baltimore, 1908; as published in *Science* 29 (1909): 839–849; later incorporated in Boas 1911c.

I propose to discuss here these problems with a view of making clear the hypothetical character of many of the generally accepted assumptions. It will be our object to attempt a formulation of the problems, and to outline certain directions of inquiry, that promise a solution of the questions involved, that, at the present time, can not be answered with scientific accuracy. It is disappointing that we have to accept this critical attitude, because the events of our daily life bring before our eyes constantly the grave issues that are based on the presence of distinct types of man in our country, and on the continued influx of heterogeneous nationalities from Europe. Under the pressure of these events, we seem to be called upon to formulate definite answers to questions that require the most painstaking and unbiased investigation. The more urgent the demand for final conclusions, the more needed is a critical examination of the phenomena and of the available methods of solution.

Let us first represent to our minds the facts relating to the origins of our nation. When British immigrants first flocked to the Atlantic coast of North America, they found a continent inhabited by Indians. The population of the country was thin, and vanished comparatively rapidly before the influx of the more numerous Europeans. The settlement of the Dutch on the Hudson, of the Germans in Pennsylvania, not to speak of other nationalities, is familiar to all of us. We know that the foundations of our modern state were laid by Spaniards in the Southwest, by French in the Mississippi Basin and in the region of the Great Lakes, but that the British immigration far outnumbered that of other nationalities. In the composition of our people, the indigenous element has never played an important rôle, except for very short periods. In regions where the settlement progressed for a long time entirely by the immigration of unmarried males of the white race, families of mixed blood have been of some importance during the period of gradual development, but they have never become sufficiently numerous in any populous part of the United States to be considered as an important element in our population. Without any doubt, Indian blood flows in the veins of quite a number of our people, but the proportion is so insignificant that it may well be disregarded.

Much more important has been the introduction of the negro, whose numbers have increased many fold so that they form now about one eighth of our whole nation. For a certain length of time the immigration of Asiatic nations seemed likely to become of importance in the development of our country, but the political events of recent years have tended to decrease their immediate importance considerably; although we do not venture to predict that the relation of Asiatics and white Americans may not become a most important problem in the future. These facts, however, are familiar to all of us and stand out clearly to our minds.

More recent is the problem of the immigration of people representing all the nationalities of Europe, western Asia and northern Africa. While until late in the second half of the nineteenth century the immigrants consisted almost entirely of people of northwestern Europe, natives of Great Britain, Scandinavia, Germany, Switzerland, Holland, Belgium and France, the composition of the immigrant masses has changed completely since that time. With the economic development of Germany, German immigration has dwindled down; while at the same time Italians, the various Slavic peoples of Austria, Russia and the Balkan Peninsula, Hungarians, Roumanians, east European Hebrews, not to mention the numerous other nationalities, have arrived in ever-increasing numbers. There is no doubt that these people of eastern and southern Europe represent a physical type distinct from the physical type of northwestern Europe; and it is clear, even to the most casual observer, that their present social standards differ fundamentally from our own. Since the number of new arrivals may be counted in normal years by hundreds of thousands, the question may well be asked, What will be the result of this influx of types distinct from our own, if it is to continue for a considerable length of time?

It is often claimed that the phenomenon of mixture presented in the United States is unique; that a similar intermixture has never occurred before in the world's history; and that our nation is destined to become what some writers choose to term a "mongrel" nation in a sense that has never been equaled anywhere.

When we try to analyze the phenomena in greater detail, and in the light of our knowledge of conditions in Europe as well as in other continents, this view does not seem to me tenable. In speaking of European types, we are accustomed to consider them as, comparatively speaking, pure stocks. It is easy to show that this view is erroneous. It is only necessary to look at a map illustrating the racial types of any European country—like Italy, for instance—to see that local divergence is the characteristic feature, uniformity of type the exception. Thus Dr. Ridolfo Livi, in his fundamental investigations on the anthropology of Italy, has shown that the types of the extreme north and of the extreme south are quite distinct—the former tall, short-headed, with a considerable sprinkling of blond and blue-eyed individuals; the latter short, long-headed and remarkably dark. The transition from one type to the other is, on the whole, quite gradual, but, like isolated islands, distinct types occur here and there. The region of Lucca in Tuscany and the district of Naples are examples of this kind, which may be explained as due to the survival of an older stock, to the intrusion of new types, or to a peculiar influence of environment.

Historical evidence is quite in accord with the results derived from the investigation of the distribution of modern types. In the earliest times we find on the peninsula of Italy groups of heterogeneous people, the linguistic relationships of many of which have remained obscure up to the present time. From the earliest prehistoric times on, we see wave after wave of people invading Italy from the north. Very early Greeks settled in the greater part of southern Italy and Phœnician influence was well established on the west coast of the peninsula. A lively intercourse existed between Italy and northern Africa. Slaves of Berber blood were imported and have left their traces. Slave trade continued to bring new blood into the country until quite recent times, and Livi believes that he can trace the type of Crimean slaves who were introduced late in the Middle Ages in the region of Venice. In the course of the centuries, the migrations of Celtic and Teutonic tribes, the conquests of the Normans, the contact with Africa, have added their share to the mixture of people on the Italian peninsula.

The fates of other parts of Europe were no less diversified. The Pyrenæan Peninsula, which at present seems to be one of the most isolated parts of Europe, had a most checkered history. The earliest inhabitants of whom we know were presumably related to the Basques of the Pyrenees. These were subjected to Oriental influences in the Pre-Mycenæan period, to Punic influences, to Celtic invasions, Roman colonization, Teutonic invasions, the Moorish conquest, and later on to the peculiar selective process that accompanied the driving-out of the Moors and the Jews.

England was not exempt from vicissitudes of this kind. It seems possible that at a very early period the type which is now found principally in Wales and in some parts of Ireland occupied the greater portion of the islands. It was swamped by successive waves of Celtic, Roman and Anglo-Saxon migration. Thus we find change everywhere.

The history of the migrations of the Goths, the invasions of the Huns, who in the short interval of one century moved their habitations from the borders of China into the very center of Europe, are proofs of the enormous changes in population that have taken place in early times.

Slow colonization has also brought about fundamental changes in blood as well as in diffusion of languages and cultures. Perhaps the most striking recent example of this change is presented by the gradual Germanization of the region east of the Elbe River, where, after the Teutonic migrations, people speaking Slavic languages had settled. The gradual absorption of Celtic communities, of the Basque, in ancient times the great Roman colonization, and later the Arab conquest of north Africa, are examples of similar processes.

Intermixture in early times was not by any means confined to peoples which, although diverse in language and culture, were of fairly uniform type. On the contrary, the most diverse types of southern Europe, northern Europe, eastern Europe and western Europe, not to mention the elements which poured into Europe from Asia and Africa, have been participants in this long-continued intermixture.

There is, however, one fundamental difference in regard to the early European migrations and the modern trans-Atlantic migration. On the whole, the former took place at a period when the density of population was, comparatively speaking, small. There is no doubt that the number of individuals concerned in the formation of the modern types of Great Britain were comparatively few as compared with the millions who come together to form a new nation in the United States; and it is obvious that the process of amalgamation which takes place in communities that must be counted by millions differs in character from the process of amalgamation that takes place in communities that may be counted by thousands. Setting aside social barriers, which in early times as well as now undoubtedly tended to keep intermingling peoples separate, it would seem that in the more populous communities of modern times a greater permanence of the single combining elements might occur, owing to their larger numbers, which make the opportunities for segregation more favorable.

Among the smaller communities the process of amalgamation must have been an exceedingly rapid one. After the social distinctions have once been obliterated, pure descendants of one of the component types decrease greatly in number, and the fourth generation of a people consisting originally of distinct elements will be almost homogeneous. I shall revert to this phenomenon later on.

It might be objected to this point of view, that the very diversity of local types in Europe proves the homogeneity of race types—as, for instance, of the northwestern European type, the Mediterranean type, the east European type, or the Alpine type; but it must be remembered that we have historical proof of the process of mixture, and that the relative number of component elements is sufficient to account for the present conditions.

I think we may dismiss the assumption of the existence of a pure type in any part of Europe, and of a process of mongrelization in America different from anything that has taken place for thousands of years in Europe. Neither are we right in assuming that the phenomenon is one of a more rapid intermixture than the one prevailing in olden times. The difference is based essentially in the masses of individuals concerned in the process.

If we confine our consideration for the present to the intermixture of European types in America, I think it will be clear, from what has been said before, that the concern that is felt by many in regard to the continuance of racial purity of our nation is to a great extent imaginary. The history of Europe proves that there has been no racial purity anywhere for exceedingly long periods, neither has the continued intermixture of European types shown any degrading effect upon any of the European nationalities. It would be just as easy to prove that those nations that have been least disturbed have lacked the stimulus to further advance and have passed through periods of quiescence. The history of Spain might be interpreted as an instance of an occurrence of this kind.

The question as to the actual effects of intermixture will not, however, be answered by a generalized historical treatment such as we have attempted here. The advocates of the theory of a degradation of type by the influx of so-called "lower" types will not be silenced by reference to earlier mixtures in Europe, the course of which can no longer be traced in actual detail for we do not know to what extent actual intermarriages have taken place, and what the development of families of mixed descent as compared with those of pure descent has been. It seems necessary that the problem should be approached from a biological standpoint. It seemed well, however, to gain first a clearer view of the historical relations of our problem. A knowledge of the events of the past tends to lay our apprehensions, that make the problem exciting, and which for this reason fill the observer with a strong bias for the results which he fears or desires.

Two questions stand out prominently in the study of the physical characteristics of the immigrant population. The first is the question of the influence of selection and environment in the migration from Europe to America. The second is the question of the influence of intermixture. A beginning of a thorough study of the former question was made as early as the time of the civil war, when Gould and Baxter, in their statistics of the enlisted soldiers, proved that the immigrant representatives of European nations were always better developed than the corresponding people in Europe. It has not been possible, up to the present time, to learn whether this differnce is due to better development here or to a process of selection, by which the weaker elements are eliminated before leaving their home country. It would be easy to ascertain the facts by an investigation of the arriving immigrants. That there is good reason to suppose that more favorable social surroundings in the United States have much to do with the better development of the immigrants is proved by the anthropometrical statistics collected by Bowditch in Boston and by Peckham in Milwaukee, who found that the children growing up in America are better developed than European children. Although much additional material has been collected on the old lines, the fundamental questions which are involved in this investigation have never received adequate attention. Statistics which I had occasion to collect recently seem to show that the development of children of immigrants is the better the longer their parents have been in the United States. I presume this merely suggests that the economic well-being of the immigrants increases, on the whole, with the length of their stay here, and that the corresponding better nutrition of the children results in better physical development. Whether, however, the whole change can be explained adequately in this manner is open to doubt. It is quite possible that the type may undergo certain changes due to environment.

In how far types must be considered as stable is a question in regard to which there is still considerable diversity of opinion. Investigators like

Kollmann maintain the absolute stability of the types now existing; while, on the other hand, indications are not absent which suggest a changeability of types, at least in certain respects. It would seem that stature may be considerably influenced by long-continued more or less favorable environment. There are investigators who maintain that the more or less energetic use of the jaws may influence the form of the head, owing to the pressure brought about by the muscles, which tend to compress the skull laterally. On the other hand, we have very clear evidence that features, like the form of the head, the form of the face and stature, are inherited from generation to generation with great persistence. As long as these questions are still so far from being settled, it seems necessary to take into consideration the possibility of a change of type in the immigrants, due to the new surroundings in which they have been placed. Some anthropologists in America have even gone so far as to claim that the geographical environment affects the European in such a way that he begins to resemble the Indian type. I have failed to find, so far, even a trace of evidence on which this opinion can be based.

The only indication that I can offer which might suggest an influence of environment is an observation which I made a number of years ago in Massachusetts, where I found that the variability of type was remarkably low, considering the mixed composition of the population—a variability which is less than the corresponding values obtained in Europe. But a sporadic observation of such a character is, of course, entirely insufficient to solve a problem of this magnitude. It would seem to my mind that one of the most important and fundamental investigations that have to be made in regard to the question of the biological assimilation of immigrants is a thorough discussion of the sameness or change of type of the second and third generations.

It has often been observed that the local types which have developed in America show a considerable amount of individualization. Some of this may very well be due to the influence of environment. It might be, for instance, that the tallness of the people of Kentucky is due to the lime-water of that area. This would be in accord with the observations made by Rœse in Gotha, who found that the stature in that city had changed with the introduction of hard water. It will certainly be possible to carry through this inquiry among a people like the Italians or Swedes, where the anthropometrical conditions of the home country are fairly well known, while for many other nationalities parallel inquiries in Europe and in America would be necessary. Even if, by extended inquiries into the physical characteristics of the descendants of immigrants, the modifications of their type should become well known, the problem would still remain: In how far do these types increase in a pure state after their migration, in how far do they tend to become extinct, and what tendency they have to mix with the rest of the population. It seems best to defer a discussion of this question until after consideration of the influence of race intermixture.

Here we may consider again the physical effect of intermixture and the propagation of mixed types independently. I regret to say that the available information in regard to this point is, if anything, more meager than that relating to the modification of types after their migration into this country. The fundamental question that must be asked is, whether the mixture of two distinct types of man tends to produce an intermediate homogeneous type in which certain of the characteristics of the parents appear blended, or whether the resultant tends to exhibit reversion to the parental types. This reversion may again be twofold. We may either find a complete reversion to one of the component parental types, or we may find a mixture of traits, some resembling the one parent, some the other parent. Obviously this question is most intimately related to the whole study of Mendelian inheritance, which occupies such a prominent place in the work of modern biologists. So far, the results obtained from a study of human types are few in number. I believe the earliest observation in regard to this subject was made by Felix von Luschan, who found as early as 1884 that the inhabitants of the south coast of Asia Minor, who are the descendants of intermarriages between a short-headed type of the central parts of Asia Minor and of the long-headed south coast type—a mixture which has continued for thousands of years—show clear evidence of alternating inheritance. In 1895 I was able to show (utilizing fairly extended observations) that the mixed blood resulting from unions of American Indians and whites shows, in regard to certain traits, a clear tendency to reversion to either parental type; while in other respects (for instance, in stature) new characteristics seem to develop. A recent inquiry into heredity among east European Jews shows that here also the children show a tendency to revert either to the father's or to the mother's type. This result is interesting, because it bears upon unions inside of a fairly uniform type of man. Other observations relate to the inheritance of abnormal traits, all of which seem to suggest, if not true Mendelism, at least the occurrence of alternating inheritance. However, the observations on mixtures of Indian and white have shown that while alternating inheritance may be found in regard to such traits as the form of the head and face, the development of the bulk of the body follows different laws. Notwithstanding these observations, the whole problem of the effects of race intermixture upon the various characteristic traits of human types is entirely unsolved.

It is not too much to say that the whole work in this field remains to be done. We do not know what weight to give to the small differences of types such as are found in Europe, and whether these differences are sufficiently great to be considered important as compared with the differences between individuals of the same geographical type, but belonging to opposite ends of the local series. We must not forget that the people of Europe in each locality are very variable, and that we may find (for instance, in Scotland) considerable numbers of individuals who will differ from one another more than do the average individuals of, let me say, Scotland and southern Italy. The question of the effects of intermixture of types can, therefore, not be treated entirely separately from the question of intermarriages among people belonging to the same locality. And it is worth considering whether the remoteness of blood relationship in different parts of Europe, as compared to the closer blood relationship inside of a narrow territory, may not outweigh all the influences of the differences of geographical types. The whole question seems to be most complex, and worthy of the most detailed and thorough study; but I do not venture to predict the anatomical and physiological effects of intermixture without a most painstaking investigation, which has not been made up to this time.

Considering our lack of knowledge of the most elementary facts that determine the outcome of these processes, I feel that it behooves us to be most cautious in our reasoning, and particularly to refrain from all sensational formulations of the problem, that are liable to add to the prevalent lack of calmness in its consideration; the more so since the answer to these questions concerns the welfare of millions of people.

The problem is one in regard to which speculation is as easy as accurate studies are difficult. Basing our arguments on ill-fitting analogies with the animal and plant world, we may speculate on the effects of intermixture upon the development of new types—as though the mixture that is taking place in America were in any sense, except a sociological one, different from the mixtures that have taken place in Europe for thousands of years; looking for a general degradation, for reversion to remote ancestral types, or towards the evolution of a new ideal type—as fancy or personal inclination may impel us. We may enlarge on the danger of the impending submergence of the northwest European type, or glory in the prospect of its dominance over all others. Would it not be a safer course to investigate the truth or fallacy of each theory rather than excite the public mind by indulgence in the fancies of our speculation. That these are an important adjunct in the attainment of truth, I do not deny; but they must not be promulgated before they have been subjected to a searching analysis, lest the credulous public mistake fancy for truth.

If I am not in a position to predict what the effect of mixture of distinct types may be, I feel confident that this important problem may be solved, if it is taken up with sufficient energy and on a sufficiently large scale. An investigation of the anthropological data of people of distinct types—taking into consideration the similarities and dissimilarities of parents and children, the rapidity and final result of the physical and mental development of children, their vitality, the fertility of marriages of different types and in different social strata—such an investigation is bound to give us information which will allow us to answer these important questions definitely and conclusively.

The final result of race mixture will necessarily depend upon the fertility of the present native population and of the newer immigrants. It has been pointed out repeatedly that the birth-rate of Americans has declined with great rapidity, and that in the second and third generations of immigrants the same decline makes itself felt. It will therefore be important to know what the relation of fertility of different types may be.

If the fertility of foreigners continues high without a corresponding higher death-rate of children, we may anticipate a gradual increase of the physical influence of the more fertile type. The immigration of the divergent types of southern and eastern Europe is, however, so recent, that this question can not be answered until at least twenty years more have elapsed.

No less important than the fertility of each immigrant type by itself is the question, in how far they tend to intermarry. The data presented in our census reports do not give a clear insight into this tendency among various nationalities. The difficulties of collecting significant statistics on the problem are very great. They appear particularly clear in the case of Italians. Married men from Italy come to the United States, earn some money, and go back to rejoin their families. They may come again, and, when conditions are propitious, they may finally send for their families to follow them. Thus we find among the Italian immigrants very large numbers who were married before they came here. It seems almost impossible to separate the contingent of couples married before their arrival here from those married after their arrival, and the chief point of interest to us lies in the intermarriages of children born in this country. It is natural that in large cities, where nationalities separate in various quarters, a great amount of cohesion should continue for some time; but it seems likely that intermarriages between descendants of foreign nationalities are much more common than the census figures would make it appear. Our experience with Americans whose grandparents immigrated into this country is, on the whole, that most social traces of their descent have disappeared, and that many do not even know to what nationalities their grandparents belonged. It might be expected—particularly in Western communities, where a rapid change of location is common—that this would result in a rapid mixture of the descendants of various nationalities. This inquiry, which it is quite feasible to carry out in detail, seems indispensable for a clear understanding of the situation.

It is somewhat difficult to realize how rapidly intermixture of distinct types takes place, if the choice of mates is left entirely to accident. I have made this calculation; and I find that in a population in which two types intermingle, and in which both types occur with equal frequency, there will be in the fourth generation less than one person in ten thousand of

328 Anthropology and Society

pure descent. When the proportion of the two original types is as nine to one, there will be among the more numerous part of the population only eighteen in one thousand in the fourth generation that will be of pure blood. Taking these data as a basis, it is obvious that intermixture, as soon as the social barriers have been removed, must be exceedingly rapid; and I think it safe to assume that one hundred years from now, in the bulk of our population, very few pure descendants of the present immigrants will be found.

Unfortunately, however, we do not know the influence of racial cohesion. Obviously this is one of the fundamental points that ought to be known in order to gain a clear insight into the effect of recent immigration. The data collected by our census and by other agencies do not contain this information, which is one of the most urgent desiderata for an understanding of the composition of the American population. I may therefore express the hope that this question may be included in the census to be organized next year, or may be otherwise provided for by an inquiry to be undertaken under the auspices of the government. Without this information, the whole discussion of the effect of intermixture will remain speculative.

No material whatever is available to answer the question whether mixture of types is favorable for the physical development of the individual, or unfavorable. Statistics collected in the Argentine Republic tend to show that with a mixture of similar types, but from remote countries, considerable changes in the proportions of the sexes develop. Observations on half-breed Indians show that a type taller than either parental race develops in the mixed blood; that the fertility of the mixed blood is increased; and I can not find any evidence that would corroborate the view, so often expressed, that the hybrid of distinct types tends to degenerate.

I have refrained entirely from a discussion of the social problem, which is no less important than the one referring to the physical types of the descendants of immigrants; and I do not intend to include this question in our consideration, which is devoted to the anthropological problem only.

I have also devoted attention essentially to the biological problems presented by the immigration of European nations, but I must not conclude my remarks without referring at least to the serious problem presented by the negro population of our country. When compared with the contrast between the negro and the white, the differences of the European types seem insignificant; and the unity of the European race, as contrasted with the negro race, becomes at once apparent.

I do not intend to take up the whole question of racial inferiority, which can not be treated adequately in the brief time that I can devote to this subject. I must confine myself to a statement of my opinion, which I have repeatedly tried to substantiate. I do not believe that the negro is, in his physical and mental make-up, the same as the European. The anatomical differences are so great that corresponding mental differences are plausible. There may exist differences in character and in the direction of specific aptitudes. There is, however, no proof whatever that these differences signify any appreciable degree of inferiority of the negro, notwithstanding the slightly inferior size, and perhaps lesser complexity of structure, of his brain; for these racial differences are much less than the range of variation found in either race considered by itself. This view is supported by the remarkable development of industry, political organization, and philosophic opinion, as well as by the frequent occurrence of men of great will-power and wisdom among the negroes in Africa.

I think we have reason to be ashamed to confess that the scientific study of these questions has never received the support either of our government or of any of our great scientific institutions; and it is hard to understand why we are so indifferent towards a question which is of paramount importance to the welfare of our nation. The anatomy of the American negro is not well known; and, notwithstanding the oft-repeated assertions regarding the hereditary inferiority of the mulatto, we know hardly anything on this subject. If his vitality is lower than that of the full-blooded negro, this may be as much due to social causes as to hereditary causes. Owing to the very large number of mulattoes in our country, it would not be a difficult matter to investigate the biological aspects of this question thoroughly; and the importance of the problem demands that this should be done. Looking into a distant future, it seems reasonably certain that with the increasing mobility of the negro, the number of full-bloods will rapidly decrease; and since there is no introduction of new negro blood, there can not be the slightest doubt that the ultimate effect of the contact between the two races must necessarily be a continued increase of the amount of white blood in the negro community. This process will go on most rapidly inside of the colored community, owing to intermarriages between mulattoes and full-blooded negroes. Whether or not the addition of white blood to the colored population is sufficiently large to counterbalance this leveling effect, which will make the mixed bloods with a slight strain of negro blood darker, is difficult to tell; but it is quite obvious, that, although our laws may retard the influx of white blood considerably, they can not hinder the gradual progress of intermixture. If the powerful caste system of India has not been able to prevent intermixture, our laws, which recognize a greater amount of individual liberty, will certainly not be able to do so; and that there is no racial sexual antipathy is made sufficiently clear by the size of our mulatto population. A candid consideration of the manner in which intermixture takes place shows very clearly that the probability of the infusion of white blood into the colored population is considerable. While the large body of the white population will always, at least for a very long time to come, be entirely remote from any possibility of intermixture with negroes, I think that we may predict with a fair degree of certainty a condition in which the contrast between colored people and whites will be less marked than it is at the present time. Notwithstanding all the obstacles that may be laid in the way of intermixture, the conditions are such that the persistence of the pure negro type is practically impossible. Not even an excessively high mortality and lack of fertility among the mixed type, as compared with the pure types, could prevent this result. Since it is impossible to change these conditions, they should be faced squarely, and we ought to demand a careful and critical investigation of the whole problem.

It appears from this consideration, that the most important practical questions relating to the negro problem have reference to the mulattoes and other mixed bloods—to their physical types, their mental and moral qualities, and their vitality. When the bulky literature of this subject is carefully sifted, little remains that will endure serious criticism; and I do not believe that I claim too much when I say that the whole work on this subject remains to be done. The development of modern methods of research makes it certain that by careful inquiry, definite answers to our problems may be found. Is it not, then, our plain duty to inform ourselves that, so far as that can be done, deliberate consideration of observations may take the place of heated discussion of beliefs in matters that concern not only ourselves, but also the welfare of millions of negroes?

Facts that could help us to shape our policies in regard to our race problems are almost entirely wanting. It has been my endeavor to show that by proper investigations much can be done to clear up these problems, which are of vital importance for the future of our nation.

SELECTION 45

American Nationalism
and World War I

NEW YORK,
Jan. 7, 1916

To the Editor of The New York Times:

Although under ordinary circumstances I should not wish to intrude upon the public my personal views regarding political matters, the bitterness of attacks upon German-Americans induces me to express concisely what I, and I believe with me many other German-Americans, feel and think. I do so because I still hope that a statement of this kind may convince some of our fellow citizens who differ from us that we who sympathize with Germany and Austria, and who strive for a more dispassionate discussion of the events of the European war on the part of both sides, have at heart the desire that our own actions should conform to what we consider right: that they should safeguard the future of our own country and help to re-establish friendly relations between the nations of the world.

At the time of my arrival here more than thirty years ago, I was filled with admiration of American political ideals. While in Europe we had grown up under the pressure of national contentions and conflicts of interests that are difficult to harmonize, I had been taught to look upon the United States as the one country that had the good fortune to be free from the pressure produced by great density of population, and that sought satisfaction in perfecting its inner development. I thought of it as a country that would not tolerate interference with its own interests, but that would also refrain from active interference in the affairs of others, and would never become guilty of the oppression of unwilling subjects. Events like the great movement westward, and the Mexican war, appeared rather as digressions from the self-imposed path of self-restraint.

A rude awakening came in 1898, when the aggressive imperialism of that period showed that the ideal had been a dream. Well I remember

Letter to the editor, New York *Times*, 8 January 1916, p. 8, published under the headline "Why German-Americans Blame America."

the heated discussions which I had that year with my German friends when I maintained that the control of colonies was opposed to the fundamental ideas of right held by the American people, and the profound disappointment that I felt when, at the end of the Spanish war, these ideals lay shattered. The America that had stood for right, and right only, seemed dead; and in its place stood a young giant, eager to grow at the expense of others, and dominated by the same desire of aggrandizement that sways the narrowly confined European states. The hope that the United States would guide the world to a saner concept of national aspirations seemed gone. What wonder if, during the period of ambitious attempts to extend our political power, many German-Americans were among those who took the view that control of alien peoples is destructive to the principles on which our nation is founded; that we have a higher duty to ourselves than to those whom, flattering ourselves, we like to call the wards of the nation. I still admire the keen insight of Carl Schurz, who, when the question first came to the front, recognized the importance of this issue, and subordinated to it all other questions as momentarily of minor importance. My political faith is still founded on the conviction that self-restraint should be the foundation of our policies.

My position in regard to other closely allied questions is determined by another consideration. In my youth I had been taught in school and at home not only to love the good of my own country but also to seek to understand and to respect the individualities of other nations. For this reason one-sided nationalism, that is so often found nowadays, is to me unendurable. The question whether this tolerant spirit is found in other nations does not concern us here. The point that concerns me is that I wish to see it realized in the country whose citizen I am. As a matter of fact, the number of people in our country who are willing and able to enter into the modes of thought of other nations is altogether too small. The American, on the whole, is inclined to consider American standards of thought and action as absolute standards, and the more idealistic his nature, the more strongly he wants to "raise" everyone to his own standards. For this reason the American who is cognizant only of his own standpoint sets himself up as arbiter of the world. He claims that the form of his own Government is the best, not for himself only, but also for the rest of mankind; that his interpretation of ethics, of religion, of standards of living, is right. Therefore he is inclined to assume the role of a dispenser of happiness to mankind. We do not find often an appreciation of the fact that others may abhor where we worship. I have always been of the opinion that we have no right to impose our ideals upon other nations, no matter how strange it may seem to us that they enjoy the kind of life they lead, how slow they may be in utilizing the resources of their countries, or how much opposed their ideals may be to ours.

Our intolerant attitude is most pronounced in regard to what we like to call "our free institutions." Modern democracy was no doubt the most wholesome and needed reaction against the abuses of absolutism and of a selfish, often corrupt, bureaucracy. That the wishes and thoughts of the people should find expression, and that the form of government should conform to these wishes is an axiom that has pervaded the whole Western World, and that is taking root even in the Far East. It is a quite different question, however, in how far the particular machinery of democratic government is identical with democratic institutions. We are not satisfied with the expression of the popular will, but, by an enormous extension of the number of elective officers, we subject the details of administration to popular control. The disadvantages of this method have led us here and there to substitute for the many elective officers a single one with almost dictatorial powers. This example shows that there is nothing sacred in the particular kind of popular control that is chosen. The technical difficulties of organizing democratic control of the Government have found a different solution in different countries. To claim as we often do, that our solution is the only democratic and the ideal one is a one-sided exaggeration of Americanism. I see no reason why we should not allow the Germans, Austrians, and Russians, or whoever else it may be, to solve their problems in their own ways, instead of demanding that they bestow upon themselves the benefactions of our régime. The very standpoint that we are right and they are wrong is opposed to the fundamental idea that nations have distinctive individualities, which are expressed in their modes of life, thought, and feeling.

Our self-sufficiency is also apt to obscure our view in regard to the attitude of various nations toward individualism and collectivism. It is rather a fortunate accident than conscious choice that enables us to allow to the individual as much freedom of action as we do. A new country, rich in resources, sparsely settled, provides openings without number. The advantages that we possess in our country are provided in England in her vast colonial possessions. On the contrary, a country as thickly settled as Germany is compelled much sooner to husband her resources and to restrict the freedom of action of the individual, because co-ordination is necessary to the well-being of the community. If we think the ends desirable we do not hesitate to bring to bear regimentation upon the freedom of the individual. The whole conservation movement can be successful only with regimentation, and it does not require much acumen to see that during the last thirty years there have occurred constant encroachments upon the freedom of action of the individual, which have been forced upon us by the exigencies of our economic situation, and it is safe to predict that these will constantly increase. Why, then, should we set up the individualism of the thinly settled young country as the standard by which the institutions of others are to be measured? I confess frankly that it was this individual freedom that will always be dear to the young that attracted me here, but maturer years have shown to me the necessity that this freedom should be co-ordinate with the necessary amount of subordination of the actions of the individual under the whole.

Applying these fundamental views to our present situation, let me explain my position in regard to the present war. I am dissatisfied particularly with our attitude toward international law, because we set up our arbitrary interpretation as an absolute standard. It is perfectly obvious that the belligerents have at heart effective warfare rather than international law, and that the new elements that enter into modern warfare make many of the former usages inapplicable in modern times. This is equally true of the modern blockade and of modern submarine warfare. If we wish to make ourselves champions of established international law we have no right to choose some laws that we consider as inviolable, while we disregard the violation of others. We must insist with equal severity on obedience to all. By not doing so, we become party to the breach of law, and forfeit the right to assume the attitude of defenders of the law. We cannot attribute, according to our alleged humanitarianism, greater virtue to those laws that protect the life of American citizens at sea than to those that protect the safety of those who live in Germany and Austria, and who are threatened by the British policy of starving out the population of these countries, only because the effects of the starvation policy are not so dramatic as the violent death of a few individuals, and bring about distress and premature death by indirect methods. I should sustain a vigorous policy, that forbids the Central Powers as well as the Entente to transgress any of the established laws. If our Government does not possess the energy or power to resist British interference I should support the policy which withdraws our protection from all those American citizens who voluntarily intrust their lives and property to the flag of any one of the belligerents. The middle course that we have taken imposes our arbitrary construction of international law upon other nations, and is, therefore, not just.

On account of the principles stated before, I am also opposed to the popular demand for preparedness. If we were neutral in spirit as well as in letter, if we did not meddle with the affairs of other continents, if we had no unfair racial discrimination against certain immigrants, the United States would have only friends among the nations. Protection of the United States should, therefore, according to my views, be based on the rectification of those policies that are apt to embroil us. We can then devote ourselves to peaceful pursuits. Shall we give up the sacred ideals of the past for the sake of playing a role in the councils of the nations, for the sake of foreign possessions, or for the sake of the exclusive control of foreign trade? I feel in duty bound to resist movements that will lead us on in these directions.

I believe this is the attitude of many German-Americans: To conform to the dictates of our conscience, to our loyalty to America, and to our love for the ideals of our youth. We decry the historical intolerance that characterizes the utterances of a great patriot of the Eastern press and of many citizens who should know better—the absurd mania of denunciation and espionage that sees a plot in every accident, such as any expert chemist would expect in a dangerous industry that is carried on by inexperienced workmen working overtime, and in every transaction that, owing to war conditions, does not proceed in a normal way.

FRANZ BOAS

 SELECTION 46

A Protest Vote
for the Socialist Party

To the Editor of The Nation:

Sir: The most important issue in the approaching election, overshadowing all other questions, appears to me the rehabilitation of our civic liberties. Under the Federal Espionage Act and similar State laws, the free expression of opinion that used to be the foundation of our liberty no longer exists. Citizens feel intimidated and, for fear of denunciation, do not dare to express their convictions and opinions even in private conversation.

I shall, therefore, vote for the Socialist party, the only one that stands for the repeal of those laws that have resulted in an abridgment of the freedom of speech and of the press, of the right of the people peaceably to assemble and to petition the government for a redress of grievances.

FRANZ BOAS

Grantwood, N. J., October 19

Letter to the editor, *The Nation* 107 (1918): 487, printed under the heading "A Sturdy Protest"; subsequently reprinted as a leaflet by the Socialist party, Bergen County, New Jersey.

SELECTION 47

Scientists as Spies

To the Editor of The Nation:

Sir: In his war address to Congress, President Wilson dwelt at great length on the theory that only autocracies maintain spies; that these are not needed in democracies. At the time that the President made this statement, the Government of the United States had in its employ spies of unknown number. I am not concerned here with the familiar discrepancies between the President's words and the actual facts, although we may perhaps have to accept his statement as meaning correctly that we live under an autocracy; that our democracy is a fiction. The point against which I wish to enter a vigorous protest is that a number of men who follow science as their profession, men whom I refuse to designate any longer as scientists, have prostituted science by using it as a cover for their activities as spies.

A soldier whose business is murder as a fine art, a diplomat whose calling is based on deception and secretiveness, a politician whose very life consists in compromises with his conscience, a business man whose aim is personal profit within the limits allowed by a lenient law—such may be excused if they set patriotic devotion above common everyday decency and perform services as spies. They merely accept the code of morality to which modern society still conforms. Not so the scientist. The very essence of his life is the service of truth. We all know scientists who in private life do not come up to the standard of truthfulness, but who, nevertheless, would not consciously falsify the results of their researches. It is bad enough if we have to put up with these, because they reveal a lack of strength of character that is liable to distort the results of their work. A person, however, who uses science as a cover for political spying, who demeans himself to pose before a foreign government as an investigator and asks for assistance in his alleged researches in order to carry on, under this cloak, his political machinations, prostitutes science in an unpardonable way and forfeits the right to be classed as a scientist.

By accident, incontrovertible proof has come to my hands that at least four men who carry on anthropological work, while employed as government agents, introduced themselves to foreign governments as representatives of scientific institutions in the United States, and as sent out for the

Letter to the editor, *The Nation* 109 (1919): 797, printed under the heading "Scientists as Spies."

purpose of carrying on scientific researches. They have not only shaken the belief in the truthfulness of science, but they have also done the greatest possible disservice to scientific inquiry. In consequence of their acts every nation will look with distrust upon the visiting foreign investigator who wants to do honest work, suspecting sinister designs. Such action has raised a new barrier against the development of international friendly coöperation.

FRANZ BOAS

New York, October 16

 SELECTION 48

Freedom to Teach

Owing to repeated conflicts between trustees and faculties of universities, we have heard much about the need of academic freedom in the sense that teaching and research should be free of outside interference, and that the personal freedom of members of the faculties should not be restricted by boards of trustees. There are other aspects of the subject, however, which have not received much attention, and which are vital for a healthy development of university life. Boards of trustees are not the only potential enemies of the freedom of the teacher. The faculties themselves are so constituted that the academic teachers are apt to consider themselves a privileged class in whose hands the development of university teaching and the advance of science rests. Universities can not be the home of the *universitas litterarum,* of the world of knowledge, if their faculties are closed corporations, and if university research and instruction are a monopoly of those who have secured recognition by appointment by the board of trustees of an established university. The younger men of this class are generally appointed on recommendation of the faculty, which, by this means, controls the character of the coming generation of teachers and investigators. A person who has knowledge that he desires to impart, but who stands outside the academic circle, has no opportunity of reaching academic students. The limitation of usefulness brought about by these conditions is most evident in cities of the size and character of Boston, Chicago, or New York. In these cities

The Nation 108 (1919): 88–89; subsequently incorporated in Boas 1945.

live numerous scholars of high accomplishment, many of whom would welcome the opportunity to formulate the results of their studies. Every serious student knows the advantage that he himself derives from the opportunity to present the result of his researches in an orderly manner, the clarifying effect of such teaching for the instructor, and the stimulating effect that it has upon the young student who is privileged to listen to such an exposition of original work. To these men the opportunity should be given to offer advanced instruction whenever they wish to do so. The university should stand for the freedom of teaching of all those qualified to teach.

It will be objected that such a policy would open the doors of the university to cranks. I do not believe that this danger is great. It might easily be guarded against if, in each science, a committee existed which could grant to investigators permission to give university instruction according to the merit of their scientific work. Such a committee should not be a faculty committee, because the very object of the plan would be to make the admission to teaching free of faculty control and to place it entirely on the basis of meritorious work. In most sciences there exist societies which have a standing sufficiently high so that a committee consisting, let us say, of their past presidents could pass on the merits of individuals; or committees consisting of representatives of various universities might perform their task. Both methods would minimize the danger that local university interests might influence the decision. It would be well if the right of affiliation with a university might be bestowed as an honor, without application, merely as a recognition of work that has reached a certain standard of excellence.

All this means that our universities ought to take the necessary steps to give up their isolation and grant to other educational and scientific agencies a voice in the control of their affairs. Without such steps no real progress is possible. We cannot continue to allow our educational affairs to be dictated by isolated bodies of trustees and faculties who necessarily look after the interests of their own institutions, without any attempt at coördination with the work of other institutions. At the present time, this method has strained our whole system well-nigh to the breaking point.

Competition of the type here advocated is unwelcome to many faculty members who like to control the work offered in their departments. In some cases there may be a dread of opposing theory or opinion, in others the fear of distracting students from the course of instruction that has been laid out for them. In still other cases the fear of losing students through outside competition may play a rôle. None of these objections, however, should stand in the way of the liberalization of the academic staff, because the control of opinion, the rigid determination of a course of study, and jealousies of competing teachers are all equally opposed to progress.

The realization of such a plan as that suggested is beset with certain financial difficulties. In those sciences in which laboratories or other costly apparatus are needed, additions to the material equipment might be necessary. The volunteer instructor should be entitled to a remuneration, the amount of which should depend on the number of his students, although allowance should be made for the total number of students in the country who devote themselves to the subject in question. If this remuneration had to be provided by the university, it might place an additional burden upon its sorely tried shoulders. On the other hand, if the attempt were made to replace some of the necessary routine teaching by the volunteer teaching here advocated, the very purpose of the move would be frustrated. The additional intellectual force should not be harnessed to routine work and used to reduce the regular university staff, but it should be rigidly confined to the kind of teaching that the individual investigator may choose for himself.

For this reason I believe that a great step in advance might be achieved if one of our many wealthy benefactors of science were to establish a fund for the remuneration of volunteer teachers who should be admitted according to the principle of merit, and whose remuneration should be determined by the success of their work. It seems probable that such a fund would be the means of giving to academic freedom an entirely new meaning. It would break down the social barriers that are raised around the academic teacher, make a clear separation between scientific achievement and social standing, and thus further the free advance of science by placing on a level of equality the academic profession and the investigators who are engaged in other occupations.

A new freedom is needed, not only for teaching but also for learning. We are wont to speak of academic freedom as freedom of the teacher, but greater academic freedom is needed also for the student. The tradition of the college and the school, in which the course of study is hedged in by innumerable rules and regulations, is still controlling in the university. Even the college student, during the last two years of work, longs for freedom to study what he wants, not merely what a faculty which believes that it knows better prescribes; and as much or little as he likes, not the amount that a faculty considers wise. This restriction of the freedom of the student is brought about, in part at least, by the rigid administrative organization of departments of instruction. Although in theory these are conceived of as purely administrative divisions, they very often work out in reality as so many schools which prevent the student from looking beyond the narrow walls that are built up around him. It would be unfair to charge the university alone with this restriction of freedom; it is to a great extent due to the attitude of the student himself, who is not ready to assert his own will and choice. Nevertheless, it remains true that the departmental organization of faculties is a hindrance to the freedom of the student. Laboratories and well-arranged seminars require administrative control, but this need not include the prescription of a detailed course of study.

One of the most potent causes of the restriction of freedom in academic life is the fact not only that the university prepares investigators and certifies by its diploma that a student is capable of conducting scientific research, but that the university diploma is also to a great extent a professional certificate. The practice of a profession requires a definite fund of knowledge, while mastery of the method of research is of lesser importance. The university diploma should be based on the mastery of a method of investigation which presupposes a knowledge of basic facts, not according to the needs of a profession, but according to the needs of research. The more sharply these two objects can be separated, the better will the university perform its task and the freer will be the student in his field of work.

❦ BIBLIOGRAPHY

For the most part, this bibliography simply gives a full citation for each of the works referred to parenthetically in the text. However, I have added a few additional titles containing material on Boas which I did not have specific occasion to cite.

The following abbreviations have been used:

AA	*American Anthropologist*
AAA	American Anthropological Association
APS	American Philosophical Society
BAAS	British Association for the Advancement of Science
BAE	Bureau of American Ethnology
GPO	Government Printing Office
IJAL	*International Journal of American Linguistics*
JAF	*Journal of American Folklore*
JRAI	*Journal of the Royal Anthropological Institute*

ABERLE, DAVID
1960 "The Influence of Linguistics on Early Culture and Personality Theory." In G. Dole and R. Carneiro, eds., *Essays in the Science of Culture.* New York: Thomas Y. Crowell, pp. 1–29.

ADAMS, RICHARD
1960 "Manuel Gamio and Stratigraphic Excavation." *American Antiquity* 26: 99.

AAA
1943 *Franz Boas, 1858–1942.* Memoir No. 61. Menasha, Wisconsin.

ANDREWS, H. J. ET AL.
1943 Bibliography of Franz Boas. In AAA 1943, pp. 67–109.

BAE
1896 Archives, BAE, in the National Anthropological Archives, Smithsonian Institution, Washington, D.C.

BENEDICT, RUTH
1943a "Franz Boas" (obituary). *Science* 97: 60–62.
1943b "Franz Boas as an Ethnologist." In AAA 1943, pp. 27–34.

BENISON, SAUL
1949 "Geography and the Early Career of Franz Boas." AA 51: 523–526.

BIDNEY, DAVID
1953 *Theoretical Anthropology.* New York: Columbia University Press.

BOAS, FRANZ (for full bibliography, see Andrews, 1943)
1885 "Baffinland: Geographische Ergebnisse einer in den Jahren 1883 und 1884 ausgeführten Forschungsreise." *Petermanns Mitteilungen,* No. 80.
1887a "The Coast Tribes of British Columbia." *Science* 9: 288–289.
1887b "Notes on the Ethnology of British Columbia." *Proceedings of the APS* 24: 422–428.

1887c   "The Occurrence of Similar Inventions in Areas Widely Apart." *Science* 9: 485–486.

1887d   "Museums of Ethnology and Their Classification." *Science* 9: 587–589, 614.

1887e   "The Study of Geography." *Science* 9: 137–141.

1888   *The Central Eskimo.* 6th Annual Report, BAE. Washington: GPO. (Cf. reprint, with introduction by Henry B. Collins. Lincoln: University of Nebraska, 1964.)

1889a   "First General Report on the Indians of British Columbia." *Report of the BAAS,* pp. 801–893.

1889b   "On Alternating Sounds." *AA* 2: 47–53.

1890   "Second General Report on the Indians of British Columbia." *Report of the BAAS,* pp. 562–715.

1891a   "Anthropological Investigations in Schools." *Science* 17: 351–352.

1891b   "Dissemination of Tales among the Natives of North America." *JAF* 4: 13–20.

1892   "The Growth of Children." *Science* 19: 256–257, 281–282; 20: 351–352.

1893   "Remarks on the Theory of Anthropometry." *Quarterly Publications of the American Statistical Association* 3: 569–575.

1894a   "The Indian Tribes of the Lower Fraser River." *Report of the BAAS,* pp. 454–463.

1894b   *Chinook Texts.* Bulletin No. 20, BAE. Washington: GPO.

1895   *Indianische Sagen von der Nord-Pacifischen Küste Amerikas.* Berlin: A. Asher.

1896a   "The Limitations of the Comparative Method of Anthropology." *Science* 4: 901–908.

1896b   "The Growth of Indian Mythologies." *JAF* 9: 1–11.

1897   "The Social Organization and the Secret Societies of the Kwakiutl Indians." *Report of the U.S. National Museum for 1895.* Washington: GPO. (Cf. Boas 1966.)

1898   "Summary of the Work of the Committee in British Columbia." *Report of the BAAS,* pp. 667–682.

1899   "Some Recent Criticisms of Physical Anthropology." *AA* 1: 98–106.

1901   "The Mind of Primitive Man." *JAF* 14: 1–11.

1902   "The Ethnological Significance of Esoteric Doctrines." *Science* 16: 872–874.

1904a   "Some Traits of Primitive Culture." *JAF* 17: 243–254.

1904b   "What the Negro Has Done in Africa." *The Ethical Record* 5: 106–109.

1905a   "The Jesup North Pacific Expedition." *Thirteenth International Congress of Americanists* (1902). New York. Pp. 91–100.

1905b   "The Negro and the Demands of Modern Life." *Charities* 15: 85–88.

1907a   "Notes on the Blanket Designs of the Chilkat Indians." In George Emmons, *The Chilkat Blanket,* Memoirs of the American Museum of Natural History 3: 351–400.

1907b   "Anthropological Research." *Science* 25: 756–757.

1909   *The Kwakiutl of Vancouver Island.* Publications of the Jesup North Pacific Expedition. New York: Stechert. 5: 301–522.

1910   Correspondence between Franz Boas and Dr. Charles D. Walcott, Secretary of the Smithsonian Institution, July to December 1909. Privately printed and distributed.

1911a   *Handbook of American Indian Languages, Part I.* Bulletin No. 40, BAE. Washington: GPO. (Cf. Holder 1966.)

1911b   *Changes in the Bodily Form of Descendants of Immigrants.* Senate Document 208, 61st Congress, Second Session. Washington: GPO.

1911c   *The Mind of Primitive Man*. New York: Macmillan.
1912a   "The History of the American Race." *Annals of the New York Academy of Sciences* 21: 177–183.
1912b   "International School of American Archaeology and Ethnology in Mexico." *AA* 14: 192–194.
1914   "Mythology and Folk-Tales of the North American Indians." *JAF* 27: 374–410.
1916a   *Tsimshian Mythology*. 31st Annual Report, BAE. Washington: GPO.
1916b   "The Origin of Totemism." *AA* 18: 319–326.
1917   "Introduction." *IJAL* 1: 1–8.
1932   "The Aims of Anthropological Research." As reprinted in Boas 1940, pp. 243–259.
1936   "History and Science in Anthropology: A Reply." As reprinted in Boas 1940, pp. 305–311.
1938   *The Mind of Primitive Man*. Rev. ed. New York: Macmillan. (Cf. reprint Free Press, 1965.)
1940   *Race, Language, and Culture*. New York: Macmillan. (Cf. reprint Free Press, 1966.)
1945   *Race and Democratic Society*. New York: J. J. Augustin. (Cf. reprint Biblo and Tannen, 1969.)
1966   *Kwakiutl Ethnography*, ed. Helen Codere. Chicago: University of Chicago Press.
1972   *The Professional Correspondence of Franz Boas*. Microfilm edition. Wilmington, Del.: Scholarly Resources Inc.
BRINTON, D. G.
1892   "The Nomenclature and Teaching of Anthropology." *AA* 5: 263–271.
BUETTNER-JANUSCH, JOHN
1957   "Boas and Mason: Particularism versus Generalization." *AA* 59: 318–324.
COATS, A. W.
1961   "American Scholarship Comes of Age: The Louisiana Purchase Exposition 1904." *Journal of the History of Ideas* 22: 404–417.
CODERE, HELEN
1959   "The Understanding of the Kwakiutl." In Goldschmidt 1959, pp. 61–75.
1966   "Introduction" to Boas 1966.
COHEN, M. R., AND NAGEL, E.
1934   *An Introduction to Logic and Scientific Method*. New York: Harcourt, Brace and World.
COLE, FAY-COOPER
1931   "The Concept of Race in the Light of Franz Boas' Studies of Headforms among Immigrants." In S. A. Rice, ed., *Methods in Social Science*. Chicago: University of Chicago Press. Pp. 582–585.
1952   "Eminent Personalities of the Half-Century." *AA* 54: 157–167.
DARNELL, REGNA
1967   "Daniel Garrison Brinton: An Intellectual Biography." Unpublished M.A. thesis, University of Pennsylvania.
1969   "The Development of American Anthropology 1879–1920: From the Bureau of American Ethnology to Franz Boas." Unpublished doctoral dissertation, University of Pennsylvania. (Cf. Darnell 1971c.)
1970   "The Emergence of Academic Anthropology at the University of Pennsylvania." *Journal of the History of the Behavioral Sciences* 6: 80–92.
1971a   "The Powell Classification of American Indian Languages." *Papers in Linguistics* 4: 71–110.
1971b   "The Revision of the Powell Classification." *Papers in Linguistics* 4: 233–258.

1971c   "The Professionalization of American Anthropology." *Social Science Information* 10: 83–103.

DARRAH, W. C.
1951   *Powell of the Colorado*. Princeton: Princeton University Press.

DELAGUNA, FREDERICA
1960   (ed.) *Selected Papers from the American Anthropologist 1888–1920*. Evanston, Illinois: Row, Peterson.

DURKHEIM, EMILE
1895   *The Rules of the Sociological Method*, ed. G. E. G. Catlin. New York: Free Press, 1966.
1912   *The Elementary Forms of the Religious Life*. Trans. Joseph Swain. New York: Free Press, 1965.

EGGAN, FRED
1954   "Social Anthropology and the Method of Controlled Comparison." *AA* 56: 743–763.
1955   (ed.) *Social Anthropology of North American Tribes*. 2nd. ed. Chicago: University of Chicago Press.

EMENEAU, MURRAY
1943   "Franz Boas as Linguist." In AAA 1943, pp. 35–38.

ERASMUS, CHARLES
1953   *Las Dimensiones de la Cultura*. Bogota: Editorial Iqueima.

FREEMAN, JOHN
1966   "University Anthropology: Early Departments in the United States." *Papers of the Kroeber Anthropological Society* 32: 78–90.

GAMIO, MANUEL
1959   "Boas Sobre Cerámica y Estratigrafía." In Goldschmidt 1959, pp. 117–118.

GILLISPIE, C. C.
1960   *The Edge of Objectivity*. Princeton: Princeton University Press.

GODDARD, P. E.
1926   "American Anthropology and Franz Boas." *American Mercury* 7: 314–316.

GOLDENWEISER, A. A.
1915   Review of Durkheim 1912. *AA* 17: 719–735.

GOLDSCHMIDT, WALTER
1959   (ed.) *The Anthropology of Franz Boas: Essays on the Centenary of His Birth*. San Francisco: Howard Chandler.

GOLDSTEIN, MARCUS
1948   "Franz Boas' Contributions to Physical Anthropology." *American Journal of Physical Anthropology* 4: 145–161.

GOSSETT, THOMAS
1963   *Race: The History of an Idea in America*. Dallas: Southern Methodist University Press.

GRUBER, JACOB
1967   "Horatio Hale and the Development of American Anthropology." *Proceedings of the APS* 111: 1–37.

HALLER, JOHN
1971   *Outcasts from Evolution: Scientific Attitudes of Racial Inferiority, 1859–1900*. Urbana: University of Illinois Press.

HALLOWELL, A. I.
1960   "The Beginnings of Anthropology in America." In Delaguna 1960, pp. 1–90.

HARRINGTON, J. P.
1945   "Boas on the Science of Language." *IJAL* 11: 97–99.

HARRIS, MARVIN
1968   *The Rise of Anthropological Theory*. New York: Thomas Y. Crowell.

HERSKOVITS, M. J.
1943   "Franz Boas as Physical Anthropologist." In AAA 1943, pp. 39–51.
1953   *Franz Boas: The Science of Man in the Making.* New York: Charles Scribner's Sons.
1956   "Further Comments on Boas." *AA* 58: 734.
1957   "Some Further Notes on Franz Boas' Arctic Expedition." *AA* 59: 112–116.
HOCKETT, C. F.
1954   "Two Models of Grammatical Descriptions." *Word* 10: 210–234.
HOLDER, PRESTON
1966   (ed.) Boas, *Introduction to Handbook of American Indian Languages* and Powell, *Indian Linguistic Families North of Mexico.* Lincoln: University of Nebraska Press.
HOWELLS, W. W.
1959   "Boas as Statistician." In Goldschmidt 1959, pp. 112–117.
HRDLIČKA, ALĔS
1943   "Franz Boas (1858–1942)." Philadelphia: *APS Yearbook 1942*, pp. 333–336.
HYMAN, S. E.
1954   "Freud and Boas: Secular Rabbis?" *Commentary* (March) 264–267.
HYMES, DELL
1961a   "On Typology of Cognitive Styles in Language." *Anthropological Linguistics* 3: 22–54.
1961b   Review of Goldschmidt 1959. *JAF* 74: 87–90.
1964   "Alfred Louis Kroeber." In Hymes, ed., *Language in Culture and Society.* New York: Harper and Row. Pp. 689–707.
1965   "Some North Pacific Coast Poems: A Problem in Anthropological Philology." *AA* 67: 316–341.
1970   "Linguistic Method in Ethnography: Its Development in the United States." In Paul Garvin, ed., *Method and Theory in Linguistics.* The Hague: Mouton. Pp. 249–325.
JACOBS, MELVILLE
1959   "Folklore." In Goldschmidt 1959, pp. 119–138.
JAKOBSON, ROMAN
1944   "Franz Boas' Approach to Language." *IJAL* 10: 188–195.
1959   "Boas' View of Grammatical Meaning." In Goldschmidt 1959, pp. 139–145.
KARDINER, ABRAM, AND PREBLE, EDWARD
1961   "Franz Boas: Icy Enthusiasm." In *They Studied Man.* Cleveland: World Publishing. Pp. 134–159.
KLUCKHOHN, C., AND PRUFER, O.
1959   "Influences during the Formative Years." In Goldschmidt 1959, pp. 4–28.
KROEBER, A. L.
1909   "Classificatory Systems of Relationship." *JRAI* 39: 77–84.
1915   "Eighteen Professions." *AA* 17: 283–288.
1935   "History and Science in Anthropology." *AA* 37: 539–569.
1943   "Franz Boas: The Man." In AAA 1943, pp. 5–26.
1952   "A Half Century of Anthropology." In *The Nature of Culture.* Chicago: University of Chicago Press. Pp. 139–143.
1956   "The Place of Boas in Anthropology." *AA* 58: 151–159.
1959   "A History of the Personality of Anthropology." *AA* 61: 398–404.
KROEBER, A. L., AND KLUCKHOHN, C.
1952   *Culture: A Critical Review of Concepts and Definitions.* Papers of the Peabody Museum of American Archaeology and Ethnology, Vol. 65.
KUNKEL, PETER
1954   "Boas, Space and Time." *AA* 56: 115.

LAUFER, BERTHOLD
1906   (ed.) *Boas Anniversary Volume: Anthropological Papers Written in Honor of Franz Boas.* New York: Stechert.
LAVIOLETTE, F. E.
1961   *The Struggle for Survival: Indian Cultures and the Protestant Ethic in British Columbia.* Toronto: University of Toronto Press.
LESSER, ALEXANDER
1968   "Franz Boas." *International Encyclopedia of the Social Sciences.* New York: Macmillan.
LEVENSTEIN, H. A.
1963   "Franz Boas as Political Activist." *Papers of the Kroeber Anthropological Society* 29: 15–24.
LÉVI-STRAUSS, CLAUDE
1963   *Structural Anthropology.* Trans. C. Jacobson and B. G. Schoepf. New York: Basic Books.
LOUNSBURY, FLOYD
1968   "One Hundred Years of Anthropological Linguistics." In J. O. Brew, ed., *A Hundred Years of Anthropology.* Cambridge: Harvard University Press. Pp. 153–225.
LOWIE, R. H.
1920   *Primitive Society.* New York: Boni and Liveright.
1937   *The History of Ethnological Theory.* New York: Farrar and Rinehart.
1943a   "Franz Boas, Anthropologist." *Scientific Monthly* 56: 183–184.
1943b   "Franz Boas, His Predecessors and His Contemporaries." *Science* 97: 202–203.
1944a   "American Contributions to Anthropology." *Science* 100: 321–327.
1944b   "Franz Boas, 1858–1942." *JAF* 57: 59–64.
1947   "Franz Boas." *Biographical Memoirs, National Academy of Science* 24: 303–322.
1948   "Some Facts about Boas." *Southwestern Journal of Anthropology* 4: 69–70.
1954   Review of Herskovits 1953. *Scientific Monthly* 78: 47.
1956a   "Boas Once More." *AA* 58: 159–163.
1956b   "Reminiscences of Anthropological Currents in America Half a Century Ago." *AA* 58: 995–1015.
McGEE, EMMA R.
1915   *Life of W. J. McGee.* Farley, Iowa: Privately printed.
MASON, J. A.
1943   "Franz Boas as an Archeologist." In AAA 1943, pp. 58–66.
MASON, O. T.
1887.   "The Occurrence of Similar Inventions in Areas Widely Apart." *Science* 9: 534–535.
MEAD, MARGARET
1959a   *An Anthropologist at Work: Writings of Ruth Benedict.* Boston: Houghton Mifflin.
1959b   "Apprenticeship under Boas." In Goldschmidt 1959, pp. 29–45.
MEAD, MARGARET, AND BUNZEL, RUTH
1960   (eds.) *The Golden Age of American Anthropology.* New York: George Braziller.
MITRA, PANCHANAN
1933   *A History of American Anthropology.* Calcutta: University of Calcutta Press.
NEEDHAM, RODNEY
1963   "Introduction" to E. Durkheim and M. Mauss, *Primitive Classification.* Chicago: University of Chicago Press.

PARMENTER, ROSS
1966   "Glimpses of a Friendship: Zelia Nuttall and Franz Boas." In June Helm,
        ed., *Pioneers of American Anthropology*. Seattle: University of Washington
        Press. Pp. 83–147.
PARSONS, TALCOTT
1949   *The Structure of Social Action*. New York: Free Press.
PASSMORE, JOHN
1957   *A Hundred Years of Philosophy*. London: Duckworth.
POWELL, J. W.
1887   "Museums of Ethnology and Their Classification." *Science* 9: 612–614.
RADCLIFFE-BROWN, A. R.
1922   *The Andaman Islanders*. Cambridge: Cambridge University Press.
1923   "The Methods of Ethnology and Social Anthropology." *South African
        Journal of Science* 20: 124–147.
RADIN, PAUL
1933   *Method and Theory in Ethnology*. New York: McGraw-Hill.
RAY, VERNE
1955   Review of Herskovits 1953. *AA* 57: 138–141.
1956   "Rejoinder." *AA* 58: 164–170.
RESEK, CARL
1960   *Lewis Henry Morgan: American Scholar*. Chicago: University of Chicago
        Press.
ROHNER, RONALD
1966   "Franz Boas: Ethnographer on the Northwest Coast." In June Helm, ed.,
        Pioneers of American Anthropology. Seattle: University of Washington
        Press. Pp. 149–222.
1967   "The Boas Canon: A Posthumous Addition." *Science* 158: 362–364.
1969   (ed.) *The Ethnography of Franz Boas*. Chicago: University of Chicago
        Press.
SAPIR, EDWARD
1915   "The Na-dene Languages: A Preliminary Report." *AA* 17: 534–558.
SHIPTON, C. K.
1943   "Franz Boas." *Proceedings of the American Antiquarian Society* 53: 15–16.
SINGER, MILTON
1968   "Culture." *International Encyclopedia of the Social Sciences*. New York:
        Macmillan.
SMITH, MARIAN
1954   Review of Herskovits 1953. *Man* 54: 111.
1959   "Boas' 'Natural History' Approach to Field Method." In Goldschmidt
        1959, pp. 46–60.
SPIER, LESLIE
1931   "Historical Interrelation of Culture Traits: Franz Boas' Study of Tsimshian
        Mythology." In *Methods in Social Science*, ed. S. A. Rice. Chicago: Uni-
        versity of Chicago Press. Pp. 449–457.
1943   "Franz Boas and Some of His Views." *Acta Americana* 1: 108–127.
1959   "Some Central Elements in the Legacy." In Goldschmidt 1959, pp. 146–
        155.
STOCKING, G. W., JR.
1960   "Franz Boas and the Founding of the American Anthropological Associa-
        tion." *AA* 62: 1–17.
1968a   *Race, Culture and Evolution: Essays in the History of Anthropology*. New
        York: Free Press.
1968b   "The Franz Boas Collection." In *The American Indian: A Conference in*

the American Philosophical Society Library. Philadelphia: Library Publication No. 2, pp. 1–19.

1968c   "The Boas Plan for American Indian Linguistics." Paper presented to Newbery Library Conference on the History of Linguistics. (To be published in D. Hymes, ed., *Studies in the History of Linguistics*. Bloomington: Indiana University Press.)

1971   "What's in a Name? The Origins of the Royal Anthropological Institute: 1837–1871." *Man* 6: 369–390.

1973a "From Chronology to Ethnology." Introduction to J. C. Prichard, *Researches into the Physical History of Man*. Chicago: University of Chicago Press.

1973b "Franz Boas." *Dictionary of American Biography*, Supplement 3.

TANNER, J. M.

1959   "Boas' Contributions to Knowledge of Human Growth and Form." In Goldschmidt 1959, pp. 76–111.

TYLOR, E. B.

1889   "On a Method of Investigating the Development of Institutions: Applied to Laws of Marriage and Descent." *JRAI* 18: 245–269.

VOEGELIN, C. F.

1952   "The Boas Plan for the Presentation of American Indian Languages." *Proceedings of the APS* 96: 439–451.

VOGET, F. W.

1970   "Franz Boas." *Dictionary of Scientific Biography*, ed. C. C. Gillispie. New York: Charles Scribner's Sons.

WAX, MURRAY

1956   "The Limitations of Boas' Anthropology." *AA* 58: 63–74.

WHITE, LESLIE

1963   *The Ethnography and Ethnology of Franz Boas*. Bulletin No. 6. Austin: Texas Memorial Museum.

1966   *The Social Organization of Ethnological Theory*. Houston: Rice University Studies 52.

WILLIAMS, J. L.

1936   "Boas and American Ethnologists." *Thought* 11: 194–209.

WOLF, ERIC

1964   *Anthropology*. Englewood Cliffs, New Jersey: Prentice-Hall.

INDEX